Doing without Concepts

Doing without Concepts

Edouard Machery

2009

OXFORD
UNIVERSITY PRESS

Oxford University Press, Inc., publishes works that further
Oxford University's objective of excellence
in research, scholarship, and education.

Oxford   New York
Auckland   Cape Town   Dar es Salaam   Hong Kong   Karachi
Kuala Lumpur   Madrid   Melbourne   Mexico City   Nairobi
New Delhi   Shanghai   Taipei   Toronto

With offices in
Argentina   Austria   Brazil   Chile   Czech Republic   France   Greece
Guatemala   Hungary   Italy   Japan   Poland   Portugal   Singapore
South Korea   Switzerland   Thailand   Turkey   Ukraine   Vietnam

Copyright © 2009 by Oxford University Press, Inc.

Published by Oxford University Press, Inc.
198 Madison Avenue, New York, New York 10016

www.oup.com

Oxford is a registered trademark of Oxford University Press

All rights reserved. No part of this publication may be reproduced,
stored in a retrieval system, or transmitted, in any form or by any means,
electronic, mechanical, photocopying, recording, or otherwise,
without the prior permission of Oxford University Press.

Library of Congress Cataloging-in-Publication Data
Machery, Edouard.
Doing without concepts / Edouard Machery.
p. cm.
Includes bibliographical references and indexes.
ISBN 978-0-19-530688-0
1. Concepts. I. Title.
BF443.M33 2009
150.1—dc22   2008020448

1 3 5 7 9 8 6 4 2
Printed in the United States of America
on acid-free paper

For Anastasia

Acknowledgments

Doing without Concepts is the (more or less recognizable) offspring of the dissertation written under the patient supervision of Daniel Andler and defended in June 2004 at the University of Paris-Sorbonne. I have presented the ideas developed in this book in many venues, and I have always benefited from the questions, comments, and criticisms made by philosophers and psychologists in the audience. Over the years, I have also profited from discussions with Gualtiero Piccinini, Tania Lombrozo, and Dan Weiskopf. Many friends and acquaintances have been punished with at least a few pages of the manuscript of this book. Special thanks are due to the members of the reading group on *Doing without Concepts* at the University of Pittsburgh—Jim Bogen, Clark Glymour, Jonathan Livengood, and Justin Sytsma—and to the members of the reading group formed around Gualtiero Piccinini's blog *Brains*—Carrie Figdor, Elisabetta Lalumera, Bryan Temples Miller, Gualtiero Piccinini, J. Brendan Ritchie, and Anna-Mari Rusanen. They were kind and patient enough to comment on the whole manuscript and their criticisms and comments have tremendously improved *Doing without Concepts*. Thanks also to those who have commented on parts of the book: Jason Byron, Carl Craver, Thomas Cunningham, Malte Dahlgrün, James Hampton, Karen Hauck, Liz Irvine, Peter Machamer, Selja Seppälä, Jonathan Surovell, and Wayne Wu. I am grateful to the two undergraduate research assistants at the University of Pittsburgh who have been working on this book: Stephen Grebinski and Jennifer Febbo. I would like also to express gratitude to the manuscript reader at Oxford University Press for his or her useful suggestions as well as to Peter Ohlin for his help and patience!

Over the years, Steve Stich has had an incredible influence on my life and career. This book is no exception. Were it not for his advice, I would never have dreamed of turning my dissertation into a book and of submitting it to Oxford University Press. Were it not for his threats, I might still be mulling over the first chapter!

This is an appropriate place to express my gratitude to my family, particularly, to my parents, Pierre and Dominique. *Merci*. And, most important, I dedicate *Doing Without Concepts* to Anastasia, with whom I have learned the true meaning of happiness.

Permissions

Portions of this book draw on the following publications:

Machery, E., Mallon, R., Nichols, S., and Stich, S. P. (2004). Semantics, cross-cultural style. *Cognition*, 92–3: B1–B12. With permission of Elsevier Limited.

Machery, E. (2005). Concepts are not a natural kind. *Philosophy of Science*, 72: 444–467. © 2005 by the Philosophy of Science Association. With permission of the Philosophy of Science Association. www.journals.uchicago.edu/toc/phos/.

Machery, E. (2006). How to split concepts. Reply to Piccinini and Scott. *Philosophy of Science*, 73: 410–418. © 2006 by the Philosophy of Science Association. With permission of the Philosophy of Science Association. www.journals.uchicago.edu/toc/phos/.

Machery, E. (2007). Concept empiricism: A methodological critique. *Cognition*, 104: 19–46. With permission of Elsevier Limited.

Machery, E. (2007). 100 years of psychology of concepts: The theoretical notion of concept and its operationalization. *Studies in History and Philosophy of Biological and Biomedical Sciences*, 38: 63–84. With permission of Elsevier Limited.

Table 6.1 is reproduced from Armstrong et al. (1983) with permission of Elsevier Limited.

The picture on the cover is reproduced by courtesy of Prof. Bastian Leibe (UMIC Research Centre, Aachen, Germany). His research with the stimulus set that is depicted on the cover was first described in the following article:

Leibe, B., and Schiele, B. (2003). Analyzing contour- and appearance-based methods for object categorization. In IEEE Conference on Computer Vision and Pattern Recognition (CVPR'03), Madison, USA, June 2003.

Contents

Introduction   3

1 Concepts in Psychology   7
    1.1 "Concept" in Psychology   7
    1.2 Evidence for the Existence of Concepts   14
    1.3 What Is a Psychological Theory of Concepts?   17
    1.4 Alternative Characterizations of the Notion of Concept   21
    1.5 Conclusion   29

2 Concepts in Philosophy   31
    2.1 "Concept" in Philosophy   32
    2.2 Concepts in Philosophy versus Concepts in Psychology   34
    2.3 How Are the Psychological and the Philosophical Theories of Concepts Connected? Peacocke's Simple Account   38
    2.4 How Are the Psychological and the Philosophical Theories of Concepts Connected? The Foundationalist Account   47
    2.5 Conclusion   50

3 The Heterogeneity Hypothesis   52
    3.1 The Received View   53
    3.2 The Heterogeneity Hypothesis   56
    3.3 Hybrid Theories of Concepts   63
    3.4 Conclusion   74

4 Three Fundamental Kinds of Concepts: Prototypes, Exemplars, Theories 76
    4.1 The Classical Theory of Concepts 77
    4.2 The Prototype Paradigm of Concepts 83
    4.3 The Exemplar Paradigm of Concepts 92
    4.4 The Theory Paradigm of Concepts 100
    4.5 Alternative Views of Concepts 108
    4.6 Three Theoretical Entities That Have Little in Common 118
    4.7 Conclusion 119

5 Multi-Process Theories 121
    5.1 Multi-Process Theories 121
    5.2 Examples of Multi-Process Theories 140
    5.3 Conclusion 150

6 Categorization and Concept Learning 151
    6.1 Categorization and Concept Learning 152
    6.2 Studying Categorization and Concept Learning 158
    6.3 Evidence for the Existence of Prototypes 163
    6.4 Evidence for the Existence of Exemplars 173
    6.5 Evidence for the Existence of Theories 183
    6.6 Organization of the Categorization Processes and of the Concept-Learning Processes 193
    6.7 Conclusion 196

7 Induction, Concept Combination, and Neuropsychology 197
    7.1 Induction 197
    7.2 Concept Combination 207
    7.3 Neuropsychology 212
    7.4 Conclusion 218

8 Concept Eliminativism 219
    8.1 Two Inconclusive Arguments against the Notion of Concept 220
    8.2 Natural Kinds and Scientific Eliminativism 230
    8.3 The Argument for the Elimination of "Concept" 241
    8.4 Objections and Replies 243
    8.5 Conclusion 245

Conclusion 247
References 253
Index of Names 277
Index of Subjects 279

Doing without Concepts

Introduction

Once at the center of philosophy, the philosophy of concepts has now been marginalized, maybe because for a few years now, it has been stalled. The contrast with the psychology of concepts is stark. Psychologists working on categorization, induction, and reasoning have continued developing and refining their theories of concepts, discovering along the way a dazzling amount of phenomena. New work on prototypes in the 1990s and early 2000s, innovative ideas on causal cognition in the first decade of the twenty-first century, the development of the neo-empiricist approach to concepts, and the promising growth of the neuropsychology of concepts have rejuvenated the field.

Philosophers of concepts have not ignored the psychology of concepts, particularly the theories developed in the 1970s and 1980s. However, rather than addressing these psychological theories in their own terms, philosophers have viewed them as attempting to answer the questions that were of interest in the philosophy of concepts. Unsurprisingly, philosophers have typically found the psychological theories of concepts to be wanting and, instead of contributing to their development, have discarded them.

This book attempts to rejuvenate the philosophy of concepts by steering it toward a new course. The key novelty is to modify philosophers' relation to the psychology of concepts. Rather than viewing the theories and models developed by psychologists as naive and deficient answers to the questions of interest in philosophy, I examine them in their own terms, without any preconception about the goals that psychologists attempt to meet. I argue that progress in the psychology of concepts and in the budding neuropsychology of concepts is conditional on psychologists and neuropsychologists eliminating the notion of concept from their theoretical vocabulary. This eliminativist proposal is the fifth and last tenet of the hypothesis that is developed at length in this book—the Heterogeneity Hypothesis:

1. The best available evidence suggests that for each category (for each substance, event, and so on), an individual typically has several concepts.
2. Coreferential concepts have very few properties in common. They belong to very heterogeneous kinds of concept.
3. Evidence strongly suggests that prototypes, exemplars, and theories are among these heterogeneous kinds of concept.
4. Prototypes, exemplars, and theories are typically used in distinct cognitive processes.
5. The notion of concept ought to be eliminated from the theoretical vocabulary of psychology.

Chapters 1 and 2 are two introductory chapters. Chapter 1 describes what concepts are taken to be in psychology and identifies the goals of psychological theories of concepts. These goals, and only these goals (not the goals that philosophers of concepts attempt to meet), provide the relevant criteria for evaluating psychological theories of concepts. I propose that in psychology, concepts are characterized as being those bodies of knowledge that are stored in long-term memory and that are used by default in the processes underlying most, if not all, higher cognitive competences when these processes result in judgments about the referents of these concepts. Theories of concepts attempt to describe the knowledge stored in concepts, the format of concepts, the cognitive processes that use concepts, the acquisition of concepts, and the localization of concepts in the brain. By doing so, they can explain the properties of people's higher cognitive competences.

Chapter 2 describes what concepts are taken to be in philosophy and identifies the goals of philosophical theories of concepts. Together, chapters 1 and 2 show that when philosophers and psychologists develop theories of concepts, they are really theorizing about different things. This conclusion undercuts many of the arguments made by philosophers against psychological theories of concepts.

Chapter 3 develops at length the Heterogeneity Hypothesis, with a special focus on the first two tenets. While most psychologists assume that there are numerous properties common to all concepts (the Received View), I propose that the class of concepts divides into kinds that have little in common. The Heterogeneity Hypothesis is also contrasted with theories of concepts that are superficially similar—namely, hybrid theories of concepts—in order to prevent their conflation.

Chapter 4 describes the theoretical entities that have been proposed by the main views of concepts developed since the 1970s—prototypes, exemplars, and theories. More recent approaches to concepts, particularly the neo-empiricist view of concepts, are also discussed. While philosophers have typically been satisfied with cartoonish versions of the psychological theories of concepts, I look closely and critically at these theories and at the models of cognitive processes developed by psychologists. This examination leads to the conclusion that given the properties that are relevant to characterize concepts, prototypes, exemplars, and theories have very little in common. This shows that if prototypes, exemplars, and theories exist, the class of concepts divides into kinds that have little in common.

Chapter 5 focuses on the fourth tenet of the Heterogeneity Hypothesis. The goal of this chapter is to investigate, in a somewhat speculative manner, the contours of those theories that assume that a single cognitive competence, for instance, inductive reasoning, is underwritten by several cognitive processes (a kind of theory I call 'multi-process theories').

Chapters 6 and 7 discuss the empirical evidence showing that prototypes, exemplars, and theories exist (Tenet 3 of the Heterogeneity Hypothesis), and that they are used in distinct cognitive processes (Tenet 4). Chapter 6 focuses on the vast research on categorization. I establish that we have at least three processes of categorization, each of which involves a specific kind of concept—namely, prototypes, exemplars, and theories.

Chapter 7 focuses on the research on inductive reasoning and concept combination. These two fields provide converging evidence for the Heterogeneity Hypothesis. Findings from the growing field of the neuropsychology of concepts are also critically assessed.

Let us take stock. Chapter 1 establishes that for psychologists, concepts are those bodies of knowledge that are used in the processes underlying the higher cognitive competences. Chapter 4 describes the main theoretical entities posited by psychologists of concepts—prototypes, exemplars, and theories—and contends that these theoretical entities have little in common. Chapters 6 and 7 show that prototypes, exemplars, and theories exist and are used in distinct categorization processes and distinct induction processes. I conclude that the class of concepts divides into kinds that have little in common.

The last chapter, Chapter 8, draws the conclusion of this line of reasoning: the notion of concept should be eliminated from contemporary psychology. Previous eliminativist arguments are considered and are judged to be inconclusive. A new type of eliminativist argument called 'scientific eliminativism'—showing that the extension of a scientific notion is not a natural kind—is developed and applied to concepts. I show that concepts are not a natural kind, and I conclude that if psychology is to progress further, the notion of concept ought to be eliminated from its theoretical vocabulary.

Here are a few practical details before pursuing at length this line of reasoning in the remainder of the book. I have attempted to restrict the footnotes to bibliographical references and terminological remarks. As a result, this book can pretty much be read without consulting them. Moreover, because I have brought together many disciplines, and because I hope to be read by diverse audiences, I have shunned the technical jargon as much as possible. When this was impossible, I have explained what the relevant technical terms meant. Because these terms do not always mean the same thing in different disciplines, I ask readers to forego their preconceptions about what these technical terms mean for them.

Finally, many of the topics discussed in this book are empirical and some might find it strange that a philosopher dabbles so thoroughly in empirical issues. Would it not be better to leave scientific questions to scientists and to focus on strictly philosophical issues? This is not my view, however. Save, maybe, for purely formal (e.g., logical) theories, philosophical claims whose correctness does not depend, however indirectly, on matters of fact are empty: they are neither true nor false. As I see it, philosophy is the pursuit of empirical knowledge by (typically, though not exclusively) conceptual means: philosophy is in the business of examining, criticizing, reforming the findings, theories, methods developed by scientists and of grasping the implications of sciences for our understanding of the world and our place in it.

1

Concepts in Psychology

The goal of this first chapter is to explain what concepts are taken to be in psychology, neuropsychology, artificial intelligence,[1] and cognitive science.[2] In section 1.1, I argue that in psychology, concepts are those bodies of knowledge that are used by default in the processes underlying the higher cognitive competences. In section 1.2, I provide some evidence that this notion of concept is not empty. In section 1.3, I clarify the nature and goals of the psychological theories of concepts: psychological theories of concepts aim at capturing the general properties of concepts—particularly what type of knowledge concepts consist of, how concepts are used in cognitive processes, and what their format is. Finally, philosophers of psychology and psychologists themselves have proposed several other ways of characterizing the notion of concept used in psychology. In section 1.4, I criticize these alternatives.

1.1 "Concept" in Psychology

Most psychologists offer vague characterizations of what they take concepts to be, while some use the notion of concept in idiosyncratic ways (e.g., Shanks 1997; Ashby and Maddox 2005: 151). The terminology is

---

[1] Artificial intelligence researchers rarely use the word "concept," preferring neologisms such as "frame" and "script."

[2] In what follows, I often use the term "psychologist" as a cover term for developmental psychologists, experimental psychologists, neuropsychologists, and cognitive scientists.

also often confusing, particularly because psychologists often use "concept" and "category" interchangeably.[3] In this section, I attempt to characterize the psychological notion of concept precisely and clearly. This characterization is both descriptive and normative. It is descriptive in that I attempt to describe what most psychologists take concepts to be. It is also normative in that I want to regiment the use of the theoretical term "concept" in psychology. I begin by introducing a few distinctions and clarifying a few notions, all of which are needed to characterize the psychological notion of concept. The point is not to define these notions as much as to clarify them to the precision needed.

In this book, I will use the term "knowledge" as psychologists do. By "knowledge," psychologists mean any contentful state that can be used in cognitive processes. So defined, "knowledge" does not refer to states that are necessarily true and justified.[4] Furthermore, "knowledge" does not refer to states that are necessarily explicit or propositional. Rather, knowledge can be implicit or explicit; it can also be propositional, imagistic, or procedural.

Psychologists divide cognition into various cognitive competences. Cognitive competences are defined functionally (see also section 5.1). Vision, proprioception, motor planning, categorization, induction, and linguistic understanding are prime examples of cognitive competences. Among cognitive competences, it is common, though not entirely uncontroversial (e.g., Stein 1995), to distinguish between higher cognitive competences and, for lack of a better word, "lower" cognitive competences. Spelling out this familiar distinction is harder than one would think because there is little agreement about the distinctive properties that characterize each type of cognition. For instance, while some take cognitive impenetrability—roughly, the property that beliefs and desires do not affect cognitive processing—to be a hallmark of lower cognitive competences (e.g., Pylyshyn 1999), others contend that lower cognitive competences are cognitively penetrable (e.g., Schyns 1999). For present purposes, suffice it to say that the lower cognitive competences encompass our perceptual competences and our motor competences, although the last stages of perception, particularly the categorization of what is perceived, belong to higher cognition. Lower cognitive competences thus include computing the layout of objects in a three-dimensional space from their projections on the retina and fine-tuning our actions to the dynamic aspects of our environments. By contrast, the processes underlying the higher cognitive competences do not take perceptual stimuli (e.g., the activation of the rods and cones) as inputs nor do they yield motor outputs

---

[3] See, e.g., Armstrong, Gleitman, and Gleitman 1983; Medin and Ortony 1989: 184; Markman 1999: 118; Roberts 1998: 335.

[4] Because philosophers assume that an individual knows a proposition p only if p is true and if this individual is justified in believing p, they might want to mentally replace "knowledge" with the expression "information and misinformation."

(e.g., the motor commands involved in grasping a particular object). They are also characterized by the following cluster of properties: they tend to be less modular than the processes underlying the lower competences; they tend to be, to some extent, under intentional control; their products are often (or can be) conscious; and they tend to be slower than the processes underlying the lower competences.[5] Categorization, deduction, induction, analogy-making, linguistic understanding, and planning—all of these are higher cognitive competences.

Psychologists explain the nature of the higher and lower cognitive competences by positing cognitive processes, that is, series of operations that access some knowledge stored in memory to bring about the functions defining the cognitive competences. The processes that underlie perception, syntactic parsing, and motor planning are often believed to access their own proprietary memory stores. For instance, our implicit syntactic knowledge is only accessed by the processes underlying syntactic processing. By contrast, the processes that underlie the higher cognitive competences are usually believed to access the same memory store—our long-term memory.[6] When we categorize something as a dog, when we make some inductive generalization about dogs, when we draw some analogy between something and dogs, and when we understand the meaning of a sentence involving "dog," we access some knowledge about dogs that is stored in a non-proprietary memory store—our long-term memory (figure 1.1).[7]

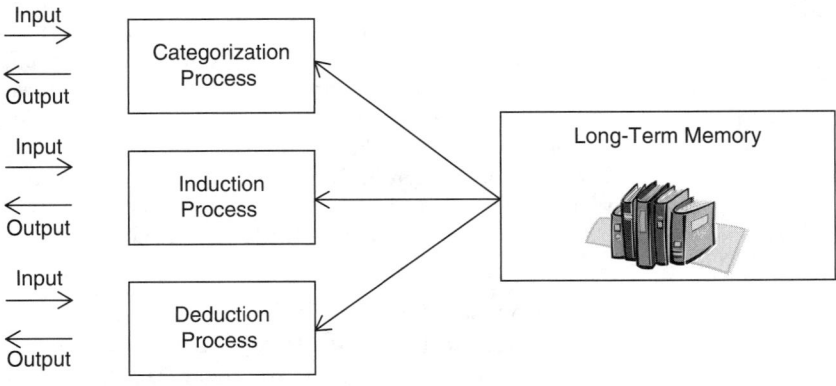

Figure 1.1 Long-Term Memory

---

[5] Clearly, not all these properties have to be possessed by the higher cognitive competences: linguistic understanding is not under intentional control and categorization can be extremely fast (Thorpe, Delorme, and VanRullen 2001). But higher cognitive competences typically possess several of these properties.

[6] If long-term memory divides into several distinct stores, as some neuropsychologists have proposed (e.g., Farah 2004; Caramazza and Mahon 2003, 2006), each of these stores is accessed by the cognitive processes underlying the higher cognitive competences.

[7] Martin and Chao 2001: 194; Barsalou et al. 2003: 84; Farah 2004: 143.

This is where the psychological notion of concept fits in. Psychologists often characterize concepts as those bodies of knowledge that are stored in long-term memory and that are used in the processes underlying the higher cognitive competences. To illustrate, Sam's concept of dog is his knowledge about dogs that is stored in his long-term memory and that is used when he categorizes something as a dog or draws some inductive inference about dogs.

This characterization of "concept" captures how psychologists of various theoretical persuasions use this theoretical term. In a recent review of his lab's work, psychologist Lawrence Barsalou, who has developed an influential neo-empiricist theory of concepts (section 4.5), proposes:

> The human conceptual system contains people's knowledge of the world. In most theories, the basic unit of knowledge is the concept. This construct is highly contentious, however.... Following psychological theories, we assume that *a concept, roughly speaking, is knowledge about a particular category* (e.g. birds, eating, happiness). Thus knowledge about birds represents the bodies, behaviors and origins of the respective entities. Knowledge plays a central role throughout the spectrum of cognitive activities. In on-line processing of the environment, knowledge guides perception, categorization and inference. In off-line processing of non-present situations, knowledge reconstructs memories, underlies the meanings of linguistic expressions, and provides the representations manipulated in thought. (Barsalou et al. 2003: 84; my emphasis)

Endorsing a different approach to concepts (viz., the theory paradigm, see section 4.4), psychologists Karen Solomon, Douglas Medin, and Elizabeth Lynch contend similarly:

> Concepts are the building blocks of thought. How concepts are formed, used, and updated are therefore, central questions in cognitive science.... Concepts serve multiple functions, and, as we will see, these functions are not independent of one another; rather, they interact with and influence each other.... A concept can be very difficult to define. However, in this paper, we will refer to a concept as *a mental representation that is used to meet a variety of cognitive functions.* (Solomon, Medin, and Lynch 1999: 99; my emphasis)

These recent characterizations are similar to older descriptions of what concepts are. For instance, in his oft-quoted review of the psychology of concepts in the 1980s, psychologist Lloyd Komatsu introduced the notion of concept as follows:

> Psychologists have traditionally equated knowing the meaning of a word with knowing (or perhaps more accurately, having) the concept labeled by a word.... In this approach, a concept is assumed to be the mental representation of a category or class (Gleitman, Armstrong, & Gleitman, 1983; Medin and Smith, 1984). The contents of such a mental representation (i.e., the intension of a word), in concert with certain assumptions about how those contents are processed, have been taken to explain a wide variety of phenomena, including people's knowledge of linguistic relations (e.g., synonymy, antinomy,

hyponymy), how people recognize the objects, events, and so on properly labeled by the word (i.e., the extension of the word), how people understand novel combinations of the word with other words, and the inferences people are able to make about an object, even, and so on, properly labeled by the word. (Komatsu 1992: 500)[8]

Although, sometimes, psychologists simply identify an individual's concept of *x* with his or her knowledge about *x* (see, for instance, Barsalou's quotation above), not every bit of knowledge about *x* is part of an individual's concept of *x*. Psychologists do distinguish between the knowledge that is stored in concepts and the knowledge that is not—for instance, between the knowledge about dogs that is stored in a concept of dog and the knowledge about dogs that is not—what I call the "background knowledge." Thus, psychologists often draw a distinction between semantic or conceptual knowledge (or memory) and encyclopedic knowledge (or memory). Semantic memory is supposed to contain the knowledge stored in concepts. By contrast, encyclopedic memory is supposed to contain the knowledge that is not stored in concepts.[9] This distinction naturally raises the following question: what distinguishes the knowledge that is stored in concepts from the background knowledge? I propose that psychologists assume, more or less explicitly, that concepts are bodies of knowledge that are used *by default* in the processes underlying the higher cognitive competences.

"Default" is used in a technical sense in artificial intelligence and computer science. Default inferences are defeasible inferences, that is, inferences that are normally drawn, except when some specific additional information is provided. Most inferences drawn by people are defeasible. When told that an object is moved, people are disposed to infer that its color has not changed, but they would not draw this inference if they were told that this object had been moved into a pail of paint. Thus, researchers on default inferences want first to emphasize that people presume that some inferential schemas are correct. Second, researchers on default inferences also highlight the fact that in some circumstances, people refrain from applying these inferential schemas.

Similarly, by using the term "default," I want to emphasize that an individual's concept of *x* is a body of knowledge about *x* that this individual presumptively takes to be relevant when she reasons about *x*, when she categorizes things as *x*, and so on. (This body of knowledge is not necessarily taken to be true: when I reason about unicorns, I use a body of knowledge about unicorns that I know not to be literally true—since there are no unicorns.) The knowledge that is stored in a concept of *x* is preferentially available when we think, reason, and so on, about *x*. So to

---

[8] See also Smith and Medin 1981: ch. 1; Barsalou 1989: 76; Medin 1989: 1469; Smith 1989: 502; Hampton and Dubois 1993: 13, 17; Barsalou 1999: 581; Murphy 2002: 92; Goldstone and Kersten 2003: 600.

[9] See, e.g., Komatsu 1992: 520–21; Markman 1999: 95; Prinz 2002: 154–161; Thompson-Schill 2003: 280.

speak, it spontaneously comes to mind. By contrast, the knowledge about *x* that is not stored in a concept of *x* is less available—it does not spontaneously come to mind. The knowledge that is not stored in a concept of *x* is used only when the knowledge that is stored in this concept is insufficient or inadequate for the task at hand. In such cases, people access their long-term memory in order to retrieve some additional knowledge about *x* that helps them deal with the task at hand (i.e., some knowledge that is not stored in the concept of *x*).

It is worth noting that the boundaries of concepts can be vague. That is, for some elements of knowledge, it might be indeterminate whether they belong to an individual's concept of *x* or to his or her background knowledge about *x*. Moreover, what is constitutive of a concept rather than of the background knowledge changes with experience (e.g., Barsalou 1987).

To summarize, many psychologists believe that there are some bodies of knowledge that are used by default in the processes underlying the higher cognitive competences (categorization, inductive reasoning, analogy-making, etc.)—or, at least, in most of them—when these processes result in judgments about the referents of these bodies of knowledge (figure 1.2).[10] This class is the extension of the theoretical term "concept." That is, within psychology, the theoretical term "concept" is commonly used as follows:

(C) A concept of *x* is a body of knowledge about *x* that is stored in long-term memory and that is used by default in the processes underlying most, if not all, higher cognitive competences when these processes result in judgments about *x*.

Note that C is not a theory of concepts. Rather, C attempts to describe what most psychologists take concepts to be. As we will see in section 1.3, theories of concepts develop specific hypotheses about the properties of the bodies of knowledge used by default in the processes underlying the higher cognitive competences—particularly about the nature of the knowledge stored in concepts, about how this knowledge is used in cognitive processes, and so on.

I end this introductory section with five important points. First, concepts are supposed to be about various types of entity. Most research has focused on concepts of classes of three-dimensional, medium-sized objects, such as animals or artifacts (Komatsu 1992: 501). These classes are usually called "categories" in the psychological literature. There has also been some research on concepts of events (Schank and Abelson 1977; Lancaster and Barsalou 1997; Gennari et al. 2002) and of substances (Malt 1994), as well as some research on abstract concepts, such as GOOD, JUSTICE, SCIENCE, or CAUSE (Hampton 1981; Mandler 1992; Barsalou 2003).[11] Finally, some psychologists have also begun studying the bodies of knowledge about

---

[10] Because nothing hangs on this, in this book, I will use "reference," "referent," and "extension" interchangeably.

[11] Names of concepts are written in small caps. Names of properties are written in italics.

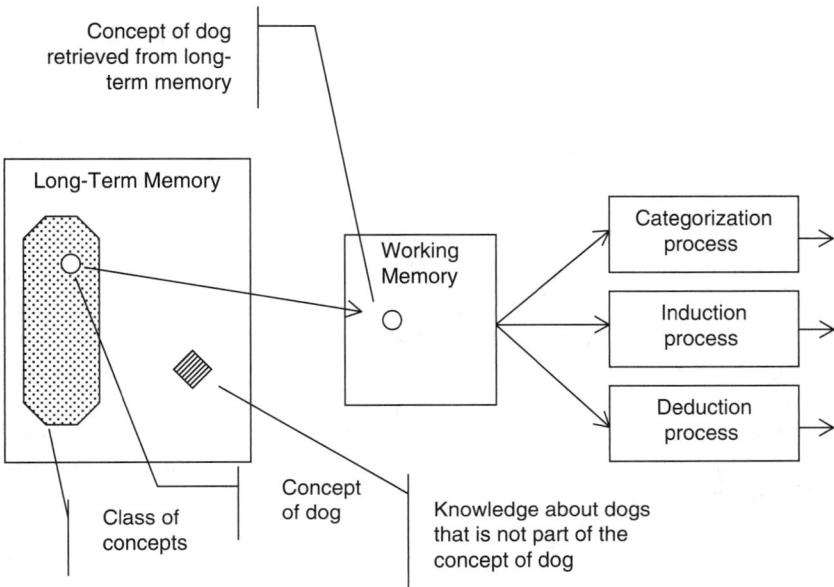

Figure 1.2 The Notion of Concept

individuals, for example, about John F. Kennedy (Rips, Blok, and Newman 2006).

Second, the characterization of concepts proposed in C is largely neutral with respect to the debate between connectionism and the classical architecture of cognition. That it is consistent with the classical approach to cognition is clear enough. I contend that to a large extent, it is also consistent with connectionism. Although they disagree with classicists about the nature of our cognitive processes, connectionists often assert that cognition is usefully described by means of theoretical notions such as plans, beliefs, goals, knowledge structures, and concepts (e.g., Smolensky 1991; Clark 1993).

This being said, connectionists might balk at some aspects of the notion of concept made explicit by C. First, connectionists typically do not distinguish between processes and memory stores, while C draws a distinction between them. Second, and more important, it is unclear whether connectionists can draw a distinction between the knowledge stored in a concept and the background knowledge. Connectionists have long argued that in a connectionist network, knowledge is implemented in the weights of the links between the nodes of this network. When a connectionist network produces some output on the basis of some input, all the weights—thus, the whole knowledge in this network—contribute to processing the input. As a result, it is unclear how to distinguish the knowledge that is used by default in cognitive processes from the background knowledge. I will leave it to connectionists to amend

C or to show that connectionism can accommodate a distinction between default knowledge and background knowledge. Prima facie, the former could be done without modifying C beyond recognition.

Third, in the psychological literature, "concept" is sometimes used interchangeably with "mental representation" (e.g., Markman 1999), "category representation" (e.g., Barsalou 1990), "knowledge representation" (e.g., Markman 1999; Hahn and Ramscar 2001), "knowledge structure" (e.g., Read 1987; Barsalou 1989: 76), "semantic representation" (e.g., Devlin, Rushworth, and Matthews 2005), and "conceptual structures" (e.g., Hahn and Ramscar 2001). C explains what is often meant by these terms. The long-term memory that is believed to store concepts is sometimes called "semantic memory" (e.g., Thompson-Schill 2003). In what follows, I will exclusively use the expressions "concept" and "long-term memory."

Fourth, I distinguish concepts from categories as follows. While a concept is a body of knowledge that is stored in long-term memory, a category is a class of objects.[12] Sam's concept of dog is a body of knowledge about a specific category, the category of dogs. Thus, categories are not in the head, as psychologists sometimes say. Rather, concepts are in the head, while categories are in the world: a concept of dog is in the head, while the category of dogs is in the world.

Finally, philosophically minded readers probably want to know how, in my view, concepts are individuated. It is important to distinguish within-individual individuation and between-individual individuation. A theory of within-individual individuation determines when two coreferential bodies of knowledge that are possessed by a single individual constitute two different concepts. In section 3.1, I propose two sufficient conditions for two coreferential bodies of knowledge to count as two distinct concepts. A theory of between-individual individuation determines when two coreferential bodies of knowledge that are possessed by two individuals are the same concept. It establishes what makes it the case that Marie's default body of knowledge about dogs and John's default body of knowledge about dogs count as the same concept of dog or, rather, as two different concepts of dog. I have no theory of between-individual individuation to offer. But there is no need to be apologetic about this because psychologists probably do not need such a theory. Psychologists attempt to identify the properties possessed by concepts in general, including Marie's and John's concepts of dog. For this purpose, it is irrelevant whether John's and Marie's concepts of dog count or do not count as the same concept.

1.2 Evidence for the Existence of Concepts

In this section, I briefly review some evidence that C applies to some bodies of knowledge stored in long-term memory (more evidence will

---

[12] I will use interchangeably "category" and "class."

be discussed in the remainder of the book). Thus, "concept" is not an empty term.

1.2.1 Default Bodies of Knowledge

Is there any reason to believe that a subset of our knowledge about, say, dogs is used by default when we reason about dogs, categorize something as a dog, and so on? From the standpoint of efficiency, it makes a lot of sense to have a body of knowledge about dogs that is used by default in the processes underlying the higher cognitive competences. We cannot retrieve from long-term memory all of our knowledge about dogs when we reason about dogs (categorize, draw analogies, etc.), since only a limited amount of information can be held in working memory at any time. As a result, if we did not have a default body of knowledge about dogs, we would have to select systematically from among all the facts that we know about dogs those that are relevant to the situations we are in. Of course, we are able to retrieve from memory those elements of knowledge that are relevant to the situations we are in. But possessing bodies of knowledge that are used by default when we categorize, draw an inductive inference, and so on, heavily reduces the need for a systematic selection of context-relevant knowledge.

Evidence concurs with this plausibility argument. A striking piece of evidence comes from linguistics: words seem to be associated with default bodies of knowledge. Consider the following sentence (Ziff 1972, quoted in Murphy and Medin 1985: 303–304):

(1) A cheetah can outrun a man

(1) is a meaningful sentence and most people would agree with it. However, as Murphy and Medin put it (1985: 303), it is true only if the cheetah is not "a 1-day old cheetah, or an aged cheetah with arthritis, or a healthy cheetah with a 100-pound weight on its back." But when we read (1), these representations of cheetahs do not come to mind. This phenomenon suggests that when a speaker utters (1) or when a hearer or a reader understands (1), he or she retrieves from memory a default body of knowledge about cheetahs.

If there are bodies of knowledge that are used by default in the processes underlying most higher cognitive competences, one would like to know the determining factors for what knowledge is included in a concept and what knowledge is part of the background knowledge. The answer to this question is currently at best tentative. Evidence suggests that frequency is an important factor. When some element of knowledge about a category is often used in categorization or in induction, this element of knowledge is likely to be part of a default body of knowledge (Barsalou 1987). Other factors may be important as well. Explicit teaching may partly determine which elements of knowledge become parts of concepts. For instance, children are explicitly taught that whales are mammals, and not fish. This element of knowledge may be part of people's concept of whale.

1.2.2 Promiscuous Bodies of Knowledge

I turn to another aspect of the notion of concept. When Sam categorizes something as a table, draws an analogy between tables and some other objects, draws an inductive inference about tables, and understands a sentence with the word "table" in it, the relevant cognitive processes are believed to retrieve by default the same body of knowledge about tables from long-term memory. By analogy to Stich's (1978) notion of the inferential promiscuity of beliefs, I call "conceptual promiscuity" the fact that the processes underlying different cognitive competences (categorization, analogy making, induction...) use the same bodies of knowledge. Note that the conceptual promiscuity of concepts is consistent with the processes underlying some higher cognitive competences tapping into proprietary memory stores, instead of tapping into a non-proprietary shared memory. The conceptual promiscuity of concepts merely requires them to be used in the processes underlying most higher cognitive competences.

Most psychologists interested in concepts endorse the conceptual promiscuity of concepts. For instance, Douglas Medin and Edward Shoben write, "*The same packet of information is employed in a wide range of contexts*, including the case where a concept is used in combination with other concepts" (1988: 158; my emphasis). And Susan Gelman and Medin concur:

> *Concepts function in enormously varied ways.* They can be used for extremely rapid identification (as when escaping from prey), organizing information efficiently in memory, problem-solving, analogizing, drawing inductive inferences, that extend knowledge beyond what is known, embodying and imparting ideological inferences, conveying aesthetic materials (e.g., metaphor, poetry), and so forth.... *In short, conceptual functions go beyond categorization.* (Gelman and Medin 1993: 158–159; my emphasis)[13]

There is also a substantial amount of evidence for the conceptual promiscuity of concepts. Much evidence will be discussed in the remainder of this book. Here, I focus on a striking finding in developmental psychology. In their book *Words, Thoughts, and Theories* (1997), Alison Gopnik and Andrew Meltzoff show that during infancy and childhood, when a specific concept changes, this change affects numerous cognitive competences and is manifest in the tasks that tap into these competences. This finding shows that the relevant concepts are used in the processes

---

[13] See also Gelman and Coley 1991: 162; Solomon, Medin, and Lynch 1999; Murphy 2002: 3; Goldstone and Kersten 2003: 601–603.

underlying several cognitive competences, consistent with the idea that concepts are promiscuous.

An example might cast some light on this idea. Gopnik and Meltzoff contend that between 15 and 18 months, children's concept of object changes in that they come to think about objects' spatial properties differently: objects' appearances and disappearances are thought by 18-month-old children, but not by younger children, to be the "consequences of movements, including invisible movements, either of objects or of the observer" (1997: 108). What matters for present purposes is that this change affects several distinct cognitive competences—particularly children's reasoning about the location of objects and their linguistic capacities.

Let us examine children's spatial reasoning first. Eighteen-month-old children, but not younger children, are able to solve Piaget's A-not-B search task (Piaget 1954). In the A-not-B search task, an object is repeatedly hidden at location A and uncovered at this location. Then, children see the object being hidden at location B. The children's task is to search for the object. Nine-month-old children fail: they search at A. Eighteen-month-old children succeed: they search at B. Although the interpretation of children's failures and successes in this task is controversial, Gopnik and Meltzoff contend that these failures and successes provide evidence for a change in children's understanding of the causes of objects' appearances and disappearances. Particularly, children come to understand that an object that is located at a location x cannot be at a location y, except if it moves or is moved from x to y.

Importantly for present purposes, this change in children's concept of object is also manifested by children's linguistic production. Around 18 months, children start using the term "gone" to refer to an object that is hidden—that is, to an object that is at a location x, but that is not visible. The appearance of this new term suggests that 18-month-old children have come to understand that the location of an object can change only if this object has moved or has been moved from one place to the other.

These findings provide evidence for the conceptual promiscuity of the concept OBJECT. The same body of knowledge about the properties of three-dimensional physical objects is used by children in the processes underlying their capacity to solve spatial problems and in the processes underlying linguistic understanding and production. Together with the numerous other examples examined by Gopnik and Meltzoff (BELIEF, ACTION, etc.), this is strong evidence for the conceptual promiscuity of concepts.

1.3 What Is a Psychological Theory of Concepts?

Since the 1970s, psychologists have proposed several theories of concepts—particularly prototype theories, exemplar theories, theory theories, and neo-empiricist theories (chapter 4). To a large extent, these theories give different answers to the same set of questions. The goal of section 1.3 is to lay out these questions.

1.3.1 Theory of Concepts versus Theory of Specific Concepts

In many areas of psychology, there is a sustained interest in specific concepts. For instance, in the 1990s, developmental psychologists have intensely studied children's concept of object.[14] In this case, the focus was on the properties that characterize a specific concept—OBJECT. There is also a sustained interest in specific classes of concepts. For example, developmental psychologist Susan Carey has focused on children's and adults' concepts of biological entities, including concepts of animals, plants, and biological events such as death or growth.[15] The focus here is on the properties that characterize a specific class of concepts—the concepts of biological entities.

Theories of concepts focus neither on specific concepts nor on specific classes of concepts. They usually aim at characterizing the properties that are true of most, if not all, concepts—the general properties of concepts.[16] This is the avowed goal of prototype theories, exemplar theories, or the recent neo-empiricist theories of concepts. Of course, specifying the general properties of concepts does not have to be the unique goal of a theory of concepts. Although it is natural to expect a theory of a class of entities *x*'s to describe the scientifically relevant properties that are true of most *x*'s—that is, to formulate inductive generalizations about this class (chapter 8)—such a theory could also purport to map scientifically relevant distinctions among subclasses of *x*'s (Medin, Lynch, and Solomon 2000). That being said, for the most part, theories of concepts have purported to identify the general properties of concepts.

1.3.2 What Are the Scientifically Relevant Properties of Concepts?

What are psychologists' generalizations about? In other words, what are the scientifically relevant properties of concepts? Theories of concepts focus on five properties of concepts: (1) the kind of knowledge stored in concepts, (2) the format of concepts, (3) their use in cognitive processes, (4) their acquisition, and (5) their neural localization. The first three properties have been more important in psychology than the last two properties.

1. *Kind of knowledge stored in concepts*: Characterizing the nature of the knowledge that is stored in a concept may be the most important goal

---

[14] See, e.g., Spelke et al. 1992; Baillargeon, Kotovsky, and Needham 1995.
[15] Carey 1985; Medin and Atran 1999; Inagaki and Hatano 2006.
[16] See, e.g., Murphy 2002: 2–3; Prinz 2002: 3.

of a theory of concepts. As we shall see at length in chapter 4, psychologists have attempted to determine whether a concept of a category x (a substance, a type of event, etc.) stores some causal knowledge about the members of x, some knowledge about their typical properties, or some knowledge about specific members of x. Characterizing the knowledge stored in concepts allows psychologists to explain various properties of human cognitive competences. For instance, the hypothesis that very early on, concepts store some causal knowledge explains why people, including young toddlers, can engage spontaneously in many kinds of causal reasoning (Gopnik et al. 2004).

2. *Format*: Psychologists have also been interested in the nature of the vehicle of concepts. Such an interest has a long history. Philosophers such as Descartes, Hume, or Kant wondered whether concepts were images, amodal symbols, or yet something else. This philosophical debate was echoed in the introspectionist phase of the psychology of concepts in the twentieth century, and it has resurfaced in recent years, when several psychologists and philosophers started arguing that rather than being amodal, the vehicles of concepts are similar to the vehicles of perceptual representations.[17] Characterizing the nature of the vehicle of concepts allows psychologists to explain various properties of our higher cognitive competences. Thus, Potter and colleagues (1986) reasoned that if concepts are images, replacing words in a sentence with pictures, for instance, replacing the word "cat" in the sentence "The cat is on the mat" with the picture of a cat, should not modify people's reading speed.[18]

3. *Use*: Concepts are used in the processes that underlie the higher cognitive competences. Specifying how they are used is an important goal of theories of concepts. Theories of concepts are often closely associated with theories of specific cognitive processes (such as the processes underlying categorization) as well as with descriptions of the general properties of the processes that use the assumed kind of concept. For instance, prototype theories typically hypothesize that the processes underlying categorization, inductive reasoning, analogy-making, and so on, have many properties in common (see chapter 4).

4. *Acquisition*: Theories of concepts have often, though not always, included hypotheses concerning how concepts are acquired.[19] There are various ways to study the acquisition of concepts. Developmental psychologists focus on how children acquire their stock of concepts. The acquisition of concepts by children has also been studied by school psychologists, who are interested in how formal teaching can improve or hinder children's acquisition of specific concepts, such as mathematical concepts.

---

[17] See, e.g., Barsalou 1999; Barsalou et al. 2003; Prinz 2002; Machery 2006b, 2007a; section 4.5 below.

[18] See also Miller and Johnson-Laird 1976; Paivio 1986.

[19] See, e.g., Rosch 1978; Carey 1985; Mandler 1992; Carey and Spelke 1994; Gopnik and Meltzoff 1997; Gopnik et al. 2004.

Concept acquisition can also be studied in adults. In fact, the study of concept acquisition in adults (usually called "concept learning") has been at the heart of the psychology of concepts (see chapter 6 below).

5. *Neural localization*: Recently, neuropsychologists have focused on the neural localization of concepts. Study of deficits involving the loss of some or all concepts—category-specific deficits and semantic dementia[20]—and more recently neuroimagery[21] are used to discover where concepts are localized. Localization is usually not pursued for its own sake, but is expected to cast some light on the nature of concepts. Neuropsychologists use their knowledge about the brains areas in which concepts are localized to infer some properties of concepts. Chapter 4 (section 4.1) and Chapter 7 discuss some of the findings in the fast-growing, but confusing field of the neuropsychology of concepts.

1.3.3 The Standard Methodology

One might wonder how psychologists can come to know what type of knowledge is stored in concepts and what their format is. Psychologists' main strategy is based on the following rationale. The properties of concepts explain how people categorize, reason inductively, draw analogies, or understand sentences. The properties of Jamie's concept of dog explain why she categorizes dogs the way she does, why she draws analogies about dogs the way she does, and so on. Similarly, the general properties of concepts explain the properties that the higher cognitive competences possess, whatever concept is involved. The general properties of concepts explain the properties of our categorization decisions, whether we categorize something as a dog, as a table, as water, or as a birthday party (*mutatis mutandis* for induction, analogy-making, etc.). In agreement with this rationale, psychologists inductively infer what kind of knowledge is stored in concepts and what the format of concepts is from subjects' performances in tasks that tap into higher cognition. We will encounter numerous examples of this methodology in this book.

Importantly, psychologists can infer what kind of knowledge is stored in concepts and what their format is from subjects' performances in experimental tasks only if they entertain some hypotheses about how concepts are used in the cognitive processes involved in solving these tasks. As argued by cognitive psychologist John Anderson (1978), without some assumptions about the nature of the cognitive processes that a given task taps into, any theory about the format of concepts can be made to be consistent with subjects' performances in this task. That is, it is always possible to cook up hypotheses about the nature of the cognitive processes used in a task that, together with the theory about the format of concepts, would accommodate

---

[20] On category-specific deficits, see, e.g., Caramazza and Mahon 2003, 2006; on semantic dementia, see, e.g., Davies et al. 2005.

[21] See, e.g., Martin and Chao 2001; Thompson-Schill 2003.

subjects' performances. The same is true for hypotheses about the kind of knowledge stored in concepts. The moral is this: testing hypotheses about the format of concepts or about what kind of knowledge is stored in concepts without developing hypotheses about the nature of the cognitive processes using these concepts is methodologically inappropriate. Psychologists ought to study concepts and cognitive processes together. Once assumptions about the processes that are involved in solving a given task have been fixed, subjects' performances in this task can be viewed as providing evidence about the format of concepts or about what kind of knowledge is stored in concepts. I call this methodology "the standard methodology." As we shall see in this book, psychologists have typically complied with the standard methodology.

1.4 Alternative Characterizations of the Notion of Concept

Tenet C (a concept of x is a body of knowledge about x that is stored in long-term memory and that is used by default in the processes underlying most, if not all, higher cognitive competences when they result in judgments about x) is not entirely uncontroversial. There are other accounts of the notion of concept in psychology and in the philosophy of psychology. In the last section of this chapter, I consider the most common alternatives.[22] First, I reject two alternatives that are inconsistent with the notion of concept expressed by C (concepts as temporary bodies of knowledge in working memory and concepts as bodies of knowledge under organismic control). Second, I critically discuss two alternatives that, though consistent with C, highlight different aspects of concepts (concepts as constituents of thoughts and concepts as categorization devices).

1.4.1 Concepts as Temporary Bodies of Knowledge in Working Memory

Barsalou has proposed that instead of being default bodies of knowledge in long-term memory, concepts are temporary bodies of knowledge in working memory. According to his proposal, concepts are constructed on the fly so that we can reason, categorize, and so on, in a context-sensitive manner.[23] Barsalou (1993: 34) recognizes that this characterization is heterodox but, nevertheless, maintains that it is needed to capture important facts about how knowledge is used in cognitive processes: we retrieve relevant, context-specific subsets of the knowledge in long-term memory. He writes (see also Komatsu 1992: 520):

---

[22] "Concept" has been used in yet other ways in the psychological literature (e.g., Michalski 1993; Shanks 1997).

[23] Barsalou 1987, 1989, 1993; see also Prinz 2002.

> The concept of *concept* is not only slippery, taking diverse forms not only across the cognitive science disciplines, but also across perspectives within disciplines. In this chapter, I develop the view that *a concept is a temporary construction in working memory, derived from a larger body of knowledge in long-term memory to represent a category*, where a category, roughly speaking, is a related set of entities from any ontological type.... Across contexts, a given person's concept for the same category may change, utilizing different knowledge from long-term memory, at least to some extent. (Barsalou 1993: 29; my emphasis)

Barsalou's characterization of concepts is inappropriate. First of all, variation across contexts of the knowledge brought to bear by a given subject on a given task is consistent with the characterization of concepts as bodies of knowledge used by default in the processes underlying the higher cognitive competences. Two facts might explain why the knowledge brought to bear on tasks varies across contexts. First, in some contexts, people might retrieve some additional knowledge about x in addition to the knowledge stored in their concept of x—that is, they might retrieve some background knowledge about x. Second, it may also be that concepts are (sometimes or often) adapted to the relevant circumstances, as has been suggested by Sperber and Wilson (1998). In this case, knowledge retrieval from long-term memory would be a two-step procedure. People would first retrieve from long-term memory the whole body of knowledge that constitutes a given concept; they would then select a subset of this body of knowledge in order to use the knowledge relevant in the present context.

What would not be consistent with the view that concepts are bodies of knowledge that are used by default in the processes underlying the higher cognitive competences is a strong variability across contexts of the knowledge brought to bear on tasks. The characterization of concepts proposed in C predicts that this variability will typically be small. And, in fact, Barsalou does contend that the knowledge used in solving experimental tasks strongly varies across contexts. To provide evidence for this view, Barsalou argues that there is a "*tremendous variability* in performances... not only in category membership, but also in typicality, definitions, and probably most other categorization tasks" (1993: 34; my emphasis).

However, the examples of "tremendous variability in performances" mentioned by Barsalou fail to show that the knowledge retrieved from long-term memory strongly varies across contexts. First, Barsalou mentions his work on ad hoc categories (Barsalou 1983; chapter 4 below). Ad hoc categories are categories for which people do not have a concept permanently stored in long-term memory; rather, people produce bodies of knowledge about ad hoc categories on the fly. For instance, when getting ready for a trip, people may think about the things to pack in a small suitcase for a trip abroad. They do not retrieve a body of knowledge about those things to pack in a small suitcase for a trip abroad from long-term memory; rather, they produce this body of knowledge on the fly. The research on ad hoc categories is extremely interesting, but it says nothing about how people think of categories for which they have some knowledge in long-term memory.

Barsalou also refers to his work on how people's evaluation of the typicality of objects with respect to specific categories changes when people are asked to take different points of view. For instance, American subjects judge that robins are highly typical birds for Americans and that swans are highly typical birds for Chinese. Barsalou takes this finding to show that how people think about birds strongly varies across contexts. This is certainly an interesting finding, but it does not show that there are no default bodies of knowledge. For, even if a default body of knowledge about birds exists, we will use our background knowledge about birds to evaluate the typicality of different species of birds from the points of view of people who are known to have very different experiences. For instance, we might reason that because swans are common birds in China, they are likely to be judged typical by Chinese. Thus, that typicality judgments vary when subjects take different points of view is consistent with the idea that we possess default bodies of knowledge.

Barsalou also reports the following findings. On two occasions (two weeks apart), subjects were asked to describe bachelors, birds, chairs, and so on (a feature production task). Overlap in the properties mentioned by different subjects on a given occasion and by the same subject across the two occasions was calculated. Barsalou and colleagues found that only 44 percent of the properties mentioned by a given subject were mentioned by another subject and that only 66 percent of the properties mentioned by a subject on a given occasion were mentioned by this very subject on the other occasion. Barsalou (1993: 32) concludes that there is "substantial flexibility in how an individual conceptualized the same category on different occasions." These findings are consistent with previous results. For instance, Barclay and colleagues (1974) have shown that when a given word is used in two different contexts, different properties become salient. When "piano" is used in a musical context, the properties of pianos related to music become salient, but when "piano" is used in a context of moving out, the properties related to their physical dimensions, such as their weight, become salient. Thus, different properties of pianos are represented in working memory in these two linguistic contexts. Together, these findings do show that there is some variability in the knowledge about x (pianos, bachelors, etc.) people rely on in different contexts.

Ironically, however, Barsalou's own findings show that the variability of the knowledge we bring to bear in different contexts is small and is thus consistent with the existence of bodies of knowledge being retrieved by default from long-term memory. In the experiment just described, Barsalou and colleagues found that, on average, seven out of ten properties listed by a given subject on a given occasion were listed on a further occasion (66 percent to be exact). This is a high correlation across occasions. This is strong evidence that, across occasions, a default concept was retrieved from long-term memory.

Besides alluding to the findings just discussed, Barsalou also proposes the following argument (1993: 34). We ought to reserve the term "concept" for the bodies of knowledge in working memory, and not for our knowledge in long-term memory, because the former, and not the latter, "control behavior." What explains people's performances in a given task is the subset of their whole knowledge that was retrieved from long-term memory during that task, namely the bodies of knowledge that were held in working memory during that task. Because "concept" is meant to pick out the bodies of knowledge that explain people's behavior and cognitive performances, "concept" should refer to the bodies of knowledge in working memory.

This argument fails to be convincing, however. Referring to default bodies of knowledge in long-term memory explains why people behave similarly in different contexts. For instance, John's default body of knowledge about fish explains why across contexts, he classifies red snappers as fish. It also explains why he classifies red snappers, trout, sharks, flounder, tuna, and guppies as fish. By contrast, referring to a body of knowledge in working memory can only explain someone's behavior in a given context. Explaining similarities across contexts is part of what the traditional notion of concept, which Barsalou wants to reject, was supposed to do. This explanatory role of the traditional notion of a concept justifies holding on to it.

1.4.2 Concepts as Bodies of Knowledge under Organismic Control

Philosopher Jesse Prinz has suggested that concepts are representations "under organismic control" (2004: 45). The idea is that these representations can be retrieved from long-term memory and manipulated intentionally. Of course, Prinz does not deny that they can also be retrieved from memory non-intentionally. Indeed, during perception, categorization takes place automatically. But Prinz maintains that to qualify as concepts, representations should also be intentionally retrievable and usable. Daniel Dennett (1993, 1996: 157) adds that concepts can also be intentionally considered. That is, concepts can be the objects of second-order mental states—not only do we have concepts, not only do we intentionally manipulate them, but we can also intentionally think about them. Thus, Prinz and Dennett propose that concepts are characterized by specific functional properties: being poised to be intentionally used and to be intentionally considered.

Prinz's and Dennett's characterization of concepts can be seen as fleshing out a common, but somewhat obscure distinction in the philosophy of mind, namely, the distinction between personal and subpersonal mental states (Dennett 1969; McDowell 1994). Mental states at the personal level are attributed to persons. This is the case of beliefs and desires: for instance, the belief that G. W. Bush has been the worst American President ever is attributed to persons. By contrast, mental states at the subpersonal level are not attributed to persons, but rather are viewed as states of parts of persons, such as brain systems. For instance, when Maria looks at people walking on the sidewalk from her office window, the identification of the edges of the volumes in her visual field is not attributed to her. Rather, edge identification is a state of her visual system.

So characterized, it is unclear why the distinction between personal and subpersonal states has been believed to pick out different kinds of mental state, rather than to be a mere linguistic accident. After all, it does not do much violence to our linguistic practices to ascribe edge identification and other prototypical subpersonal states to persons, nor does it to view beliefs, desires, concepts, and emotions as states of brain systems. Indeed, linguistic practices are labile. States, such as edge identification, are commonly ascribed to persons in neuropsychology.

One might object that it is a conceptual truth that beliefs, desires, and emotions are states of persons, while edge identification and sentence parsing are states of parts of persons. On this view, by ascribing beliefs to parts of individuals, neuropsychologists and others either are committing a conceptual mistake or are changing the subject, that is, are no longer talking about beliefs, but about other states. This objection ought to be resisted, however. The linguistic practices of the objector are assumed to define what counts as conceptual truths, and deviances from her linguistic practices are assumed to be conceptual mistakes. But there is simply no reason to grant the objector's linguistic practices such a status.

So, is the distinction between states at the personal level and states at the subpersonal level a mere linguistic quirk? Not necessarily. Prinz's and Dennett's characterization of the notion of concept might be seen as clarifying this distinction. Personal states have some specific functional properties: they can be intentionally used and considered. Subpersonal states do not have these functional properties. According to this proposal, human beliefs and desires are personal, while edge identification and syntactic parsing are not. Note that when the distinction is drawn this way, it does not make sense to claim that the same state can be characterized both at the subpersonal and the personal levels. Instead, some states are personal, while others are subpersonal, depending on their functional properties.

Clearly, Prinz and Dennett emphasize important functional properties of some mental states. However, two questions are raised by their approach. First, is the class of bodies of knowledge used by default in the processes underlying the higher cognitive competences characterized by the functional properties highlighted by Prinz and Dennett? If not, should we use the term "concept" to refer to the class of bodies of knowledge that have these functional properties or should we prefer the characterization of concepts proposed in C?

The answer to the first question is probably negative. Certainly, some of the bodies of knowledge that are used by default in the processes underlying the higher cognitive competences can be intentionally used and some can become the objects of second-order thoughts. However, there is no reason to believe that all can be.

If this is the case, one could use the term "concept" to refer only to those bodies of knowledge that can be intentionally used in higher cognitive processes and that can be the objects of second-order thoughts rather than to the bodies of knowledge used by default in the processes underlying the higher cognitive competences. However, this proposal should be resisted because it does not capture the use of "concept" in psychology, neuropsychology, and cognitive science. Indeed, numerous psychologists call "concepts" some bodies of knowledge that are incidentally acquired—that is, that are acquired without people being aware that they have acquired them—and that are only used in implicit processes—that is, in processes that do not require intentional control (e.g., Ashby et al. 1998).

1.4.3 Concepts as Constituents of Thoughts

In the philosophy of psychology, concepts are usually introduced as constituents, components, or parts of thoughts. For instance, in their recent review of the philosophy and psychology of concepts, Eric Margolis and Steve Laurence introduce the notion of concept as follows: "Thoughts are seen as having constituents or parts, namely, concepts" (2004: 190).[24] Some psychologists endorse this characterization. Solomon and colleagues introduce the notion of concept by means of the common metaphor of "building blocks of thoughts" (1999: 99).

Characterizing concepts as constituents of thoughts is consistent with characterizing them as bodies of knowledge used by default in the processes underlying the higher cognitive competences, as proposed in C, since these bodies of knowledge could also be constituents of thoughts. Indeed, some psychologists characterize concepts both as constituents of thoughts and as those bodies of knowledge that are used by default in the processes underlying the higher cognitive competences (e.g., Solomon, Medin, and Lynch 1999).

Nonetheless, the characterization of concepts proposed in C is to be preferred to the characterization of concepts as constituents of thoughts. My first and main qualm with the characterization of concepts under consideration is that the notions of component and constituent and, *a fortiori*, metaphors like "building blocks" are typically not fully explained. As a result, what this characterization of "concept" amounts to is not entirely clear.

Of course, a well-known account of the notion of constituent can be found in the language-of-thought hypothesis.[25] According to the language-of-thought hypothesis, mental states, such as beliefs, desires, and other

---

[24] See also Fodor 1998: 26; Prinz 2002: 2.
[25] Fodor 1975; Newell and Simon 1976; Pylyshyn 1984; Fodor and Pylyshyn 1988; Van Gelder 1990.

propositional attitudes, are representations. Like other representations, such as paintings or sentences, mental states consist of a vehicle endowed with some semantic properties, such as reference, sense, or truth conditions (the content of the representation). The vehicle of the representation is the physical entity that has these semantic properties. A second tenet of the language-of-thought hypothesis is that there are two kinds of mental representation. Some mental representations are simple (or primitive), while other representations are complex, that is, made out of simpler representations (and, ultimately, out of simple representations) according to rules of composition, often called "grammar" or "syntax." The content of a complex representation is a function of the content of the simpler representations out of which it is made together with the relevant rules of composition.

Let us focus on the second tenet of the language-of-thought hypothesis. In any representational scheme that distinguishes simple and complex representations, a specific operation on vehicles must correspond to each rule of composition (Van Gelder 1990). For instance, in some logical systems, the following operation on vehicles corresponds to conjunction: the conjunction of $\ulcorner \Psi \urcorner$ and $\ulcorner \Phi \urcorner$ is to be written $\ulcorner (\Psi \mathbin{\&} \Phi) \urcorner$.[26] As Van Gelder (1990) correctly argued, according to the language-of-thought hypothesis, the operations on vehicles corresponding to the rules of composition are structural relations between vehicles. Spatial concatenation of written words of natural languages and temporal concatenation of spoken words of natural languages are two possible structural relations between simpler representations. The conjunction of two sentences in English, for instance, of "The dog is on the mat" and "The beer is in the fridge," corresponds to a spatial relation between each sentence: the first sentence is written on the left of "and" while the second sentence is written on the right of "and." Thus, the conjunction of these two sentences is "The dog is on the mat and the beer is in the fridge." If token mental representations are brain states, then, according to the language-of-thought hypothesis, a brain state that realizes a complex mental representation consists in several brain states, which realizes the compounded simple representations, standing in some structural relation. This point was put very clearly by Fodor and Pylyshyn, "The symbol structures in a classical model are assumed to correspond to real physical structures in the brain and *the combinatorial structure* of a representation is assumed to have a counterpart in structural relations among physical properties of the brain" (1988: 13). According to the language-of-thought hypothesis approach, the notion of constituency has thus a very clear sense.

However, if one rejects or even remains noncommittal about the language-of-thought hypothesis, the notions of constituent and

---

[26] A given rule of composition, such as conjunction, often corresponds to different operations on vehicles in different representational systems. For instance, besides the operation mentioned in the text, conjunction may also correspond to the following operation on vehicles: The conjunction of $\ulcorner \Psi \urcorner$ and $\ulcorner \Phi \urcorner$ is to be written $\ulcorner K\, \Psi \Phi) \urcorner$.

component should be clarified. Although I am confident that this can be done (for some suggestions, see Van Gelder 1990), typically, no explanation is given of what is meant by these notions (e.g., Prinz 2002: 2).

The second reason for preferring C to the characterization of concepts as constituents of thoughts is that this characterization often plays little role in the experimental psychology of concepts, while the characterization proposed in C is indeed central to this field. Psychologists working on categorization (see chapter 6 below) and on induction (see chapter 7 below) focus on the nature of the knowledge in long-term memory and on how this knowledge is used in cognitive processes. Obviously, this is congenial to the idea that concepts are bodies of knowledge that are used by default in the processes underlying the higher cognitive competences.

One might object that psychologists are also working on concept combination (for a review, see also Murphy 2002: ch. 12). Does this suggest that the notion of a concept as a component of thoughts plays an important role in psychology? I doubt it. The field of concept combination focuses on how people produce bodies of knowledge about classes for which we have no concept permanently stored in long-term memory. For instance, most people do not store in long-term memory a body of knowledge about Oxford graduates who are carpenters. But people are able to create a temporary body of knowledge about Oxford graduates who are carpenters out of the bodies of knowledge about Oxford graduates and about carpenters. This is what the psychology of concept combination is about, as we will see in more detail in chapter 7. This field is not built on and does not require the notion of concepts as constituents of thoughts. To conclude, although the characterization of concepts as constituents of thought is not inconsistent with the characterization proposed in C, the latter characterization should be preferred to the former.

1.4.4 Concepts as Categorization Devices

It is sometimes proposed that concepts are categorization devices. That is, concepts are those bodies of knowledge that allow us to categorize. For instance, developmental psychologists Susan Jones and Linda Smith write, "We use the word *concept* to refer to the represented structure (or intension) that allows members of a category to be recognized" (1993: 114). Some philosophers of psychology explicitly concur (Prinz 2002: 9).

This characterization of concepts is consistent with the characterization of concepts proposed in C. By characterizing concepts as categorization devices, neither Jones and Smith nor Prinz intend to deny that concepts are also used in the processes underlying other higher cognitive competences. Moreover, those psychologists that highlight the conceptual promiscuity of concepts do not deny that concepts are categorization devices.

Still, we should prefer C to Jones and Smith's way of characterizing concepts. Characterizing concepts as categorization devices fosters some research habits that may have been useful at some point, but are now detrimental. Psychological research on concepts has been closely tied to the study of categorization (chapter 6). As Solomon and colleagues have observed, "until recently, the study of concepts has largely been the study of categorization" (1999: 99). This has been fruitful, leading to the discovery of many psychological phenomena that have to be accounted for by any theory of concepts. However, this focus on categorization probably led psychologists to pay less attention to the role of concepts in other cognitive competences, such as induction. This is unfortunate. If concepts are promiscuous, concepts probably have the properties they have because they are used in the processes underlying several distinct higher cognitive competences, not just in the process(es) underlying categorization. That is, what kind of knowledge is stored in concepts and how this knowledge is used results from the demands of all the cognitive processes that use concepts. Focusing on categorization may thus lead to a partly erroneous view of concepts. Several psychologists have come to this conclusion. Thus, in the last pages of his book on concepts, psychologist Gregory Murphy writes, "Researchers need to acknowledge a wide range of data rather than focusing on a single paradigm. In some cases, I believe that researchers have made claims that are clearly disconfirmed outside their particular specialty without a single sign of shame" (2002: 497). Commenting on some formal models of concepts and concept learning (which are also models of categorization), he also writes:

> One reason I have not spent more time on such models, which are of intense interest to contemporary researcher, is that they are all wrong. Of course, that is true of all our current theories.... More important, most of the models are limited to a single kind of situation or concept type. Most are directed toward concept learning but have nothing to say about induction, hierarchical structure, word meaning, or conceptual combination. (Murphy 2002: 478)

Characterizing concepts as bodies of knowledge used by default in the processes underlying the higher cognitive competences and not as categorization devices goes a long way toward countering the prevailing focus on categorization. This characterization highlights the fact that concepts are used in the processes underlying many higher cognitive competences (the conceptual promiscuity of concepts) and invites psychologists to study the role of concepts in several higher cognitive competences. Thus, the characterization of concepts expressed by C should be preferred to the characterization of concepts as categorization devices.

1.5 Conclusion

In this chapter, I have explained in detail what the term "concept" is meant to refer to in psychology. I have argued that concepts are characterized as bodies of knowledge that are used by default in the processes underlying the higher cognitive competences. Textual evidence suggests that this characterization captures psychologists' use of the term "concept."

I have briefly provided some evidence that so characterized, "concept" picks out a class of mental states. I described what a theory of concepts is about: a theory of concepts should describe the kind of knowledge stored in concepts, the way they are used in cognitive processes, their format, their acquisition, and their neural localization. Finally, I contrasted this characterization of "concept" with other characterizations in psychology and in the philosophy of psychology. I have argued that all things considered, the characterization proposed in this book is to be preferred to these alternative characterizations.

2

Concepts in Philosophy

In this chapter, the contemporary philosophy of concepts is critically evaluated. I begin by characterizing the most relevant meaning of the term "concept" in philosophy—concepts as capacities for having propositional attitudes (section 2.1).[1] In section 2.2, I argue that when philosophers and psychologists develop theories of concepts, they are really theorizing about different things. This conclusion undercuts many of the arguments made by philosophers against the theories of concepts developed by psychologists. It also raises the following question: if the philosophical theories of concepts and the psychological theories of concepts are really about different things and, as a result, do not compete with each other, how might they be related? In the last two sections, I discuss two answers to this question. In section 2.3, I criticize at some length a proposal made by Christopher Peacocke (1992)—"the Simple Account": philosophers should determine the necessary and sufficient conditions for possessing a concept and psychologists should explain how the human mind meets these conditions. In section 2.4, I focus on a second proposal—"the Foundationalist Account": while psychologists explain behavior and cognition by ascribing contentful mental states, philosophers explain how people can have contentful states.

---

[1] My goal is to elucidate the debates among contemporary philosophers writing on concepts. It is clear that in the past, philosophers writing on concepts have often focused on different issues than contemporary philosophers. Particularly, the questions of interest for seventeenth- and eighteenth-century philosophers were often psychological.

2.1 "Concept" in Philosophy

2.1.1 What Are Concepts?

The term "concept" is used in several different ways in philosophy. Because I am interested in comparing the theories of concepts developed by philosophers and by psychologists, the most relevant use is to be found in the contemporary philosophy of mind and in the philosophy of psychology, for instance, in the writings of Evans, Fodor, Laurence and Margolis, and Peacocke. People have beliefs, desires, opinions, wishes—what are called "propositional attitudes" in philosophy. Beliefs, desires, and their likes are intentional states. Beliefs and their likes can be true or false, while desires and their likes can be satisfied or unsatisfied. For instance, Jean's belief that Nicolas Sarkozy is the president of France is true if and only if Nicolas Sarkozy is the president of France. Jean's (bygone) desire that Nicolas Sarkozy was not elected president of France would have been satisfied if and only if Nicolas Sarkozy had not been elected president of France. Jean's belief and Jean's desire are both about presidents. Thus, Jean's mind is such that he can have desires, beliefs, and other propositional attitudes about presidents as such.[2] This is where the philosophical notion of concept fits in. Having a concept of president is being able to have beliefs, desires, and so on, that are about presidents as such. More generally,

(C_Φ) Having a concept of x is being able to have propositional attitudes about x as x.

Jean can have intentional states like the belief that the president is a crook because he is able to have beliefs or desires about presidents and about crooks as such, that is, because he possesses the concept of president and the concept of crook.[3]

2.1.2 What Are Theories of Concepts?

Explaining in virtue of what one can have the belief that the president is a crook depends on explaining in virtue of what one can have propositional attitudes in general about presidents as such and about crooks as such—and the latter is what a theory of concepts is about. It spells out the properties in virtue of which people can have beliefs, desires—in general,

---

[2] I use "propositional attitudes about presidents as such" liberally. One might hold that the belief that Nicolas Sarkozy is president is about Nicolas Sarkozy and not about presidents. By contrast, I take this belief to be about Nicolas Sarkozy and about presidents.

[3] In most discussions of the notion of concept, the representational theory of mind is taken for granted (Fodor 1994, 1998; Margolis and Laurence 1999; Prinz 2002; Peacocke 2004: 98). The notion of concept introduced in C_Φ is also consistent with other views of our mental states, for instance, with ascriptionist views of mental states (Peacocke 1992: 36–40).

propositional attitudes—toward the objects of their attitudes. A theory of concepts is thus a semantic theory for our propositional attitudes: it explains how our thoughts can have the content they have.

Theories of concepts come under different guises. Some theories are explicitly reductionist and naturalistic. They aim at specifying in non-intentional terms the conditions that are necessary and sufficient for having a concept of x, that is, for being able to have propositional attitudes about x as x. Other theories are merely naturalistic. They aim at specifying in non-intentional terms the sufficient conditions for having a concept of x. Other theories reject both the naturalistic and the reductionist constraints.[4]

2.1.3 A Worry for the Individuation of Concepts

Philosophical theories of concepts of the kind considered so far are typically supposed to explain how concepts are individuated. That is, they are supposed to explain what distinguishes our capacity to have propositional attitudes about x as x from our capacity to have propositional attitudes about y as y. For instance, they are supposed to explain what distinguishes our capacity to have propositional attitudes about dogs as such from our capacity to have propositional attitudes about cats as such or what distinguishes our capacity to have propositional attitudes about triangles as such from our capacity to have propositional attitudes about trilateral figures as such.

Philosophers have rarely explained why they believe that there is a single correct way of individuating concepts. Many entities can be legitimately individuated in several ways. Languages and dialects are good examples (Brigandt 2005). One can give opposite answers to the question "Do the Quebecois and the French both speak French?" depending on how French is individuated. There is little ground for arguing that one and only one of these ways of individuating French is correct. The existence of several individuation principles is not limited to languages and dialects. Organs such as hearts or eyes can be individuated in numerous ways, for instance, in a phylogenetic way and in a functional way. According to the first kind of individuation, two organisms have the same organ if and only if they possess the relevant organ by virtue of common descent. According to the second kind of individuation, two organisms have the same organ if and only if the relevant organ fulfills the same function. Depending on how organs are individuated, opposite answers might be given to the question "Do humans and cephalopods have eyes?"

I do not know whether concepts (as characterized by C_Φ) can be legitimately individuated in several ways, as can languages, dialects, and organs. However, I know of no explicit discussion of why there has to be a

---

[4] Although the discussion so far differs somewhat from typical introductions of the notion of concept in the philosophy of mind (compare with, e.g., Laurence and Margolis 1999; Margolis and Laurence 2004), it is, I believe, uncontroversial (see, e.g., Peacocke 2004: 98; Weiskopf and Bechtel 2004: 48).

single way of individuating concepts, as seems to be assumed by most theories of concept individuation. It might be that philosophers have been swayed by the following argument: because different ways of individuating concepts would lead to different ways of individuating propositional attitudes and because there is a single correct way of individuating propositional attitudes, there is a single way of individuating concepts. However, this argument is unconvincing, because the second premise is as controversial as the conclusion it is supposed to support: propositional attitudes can probably be individuated in various ways.

2.2 Concepts in Philosophy versus Concepts in Psychology

2.2.1 Two Distinct Theoretical Projects

In the philosophy of mind, in the philosophy of psychology, and, sometimes, in psychology, it is assumed that the theories of concepts developed by philosophers and the theories of concepts developed by psychologists, neuropsychologists, or, more generally, cognitive scientists aim at answering the same questions.[5] As a result, most philosophers put on equal footing philosophical theories of concepts (e.g., Fodor's theory of concepts) and psychological theories of concepts (e.g., prototype theories) and evaluate their virtues with respect to the same set of criteria.[6]

The assumption that philosophical and psychological theories aim at answering the same questions is however mistaken: theories of concepts in philosophy and theories of concepts in psychology have in fact entirely different goals. As we saw in section 1.3, psychologists working on concepts are interested in the properties of the bodies of knowledge that are used by default in the processes underlying the higher cognitive competences. Their goal is to determine what kind of knowledge is used by default in the processes underlying the higher cognitive competences, how this knowledge is used in these processes, how it is acquired, and where it is located in the brain. By doing so, they hope to explain various properties of the higher cognitive competences—how we categorize, make inductions, or draw analogies. But what psychological theories of concepts do not do, and are not supposed to do, is to explain what makes it the case that we can have propositional attitudes about the objects of our attitudes.

By contrast, as we saw in the first section of this chapter, philosophers are typically interested in what conditions have to be fulfilled for having

---

[5] There are a few exceptions, however. Peacocke clearly distinguishes the notion of concept used in psychology from the notion of concept used in philosophy. In *A Theory of concepts*, he notes that "in the literature of the cognitive sciences, the term 'concept' is often assigned a different sense from that chosen here" (1992: 3). The discussion in section 2.2 vindicates Peacocke's claim.

[6] See, particularly, Rey 1983, 1985; Margolis 1994, 1995; Fodor 1994, 1998; Millikan 1998, 2000; Laurence and Margolis 1999; Prinz 2002; Margolis and Laurence 2004.

attitudes about the objects of our attitudes. In contrast to psychologists, their goal is not to characterize the properties of the bodies of knowledge that are used by default when we categorize, when we reason inductively or deductively, and when we draw analogies. Nor do they hope to explain the properties of the higher cognitive competences.

2.2.2 Objections and Replies

Philosophers of psychology have typically assumed that the notion of concept captured by C was psychologists' answer to the question of how we can have propositional attitudes about the objects of our attitudes. That is, philosophers have typically assumed that psychologists believe that we can have propositional attitudes about the objects of our attitudes because we have specific bodies of knowledge about them. I now criticize three arguments that might be proposed to support this (mistaken) interpretation of the psychological theories of concepts.

First, one might point out that some theories of concepts and categorization in psychology are very similar to some theories of reference in philosophy (that is, to theories that explain in virtue of what words refer to what they refer). This might be taken to suggest that psychological theories of concepts really attempt to explain how we can have attitudes about the objects of our attitudes. For instance, according to Searle (1958), a proper name refers to the entity that satisfies most of the predicates that competent speakers associate with this proper name. "Gödel" refers to Gödel because Gödel satisfies most of the predicates that competent speakers associate with "Gödel." According to prototype theorists, roughly, we decide that an object z is a P when z possesses a sufficient number of the typical properties of the P's (e.g., Hampton 1979, 1993; chapters 4 and 6 below). We decide that Fido is a dog because Fido possesses most of the properties that are typical of dogs.

Although there is a family resemblance between Searle's theory of reference and prototype theories of categorization, they are really about different things. Searle's theory explains how words refer, while the prototype view explains how we categorize, that is, how we decide whether an object belongs to a category—what type of knowledge we use and how we use this knowledge. The first issue is semantic; the second is psychological. These two issues are different and should be distinguished.

Second, one might contend that many psychologists view their own theories of concepts as explaining how we can have propositional attitudes about the objects of our attitudes. Prototype theorists often say that the hypothesis that concepts are prototypes explains why membership in the extension of concepts is graded, implying that prototype theories characterize the reference relation between our thoughts and their objects. Similarly, Carey, a theory theorist, often compares her theory of concepts to Kuhn's descriptivist theory of reference (e.g., Carey 1991).

Philosophers have regularly taken psychologists at their word. For example, Margolis contends that Carey's theory of concepts is best seen as a semantic theory: "The theory analogy, once plainly put, amounts to the view that concepts have their semantic properties by virtue of their roles in restricted knowledge structures" (Margolis 1995: 68). Fodor (1994, 1998) endorses a similar interpretation of the psychological theories of concepts. And he concludes that as semantic theories, they are worthless.

Psychologists' explicit interpretation of their own theories might seem at odds with my claim that the notion of concept in psychology (as captured by C) is not intended to be an answer to the philosophical question of how we can have propositional attitudes about the objects of our attitudes, but appearances are misleading. In many cases, psychologists' semantic claims are in fact psychological claims under disguise (see also Hampton 2007). When prototype theorists refer to the gradedness of category membership, they have in fact in mind various properties of people's judgments about categories. Sometimes, prototype theorists refer to the fact that people's confidence that objects belong to a given category varies across objects (e.g., Hampton 1979); sometimes, they refer to the fact that subjects judge that category members are more or less typical of their categories; sometimes they refer to the fact that subjects judge that the membership in some categories (e.g., the category of bullies) is graded (e.g., Kamp and Partee 1995). These properties of people's judgments about categories are assumed to be relevant for understanding the nature of the bodies of knowledge used by default in the processes underlying the higher cognitive competences. In other cases, psychologists' commitment to specific theories of reference can be disentangled from their theory of concepts. Carey is a prime example. Her psychological theory of concepts is to a large extent independent from her endorsement of a descriptivist theory of reference. Her work primarily bears on what type of knowledge children possess, how they use this knowledge in reasoning, and how they acquire this knowledge. Focusing on her semantic theory instead of her theory of children's knowledge, knowledge use, and knowledge acquisition is uncharitable.

Third, one might contend that a good theory of concepts ought to satisfy both philosophers' and psychologists' interests: it ought to explain what type of knowledge is used in the processes underlying the higher cognitive competences, and it ought to explain how we can have propositional attitudes about the objects of our attitudes (Prinz 2002). I am unconvinced. It would certainly be nice to have a correct philosophical theory of concepts and a correct psychological theory of concepts. However, a psychological theory of concepts would not be incomplete for failing to explain how one can have propositional attitudes about the objects of our attitudes; *mutatis mutandis* for a philosophical theory of concepts. Psychologists and philosophers have different goals—explaining the properties of the higher cognitive competences by characterizing the bodies of knowledge used by default in the processes underlying these competences and explaining how we can have propositional attitudes about the objects of our attitudes—and, as they should, they evaluate their theories according to different criteria.

2.2.3 Undermining Philosophers' Objections against Psychological Theories of Concepts

Does it really matter if one fails to distinguish between what psychological theories of concepts and what philosophical theories of concepts are about? The answer is a resounding yes. A clear distinction is needed to avoid futile arguments between philosophers and psychologists.

If psychologists' interests have little to do with philosophers', there is little point in evaluating psychological theories of concepts according to the criteria used to evaluate philosophical theories of concepts. Psychological theories of concepts should not be blamed for being unable to explain what enables us to have propositional attitudes about the objects of our attitudes.

This point invalidates numerous objections made by philosophers against psychological theories of concepts (Rey 1983, 1985; Fodor 1994, 1998; Margolis 1994, 1995; Laurence and Margolis 1999). These objections make sense only if psychologists' theories of concepts constitute answers to the question of how we can have propositional attitudes about the objects of our attitudes. Take, for instance, Margolis's (1994) criticism of prototype theories (see also Laurence and Margolis 1999). Margolis argues that prototype theories are inconsistent with Kripke's and Putnam's insights about the causal-historical nature of reference. According to Kripke and Putnam, a term can refer even when speakers have few true beliefs about the referent of this term. Philosophers have generalized this idea to propositional attitudes: we can have a propositional attitude about x as such even when we have few true beliefs about x. Margolis claims that this property is inconsistent with prototype theories. The reason is that, like many philosophers, Margolis takes prototype theories to explain how we can have attitudes about the objects of our attitudes. For Margolis, prototype theories contend that to be able to have propositional attitudes about x as such is to know which properties are typically true of x. For this reason, he takes them to be refuted by Kripke's insight. However, Margolis's argument is obviously pointless when it is recognized that prototype theories, like the other psychological theories of concepts, do not attempt to explain how we can have attitudes about the objects of our attitudes.

The reverse is also true, of course. There is little point in blaming some philosophical theories of concepts, such as Fodor's theory, for being unable to explain how we reason, how we categorize, how we draw analogies, or how we induce (as does, e.g., Prinz 2002). For, simply, a philosophical theory of concepts is not in the business of providing such explanations.

2.3 How Are the Psychological and the Philosophical Theories of Concepts Connected? Peacocke's Simple Account

I have shown that philosophical theories of concepts and psychological theories of concepts have different goals. This raises the question of how these two types of theory should be connected. In the remainder of this chapter, I consider two different answers to this question.

2.3.1 The Simple Account

Philosopher Christopher Peacocke has developed one of the most influential philosophical theories of concepts (1992, 1996, 1998, 2004). Peacocke proposes that to possess a concept of x is to be disposed to find primitively compelling some specific judgments or some specific inferences about x. An inference or a judgment is found primitively compelling if and only if (1) one finds it compelling and (2) one does not find its justification answerable to something else. A judgment J made in circumstances C is primitively compelling if and only if one finds that making J in circumstances C is self-justificatory. Peacocke illustrates his theory of concepts with the concept AND. He proposes that an individual possesses the concept AND if and only if she is disposed to find primitively compelling the inferences that instantiate the rules of and-introduction and of and-elimination (Peacocke 1992: 6; figure 2.1).

To give another example, an individual possesses the concept SQUARE only if she is disposed to find primitively compelling a judgment that a seen square object is square when this object is presented visually with the right orientation in the right conditions and when she takes her experience at face value (1992: 74). For each concept, the inferences or judgments that are constitutive of the possession of this concept can be specified a priori.

In Chapter 7 of *A Theory of Concepts*, Peacocke explicitly connects his theory of concepts with psychology (see also Peacocke 1996). He proposes a division of labor between psychologists and philosophers, which he calls the "Simple Account." Philosophers should specify a priori the possession conditions of specific concepts, such as BELIEF, SQUARE, or RED. Psychologists should then describe the nature of the states and processes required for someone to meet the possession conditions independently established by philosophers:

$$\frac{P \quad Q}{\therefore P \& Q} \qquad \frac{P \& Q}{\therefore P} \qquad \frac{P \& Q}{\therefore Q}$$

Rule of and-introduction   Rules of and-elimination

Figure 2.1 Form of the Inferences That Someone Has to Find Primitively Compelling in Order to Possess the Concept AND

Simple Account: When a thinker possesses a particular concept, an adequate psychology should explain why the thinker meets the possession condition. (Peacocke 1992: 177)

One can identify three different tasks for psychologists in Peacocke's exposition of the Simple Account. First, psychologists should characterize the nature of the mental states that are mentioned in the possession conditions of concepts. For example, describing the possession conditions for an observational concept such as SQUARE involves mentioning some specific perceptual states. Psychologists should describe the nature of these perceptual states. The second task consists in characterizing the computations that explain the formation of judgments or the transitions between judgments that are mentioned in the possession conditions of concepts. For instance, possessing the concept SQUARE involves finding some perceptual judgments, such as the judgment that a seen object is square, primitively compelling. Psychologists should explain how people form the judgment that a seen object is square. The last task consists in accounting for our feeling that some judgments or some inferences are primitively compelling.

2.3.2 Subordinating Psychology to Philosophy?

There are numerous reasons to resist Peacocke's Simple Account. First, contrary to what we are looking for, the Simple Account says absolutely nothing about the collaboration between the actual psychology of concepts and the philosophy of concepts. Rather, it describes the collaboration of a whole discipline—psychology—with the philosophy of concepts. Peacocke's imagined psychology of concepts would indeed encompass the psychology of perception (because psychologists would have to characterize the perceptual states mentioned in the possession conditions of concepts), the psychology of judgment and reasoning (because psychologists would have to characterize the judgments and inferences mentioned in these possession conditions), and the psychology of our meta-representational capacities (because psychologists would have to account for our feeling that some judgments or inferences are primitively compelling).

Furthermore, the Simple Account advocates some kind of subordination of psychology to the philosophy of concepts. Philosophers spell out a priori the possession conditions of a given concept or of a type of concept. Psychologists investigate how people meet these possession conditions. The abysmal record of the attempts to subordinate science to philosophy ought to give us pause.

2.3.3 Peacocke's Commitment to the Analytic/ Synthetic Distinction

Additionally, Peacocke's views about what philosophers have to bring to a joint venture between psychology and philosophy stands on shaky grounds because his theory of concepts is committed to the possibility of drawing the analytic/synthetic distinction. But, as Quine (1951) has persuasively argued, there is no non-circular way to draw this distinction.

Although Peacocke has repeatedly denied such a commitment (e.g., 2004: 92–93), I am not convinced by his denial. Peacocke contends that we get some a priori knowledge when we make explicit what is involved in possessing concepts. Take one of Peacocke's pet examples, the mathematical concept of limit. It is possible to possess the concept of limit without being able to explain what limits are. By making explicit what is constitutive of having the concept LIMIT, one gains some a priori knowledge about what limits are. That is, one acquires some justified true beliefs about limits. The issue of interest is what makes these beliefs true. I see but one answer consistent with Peacocke's theory. For Peacocke, the reference of the concept LIMIT is determined by its possession conditions. That is, limits are those entities that make the judgments or inferences that constitute the possession conditions of the concept LIMIT true or truth-preserving. Thus, for Peacocke, our knowledge about limits acquired by spelling out the possession conditions of LIMIT is true because what is constitutive of possessing the concept LIMIT determines what limits are. If this is correct, Peacocke's theory of concepts seems to entail that some propositions are analytically true after all, namely those propositions about the referent of a concept that result from making explicit what is constitutive of the possession of this concept.

Be that as it may, there is another problem in this vicinity. Peacocke can only deny a commitment to the analytic/synthetic distinction because he endorses a narrow notion of analyticity—"true purely in virtue of meaning" (2004: 92). According to Peacocke, some judgments or transitions between judgments are justified by virtue of the concepts involved in these judgments. For instance, it follows from what is constitutive of possessing the concept RED that one is justified in judging that a seen object is red if one takes one's experience of a red object at face value. Some transitions between judgments are also truth-preserving by virtue of the concepts involved. It follows from what is constitutive of possessing the concept AND that the inferences that follow the rule of and-introduction are truth-preserving. If one defines analyticity as true purely in virtue of meaning, then neither the judgments that are justified by virtue of the concepts involved in them nor the inferences that are truth-preserving by virtue of the concepts involved in them are analytic. However, it is unclear why the notion of analyticity should be so narrowly defined. The distinction between analytic and synthetic can be naturally extended to justification and to the preservation of semantic properties (Boghossian 1996). Particularly, a belief that p is analytically justified if and only if it is justified purely in virtue of the concepts involved in having this belief. When the notion is so broadened, it is clear that Peacocke's theory of concepts is committed to the analytic/synthetic distinction.

The moral is this: rather than denying a commitment to the analytic/synthetic distinction, Peacocke should embrace this distinction and attempt to defend it (as has been done by, e.g., Boghossian 1996). It remains to be seen whether this can be done.

2.3.4 A Methodological Objection to the Simple Account

Rather than arguing against the attempts to salvage the analytic/synthetic distinction, I turn to a different objection against the Simple Account. I argue that Peacocke's method for spelling out the possession conditions of concepts is inadequate. In *A Study of Concepts*, Peacocke says little about how these possession conditions are to be spelled out. The most developed attempt at explaining the recommended method is to be found in his article, "Implicit conceptions, understanding and rationality" (1998: 44–51; see also Peacocke 1996: 442–443). Using the example of how someone might come to endorse the truth-table for the disjunction, Peacocke writes:

> [T]he reflection involves *a simulation exercise*. The thinker imagines—to start with one of the cases—that A is true and B is false. His aim is to address the question of whether the alternation 'A or B' should be regarded as true or false in *the imagined circumstances*. As in any other simulation exercise, *he then exercises a capacity off-line*. This capacity is *the very same, understanding-based capacity he would be exercising in a real case* in which he had the information that A is true and B is false and has to evaluate the alternation 'A or B'. As in the corresponding real case, in the imaginative exercise he goes on to hold that 'A or B' is true in the simulated circumstances.... Next our thinker proceeds to consider imaginatively another case.... As he goes through the cases... he comes rationally to accept the axiom or rule as valid. (Peacocke 1998: 45; my emphasis)

Peacocke proposes that this method applies to everyday concepts, such as TABLE, as well as to mathematical concepts, such as LIMIT.

One can distinguish three steps in Peacocke's brief description of the method for spelling out the possession conditions of concepts. First, the imaginative step: philosophers are invited to imagine numerous counterfactual circumstances. Second, the simulative step: philosophers are invited to decide whether the concept at hand applies in the imagined counterfactual circumstances—that is, philosophers are invited to make counterfactual judgments. According to Peacocke, philosophers arrive at such counterfactual judgments by simulating the judgments they would make if they believed the counterfactual circumstances were actual—that is, they pretend that the antecedents of these counterfactual judgments are actual, and they make the very judgments they would make if they really took the antecedents to be actual. The resulting judgments become the consequents of the counterfactual judgments. Third, the reflective step: the pattern of counterfactual judgments is used to determine what it is to possess the concept at hand.[7]

Why should philosophers focus on counterfactual judgments rather than on non-counterfactual judgments? Counterfactual judgments allow philosophers to tell apart what we take to be true of the objects of our judgments independently of the way the world actually is from what we take to be true of them because of our knowledge of the actual world. Thus, counterfactual judgments allow philosophers to identify the judgments we make about the objects of our judgments by virtue of having concepts of these objects—or so the argument goes. To illustrate, because I judge that if water were never sold in bottles, it would still be water, I do not judge that water is sold in bottles by virtue of having the concept of water. Thus, being disposed to judge that water is sold in bottles is not part of the possession conditions of the concept of water.[8]

It is essential to Peacocke's methodology that when we make a counterfactual judgment, the consequent of this judgment is the very judgment we would make if we were to believe that the antecedent is actual. Consider an example. Suppose that we judge that if cats turned out to be robots controlled from Mars, they would still be cats. Then, philosophers might conclude that being disposed to infer that something is an animal if it is a cat (or being disposed to find this inference primitively compelling) is not part of the possession conditions of the concept of cat. But suppose now that we come to believe that cats are robots controlled from Mars (maybe because we are under hypnosis) and that in these circumstances, we judge that what we took to be cats are not cats after all. In this case, the consequent of the counterfactual judgment that if cats turned out to be robots, they would still be cats would differ from the judgment we would make if we believed that cats are robots. If such a discrepancy were to happen, our counterfactual judgment about cats would be of no use for identifying what we are committed to by virtue of having the concept of cat.

So, are the consequents of counterfactual judgments the very judgments we would make if we were to take the antecedents to be actual? Peacocke assumes they are because he takes the counterfactual judgments to result from a process of simulation. He contends that when we make a counterfactual judgment, we pretend that the antecedent is actual and we simulate a judgment—the very judgment we would make if we really took the antecedent to be actual (rather than merely pretending). I call this

---

[7] Williamson (2007) also appeals to off-line simulation to explain how we can come to know the truth of counterfactuals. The argument developed against Peacocke could probably be applied, *mutatis mutandis*, against Williamson's proposal.

[8] Judgments that express a posteriori necessary propositions, such as the proposition that water is H_2O, raise a prima facie difficulty for this methodology. The reason is that although we do not judge that water is H_2O by virtue of having the concept of water, we do judge that if some substance were not H_2O, it would not be water. Two-dimensional theories of meaning might provide a solution to this problem (e.g., Chalmers 2006).

account of counterfactual judgment "the Simulation Model." It is similar to many models of counterfactual judgments in the philosophical literature (e.g., Nichols et al. 1996) and in the psychological literature (e.g., Dias and Harris 1990; Peterson and Riggs 1999).

If, as will be suggested below, the Simulation Model is wrong—that is, if counterfactual judgments do not result from pretending that the antecedent is actual and from simulating a judgment—then it is possible that the consequents of counterfactual judgments are not the judgments we would make if we took their antecedents to be actual. For, if we do not pretend and simulate when we make a counterfactual judgment, it is plausible that we appeal to some specific beliefs—some kind of theory—about what would be what if things were not as they actually are. For instance, when we judge that if we were on Twin-Earth, XYZ would not be water, we might appeal to the belief that a substance would not be water if it did not have the chemical structure it actually has (H_2O). Because we do not appeal to this type of belief when we make non-counterfactual judgments, the consequents of counterfactual judgments would then differ from the judgments we would make if we took the antecedents of these judgments to be actual. The failure of the Simulation Model would thus have dire consequences for Peacocke's methodology, because, as we have seen, it is central to his methodology that the consequents of our counterfactual judgments are the judgments we would make if we took the antecedents to be actual.

So, is the Simulation Model correct? The literature on counterfactual reasoning has yet to reach any consensus about how people make counterfactual judgments.[9] However, some findings about autism tentatively suggest that we do not make counterfactual judgments by pretending that the antecedents of the counterfactual judgments are actual and by making the judgments we would make if we took the antecedents to be actual. Additionally, the best evidence for the Simulation Model—the improvement of young children's counterfactual reasoning when children are prompted to pretend—in fact fails to support it. Thus, it is at best unclear whether we make counterfactual judgments by simulating a non-counterfactual judgment. I consider these two points in turn.

The absence of pretend play at the end of children's second year is a reliable sign of autism, although there is no consensual explanation for this absence. While all normal children engage in pretend play around eighteen months (using an object, say, a banana, as if it were another object, say, a telephone), autistic children do not. Although it was claimed that autistic children are unable to understand pretense and to engage in pretense, additional research has shown that autistic children can understand pretense acted by adults and, when prompted, can themselves engage in

---

[9] Nichols et al. 1996: 53–59; Roese 1997; Peterson and Riggs 1999; Nichols and Stich 2003.

pretense. However, autistic children's pretense differs from normal children's pretense, in that it is stereotypical and lacks creativity. Additionally, autistic children lack the motivation to spontaneously engage in pretense (for references on autism and pretense, see Leevers and Harris 2000). Because pretense is a key element of the Simulation Model, if people make counterfactual judgments by simulating judgments, autistic children should not engage in counterfactual reasoning spontaneously and fluently.

So, are autistic children able to engage in counterfactual reasoning? According to a small body of evidence, the answer is, yes, for at least some autistic children. I will start with the most controversial findings and move to a more convincing body of evidence. Scott and colleagues (1999) presented autistic children with a false universally quantified proposition, for instance, the proposition that all cats bark, and a singular proposition, for instance, the proposition that Rex is a cat. Autistic children were then asked whether Rex barks. Surprisingly, autistic children did better than normal children on this task. Scott and colleagues concluded their study by stating that "abstract counterfactual reasoning appears to be intact in children with autism" (1999: 349). Because autistic children's capacity for pretense is impaired, this finding speaks against the idea that counterfactual judgments involve pretending that the antecedent of the counterfactual judgment is actual.

Scott and colleagues' (1999) finding has been challenged by Leevers and Harris (2000). Leevers and Harris hypothesized that Scott and colleagues' finding might be an experimental artifact. Scott and colleagues' task required children to answer affirmatively, and autistic children have a tendency to give affirmative answers. This tendency can explain why autistic children gave numerous correct answers. Leevers and Harris found that when a negative answer was the correct answer, autistic children gave mostly incorrect answers.[10] What is more, it is dubious that the task used by Scott and colleagues really involved any counterfactual reasoning, for this task can be successfully completed by applying the rules of deductive logic.

Others findings suggest more clearly that at least some autistic children can reason counterfactually. Peterson and Bowler (2000) told autistic children a story describing the consequences of an event. Children were then asked what would have happened if the event had not taken place. Peterson and Bowler found that half of the autistic children were able to reason counterfactually. Similarly, in Grant and colleagues' (2004) study, autistic children and adolescents were told a story. They were then asked what would have happened if an event described in the story had not happened. Grant and colleagues found that more than a third of autistic children and adolescents engaged in correct counterfactual reasoning (Grant, Riggs, and Boucher 2004: 182, table 3). Unfortunately, in these two articles, no information is given about the subjects' capacity for

---

[10] It is noteworthy that Leevers and Harris (2000: 81) contend that autistic children are able to engage in counterfactual reasoning.

pretense. Thus, it is impossible to reject the hypothesis that those autistic children who were able to reason counterfactually also had a preserved capacity for pretense. However, in both experiments, autistic subjects were diagnosed as autistic according to the criteria laid out in the DMS-III (Peterson and Bowler 2000) or in the DSM-IV (Grant, Riggs, and Boucher 2004). These criteria include abnormal pretend play, suggesting that a normal capacity for pretense is not required for counterfactual reasoning.

This small body of evidence about autistic children's capacity to engage in counterfactual reasoning casts some doubt on the Simulation Model and thus on the claim that the consequents of philosophers' counterfactual judgments are those judgments they would make if they took the antecedents of these counterfactuals to be actual.

I turn now to the second point: the strongest evidence for the Simulation Model in fact fails to support it. A robust finding in the study of the development of counterfactual judgments and counterfactual reasoning is that prompting children to use their imagination helps normal children and children with moderate learning difficulties to engage in counterfactual reasoning and to make counterfactual judgments. This finding seems to support the Simulation Model: performance is improved because instructions to rely on their imagination prompt children to pretend that the antecedent of the counterfactual is actual, which enables them to simulate a non-counterfactual judgment (e.g., Dias and Harris 1990).

However, Leevers and Harris (2000) have convincingly argued that appearances are misleading. In their view, prompting imagination improves the performance of normal children because it makes clear that the antecedent is to be accepted in spite of its falsehood: "Instruction boosts logical performance by clarifying the experimenter's intention that a false proposition be accepted as a basis for reasoning and that children with autism have difficulty grasping this intention" (2000: 64).

If Leevers and Harris's explanation is correct, the effect of instructions might last for some time. By contrast, if instructions to imagine prompt children to pretend that the antecedent is actual, then the effect of these instructions should not last for a long time. Consistent with their explanation, Leevers and Harris found that the improvement of children's performances lasted for at least a week.

Additionally, Leevers and Harris (2000) noted that various types of instruction have the same effect as the instructions to imagine. This suggests that instructions might not improve children's performances in counterfactual tasks by prompting children to pretend that some propositions are actual, but rather by making it clear to children that the false proposition has to be accepted in spite of its falsehood. Thus, the effect of the instructions to imagine on children's performances in tasks involving counterfactual judgments and reasoning is no clear evidence for the Simulation Model.

To summarize, Peacocke's method for discovering the possession conditions of concepts is committed to a specific account of counterfactual judgments—the Simulation Model. However, some evidence suggests that we do not make counterfactual judgments by simulating, and the best evidence for the Simulation Model has been found to be lacking.

2.3.5 Objections and Replies

Several replies to the methodological argument developed in the previous pages could be made on behalf of Peacocke. First, Peacocke might argue that there may be at least two pretense mechanisms—one involved in pretend play and one involved in counterfactual reasoning. If this were the case, the finding that some autistic children do not spontaneously engage in pretend play while being able to make counterfactual judgments would not be evidence that counterfactual judgments do not involve pretense. There are two main problems with this line of argument. It is clearly ad hoc. It is also at odds with the assumption, typically made by philosophers and psychologists who emphasize the importance of simulation in cognition, that there is a single pretense mechanism.

A second reply would go as follows. Peacocke did not intend to describe how we typically make counterfactual judgments. Rather, he intended to describe how philosophers should make counterfactual judgments if they are to use their counterfactual judgments to formulate the possession conditions of concepts. And, so the objection goes on, none of the findings mentioned above shows that people cannot make counterfactual judgments by simulating non-counterfactual judgments. The main problem with this reply is that if people do not typically make counterfactual judgments by simulating non-counterfactual judgments, then it is unclear whether they can make counterfactual judgments in this way, for it is unclear whether people can change the way they typically make counterfactual judgments. And, to the best of my knowledge, philosophers are people too. Notice that it is no good to reply that we know very well, introspectively, that we can make counterfactual judgments by simulating noncounterfactual judgments, for, as is typically emphasized by psychologists, introspection says little about the processes that produce our judgments.

Third, Peacocke could reply that counterfactual judgments that are not underwritten by a simulation process can also be used to determine the possession conditions of concepts. However, as we have already seen, this reply is dubious. It is crucial for Peacocke's methodology that the consequents of counterfactual judgments be the very judgments we would make if we took the antecedents to be actual. If we do not simulate when we make a counterfactual judgment, it is possible that the consequents of the counterfactual judgments are not the judgments we would make if we took the antecedents to be actual.

Finally, Peacocke might well argue that there are other methods for identifying a priori the possession conditions of concepts. After all, he takes himself to be describing only one such method (e.g., 1996: 443).

This might well be. But, as far as I know, Peacocke has not developed this idea in any detail, so it is impossible to assess it properly.

Let us take stock. Peacocke proposes a specific connection between the philosophy of concepts and psychology. Psychologists interested in concepts should explain how people can meet the possession conditions specified a priori by philosophers. Peacocke's Simple Account suffers from many problems. It fails to connect the actual psychology of concepts with the philosophy of concepts. It subordinates psychology to a specific field within philosophy. It is committed to the analytic/synthetic distinction. Most important, the method recommended for discovering the possession conditions of concepts is very sketchy. When it is spelled out at greater length, Peacocke seems to be committed to a specific account of how philosophers make counterfactual judgments—the Simulation Model. But evidence is at best lacking that this is how people make these judgments. We are thus left in the dark concerning how possession conditions are to be spelled out. As long as some other method has not been developed in some detail, one should, at the very least, question whether the project of spelling out the possession conditions of concepts can be completed. If it cannot be completed, Peacocke's proposal for connecting the philosophy of concepts with psychology is vacuous. Unsurprisingly, more than fifteen years after the publication of *A Theory of Concepts* in 1992, the interdisciplinary research program sketched by Peacocke has yet to see the light.

2.4 How Are the Psychological and the Philosophical Theories of Concepts Connected? The Foundationalist Account

2.4.1 Securing the Foundations of Psychology

Psychologists of concepts take for granted that when we reason about, say, dogs, categorize something as a dog, or draw some analogy between someone and dogs, we use some knowledge about dogs (figure 1.2). But they do not explain how we can have any knowledge or any other propositional attitude about dogs (or anything else). This suggests that the philosophy of concepts might play a foundational role: philosophers' job might be to explain something that is taken for granted by psychologists—namely, how we can have propositional attitudes about the objects of our attitudes. I call this proposal "the Foundationalist Account."

2.4.2 The Argument from the Variability of Propositional Attitude Ascriptions

In the remainder of this chapter, I consider an argument that casts doubt on the methods used by philosophers to implement the Foundationalist Account. How can a philosophical theory of concepts be developed? The most natural strategy is to focus on the propositional attitudes we are most familiar with (beliefs, desires, wishes, etc.) by contrast to the propositional attitudes used by psychologists to explain our cognitive competences or our behavior (e.g., Chomsky's cognizing). The ascription of the latter attitudes is often controversial. Furthermore, psychologists have not developed specific principles for the ascription of these attitudes; rather, their ascription piggybacks on the way people ascribe familiar propositional attitudes, such as beliefs and desires. Focusing on these familiar propositional attitudes, philosophers could compare the situations in which people are in a position to have beliefs and desires about something, for example, cats, water, and democracy, and the situations in which people are not in such a position. Then, they could identify the conditions people must meet in order to have propositional attitudes about the objects of their attitudes.

The next question is "How do we know what beliefs and desires people have?" As philosophers have often pointed out, beliefs and desires are similar to theoretical entities in that their existence has to be inferred. We ascribe beliefs and desires to people on the basis of our knowledge of what people say and of what they do. For example, if a person says that G. W. Bush is the worst American President ever, *ceteris paribus*, we ascribe to her the belief that G. W. Bush is the worst American President ever. There are different views about the cognitive mechanisms that underlie the ascription of attitudes (e.g., Nichols and Stich 2003; Goldman 2006), but this matters little for present purposes. What matters is that we have no access to people's propositional attitudes except through the inferential ascription of propositional attitudes. Since theories of concepts aim at specifying the conditions for having propositional attitudes, these ascriptions are the data theories of concepts depend on.

To substantiate their claims about concepts, philosophers of concepts have often relied on the ascription of propositional attitudes to individuals described in thought-experiments that describe strange situations. These thought-experiments are needed to discriminate between the competing theories of concepts because in real-life situations, these theories of concepts ascribe to people the same stock of concepts. Some thought-experiments probe whether readers would ascribe beliefs or whether they would rather refrain from ascribing beliefs to the individuals described in these thought-experiments. For instance, in a well-known article (1979), Tyler Burge describes an individual, Oscar, who is convinced that he has arthritis in his thigh. Burge then asks the reader to imagine a situation that is almost identical to Oscar's situation. In this second situation, Oscar is also convinced that he has arthritis in his thigh. The only difference between the two situations is that in the English spoken in the second situation, "arthritis" is used to refer to ailments in the ankles and to ailments in the thigh. The reader is invited to share Burge's intuitions that Oscar in the first situation has (false) beliefs about arthritis, while Oscar in the second situation has no belief about arthritis. Thus, in the first situation, but not in the second situation, Oscar has the concept of arthritis, even though the only difference between the two situations is in the language spoken in Oscar's linguistic community. Burge concludes that the capacities to have propositional attitudes about the objects of our attitudes—concepts—supervene on social facts. Other thought-experiments probe whether readers would ascribe the same belief or different beliefs to two individuals described in thought-experiments (e.g., Stich 1983).

The philosophical methodology just described assumes that the ascription of propositional attitudes to the individuals described in the thought-experiments used by philosophers is uniform. If there were some variation in people's ascription of propositional attitudes and if there were no reason to prefer some ascriptions to others, it would be unclear how one should proceed to build a theory of concepts. For it would be unclear which ascriptions of propositional attitudes a theory of concepts should strive to accommodate. Thus, suppose that people disagree about whether in the second situation described by Burge (1979), Oscar has beliefs about arthritis. Then, it would be unclear whether, as Burge has claimed, the possession of concepts really supervenes on social facts.

Thus, a crucial (but yet to be completed) task is to determine whether there is some substantial variation in the ascriptions of propositional attitudes that are relevant for evaluating the competing theories of concepts. As long as it has not been empirically established that there is no such variation or as long as it has not been convincingly argued that this variation is irrelevant, it is questionable whether the project of building a philosophical theory of concepts can be completed by means of the traditional philosophical methodology.

This task is particularly pressing because the little evidence there is shows that the intuitions triggered by some famous thought-experiments that are relevant for the philosophy of concepts do vary. Based on Stich's (1983) discussion of the ascription of propositional attitudes, psychologist Claire Hewson (1994) investigated people's judgments of belief identity. Subjects were presented with several stories, including the following story:

> This story is about two men, Tom and Dick. Tom is a contemporary of ours, a young man with little interest in politics or history. From time to time he has heard bits of information about Dwight David Eisenhower. We can assume that most of what Tom has heard is true, though there is no need to insist that all is true. Let us also assume that each time Tom heard something about Eisenhower, Eisenhower was referred to as 'Ike'. Tom knows that this must be a nickname of some sort, but he has no idea what the man's full name might be and doesn't very much care. Being little interested in such matters, Tom remembers only a fraction of what he has heard about Ike; that he was both a military man and a political figure; that he played golf a lot... and perhaps another half dozen facts. He has no memory of when or where he heard these facts, nor from whom. Dick, in this story, is a young man in Victorian England. Like Tom, he is bored by politics and history. Dick has heard some anecdotes about a certain Victorian public figure, Regina Angell-James, who,

for some reason that history does not record, was generally called 'Ike'. Angell-James and Eisenhower led very different careers in different places and times. However, there were some similarities between the two men. In particular, both were involved in politics and the military, both liked to play golf, and both had a penchant for malapropisms. Moreover, it just so happens that the few facts that Dick remembers about Angell-James coincide with the few facts Tom remembers about Eisenhower. What is more, Dick would report these facts using the very same sentences that Tom would use, since the only name Dick knows for Angell-James is 'Ike'. Now, suppose that one fine day in 1880 one of Dick's friends ask him what he knows about Ike. Dick replies "He was some kind of politician who played golf a lot." A century later, one of Tom's friends asks him an identically worded question, and Tom gives an identically worded reply.

Subjects were then asked the following question: do Tom and Dick have the same or different beliefs when they say, "He was some kind of politician who played golf a lot"?

For present purposes, Hewson's main finding is that there is substantial disagreement among subjects about whether the two individuals described in this and other probes have the same belief. This finding belies any a priori assumption that people will agree on which attitudes should be ascribed to the individuals described in the thought-experiments that are relevant for the philosophy of concepts. Barring some extensive empirical investigation of people's ascriptions of propositional attitudes to the individuals described in these thought-experiments, the favorite methodology of philosophers for implementing the Foundationalist Account is thus subject to caution.

Importantly, even if we were to reject philosophers' favorite methodology, this would not entail that the Foundationalist Account cannot be implemented. After all, there might be other methods for studying the relation between thoughts and their objects, even though there is currently no recognized alternative method. However, important as it is, developing such a method is a topic for another book.

2.5 Conclusion

The common wisdom in the philosophy of psychology and in the philosophy of mind is that theories of concepts in philosophy and in psychology share the same goals and should be evaluated according to the same criteria. Together, Chapters 1 and 2 show that this common wisdom is mistaken. "Concept" in psychology refers to a specific class of bodies of knowledge, assumed to be used by default in the processes underlying most higher cognitive competences, and a theory of concepts in psychology attempts to describe the properties of these bodies of knowledge in order to explain the properties of the higher cognitive competences. "Concept" is used in various ways in philosophy. Of particular relevance here is the idea that a theory of concepts spells out the conditions under which one can have propositional attitudes about the objects of one's attitudes. When the goals of theories of concepts in philosophy and in psychology are clearly explained and properly distinguished, most philosophical attacks against the psychological theories of concepts are decisively undermined.

Two proposals for bringing together the philosophy of concepts and the psychology of concepts—Peacocke's Simple Account and the Foundationalist Account—have been discussed. Peacocke proposed that psychologists should explain how people meet the possession conditions spelled out by philosophers. The Simple Account fails to bring together the actual psychology of concepts and the philosophy of concepts; it is also committed to the analytic/synthetic distinction; and it does not tackle seriously the methodological question of how possession conditions are to be spelled out. The Foundationalist Account purports to provide folk and scientific ascriptions of contentful states with an account of content. However, because philosophers' method for implementing the Foundationalist Account is questionable, it is unclear whether this project can really be completed.

3

The Heterogeneity Hypothesis

In chapters 1 and 2, I clarified what "concept" is meant to refer to in psychology and in philosophy and what the goals of psychological theories of concepts are. I now turn to the central task of this book—developing a new picture of the organization of our knowledge in long-term memory. In short, I contend (1) that the best available evidence (to be reviewed in chapters 6 and 7) suggests that for each category of objects (for each substance, type of event, and so on), an individual typically has several concepts, that is, again, several bodies of knowledge that are by default retrieved from long-term memory and used when he or she categorizes, reasons inductively or deductively, or makes analogies. For instance, instead of having a single concept of dog, an individual has in fact several concepts of dog. Moreover, I propose (2) that coreferential concepts have very few properties in common. Coreferential concepts belong to very heterogeneous kinds of concept. For example, an individual's concepts of dog share very few properties with each other. Each concept of dog belongs to a kind of concept that has very little in common with the kinds of concept the other concepts of dog belong to. I call these kinds "the fundamental kinds of concept." Further, I argue (3) that evidence strongly suggests that prototypes, exemplars, and theories are among the fundamental kinds of concept (chapters 4, 6, and 7).[1] I also propose (4) that prototypes, exemplars, and theories are often used in distinct

---

[1] See chapter 4 on these notions.

cognitive processes (chapter 5). For instance, instead of categorization being underwritten by a single cognitive process, we have at least three categorization processes, one for each of the fundamental kinds of concept distinguished in this book—namely, prototypes, exemplars, and theories (chapter 6). Finally, I argue (5) that the notion of concept ought to be eliminated from the theoretical vocabulary of psychology because it might prevent psychologists from correctly characterizing the nature of our knowledge in long-term memory and its use in cognitive processes (chapter 8). Together, these five tenets form a view of concepts that I call "the Heterogeneity Hypothesis."

The Heterogeneity Hypothesis stands in sharp contrast with the dominant view of concepts in psychology—"the Received View." The Received View denies each of the five tenets of the Heterogeneity Hypothesis. Proponents of the Received View propose that each category of objects (each substance and so on) is typically represented by a single concept. More important, they take the class of concepts to be a homogeneous class. For them, psychological theories of concepts should spell out the general properties of concepts, that is, the properties that are common to most, if not all, concepts (section 1.3). As a result, proponents of the Received View maintain that the term "concept" is an important theoretical notion in psychology.

This chapter develops the Heterogeneity Hypothesis in greater detail, with a special focus on its first and second tenets. In section 3.1, I flesh out the Received View. In section 3.2, I elaborate on the first and second tenets of the Heterogeneity Hypothesis: for each category of objects (for each substance, for each type of event, and so on), we have several concepts, and these concepts belong to kinds of concept that have little in common. In section 3.3, I contrast the Heterogeneity Hypothesis with theories of concepts that are superficially similar—namely, hybrid theories of concepts—in order to prevent their conflation.

3.1 The Received View

3.1.1 What Is the Received View?

Psychologists are fully aware that there are plenty of differences between concepts and between kinds of concept. Some exciting research has highlighted the similarities and differences between particular concepts. For example, Carey has studied the development of the concepts of animal and of person among normal and abnormal preschoolers.[2] In substance, she claims that young children's concept of animal is based on their concept of person, while older children's concepts of animal and of person are independent from each other. Psychologists have also emphasized the differences

---

[2] See, e.g., Carey 1985; Carey and Johnson 2000; but see Sousa, Atran, and Medin 2002.

between kinds of concept. For instance, Gelman has emphasized the differences between concepts of artifacts and concepts of animal species.[3]

Psychologists' interest in the differences between concepts and between kinds of concept should not be conflated with a belief that there are only few properties common to all (or most) concepts. In fact, psychologists typically expect that over and beyond the differences between concepts and between kinds of concept, concepts (or, maybe, most concepts) share many scientifically relevant properties.[4] In other words, they expect the class of concepts to yield numerous inductive generalizations—principally about what type of knowledge is stored in concepts and how they are used in cognitive processes, but also about what their format is, how they are acquired, and where they are localized in the brain (section 1.3).

This view is rarely made explicit, but it has been nicely put by Murphy (see also Keil 1987: 175; Goldstone and Kersten 2003: 599):

> The psychology of concepts cannot by itself provide a full explanation of the concepts of all the different domains that psychologists are interested in. This book will not explore the psychology of concepts of persons, musical forms, numbers, physical motions, and political systems. *The details of each of these must be discovered by the specific disciplines that study them*; to fully understand people's musical concepts will require much research into the psychology of music, rather than being predictable solely from what we know of concepts per se. *Nonetheless, the general processes of concept learning and representation may well be found in each of these domains.* For example, I would be quite surprised if concepts of musical forms did not follow a prototype structure . . . did not have a preferred level of categorization . . . and did not show differences depending on expertise or knowledge. . . . Spelling out what categories people have of musical forms, what levels of representations there are, and what knowledge influences the concepts is primarily part of the psychology of music rather than the psychology of concepts. But once the basic elements of musical concepts have been identified, *the concepts will likely be found to follow the principles identified in other domains.* (Murphy 2002: 2–3; my emphasis)[5]

The Received View is also explicitly endorsed in some form or other by several philosophers of psychology.[6] Notably, Prinz writes:

> *An adequate theory of concepts must have sufficient expressive power or breath to accommodate the large variety of concepts that we are capable of possessing.* The human conceptual repertoire ranges from the sensory to the abstract. We have concepts of readily observable states within ourselves, like PAIN, theoretically derived concepts, such as ELECTRON, and seemingly formal concepts, such as

---

[3] Gelman and Markman 1986, 1987; Gelman 1988; Gelman and Wellman 1991; for a book-length treatment of this question, see Gelman 2003.

[4] For some dissenting voices, see Keil 1989; Ashby et al. 1998; Hahn and Chater 1998; Smith, Patalano, and Jonides 1998; Knowlton 1999; Pinker and Prince 1999; Ashby and Waldron 2000; Ashby and Ell 2002; Maddox et al. 2004; Ashby and O'Brien 2005.

[5] Murphy himself is reluctant to endorse this view.

[6] Laurence and Margolis 1999: 72; Danks 2007.

NUMBER. We have concepts of natural kinds, such as FROG, artifacts, such as BOAT, and social kinds, such as MOTHER or DEMOCRACY. (Prinz 2002: 3; my emphasis)

Moreover, the Received View implicitly underlies much theorizing about concepts in psychology. It is well-known that various approaches to concepts have been proposed since the development of the prototype paradigm of concepts in the 1970s (chapter 4). Strikingly, none of these approaches is supposed to characterize exclusively a subset of the class of concepts, in contrast to the whole class of concepts. On the contrary, they are assumed to characterize most, if not all, concepts.

Finally, the Received View underwrites the empirical controversies between psychologists studying concepts. Since the 1970s, psychologists have looked for phenomena—for instance, properties of categorization judgments—that were predicted by their favored theory of concepts, but that were hard to account for by rival theories. With such phenomena in hand, psychologists have often concluded that their favored theory was likely to be correct, while rival theories were likely to be incorrect. This kind of argument supposes that a single theory of concepts should be able to account for all the relevant phenomena. If, contrary to the Received View, the class of concepts divides into several kinds that have little in common, the distinct theories of concepts that characterize these kinds of concept will account for different phenomena, and the fact that theory A, but not theory B, explains some phenomenon, such as a property of some categorization judgments, will not necessarily constitute evidence against theory B.

3.1.2 Is the Received View a Strawman?

I suspect that the claim that the Received View is commonly endorsed by psychologists of concepts will be met with skepticism in some quarters. Some may object that I am building a strawman, and they may claim that in fact, most psychologists take for granted the diversity of concepts. This objection should be resisted, for if many psychologists recognize that there are differences between kinds of concept, hardly any psychologist contends that concepts divide into kinds that have very few properties in common.

As an example, consider Medin and colleagues' (2000) article on the diversity of concepts. They argue that in the search for the general properties of concepts, psychologists have insufficiently paid attention to the differences between kinds of concept. They provide some evidence that these differences are scientifically important and invite psychologists to focus on them:

> This paper discusses recent research demonstrating that useful distinctions may be made among kinds of concepts, including both object and nonobject concepts. We discuss three types of criteria, based on structure, process, and content, that may be used to distinguish among kinds of concepts. (Medin, Lynch, and Solomon 2000: 121)

Medin and colleagues recognize the diversity of concepts, but, crucially, they do not deny that there are general properties of concepts and that the correct theory of concepts has to describe these properties. Medin and colleagues want psychologists to find out the general properties of concepts and to map the important differences between kinds of concept. This is transparent when they rely on an analogy between kinds of concept and kinds of living things:

> To use an analogy with biological kinds, there are interesting properties that all living things share, but there are further interesting generalizations that may hold only for mammals or only for primates or only for human beings. *Treating all concepts as being of the same type may be useful for some purposes* but we may be missing important principles that apply robustly only for subsets of concepts. (Ibid. 122–123; my emphasis)

For present purposes, the moral is that even those, like Medin and colleagues, who emphasize the differences between kinds of concept are often committed to the Received View.

Similar considerations apply to an apparent exception to the Received View. Some psychologists contend that their favored theory of concepts applies to the concepts of three-dimensional physical objects, while remaining noncommittal about its application to concepts of events or of substances.[7] This is not tantamount to rejecting the Received View. It is unclear whether these psychologists propose that there are only few properties common to concepts of three-dimensional physical objects, to concepts of substances, and to concepts of events. Rather, they may merely endorse the much less controversial claim that concepts of events and concepts of substances are likely to differ from concepts of physical objects in several important ways.

Finally, even when psychologists contend that few properties are shared by the concepts of physical objects, the concepts of events, and the concepts of substances, their views are still at odds with the Heterogeneity Hypothesis. The Heterogeneity Hypothesis proposes that (1) for a given category of objects (for a substance, etc.), we have several concepts, each of which belongs to a different kind of concept, and that (2) there are few properties common to these kinds of concept. Thus, if the Heterogeneity Hypothesis is correct, it is mistaken to believe that the class of concepts of physical objects yields many interesting generalizations.

3.2 *The Heterogeneity Hypothesis*

Concepts could be heterogeneous in various ways. It is thus illuminating to contrast the Heterogeneity Hypothesis with other types of conceptual heterogeneity. I first describe two types of conceptual heterogeneity that I reject: Scope Pluralism and Competence Pluralism. Then, in the

---

[7] See, e.g., Smith and Medin 1981; Komatsu 1992: 501.

following subsection, I present the type of conceptual heterogeneity that is defended in this book.

3.2.1 Two Types of Conceptual Heterogeneity: Scope Pluralism and Competence Pluralism

A first type of conceptual heterogeneity—Scope Pluralism—is characterized by the following two tenets. (1) Different types of entity, such as artifacts and animals or, alternatively, events, substances, and physical objects, are represented by different kinds of concept and (2) these kinds of concept have little in common. Komatsu has speculated along such lines: "These different sorts of words [natural kind terms, artifact terms, etc.] may be associated with mental representations that encode different sorts of information, are established through different means (discovery vs. convention), and tend to be used in different sorts of ways" (1992: 513). Few properties could be shared by DOG and TABLE because, in general, concepts of biological kinds and concepts of artifacts could have little in common.[8] Alternatively, few properties could be shared by BIRTHDAY, DOG, and WATER because, in general, concepts of events, concepts of physical objects, and concepts of substances could have little in common.

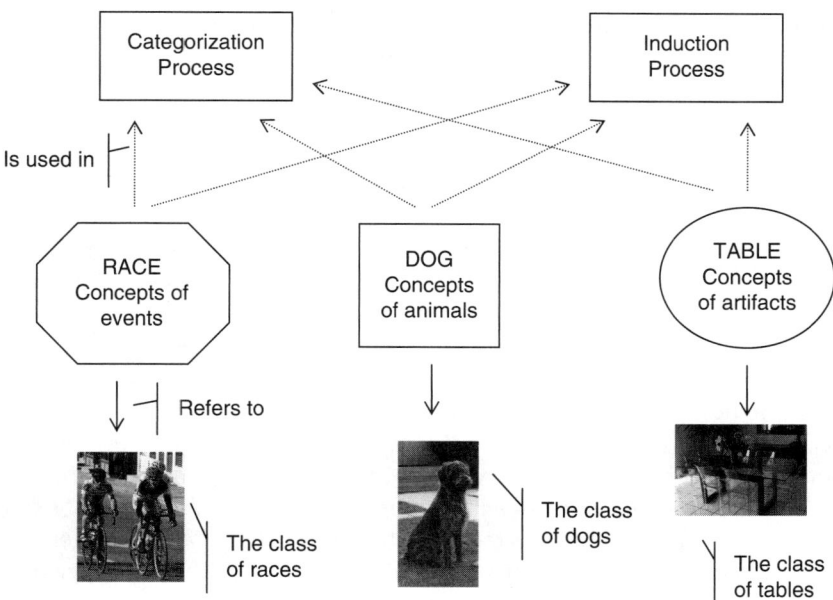

Figure 3.1 Scope Pluralism

---

[8] Millikan (1998, 2000) has argued that concepts of what she calls "substances" differ from other kinds of concept. This is an instance of Scope Pluralism. For another instance, see Pinker and Prince 1999.

Notice that, according to scope pluralism, each category or each event is typically represented by a single concept (figure 3.1).

Criticizing a short exposition of the ideas developed in this book (Machery 2005), Piccinini and Scott (2006) have defended the plausibility of Scope Pluralism. They propose that some entities (e.g., some abstract entities) might be represented by "non-similarity-based concepts," while other entities (e.g., most classes of physical objects) are represented by "similarity-based concepts."

I disagree with their proposal (Machery 2006a) because, in contrast to Piccinini and Scott, I believe that many entities are simultaneously represented by one or several "similarity-based concepts"—for example, a prototype and a set of exemplars—and by a "non-similarity-based concept"—either a theory or a definition. Much evidence will be presented in this and subsequent chapters (see, particularly, sections 3.3, 6.3–6.6, and 7.1–7.2 below).

Consider now a second type of conceptual heterogeneity—Competence Pluralism. One could propose (1) that different kinds of concept are involved in different cognitive competences and (2) that these kinds have little in common. For example, a concept of dog used when we categorize something as a dog could have little in common with a concept of dog used when we reason inductively about dogs because, in general, concepts that are used when we categorize and concepts that are used when we reason inductively could have little in common.[9] Komatsu has also speculated along these lines: "An object category may be represented in more than one way, each implicated in a different task (e.g., classification, deduction, judgments of similarity)" (1992: 501).

According to Competence Pluralism, every category (substance, type of event, etc.) is represented by several concepts, one for each cognitive competence. The class of dogs is represented by several concepts of dog. Moreover, the concepts of a given category (substance, etc.) belong to kinds of concept that have little in common with each other (figure 3.2).

In their critical discussion of Machery (2005), Piccinini and Scott (2006) have also defended the plausibility of Competence Pluralism. They distinguish between two types of cognitive competence, namely, those competences that involve language, such as understanding lexical compounds, and those competences that do not, such as perceptual discrimination.[10] They propose that two very different kinds of concept might be used in these two types of competence. The linguistic competences might recruit some representations of classes that are different from the representations of classes recruited by the non-linguistic competences.

I am unconvinced (Machery 2006a). There is a wealth of evidence that lexicalized concepts (that is, concepts that are expressed by a word), which

---

[9] If Competence Pluralism were correct, the notion of concept presented in chapter 1 would have to be modified. For the notion of concept presented in chapter 1 assumes that concepts are the inputs to the cognitive processes underlying most higher cognitive competences.

[10] They use the term "task" to refer roughly to what I call "competence."

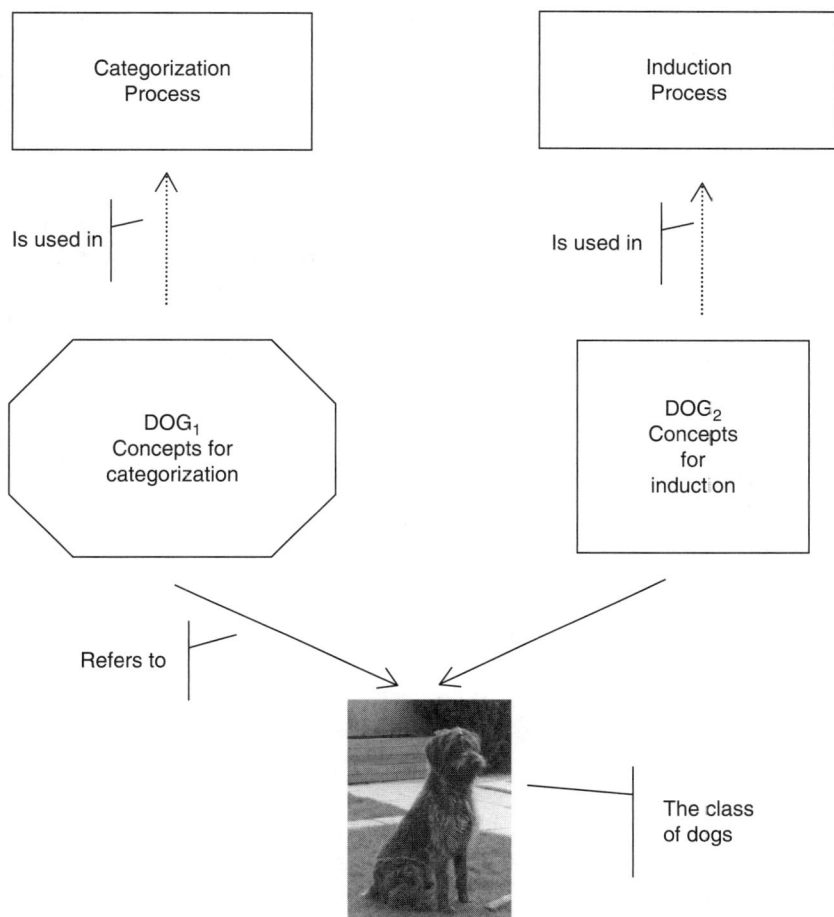

Figure 3.2 Competence Pluralism

can be recruited by the linguistic competences, and non-lexicalized concepts, which cannot be recruited by these competences, have very similar properties. Consider, for instance, typicality. It is well-known that typical objects are categorized more quickly and more accurately than atypical objects. The membership of typical objects in a given category is also learned more quickly than the membership of atypical objects in this category. For present purposes, the important point is that these properties are common to lexicalized concepts and to non-lexicalized concepts (e.g., Rosch and Mervis 1975). We decide more quickly that a robin is a bird than that a penguin is a bird. Similarly, when subjects learn to classify meaningless, abstract, and non-lexicalized figures into different categories and are then asked to classify new figures into these categories, typical figures are classified more quickly and more accurately than atypical figures. The similarity between lexicalized and non-lexicalized concepts shows that it is not the case that very different kinds of concepts are used in linguistic tasks and in non-linguistic tasks. Thus, Piccinini and Scott's defense of Competence Pluralism fails.

3.2.2 The Heterogeneity Hypothesis

I reject both Scope Pluralism and Competence Pluralism. First, with Competence Pluralism and against Scope Pluralism, I propose that most categories of physical objects, most types of event, and most substances are represented by several concepts that belong to kinds that have little in common. For example, according to the Heterogeneity Hypothesis, we have several concepts of dog, say, DOG_1, DOG_2, and DOG_3, each of which belongs to a different kind of concept. (In section 3.3, I explain why these bodies of knowledge should be thought of as three distinct bodies of knowledge [three concepts] rather than as the components of a single body of knowledge [of a single concept].) There are few properties common to DOG_1, DOG_2, and DOG_3 because, in general, the corresponding kinds of concept (the fundamental kinds of concept) have little in common. Particularly, as will be shown from chapters 4 to 7, concepts that belong to distinct fundamental kinds store different types of knowledge about their reference and are used in different types of cognitive process.

Second, with Scope Pluralism and against Competence Pluralism, I propose that concepts do not vary across cognitive competences. We use DOG_1, DOG_2, and DOG_3 to categorize, to reason inductively, and to reason deductively (figure 3.3).

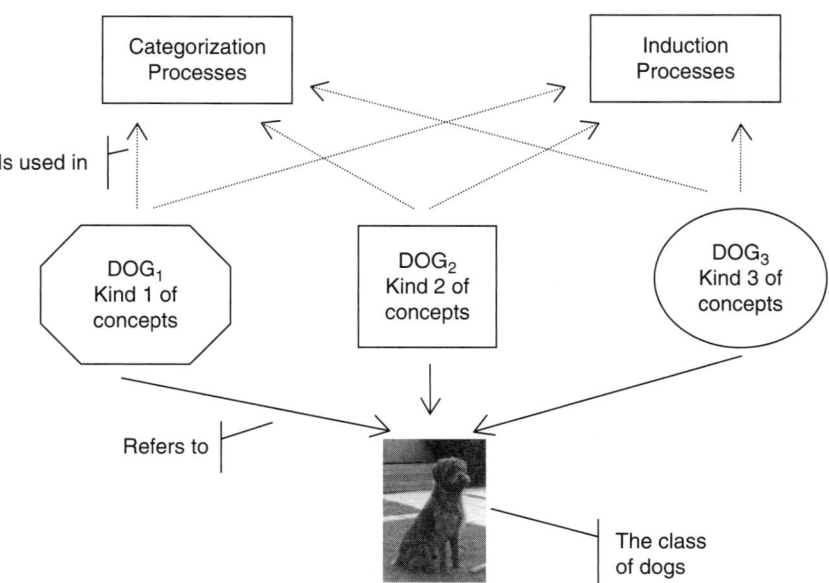

Figure 3.3 The Heterogeneity Hypothesis

The Heterogeneity Hypothesis 61

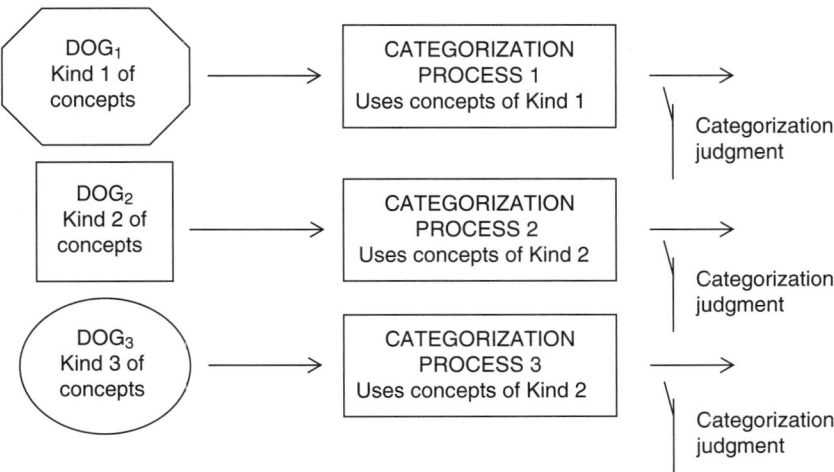

Figure 3.4 Several Categorization Processes

A word is needed about how these different kinds of concept are supposed to be used to categorize, to reason inductively, and to understand a language. Consider the case of categorization. I propose that each fundamental kind of concept is used in a distinct categorization process. That is, we have several categorization processes, each defined over a fundamental kind of concept (figure 3.4). The same is true of several other competences (more on this in chapter 5).

3.2.3 Complications

The Heterogeneity Hypothesis is domain-general. It does not assume that the nature of our conceptual knowledge varies across domains, such as biology and psychology, or across types of entity, such as physical objects and events. Typically, the same kinds of concept are to be found across domains and across types of entity. More specifically, across domains, classes of physical objects, substances, and events are typically represented by a prototype, by a set of exemplars, and by a theory (chapter 4).

However, I fully realize that this is likely to turn out to be a simplification. First, it may well be that in some domains or for some types of entity, the bodies of knowledge that are used by default in the processes underlying the higher cognitive competences turn out to be of a different nature than the concepts used in other domains or for other types of entity. To give a speculative example, it could be that in the moral domain, moral properties like *good* are not represented by a prototype, a set of exemplars, and a theory, but rather by a set of exemplars and an ideal (see chapter 4 on the notion of ideal). The moral domain would thus be an exception to the generalization proposed by the Heterogeneity Hypothesis.

Furthermore, the Heterogeneity Hypothesis proposes a synchronic diversity of concepts. Concepts could also differ diachronically. That is, it could be that the nature of concepts varies across times. Particularly, the concepts possessed by children and by adults could belong to kinds that have little in common. This is in fact a common proposal in the psychological literature. Vygotsky (1986) has proposed that young children's concepts, but not adults', are images. Thus, according to Vygotsky, the vehicles of children's and adults' concepts are different (see also Inhelder and Piaget 1969 and the discussion in Keil et al. 1998). Some psychologists have also proposed that the nature of concepts varies with experience (e.g., Homa, Sterling, and Trepel 1981; Smith and Minda 1998). For instance, the concept of kangaroo possessed by a European and the concept of kangaroo possessed by an Australian who has an extensive, first-hand experience with kangaroos could belong to kinds that have little in common. This last consideration suggests that there could be some individual differences as well as some cross-cultural differences in the kinds of concept possessed by people (on the latter, see Nisbett 2003).

Finally, it might well be that some categories of physical objects (or some substances, etc.) are represented by a single concept and thus are exceptions to the Heterogeneity Hypothesis. For example, when I learn what a transcendental argument is, I might first acquire a definition and, later, acquire exemplars of transcendental arguments. In the first step, I would have a single concept of a transcendental argument.

Evidence might bear out some of these potential complications. Importantly, if this were the case, the overall perspective developed in this book would still hold, even though some of the claims made by the Heterogeneity Hypothesis would have to be modified. Indeed, these complications would provide further support to the main moral of this book: few generalizations are true of the class of concepts, and the notion of concept is inappropriate for psychology. However, because current evidence does not clearly support the speculations entertained here, I will focus on the Heterogeneity Hypothesis in the remainder of the book.

3.2.4 The Argumentative Strategy

Why should we endorse the Heterogeneity Hypothesis? In the following chapters, I will pursue the following argumentative strategy. In the recent psychological literature, various research programs have aimed at characterizing the class of bodies of knowledge denoted by the notion of concept—primarily, the prototype paradigm of concepts (e.g., Hampton 1979, 2006; Smith 2002), the exemplar paradigm of concepts (e.g., Medin and Schaffer 1978; Nosofsky 1986), and the theory paradigm of concepts (e.g., Carey 1985; Murphy and Medin 1985; Gopnik and Meltzoff 1997). I argue that these research programs have characterized this class in very different ways. They posit entities—prototypes, exemplars, and theories—that have little in common (chapter 4). These theories assume that all concepts (or, at least, most of them) are prototypes, or exemplars, or theories. I propose instead that in order to provide a satisfactory explanation of the properties of our higher cognitive competences, we need to assume that the class of concepts divides, at least, into exemplars, prototypes, and theories (chapters 6 and 7).

Consider the case of categorization. Psychologists have discovered many properties of the capacity to categorize. Theories of concepts and theories of the process(es) underlying categorization aim at explaining these properties. I will show in chapter 6 that to explain them, one needs to assume that for many categories, substances, events, and so on we possess at least three coreferential concepts—a prototype, a set of exemplars, and a theory—used in three distinct categorization processes. By contrast, psychologists who only posit the existence of, say, prototypes are unable to account for all the properties of our capacity to categorize (*mutatis mutandis* for exemplars and theories).

It is worth emphasizing three important aspects of this argumentative strategy. First, I need to show that the theoretical entities assumed by the main paradigms of concepts have little in common. Merely showing that there are differences between kinds of concept will not do, for, as we saw, psychologists who endorse the Received View are not committed to denying the existence of these differences. Moreover, I need to show that if they exist, exemplars, prototypes, and theories are used by default in the processes underlying our higher cognitive competences. This is a necessary condition for these bodies of knowledge to count as concepts. Otherwise, it could be that concepts are prototypes, while exemplars and theories belong to our background knowledge (or that concepts are exemplars, while prototypes and theories belong to our background knowledge, and so on). Finally, this argumentative strategy is clearly empirical. It involves reviewing a large body of empirical evidence (chapters 6 and 7). Moreover, new empirical findings could lead to a different conclusion. For instance, psychologists might discover that all concepts are located in the same brain area. The claim that prototypes, exemplars, and theories have few scientifically relevant properties in common would then be falsified.

3.3 Hybrid Theories of Concepts

The Heterogeneity Hypothesis may remind those readers who are acquainted with the psychology of concepts of hybrid theories of concepts. Indeed, Piccinini and Scott (2006) have emphasized the need to distinguish clearly the Heterogeneity Hypothesis from these theories. In this last section, I clarify the distinction between the Heterogeneity Hypothesis and hybrid theories of concepts, and I argue that the latter are unsatisfactory models of concepts.

3.3.1 What Are Hybrid Theories of Concepts?

Although hybrid theories of concepts come in many forms, they share some common features.[11] They typically propose that concepts are characterized by the following four properties:

1. A concept C is divided into several parts ($P_1, P_2 \ldots$).
2. Each part stores a distinct type of knowledge (e.g., knowledge about the typical properties of the instances of C, causal knowledge about the instances of C, etc.).
3. These parts are necessarily linked to each other: when one of the parts is used, say, to categorize, we can *ipso facto* use the other parts of the concept for other purposes; for instance, we can use them to reason deductively or inductively.
4. These parts are coordinated: the parts of a given concept do not produce inconsistent outcomes, for instance, inconsistent categorization judgments.

Coordination (Tenet 4) might result from the following circumstances:

- Different cognitive competences involve different parts of concepts: for instance, P_1 might be involved in categorization, while P_2 might be involved in induction.
- When a given competence involves several parts of a concept, these parts are used in a single cognitive process: if categorization involves P_1 and P_2, a single categorization process uses both P_1 and P_2.
- When the parts of a concept are used in several distinct cognitive processes underlying a given competence, one of these parts provides a criterion of correctness: if P_1 and P_2 are used in two different categorization processes, when P_1 and P_2 yield different categorization judgments, one of them is assumed to provide the correct categorization judgment (e.g., Armstrong, Gleitman, and Gleitman 1983: 292; Gelman 2004: 252).

It is noteworthy that proponents of hybrid theories of concepts have usually failed to explain what is meant by claiming that several bodies of knowledge are the parts of a single concept, in contrast to being distinct concepts. The third and the fourth tenets are meant to fill this gap, by making explicit the views past and current hybrid theories of concepts are committed to. They constitute two necessary and jointly sufficient conditions for two coreferential bodies of knowledge to be parts of the same concept, rather than two distinct concepts. Importantly, if

---

[11] Rips, Shoben, and Smith 1973; Smith, Shoben, and Rips 1974; Miller and Johnson-Laird 1976; Osherson and Smith 1981; Keil 1989; Gelman 1990, 2004; Nosofsky, Palmeri, and McKinley 1994; Keil et al. 1998; Anderson and Betz 2001.

some proponents of hybrid theories were to reject these two tenets, they would have to explain what is meant by saying that, say, a definition of x and a prototype of x are two distinct parts of the same concept of x.

By the same token, the third and fourth tenets explain what it means for different bodies of knowledge to be distinct concepts—that is, what functional properties our bodies of knowledge should possess in order to count as distinct concepts. They constitute two sufficient conditions for two coreferential bodies of knowledge to be distinct concepts, rather than parts of the same concept: two bodies of knowledge about the same entity count as two distinct concepts if they fail to satisfy either Tenet 3 or Tenet 4.

To summarize, to say that a concept of x has several parts is to say that several bodies of knowledge about x's are so organized that (Tenet 3) if I categorize an x on the basis of one of these bodies of knowledge, then I can reason inductively about this x on the basis of the other bodies of knowledge (*mutatis mutandis* for deduction, analogy making, etc.) and that (Tenet 4) these bodies of knowledge do not produce inconsistent categorization judgments (*mutatis mutandis* for the other higher cognitive competences).

Two examples may cast some light on hybrid theories of concepts. Osherson and Smith (1981) have proposed that concepts are made of two parts, a core and an identification procedure. Specifically, they propose that the core of a concept consists of a definition, while the identification procedure consists of a prototype:

> We can distinguish between a concept's *core* and its *identification procedure*; the core is concerned with those aspects of a concept that explicate its relation to other concepts, and to thoughts, while the identification procedure specifies the kind of information used to make rapid decisions about membership.... We can illustrate with the concept *woman*. Its core might contain information about the presence of a reproductive system, while its identification procedure might contain information about body shape, hair length, and voice pitch. Given this distinction, it is possible that some traditional theory of concepts correctly characterize the core, whereas prototype theory characterizes an important identification procedure. (Osherson and Smith 1981: 57)

To anticipate the next chapter, a definition represents a set of properties that are deemed to be necessary and sufficient for belonging to a category; roughly, a prototype represents the properties that are deemed to be typical of a category. Thus, the core and the identification procedure are assumed to store two different types of knowledge about the extension of the concept. This illustrates the first two tenets.

Osherson and Smith propose that some cognitive competences involve only one of these two parts. Particularly, concept composition is assumed to involve exclusively the core: when we create a complex body of knowledge about pet fish, we use only the knowledge stored in the core of the concepts FISH and PET. For Osherson and Smith, other competences, such as categorization, involve both the definition and the prototype: categorization is underwritten by two distinct processes—a prototype-based process and a definition-based process. Osherson and Smith contend that we categorize objects by means of the prototype when we need to identify quickly their category membership. This categorization is reliable, but defeasible. We categorize objects by means of the definition when we need to be sure of their category membership. Importantly, definition-based categorization is the ultimate touchstone of the category membership of an object. Prototype-based categorization is defeated when it contradicts the definition-based categorization. That is, our prototype-based categorization process and our definition-based categorization process are so organized that when they yield different outputs, one of them (i.e., the definition-based process) provides a criterion of correctness. This illustrates Tenet 4 above.

Consider now the model of concepts and categorization proposed by Robert Nosofsky and colleagues (1994)—RULEX (for "rules plus exemplars"). According to RULEX, a concept consists of two parts, a rule and a set of exemplars. A rule is, roughly, equivalent to a definition. An exemplar is a representation of a category member. This illustrates the first two tenets. During categorization, these two parts are used as follows. When people have to categorize an object in one of two categories, A and B, they first apply a rule that discriminates most members of A from most members of B. Then, they check out whether this object is not one of the known exceptions to the rule (figure 3.5).

This model illustrates the fourth tenet: RULEX supposes that a single categorization process uses both parts of our concepts (rule and exemplars), so that the parts of a given concept do not produce inconsistent categorization judgments.

3.3.2 Contrast between Hybrid Theories of Concepts and the Heterogeneity Hypothesis

Hybrid theories of concepts were proposed at the end of the 1970s and at the beginning of the 1980s for several reasons. They were sometimes motivated by the desire to save the view that concepts consist of definitions

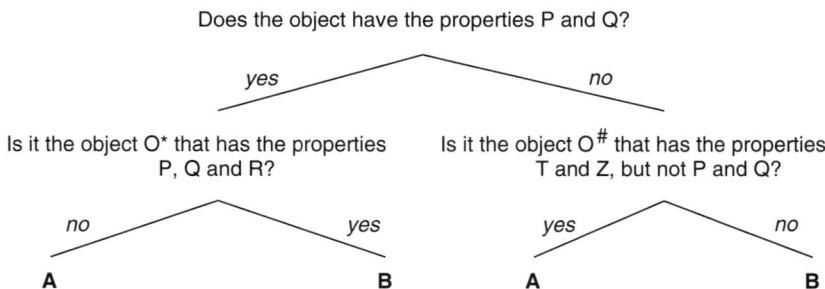

Figure 3.5 The Categorization Procedure of RULEX (inspired by Nosofsky et al. 1994:55)

(section 4.1). If concepts consist of two parts, a definition and an additional part, experimental findings that cannot be explained by assuming that concepts consist of definitions might be explained by supposing that subjects performed the way they did because they relied on this additional part of concepts to complete the experiments. Hybrid theories of concepts were also motivated by what was viewed as the shortcomings of the new theories of concepts proposed in the 1970s, such as the prototype theories. For instance, Osherson and Smith (1981) endorsed the hybrid theory of concepts described above on the grounds that prototypes do not compose. Since prototypes do not compose, but concepts do, concepts cannot be identical to prototypes; rather, prototypes are merely a part of concepts—or so they reasoned.

The popularity of hybrid theories decreased in the 1980s and early 1990s, but many new hybrid theories of concepts have recently been proposed.[12] The motivation behind these theories is to a large extent similar to the motivation behind the Heterogeneity Hypothesis. As we shall see at length in chapters 6 and 7, different findings about higher cognition are best explained by different theories about concepts. Hybrid theories of concepts explain this fact by postulating that concepts have different parts. The Heterogeneity Hypothesis explains this fact by postulating several coreferential concepts that belong to different kinds.

So, what are the differences between the Heterogeneity Hypothesis and hybrid theories of concepts? These differences result from the third and the fourth tenets proposed above. If several bodies of knowledge are the parts of a given concept, when I use a specific body of knowledge about x to categorize, I can *ipso facto* use other bodies of knowledge about x to reason inductively or deductively (Tenet 3). Moreover, when several bodies of knowledge are the parts of a given concept, these bodies of knowledge cannot yield conflicting outcomes about x, for instance, inconsistent categorization judgments. Often, one of the parts is assumed to provide a criterion of correctness (Tenet 4).

Let us focus first on Tenet 3. It is a fact that my different bodies of knowledge about the same entity are often linked. For instance, my bodies of knowledge about water—my knowledge about the molecular structure of water, my knowledge about the typical properties of water, and my knowledge of specific bodies of water—are linked. Thus, if I know that a liquid in a glass on my desk is made of H_2O, I can infer that this liquid is likely to have the typical taste and smell of water and that it is likely to have the same taste as the glass of water I had earlier today.

How does the Heterogeneity Hypothesis accommodate this fact? First, it is important to keep in mind that being linked is a necessary property, but not a sufficient property for being parts of a single concept.

---

[12] Nosofsky, Palmeri, and McKinley 1994; Keil et al. 1998; Anderson and Betz 2001; Gelman 2004.

Thus, many concepts that, in anybody's views, are distinct are linked. Like anybody else, proponents of hybrid theories of concepts grant that my bodies of knowledge about dogs and about mammals are not parts of the same concept. Rather, they are distinct concepts. Nonetheless, my knowledge in long-term memory is so organized that when I classify an animal as a dog, I can *ipso facto* use my knowledge about mammals to draw some conclusions about this animal. Because many concepts that are clearly distinct are linked, the fact that coreferential bodies of knowledge are linked is perfectly consistent with the Heterogeneity Hypothesis.

So, do hybrid theories of concepts and the Heterogeneity Hypothesis agree on Tenet 3? That is, do they agree that the bodies of knowledge about the same category (substance, etc.) are linked? Not entirely. For the sake of simplicity, let us focus on a toy hybrid theory of concepts, which proposes that concepts have two parts, a prototype and a definition. With respect to Tenet 3, this hybrid theory would differ from the Heterogeneity Hypothesis in the following way (*mutatis mutandis* for the other hybrid theories of concepts). This toy hybrid theory contends that, necessarily, the prototype of x can be used in our cognitive processes when the definition of x has been used, and vice-versa. The Heterogeneity Hypothesis agrees that often, but not necessarily, the prototype of x can be used in our cognitive processes when the definition of x has been used, and vice-versa. But it also contends that it might happen that a prototype of x cannot be used in our cognitive processes when a definition of x has been used, and vice-versa. According to the Heterogeneity Hypothesis, being linked is a contingent property of our bodies of knowledge.

Consider now Tenet 4. The difference between the Heterogeneity Hypothesis and hybrid theories of concepts is more clear-cut with respect to this tenet. The Heterogeneity Hypothesis, but not hybrid theories of concepts, predicts that the coreferential bodies of knowledge it posits will occasionally lead to conflicting outcomes, such as inconsistent judgments. Moreover, no body of knowledge should be treated as the criterion of correctness for solving the conflict between these outcomes, for instance, between inconsistent categorization judgments. That is, the Heterogeneity Hypothesis predicts the existence of cognitive conflicts. According to hybrid theories of concepts, such cognitive conflicts should not happen.

3.3.3 Against Hybrid Theories of Concepts: Malt's Findings

We just saw that there are two differences between the Heterogeneity Hypothesis and hybrid theories of concepts. First, for the latter, but not for the former, coreferential bodies of knowledge are necessarily linked. Second, for the latter, but not for the former, the coreferential bodies of knowledge do not lead to cognitive conflicts. In the remainder of this chapter, I will focus on the second difference: evidence suggests that the coreferential bodies of knowledge often yield conflicting outcomes. Thus, these bodies of knowledge are probably not organized in the way that hybrid theories of concepts propose.

I will review further findings in later chapters (see, particularly, sections 6.5 and 7.1.4). Here, I focus on two types of findings that illustrate the cognitive conflicts resulting from the existence of several coreferential bodies of knowledge. I first discuss Barbara Malt's important, but controversial findings about the way people conceptualize water (Malt 1994).[13] Then, I present some linguistic evidence.

Malt systematically collected examples of liquids that are not usually called "water," but that are similar to water in various respects. Examples included tea, coffee, and tears. She also systematically collected instances of liquids that are usually called "water," such as lake water. In the first experiment, subjects were presented with the former liquids and were asked to evaluate the percentage of H_2O in these liquids. A second group was given the same task with respect to the latter liquids. The most relevant result was that many liquids that are not called "water" were judged to have a higher proportion of H_2O than many liquids that are called "water." For instance, tea was judged to be made of 91 percent, coffee of 89 percent, and tears of 89 percent of H_2O, while ocean water and puddle water were judged to be made of 80 percent of H_2O. An analysis of people's judgments also revealed that four dimensions determine whether a liquid is called "water": its chemical composition, its origin, its current location, and its use to humans. A plausible interpretation of this analysis is that a liquid is called "water" if it is sufficiently similar to prototypical bodies of water along these four dimensions.

On the other hand, we believe that water is H_2O. Many might even have the intuition that water is essentially H_2O: necessarily, something is water if and only if it is constituted by molecules of H_2O. This belief about water suggests that in a given context, of two liquids that are made of a high proportion of H_2O, the one which is believed to contain the higher proportion of H_2O is more likely to be judged to be water.

Thus, we have some knowledge about prototypical bodies of water, and this knowledge underwrites which liquids are called "water." We also have some knowledge about what water necessarily is—namely, H_2O. We can use this knowledge to decide whether a liquid is water. As a result, we might make conflicting judgments about whether specific liquids are water. Importantly, none of these two bodies of knowledge provides a criterion of correctness for deciding whether a liquid is water. This should not be the case if they were parts of a single concept, WATER. Rather, this suggests that they really are two different concepts, $WATER_1$ and $WATER_2$.

Or does it? Abbott (1997, 1999) has argued that Malt's findings say nothing about our concept(s) of water. She correctly emphasizes that not calling something ⌜x⌝, for example, not calling a liquid "water," is not

---

[13] See also Malt 1993; Chomsky 1995; Laporte 1998; Strevens 2000.

tantamount to believing that it is not an *x*, for instance, that it is not water. In many situations, we might not want to call a liquid "water," although we believe that this liquid is water. For how we call something depends both on what we believe this thing to be and on our beliefs about how others will interpret what we say. Consider the following case. Objects usually belong to embedded classes. Fido is a Rottweiler, but it also a dog, a mammal, and an animal. In most contexts, referring to Fido as a mammal would be pragmatically infelicitous, for predicates that are both common and more specific could truthfully be used in these contexts. Thus, referring to Fido as an animal would convey some conversational implicature. Consider another case. A class, such as pigeons, can be the extension of several terms, including some technical terms. In most contexts, using a technical term is pragmatically inappropriate. Using such a term would convey the conversational implicature that something specific is intended by the use of this term. Abbott proposes that the same is true of tea, coffee, and tears. We believe that coffee is water, but, for pragmatic reasons, we do not call it "water":

> The difference is not that one substance (e.g., the stuff coming out of your eyes) is not water and the other stuff is water. They are both water. The difference is only that one is *called* 'water' and the other is not. And that only goes to show that we need to distinguish what something is from what it may be called on particular occasions. (Abbott 1997: 315)

If this explanation were correct, then we would have no conflicting judgments about water. Malt's findings would not raise any difficulty for hybrid theories of concepts.

Abbott offers two arguments in support of her interpretation of Malt's findings. In contrast to tap water or swamp water, tea, coffee, and tears are associated with specific terms, namely "tea," "coffee," and "tears." As a result, tea, coffee, and tears are called, respectively, "tea," "coffee," and "tears," and not "water." Calling them "water" would be pragmatically infelicitous. Because there is no specific term for "tap water," we call tap water "water." Furthermore, "tea," "coffee," and "tears" are associated with descriptive elements. For instance, "tear" might be associated with the belief that tears flow from the eyes. Calling tears "tears" conveys this descriptive information.

There is little doubt that the use of "water" is affected by various pragmatic considerations. For instance, water is always more or less pure. The degree of impurity below which a liquid is not called "water" probably varies across communicational contexts. In a chemistry class, this degree might be very high. When we ask whether a lake contains water, this degree is probably much lower (and quite low for some lakes).

However, pace Abbott, it is not the case that for pragmatic reasons, we merely do not call coffee (or several other liquids used in Malt's experiments) "water," although we believe that coffee is water.[14] First, Abbott owes us an explanation of why there are specific terms for tea, coffee, and

---

[14] For further discussion, see Laporte 1998; Strevens 2000.

tears, but not for tap water or swamp water. Is it not precisely because we judge that the latter, but not the former are water?

Second, the cases of coffee and tea contrast with those cases in which we believe that an *x* is a *y*, although we do not refer to this *x* as a ⌜*y*⌝. We believe that Perrier is water, although we typically do not call Perrier "water." But, when we are asked whether Perrier is water, we give a positive answer because there is nothing pragmatically inappropriate in answering the question this way. To make this more vivid, suppose that you are buying some groceries with a friend. If pointing toward a bottle of Perrier, you were to ask,

(1) Is this bottle of Perrier a bottle of water?

your friend would give an affirmative answer. Because we reply to a question, the pragmatic rule that, everything being equal, one should use the expression that is the most informative is waived. By contrast, when we are asked whether iced coffee is water, we give a negative answer. Thus, I would give a negative answer, if I were asked by someone pointing toward a bottle of iced coffee:

(2) Is this bottle of iced coffee a bottle of water?

The contrast between "Perrier" and "coffee" refutes Abbott's first argument. It shows that our reluctance to say that iced coffee is water does not result from the availability of a more specific term for iced coffee. It also refutes Abbott's second argument. "Perrier" is associated with descriptive elements. Still, we answer that Perrier is water, when asked (1), but not that iced coffee is water, when asked (2). This contrast shows that our reluctance to say that iced coffee is water does not result from "coffee" being associated with descriptive elements. Thus, Abbott's two arguments fail to support her claim that we think that coffee (tears, etc.) is water, although we do not call it "water."

Before considering the linguistic evidence against hybrid theories of concepts, it is worth mentioning a different objection to the relevance of Malt's findings for the truth of hybrid theories of concepts. One might question whether the findings about the way we conceptualize a single substance, namely, water, are sufficient to cast serious doubts on hybrid theories of concepts. Why would we assume that the findings about the concept(s) of water generalize to other concepts? In reply, I note that other findings about cognitive conflicts are problematic for these theories. It is also unclear why we would conceptualize water in an abnormal way. Water is an ordinary substance, and we probably think about water or classify liquids as water several times a day. Thus, WATER is probably a representative concept.

3.3.4 *Against Hybrid Theories of Concepts: Linguistic Evidence*

Linguistic evidence concurs with Malt's psychological evidence. According to hybrid theories of concepts, a sentence ⌜*x* is a P⌝ should typically not be ambiguous. For the parts of a given concept of P are not supposed to be independent ways of thinking about P. By contrast, according to the Heterogeneity Hypothesis, a lexical item will typically be associated with different concepts. As a result, a sentence ⌜x is a P⌝ will sometimes be ambiguous. Linguistic evidence supports the Heterogeneity Hypothesis. Consider the following sentences:

(3) A penguin is a bird
(4) A whale is a fish
(5) Tina Turner is a grandmother
(6) Zombies are alive
(7) Onions are lilies
(8) Tomatoes are vegetables

Each of these sentences is true under one reading and false under another one (for consistent empirical evidence, see Machery and Seppälä 2008). Hedges, such as "in a sense" and "in another sense," make this type of ambiguity particularly salient.[15] Consider:

(9) In a sense, tomatoes are vegetables
(10) In another sense, tomatoes are not vegetables

Moreover, men get sometimes insulted as follows:

(11) You are a woman
(12) You are not a man

This linguistic evidence suggests that consistent with the Heterogeneity Hypothesis, predicates such as "bird," "fish," "grandmother," or "woman" are associated with different concepts.

Proponents of hybrid theories might make several objections to this conclusion. First, they might point toward sentences that are not ambiguous in the way (5)–(10) are. Consider:

(13) Fool's gold is gold
(14) Fake dollars are dollars

Some might judge that these two sentences are simply false. In reply, I note that my intuitions are not so clear: in some sense, fake dollars are dollars. More important, when "fake" and a few other qualifiers qualify a predicate, this predicate might come to express a specific concept among the concepts it can express. For instance, when "fake" qualifies "dollar," "dollar" might express a concept of dollar according to which a dollar is essentially issued by the Federal Reserve. This linguistic hypothesis assumes that a given predicate expresses several concepts. If this is correct, sentences such as (13) and (14) do not raise any difficulty for the Heterogeneity Hypothesis.

---

[15] For a semantic theory that is congenial with the views developed here, see Pietroski 2003.

Another objection focuses on what people mean when they agree that sentences (3)–(8) might be both true and false. Consider (8). One might suggest that when people judge that (8) is false, they interpret it literally. When people judge that (8) is true, they do not interpret it literally. Rather, they take (8) to claim that tomatoes look like vegetables, which they take to be true, maybe because tomatoes and typical vegetables are used similarly. Under this interpretation, people do not make inconsistent judgments: people believe that tomatoes are not vegetables, and they believe that they are used like vegetables. According to this interpretation, the linguistic evidence discussed above does not provide evidence that words such as "tomato" are associated with several concepts of tomato.

The proposed interpretation of people's reading of sentences (3)–(8) is not convincing, however. Consider:

(15) Prague looks like Paris
(16) Prague is Paris

Like many tourists, I take (15) to be true, but I do not take (16) to be both true and false. Rather, read without context, I take (16) to be false. However, (16) should be true under one reading if the correct explanation of why people take (8) to be both true and false is that when they take it to be true, they interpret it as meaning that tomatoes are like vegetables in some respects.[16]

Some might find it really hard to stomach that sentences such as (3)–(8) might be both taken to be true and false, when read literally. After all, Tina Turner is a grandmother, whales are not fish, and tomatoes are not vegetables (e.g., Rey 1983: 246). I would like to propose a speculative explanation of people's resistance to the idea that sentences (3)–(8) might be taken to be both true and false, when read literally. When people are judging that it is simply mistaken to assert that tomatoes are vegetables, they are entertaining one of their coreferential concepts of tomato. For these people, "tomato" might express by default this concept. For this reason, they might find it hard to see how (8) might be both true and false, when read literally. Importantly, that some people are judging that it is simply mistaken to assert that tomatoes are vegetables does not show that they do not have other concepts of tomato. For, as illustrated by Malt's work on how people conceptualize water, these other concepts might be used when we categorize or in other contexts, although they might not be spontaneously expressed by the relevant words.

---

[16] Alternatively, I could concede that when we agree with (8), we read it as a comparison, while we disagree with (8) when we read it as a literal assertion. I could then contend that the fact that we have several coreferential concepts of vegetables explains why we can read (8) both as a literal assertion (leading us to disagree with it) and as a comparison (leading us to agree with it). One of our concepts of vegetables is by default expressed by "vegetable"— which explains why read literally, (8) is judged to be false. But, in some contexts, for instance, when we read (8) as a comparison, a different concept of vegetables comes to be expressed by "vegetables."

Let us consider another objection to the linguistic evidence presented above. Proponents of hybrid theories of concepts might ask why words are not systematically ambiguous if it is really the case that most predicates are associated with several concepts. There are two mutually consistent replies to this objection. Words might have default readings. For instance, one of the coreferential concepts of water assumed by the Heterogeneity Hypothesis might be the default reading of "water." A special context or a hedge might be required for "water" to express the other concepts of water. If this is the case, in most linguistic contexts, a sentence ⌜x is a P⌝ should not be ambiguous, although it has the potential to be ambiguous in some contexts. Furthermore, it is likely that in most contexts, speakers would judge that a sentence ⌜x is a P⌝ has the same truth-value for all the potential coreferential concepts that might be associated with ⌜P⌝. Consider, for instance, the way we conceptualize grandmothers. Suppose that we have two concepts, a prototype of grandmothers that represents grandmothers as grey-haired, old women and a definition of grandmothers that represents grandmothers as being necessarily mothers of a parent. Suppose also that the predicate "grandmother" can be associated with either concept. Because many grey-haired, old women are also mothers of a parent, we would judge that these women are grandmothers for the two concepts of grandmother expressed by "grandmother." As a result, we might fail to realize that "grandmother" might express two distinct concepts.

Let us consider a last reply on behalf of hybrid theories of concepts. A proponent of such theories might concede that Malt's findings and the linguistic evidence discussed above strongly suggest concepts are not essentially coordinated. But she might insist that the parts of a concept need not be coordinated. That is, she might reject Tenet 4 of the characterization of hybrid theories (section 3.3.1). The problem with this move is that without this tenet, we are left with little understanding of what is meant by "a part of a concept." It becomes unclear what hybrid theories of concepts amount to.

3.4 Conclusion

In this chapter, I have developed the central hypothesis of this book—the Heterogeneity Hypothesis. This hypothesis consists of 5 tenets:

1. The best available evidence suggests that for each category (for each substance, event, and so on), an individual typically has several concepts.
2. Coreferential concepts have very few properties in common. Thus, coreferential concepts belong to very heterogeneous kinds of concept.
3. Evidence strongly suggests that prototypes, exemplars, and theories are among these heterogeneous kinds of concept.

4. Prototypes, exemplars, and theories are used in distinct cognitive processes.
5. The notion of concept ought to be eliminated from the theoretical vocabulary of psychology.

I have spelled out Tenets 1 and 2. Against other forms of conceptual heterogeneity, such as Scope Pluralism, I argue that most categories of physical objects, most substances, most events, and so on are represented by several concepts. I also propose that these coreferential concepts belong to very heterogeneous kinds of concept. Against Competence Pluralism, I propose that concepts do not vary across cognitive competences. In some respects, the Heterogeneity Hypothesis is similar to the hybrid theories of concepts developed by psychologists of concepts. While proponents of hybrid theories have said little about the notion of a part of a concept, I have tried to flesh it out. A key difference between these theories and the Heterogeneity Hypothesis is that for the former, the hypothesized coreferential bodies of knowledge are not supposed to produce conflicting outcomes, such as inconsistent judgments. Hybrid theories are thus badly equipped to account for the frequent conflicts in cognition.

4

Three Fundamental Kinds of Concept: Prototypes, Exemplars, Theories

Since the rejection of the so-called classical theory of concepts, according to which concepts are definitions, three paradigms have successively emerged in the psychology of concepts: the prototype paradigm,[1] the exemplar paradigm,[2] and the theory paradigm.[3] The first two paradigms are occasionally assimilated under the heading "similarity-based" views (e.g., Komatsu 1992) or under the heading "probabilistic views" (e.g., Medin 1989), and the theory paradigm is sometimes called "the knowledge approach" (Murphy 2002) or "explanation-based views" (Komatsu 1992). These three paradigms are not detailed theories of concepts. Rather, they are general outlines, which can be developed in various ways by specific theories of concepts. For instance, instead of a unique prototype theory of concepts, there is a family of prototype theories that share some commitments, but that develop them differently. The prototype paradigm captures these shared commitments.

In this chapter, I describe the main paradigms of concepts in the contemporary psychological literature on concepts.[4] I argue that they

---

[1] Posner and Keele 1968, 1970; Rosch and Mervis 1975; Rosch 1978; Hampton 1979, 2006.
[2] Medin and Schaffer 1978; Nosofsky 1986.
[3] Carey 1985; Murphy and Medin 1985; Gelman and Markman 1986; Keil 1989.
[4] There are many good reviews of the psychological literature on concepts: Smith and Medin 1981; Medin 1989; Komatsu 1992; Hampton 1997c; Prinz 2002: chs. 2–4; Murphy 2002; Goldstone and Kersten 2003. This chapter owes much to these reviews.

posit three theoretical entities—prototypes, exemplars, and theories—that have little in common. Thus, this chapter establishes the following conditional claim: if it can be shown that the class of concepts includes these three types of entities, then concepts divide into kinds that have little in common.

In section 4.1, I briefly review the classical theory of concepts. In the following three sections, I focus successively on the three main contemporary paradigms of concepts—the prototype paradigm of concepts, the exemplar paradigm of concepts, and the theory paradigm of concepts. As explained in chapter 1, a theory of concepts should determine what kind of knowledge is stored in concepts and, at least in general terms, what kind of cognitive process uses concepts. Ideally, it should also characterize the format of concepts, cast some light on concept acquisition, and, increasingly, localize concepts in the brain. In these three sections, I consider how the main paradigms of concepts deal with these tasks, particularly with the first two. In section 4.5, I consider some alternative views of concepts—particularly, the neo-empiricist view of concepts[5] and the view that concepts are ideals.[6] In section 4.6, I show that the three main paradigms of concepts posit very different kinds of concept.

4.1 The Classical Theory of Concepts

4.1.1 The Psychology of Concepts before the 1970s

The first section of psychologist Sarah C. Fisher's monograph (1916: 2–32) is a useful entry point to the psychological literature on concepts and concept acquisition in the nineteenth century (see also Moore 1910: 76–115). Fisher correctly notes that the philosophical speculations about the nature of our knowledge paved the way for the experimental work in psychology. Like contemporary psychologists, Descartes, Locke, and Hume were interested in empirical issues, such as how concepts are acquired, how concepts are used, and whether concepts are images. Their speculations were echoed in the theoretical controversies in psychology during the second half of the nineteenth century, for instance, in Wundt's (Boring 1950) or in Taine's work (Taine 1870). However, little experimental work on concepts took place before the end of the nineteenth century. At the juncture of the nineteenth and twentieth centuries, two experimental approaches to concepts emerged. Ribot (1891, 1899) focused on what people are aware of when they read or hear a word (see also Binet 1903). Other psychologists examined what kind of knowledge people acquire from encountering category members and how they use this knowledge to categorize other category members (Grünbaum 1908;

---

[5] Barsalou 1999, 2008; Prinz 2002; Machery 2006b, 2007a.
[6] Barsalou 1983, 1985.

Moore 1910). To use a modern vocabulary, these two experimental approaches focused respectively on linguistic understanding and on concept learning. Noticeably, these two approaches still structure the contemporary psychology of concepts.[7]

Naturally, during the twentieth century, psychologists have characterized concepts in various ways. Introspective psychologists thought that humans acquire some consciously accessible knowledge about category members,[8] while behaviorists identified concepts with a mere disposition to associate category members with a given name.[9] Nonetheless, above and beyond these differences, introspective psychologists, functional psychologists (e.g., Hull 1920), and, later, behaviorists (e.g., Smoke 1932) concurred in using the theoretical term "concept" to refer to that which is acquired from encountering category members and which enables us to decide whether entities belong to a given category. These psychologists were interested in understanding the process of acquisition—often called "abstraction"—as well as the end product of this process, the concept itself. In this respect, they do not differ from contemporary psychologists and neuropsychologists interested in concepts.

4.1.2 The Classical Theory of Concepts: Main Ideas

Most psychologists interested in concepts before the end of the 1960s endorsed what is known as the classical theory of concepts. According to this theory, a concept of a class of objects consists of a body of knowledge about which properties are separately necessary and jointly sufficient for belonging to this class. The concept BACHELOR may consist of the belief that bachelors are unmarried, adult men. When we categorize someone as a bachelor, when we reason about bachelors, we use by default this definition.[10]

To clarify, when the classical theory of concepts asserts that the concept of a class is a definition, it does not propose that people know the real conditions of membership in this class (if there are such conditions); rather, it proposes that people view a set of properties as necessary and sufficient conditions of membership in this class. This distinction is similar to Locke's distinction between the nominal essence and the real essence of a class (Locke [1690] 1979).

The classical theory of concepts is usually associated with a specific theory of concept acquisition and of categorization. Acquiring a concept

---

[7] See, for instance, Murphy 2002: chs. 1–6 on concept learning and chs. 11–12 on linguistic understanding.

[8] Moore 1910; Fisher 1916.

[9] Kuo 1923; Gengerelli 1927; Smoke 1932.

[10] For the sake of simplicity, in this chapter and in the following ones, I focus mostly on concepts of categories of physical objects ("categories" for short). However, my claims about concepts of categories are intended to apply, *mutatis mutandis*, to concepts of substances, concepts of events, and so on. These claims can be easily modified to fit the relevant concepts.

of a category consists of coming to believe that some properties are necessary and sufficient for belonging to this category. Categorizing in a category consists of checking whether the object to be categorized (what I will henceforth call the "target") possesses the properties that are believed to be necessary and sufficient for belonging to this category.

These ideas have often been explicitly endorsed.[11] They were also assumed in the experiments most psychologists ran before the end of the 1960s.[12] For instance, to study introspectively the formation of concepts, Fisher (1916) created several drawings of abstract shapes (figure 4.1). Categories of ten figures were created. All the figures within a given category shared a common part, which defined the category. A meaningless name—"Zalof," "Deral," "Tefoq," and "Kareg"—was associated with each category. Fisher presented the members of a given category in succession. Subjects were supposed to examine the category members in order to be able to define the name of the category—that is, they were supposed to determine what part was necessary and sufficient for being a member of the category. Subjects were asked to introspect their mental states during the experiment (see Machery 2007b for further detail).

This is, of course, not to say that before the end of the 1960s, all psychologists have blindly endorsed the classical theory of concepts. Noticeably, Bruner and colleagues (1956) did study the acquisition of non-classical

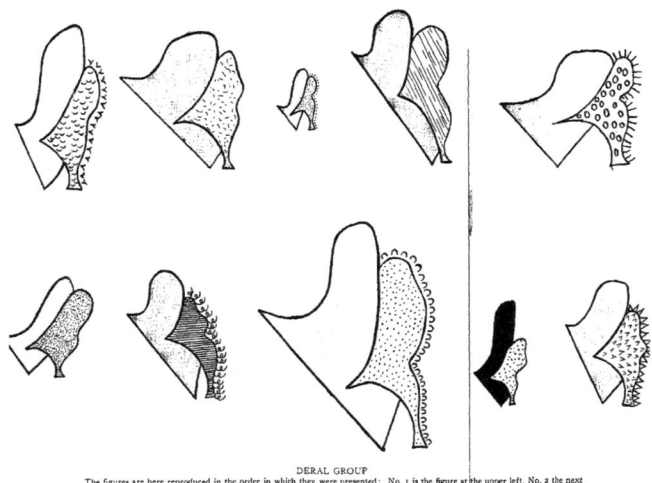

Figure 4.1 An Example of Fisher's Stimuli, the Deral Group (from Fisher 1916, appendix, colored original)

---

[11] Hull 1920; Katz and Fodor 1963.
[12] Hull 1920; Gengerelli 1927; Smoke 1932; Conant and Trabasso 1964. See Machery 2007b on the experimental designs used in the psychology of concepts since the beginning of the twentieth century.

concepts, including concepts of categories that were characterized by a disjunction of properties. However, the bulk of the research on concepts up to the end of the 1960s assumed the classical theory of concepts.

4.1.3 Are Concepts Definitions?

The classical theory of concepts has been widely rejected in the psychological literature on concepts. Since the reasons for this rejection have been reviewed elsewhere,[13] I will be brief.[14] First, it is often noticed that two thousand years of conceptual analysis in philosophy have been fruitless. There is no agreed upon definition of good, justice, or knowledge. Many philosophers have renounced the hope of finding such definitions. If concepts were definitions, surely philosophers would have managed to define good, justice, or knowledge.

More mundane concepts also seem to be impossible to define, a point made by Wittgenstein (1953) with respect to concepts like GAME.[15] More recently, Fodor (1981) has shown that defining the concept of painting is fraught with the very difficulties that hamper the conceptual analysis of abstract concepts: for every proposed definition, it is possible to find a case that falsifies it.[16] This is evidence for the generalization that save maybe for a few exceptions, concepts are not definitions.

Other pieces of evidence are even harder to accommodate. Suppose that a concept is defined by means of another. For example, to murder has been defined as to kill intentionally together with some other conditions. Prima facie, this predicts that processing MURDER would take longer than processing KILL. However, several experiments run by Fodor and colleagues (1980) show that this is not the case. These two concepts are processed at the same speed. Importantly, the examples used by Fodor and colleagues are among the best cases for the claim that concepts are definitions.

A proponent of the classical theory of concepts could demur. To explain Fodor and colleagues' finding, she could perhaps contend that definitions are chunked—that is, processed as units. However, this kind of ad hoc reply will not work with the main problem for the classical theory of concepts. The nail in the coffin of the classical theory is that it has very little explanatory power. It fails to explain the phenomena that have been found in the psychology of concepts since the 1970s. For example, it does not

---

[13] Smith and Medin 1981: ch. 3; Hampton 1993, 1997c; Laurence and Margolis 1999; Murphy 2002: ch. 2; for a critical discussion, see Jackendoff 1992: 48 et seq.; Margolis 1994.

[14] Not all arguments against the classical theory of concepts are convincing. It is often said that vagueness—the existence of objects that are neither clearly members nor clearly nonmembers of the relevant category—is inconsistent with the classical theory (e.g., Hampton 1993). This is, of course, not the case. Definitions result in vagueness when the elements of these definitions are themselves vague.

[15] See also Ryle 1951 on THINKING and WORK.

[16] See also Hampton 1979 and McNamara and Sternberg 1983.

explain the fact that typical *x*'s are categorized more quickly and more reliably than atypical *x*'s (Rosch and Mervis 1975; ch. 6). More generally, most psychologists agree that there are very few, if any, experimental results that are best explained by the hypothesis that concepts are definitions (Murphy 2002: 39).

4.1.4 The Return of Definitions?

The case against definitions would seem to be closed. However, a few psychologists and linguists have remained faithful to the classical theory of concepts. Moreover, there is a recent surge of interest in definitions among neuropsychologists.

Some psychologists endorse some form of Scope Pluralism (section 3.2): the nature of concepts varies across domains or across types of entity. For instance, Pinker and Prince (1999) propose that in some domains, concepts are definitions, while in other domains, concepts are prototypes or exemplars.[17] They suggest that kinship concepts (e.g., UNCLE) and legal concepts (e.g., BATTERY) are well characterized by the classical theory.

Rather than endorsing some form of Scope Pluralism, a few psychologists contend that for most categories, we have both a definition and another type of concept, for instance, a set of exemplars. Some propose that the former and the latter should be thought of as parts of the same concept, endorsing a hybrid theory of concepts. For instance, as we saw in the previous chapter, Nosofsky and colleagues (1994) have proposed a model of this type, called "RULEX" (section 3.3).

Others psychologists have adopted a position similar to the Heterogeneity Hypothesis. Particularly, Gregory Ashby and colleagues propose that a definition of a category and a prototype of this category form two concepts, instead of being two parts of a single concept (Ashby et al. 1998; Ashby and Ell 2001). In what follows, I argue against the resurgent idea that we store definitions in long-term memory, be they thought of as parts of concepts or as full-blown concepts.

First, I need to comment on the terminology used by the psychologists and neuropsychologists interested in definitions. They usually speak of "rules," "rule-based" systems, or systems dedicated to the acquisition of "rules." This is problematic.[18] While rules are assumed by these psychologists to stand in contrast to prototypes, it is unclear why prototypes do not count as rules. Deciding that an object is a dog on the basis of a hypothetical prototype of dog is, roughly, to apply the rule that an object is a dog if and only it possesses a sufficient number of the properties that are typical of dogs

---

[17] They concede that some words may express both a definition and a prototype. In these cases, they come close to endorsing the Heterogeneity Hypothesis (Pinker and Prince 1999: 254–255).

[18] Gigerenzer and Regier 1996; Hahn and Chater 1998; Marcus 2005; Pothos 2005.

(section 4.2). To preserve the contrast intended by psychologists, the notion of definition is to be preferred to the notion of rule.

I consider two reasons for the return of definition. First, some psychologists have emphasized that people, particularly children, are sometimes told definitions. For example, children may be told that an uncle is a brother of a parent. As a result, people could acquire the habit of looking for definitions of categories (Palmeri and Gauthier 2004: 296). However, the importance of this consideration is questionable. Several concepts, such as OBJECT or AGENT, may be innate. Scores of concepts are also learned before children are explicitly told definitions. Moreover, as noted above, for many categories, there is simply no definition to learn.

Second, and most important, some recent neuropsychological experiments provide evidence that some brain regions are specifically involved in learning definitions.[19] Thus, Ashby and Ell write, "Different brain regions are implicated according to whether the category-learning task involves explicit rules, prototype distortion or information integration" (2001: 204). There is evidence that the right dorsolateral prefrontal cortex, the anterior cingulate, and the right caudate nucleus are involved when subjects learn the definitions of well-defined categories.

This line of neuropsychological research is, I now argue, theoretically misguided. Scores of experiments in the 1950s and 1960s (e.g., Bruner, Goodnow, and Austin 1956; Conant and Trabasso 1964) showed that people are able to acquire concepts of well-defined categories. A considerable amount of information was acquired about issues such as how difficult it is to acquire different types of definition, how people select hypotheses about which definition distinguishes category members from other items, and so on. When this research tradition was attacked at the end of the 1960s, our capacity to form definitions from encountering members of well-defined categories was not questioned. Rather, psychologists questioned the ecological validity of the findings about concepts of well-defined categories. What was judged problematic with this line of research was whether subjects learn concepts of experimental, well-defined categories in the same way as we learn concepts in our everyday life and whether concepts of well-defined categories are similar to the concepts acquired outside the lab. Psychologists concluded negatively. Recent research in neuropsychology falls prey to the same objection. Certainly, people can learn concepts of well-defined categories, and, certainly, this capacity involves some brain areas. However, this fact does not give any new reason to believe that save for a few concepts, people learn definitions, store definitions in long-term memory, and use definitions in categorization and other cognitive competences outside the lab.

---

[19] Ashby et al. 1998; Smith, Patalano, and Jonides 1998; Ashby and Ell 2001; Ashby and Maddox 2005.

In fact, the recent work on definitions in neuropsychology tentatively suggests that the capacity to learn the concepts of well-defined categories in experimental settings has little to do with the acquisition of concepts in the real world. The dorsolateral prefrontal cortex and the cingulate cortex are involved, among other things, in the attentional monitoring of performances.[20] If acquiring the concepts of well-defined categories is not an ecologically valid task, people should not have a dedicated cognitive system for completing this task. Acquiring these concepts, that is, acquiring definitions, would then involve the neural systems that underlie the attentional monitoring of performances. Since the dorsolateral prefrontal cortex and the cingulate cortex are precisely involved in what neuropsychologists call "rule learning," we can tentatively conclude that learning the definition of a well-defined category is an unusual task, for which there is no dedicated cognitive system. If this is correct, studying how people learn the definitions of categories in experimental settings says little about concept acquisition in the real world.

4.2 The Prototype Paradigm of Concepts

4.2.1 Statistical Knowledge

The prototype paradigm was developed in the 1970s to replace the classical theory of concepts. This happened quickly. Psychologists Eleanor Rosch,[21] Carolyn Mervis, Michael Posner, Lance Rips, Edward Smith, and James Hampton played an important role in the emergence and quick success of this new view of concepts.[22] This theoretical and empirical development in psychology was congruent with the research on knowledge representation in artificial intelligence.[23]

The prototype paradigm of concepts is built around the idea that concepts are prototypes.[24] In turn, a prototype of a class is a body of statistical knowledge about the properties deemed to be possessed by the members of this class.[25] While the classical theory of concepts assumes that when we categorize or when we reason, we have in mind some properties that we take to be necessary and jointly sufficient for belonging to the class at hand, the prototype paradigm of concepts assumes that we have in mind

---

[20] Wood and Grafman 2003; Beer, Shimamura, and Knight 2004.
[21] Rosch's ideas have constantly evolved. In a well-known article (1978), she argues that her findings are consistent with several theories of concepts.
[22] Posner and Keele 1968, 1970; Rips, Shoben, and Smith 1973; Smith, Shoben, and Rips 1974; Rosch 1973, 1975, 1978; Rosch and Mervis 1975; Rosch et al. 1976; Hampton 1979, 1981.
[23] See, e.g., Schank and Abelson 1977.
[24] See, e.g., Rosch and Mervis 1975; Smith et al. 1988; Smith and Minda 2002.
[25] The term "prototype" is used ambiguously to designate the most typical member of a category (e.g., Rosch and Mervis 1975) and the representation of a category (e.g., Hampton 1979). I use the term in this second sense.

some properties that are characterized statistically—for instance, the properties that are believed to be typically possessed by the members of this class.

Prototype theories of concepts vary, depending on how they characterize the nature of the statistical knowledge stored in prototypes. Depending on the theory, prototypes consist of knowledge about properties that objects either possess or do not possess or about properties that objects possess to some degree. The property *having wings* is an instance of the first type of property. The property *being sweet* is an instance of the second type of property: a substance can be more or less sweet. This second type of property can have a discrete number of values or can be continuous. Prototype models that focus on the first type of property are usually called "featural models," while models that focus on the second type of property are usually called "dimensional models" (Smith and Medin 1981).[26]

Moreover, depending on the theory, prototypes represent the typical properties of categories (e.g., Rosch 1975), the cue-valid properties of categories (e.g., Hampton 1993), or the properties that are both cue-valid and typical. A property P is typical of a class C if and only if the probability that an object possesses P given that it is a member of C is high. *Having four legs* is a typical property of dogs. Knowing which properties are typical of a class is particularly useful when you have to draw inductions about the members of this class. A property P is highly cue-valid for a class C if the probability that an object belongs to C given that it possesses P is high (e.g., Smith and Medin 1981: 79). *Barking* is a highly cue-valid property of dogs, while *having four legs* is not a highly cue-valid property of dogs. Knowing which properties are highly cue-valid for a class is particularly useful when you have to decide whether objects belong to this class. Finally, prototypes could also store some knowledge about the properties that maximize some weighted function of typicality and cue-validity (e.g., Jones 1983).[27]

According to some theories, prototypes merely store some knowledge about which properties are typical (or cue-valid). According to other theories, prototypes also store the degree of typicality (or of cue-validity) of the typical (or cue-valid) properties. In addition, dimensional models of prototypes vary, depending on what type of knowledge prototypes are assumed to store. As noted by Barsalou (1990), prototypes could store some knowledge about the modal value or the mean value of the relevant properties.

---

[26] On dimensional models of concepts, see Markman 1999: ch. 2; Gärdenfors 2000; Rogers and McClelland 2004.

[27] In the psychological literature, the vocabulary is not completely fixed. What I have called "typicality" is sometimes called "category-validity" (e.g., Murphy and Medin 1985: 293; Murphy and Lassaline 1997: 104; Prinz 2002: 154–155). What I have called "cue-validity" is sometimes called "diagnosticity."

There is no reason to assume that all prototypes store the same type of statistical knowledge. On the contrary, if prototypes are tailored to the categories they represent, they are likely to store different types of statistical knowledge. Suppose that the members of a given category possess some properties that have an infinite number of values, such as *being sweet*. If the values of these properties are normally distributed, then knowing the mean value and, maybe, the standard deviation for these properties is an efficient way of describing this category. By contrast, knowing the mean value of the properties possessed by the members of a category will lead to incorrect categorizations if the distribution of the values of these properties is highly skewed. Thus, one might expect prototypes to store different types of statistical knowledge, depending on the nature of the represented categories.

Critics of prototype theories often assume that prototype theories are empiricist (e.g., Keil 1989)—that is, that prototypes represent only the perceptual properties of category members, such as their shape, form, or color. However, prototypes might represent any kind of property: "A moment's consideration shows that a model that is limited to representing purely perceptual information with no deeper structural, functional or abstract attributes is simply a 'straw man' as a model for representing concepts" (Hampton 1998: 138). Thus, prototype theories can, but need not, be empiricist.

Prototype theorists need to explain why our concepts represent only some of the numerous typical (or cue-valid) properties of the members of a category. I call this explanatory task "the selection problem." Psychologists have repeatedly highlighted this issue (e.g., Smith and Medin 1981), but to no avail. Little progress has been made in this area.

Finally, prototype theorists need not claim, and typically do not (e.g., Hampton 2001), that our knowledge about a category boils down to the body of statistical knowledge that is stored in the concept of this category. Prototype theorists might propose that even if our concept of a class consists of a prototype, we also have some other kinds of knowledge about this class. What would distinguish the prototype from these other kinds of knowledge is that the former, but not the latter, would be used by default in the processes underlying the higher cognitive competences (section 1.1).

4.2.2 Two Examples

I will illustrate the prototype paradigm of concepts with two models of prototypes. I consider first the featural model proposed by Hampton in 1979 under the name "polymorphous concepts." Hampton describes his model as follows:

> *A polymorphous concept* can be defined as one in which an instance is classified as belonging to a certain class, if and only if it possesses at least a certain

number of a set of features, none of which need be necessary or sufficient in itself.... If in addition... we allow for differential weighting of the features, then the polymorphous concept becomes essentially equivalent to the idea of a prototype concept, developed by Rosch (1975). (Hampton 1979: 450–451)

Basically, in this model, a prototype is a list of properties (also called "features" or "attributes") that are used to decide whether objects belong to the represented class.

Hampton does not say much about what characterizes the properties that are represented by prototypes, although he briefly refers to the notion of cue-validity (Hampton 1979: 451). To determine which properties are represented by prototypes, Hampton used the following procedure, called the "feature listing task" or "property listing task." Subjects were asked to describe different categories, such as the category of vehicles. They were invited to list as many properties of vehicles as possible. Properties were then pooled across subjects. The properties that had been listed most frequently were assumed to be represented by the concept of vehicle. This criterion is called "production frequency." Production frequency is correlated with how important subjects think a property is for defining the category in question.

The representation of the concept VEHICLE obtained with this procedure (figure 4.2) does not correspond exactly to the concept of vehicle possessed by any of Hampton's (1979) subjects. It is an abstraction out of their concepts. But, since the variables used in Hampton's studies are aggregate variables (mean typicality, mean reaction time, etc.), this should not be viewed as a problem for Hampton's approach.

The idea that property listing is a sound procedure for characterizing the knowledge stored in concepts has been criticized by some psychologists.[28] According to Barsalou (1993), this method is unprincipled: it assumes, without justification, that the knowledge stored in concepts is introspectively available. Relying on the introspection of many subjects, as is done by Hampton and others, does not alleviate this difficulty. Moreover, only these properties that can be easily expressed linguistically are listed: knowledge that cannot be easily formulated, but that may be part and parcel of a concept is not accessed by this task. Additionally, one might worry that the properties that are listed are determined by pragmatic factors. Tversky and Hemengway (1984) have argued that subjects preferentially list the properties that distinguish the instances of the concept presented in the experiment from implicit or explicit contrast classes. For instance, *having two legs* is usually not listed for the concept EAGLE because most other birds have two legs. Similarly, pragmatic considerations explain why *does not fly* is mentioned for PENGUIN, but not for DOG. Another

---

[28] See the discussion in Hampton 1979: 442; for a more critical approach, see Armstrong Gleitman, and Gleitman 1983; Murphy and Medin 1985: 299 et seq.; Barsalou 1993: 43 et seq.

VEHICLE
1 Carries people or things
2 Can move
3 Moves along
4 Has wheels
5 Is powered, has an engine, uses fuel
6 Is self-propelled, has some means of propulsion
7 Is used for transport
8 Is steered, has a driver controlling direction
9 Has a space for passengers or goods
10 Moves faster than a person on his own
11 Man-made

Figure 4.2 The Prototype of Vehicle according to Hampton's (1979) Model (inspired by Hampton 1979: 459)

difficulty with the property listing task is that subjects' performances are not perfectly reliable: subjects list different properties across occasions (Barsalou 1993; section 1.3). This is to be expected if pragmatic factors are important in this task. Finally, psychologists typically amend the lists made by subjects, crossing out absurd properties, identifying synonyms, and even adding some properties.

These objections do not justify rejecting the property listing task. Although introspection occasionally misleads, there is little reason to doubt that when concepts can be introspected, we have a partial, but accurate introspective grasp of the knowledge they store. Furthermore, although it is not perfect, reliability between and within subjects is rather substantial (Hampton 1979; see section 1.3). The role of pragmatic factors in the property listing task and the fact that this task is linguistic merely show that property listing may not provide a complete description of the knowledge stored in concepts. Even so, property listing may still yield a partial description of this knowledge. In brief, in spite of its limits, the property listing task remains useful. It provides the partial description of the knowledge stored in concepts that is needed to test claims about concepts and cognitive processes.

Hampton's (1979) model contrasts with the model of prototypes developed by Smith and colleagues (1988).[29] It is now widely recognized that the models that are similar to Hampton's model are too simple.[30] These models assume that concepts store very little knowledge about the categories they denote and that cognitive processes typically use very little knowledge. By contrast, Smith and colleagues assume that concepts store a large amount of knowledge:

> In our view, a prototype is *a prestored representation of the usual properties associated with the concepts' instances*.... Thus, an apple prototype will include properties such as having seeds, properties that are part of our commonsense knowledge about apples. Earlier work on prototypes indicated that a concept's prototype includes properties that are not strictly necessary for concept membership (e.g., Rosch 1973; Smith, Shoben, and Rips 1974). The prototype of apple, for example, includes the nonnecessary properties of red, round, and smooth. Subsequent work has shown that the contents of a prototype must include *far more than a list of properties.* (Smith et al. 1988: 487; my emphasis)

Smith and colleagues' prototype model distinguishes two types of knowledge, the knowledge about what they call "attributes" and the knowledge about what they call "values." Attributes are kinds of property or variables, while values are properties. Color is an attribute, while red and blue are values. Smith and colleagues propose that concepts store some knowledge about the distribution of properties among the members of the denoted class (figure 4.3). Instead of storing merely some knowledge about the most common color, the prototype of apple is assumed to store some knowledge about how often apples are red, how often apples are blue, and so on. Values are weighted for their salience, which is supposed to reflect their subjective frequency and their "perceptibility." Attributes are weighted for their diagnosticity, which is defined as "a measure of how useful the attribute is in discriminating instances of the concept from instances of contrasting concepts" (1988: 487).

To characterize the knowledge stored in prototypes, Smith and colleagues relied on the property listing task (1988: 497–500). Subjects were asked to list the properties of various types of fruits (e.g., apples) and vegetables (e.g., carrots).[31] For each fruit and each vegetable, the properties listed by all subjects were pooled together. Two judges classified these properties (or values) into attributes. For instance, *red* and *yellow*

---

[29] Hampton (1993) presents a related model.
[30] Barsalou 1993: 37 et seq.; Hampton 1993: 73.
[31] "The instructions...informed subjects that for each instance, they were to write down all its properties they could think of, and that they had 90 seconds to do this" (Smith et al. 1988: 497).

APPLE			
Attributes		**Values**	
Color	1	Red	27
		Green	3
		Brown	-
Shape	0.5	Round	25
		Cylindrical	5
		Square	-
Texture	0.25	Smooth	24
		Rough	4
		Bumpy	2

Figure 4.3 The Prototype of Apple according to Smith et al.'s (1988) Model (inspired by Smith et al. 1988: 490)

were classified as being colors. Interestingly, the same attributes emerged across all fruits and across all vegetables (1988: 498; see also table 1, p. 500). The number of mentions of a property for a given fruit (or vegetable) was taken as a measure of its weight in the concept of that fruit. The weight of each property represented by the concepts FRUIT and VEGETABLE was determined by averaging its weight for each fruit and for each vegetable. The diagnosticity of an attribute in the concepts FRUIT and VEGETABLE was a function of how useful it was in discriminating fruits and vegetables. Smith and colleagues measured the degree of association of each attribute with fruits, but not vegetables, and vice-versa (for more detail, see Smith et al. 1988: 498).

Some psychologists contrast Smith and colleagues' (1988) model (and similar models) with the prototype models, calling the former "frame theories" or "schema theories" (e.g., Komatsu 1992). However, there is no reason to restrict the label "prototype" to the simplest models, such as Hampton's (1979) model. As noted by Smith and colleagues themselves, their model develops the key insight of the prototype paradigm: concepts store some statistical knowledge about category members.[32]

---

[32] Several other models of concepts should also be classified as prototype models. This is the case of scripts (Shank and Abelson 1977). According to this approach, events, such as going to the restaurant, are characterized as sequences of typical events. Decision bound theory (Ashby and Gott 1988) is also a version of the prototype paradigm.

4.2.3 Prototype-Based Models of Cognitive Processes

Prototype theories of concepts have been associated with rather detailed models of the cognitive processes underlying the higher cognitive competences. Although different cognitive processes are typically modeled differently and although there are often several prototype-based models for a given cognitive competence, one can identify a few key properties of these models.

Their most important property is that cognitive processes are assumed to involve the computation of the similarity between prototypes and other representations (e.g., Hampton 1998, 2006). Consider the following toy example. I see Fido and I categorize it as a dog. This categorization judgment results from the following processes (figure 4.4). The prototype of dog is retrieved from long-term memory (together, maybe, with other prototypes); this prototype is compared or, as psychologists usually say, is "matched" with a representation of Fido; the similarity between these two representations is computed; the degree of similarity depends on how many properties are represented by both the prototype and the representation of Fido; the judgment that Fido is a dog follows from the high degree of similarity between the prototype of dog and the representation of Fido.

The second property of these models is that the similarity computation is usually assumed to be linear.[33] In linear models, a property that is shared by the target and the prototype increases the similarity between the target and the prototype independently of whether they share other properties. To illustrate, the fact that my neighbor's dog, Fido, has a property that matches my prototype of dog (say, *barking*) increases the similarity between the representation of Fido and the prototype of dog independently of whether Fido and my prototype of dog match in other respects. To put it more technically, properties are independent cues for categorization.

Strictly speaking, the linearity of the similarity function is not required by prototype models. A few prototype models of categorization rely on non-linear functions.[34] However, as will be shown in section 4.3.3, linear functions fit the gist of prototype-based models of cognitive processes.

Finally, prototype-based models of cognitive processes, for instance, prototype-based models of categorization, are typically integrative (Berretty, Todd, and Martignon 1999). That is, it is assumed that prototype-based cognitive processes combine several cues to produce their outputs. For instance, to decide whether a target is a dog, we are assumed to take always into consideration several of its properties.[35]

---

[33] Medin and Schaffer 1978: 215; Hampton 1993: 74.

[34] Nosofsky 1992; Smith and Minda 1998.

[35] For non-integrative models of cognitive processes, including categorization, see Gigerenzer, Todd, and the ABC Research Group 1999.

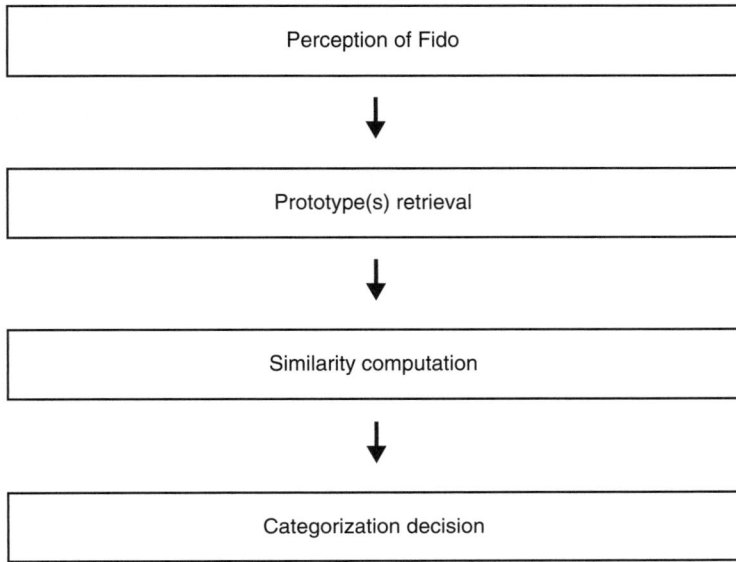

Figure 4.4 Successive Psychological Processes in Categorization

4.2.4 Example

The previous section has highlighted the core ideas of prototype-based models of cognitive processes. Such models have been developed for various cognitive processes, including reasoning under uncertainty (Smith and Osherson 1989), inductive inference (Smith 1989; Osherson et al. 1990; Sloman 1993), concept combination (Hampton 1987, 1997a; Smith et al. 1988; Costello and Keane 2000, 2005), and deductive reasoning (Sloman 1998). Some of these models will be described in later chapters. To illustrate the gist of these models, I focus here on a prototype-based model of categorization.

There are several prototype-based models of categorization. These models are rarely full-blown models of the categorization process. As Barsalou (1990) has pointed out, typically little is said about the search in long-term memory, that is, about the second step of the categorization process (figure 4.4). Particularly, we are typically not told how prototypes are selected, that is, what determines whether a specific prototype is retrieved from memory in order to be involved in the categorization process. Prototype-based models usually focus only on the last two steps of the categorization process. They specify how the similarity between a prototype and a target is computed—they specify the similarity measure; they also specify how the decision to categorize the target is made, based on its similarity with the prototype—they specify the decision rule. Additionally, the description of the last two steps of the categorization process rarely qualifies as a full-fledged process model. For instance, typically, nothing is said about whether the matching process between the representation of the target and the prototype is done serially (a property at a time) or in parallel (all properties at the same time).

Hampton (1993) is a good illustration of prototype-based models of categorization.[36] His model consists of a prototype model of concepts, a similarity measure, and a decision rule. The prototype model of concepts is similar to Smith and colleagues' (1988) model described above. The similarity measure is the following (1993: 73–74):

$$S(x, C) = f(w(x, i)) \tag{1}$$

where $S(x, C)$ is the similarity between the target x and the prototype of the category C and $w(x, i)$ is the weight of the value (e.g., *red*) possessed by x for the ith attribute represented by the prototype (e.g., *color*).

Hampton notes, "The simplest, and most common assumption for the function f is a linear combination rule, such that the similarity is proportional to the sum of the attribute-value weights possessed by an instance" (1993: 74). Thus,

$$S(x, C) = \sum_{i=1}^{n} w(x, i) \tag{2}$$

Hampton's decision rule for categorization is a simple deterministic rule (74):

$$S(x, C) > t \rightarrow x \in C \tag{3}$$

where t is a criterion (or threshold) on the similarity scale.

Noticeably, this rule says nothing about the cases where the similarity of the target to two different prototypes is above threshold. Finally, Hampton's model assumes that the same process of similarity evaluation underlies both typicality judgments (how typical an object is of its category) and categorization judgments. Typicality ratings are supposed to be monotonically related to similarity.

Thus, Hampton's model of the categorization process involves a matching process between representations as well as a linear measure of the similarity between a prototype and other presentations. These are the trademarks of prototype-based models of cognitive processes.

4.3 The Exemplar Paradigm of Concepts

4.3.1 Knowledge about Particulars

A few years after the development of the prototype paradigm, a very different paradigm of concepts was proposed by Lee Brooks (1978) and

---

[36] For other models, see Osherson and Smith 1981; Smith and Medin 1981; Smith and Minda 1998.

Douglas Medin (Medin and Schaffer 1978). Medin's and Brooks's groundbreaking ideas have been developed in detail in the 1980s and 1990s, leading to many exemplar models of concepts.[37] Despite its success, the exemplar paradigm of concepts has not entirely replaced the prototype paradigm. Proponents of these two paradigms have accumulated findings that were deemed to be easily explicable by their favored paradigm, but problematic for the alternative paradigm.

The exemplar paradigm of concepts is built around the idea that concepts are sets of exemplars. In turn, an exemplar is a body of knowledge about the properties believed to be possessed by a particular member of a class.[38] When we categorize, when we reason, and so on, we have by default in mind a set of exemplars (or, in some models, an exemplar drawn from a set of exemplars stored in long-term memory).[39] Medin and Schaffer have well captured the gist of the exemplar paradigm:

> The general idea of the context model [the name of their model] is that classification judgments are based on the retrieval of stored exemplar information.... This mechanism is, in a sense, a device for reasoning by analogy inasmuch as classification of new stimuli is based on stored information concerning old exemplars.... Although we shall propose that classifications derive from exemplar information, we do not assume that the storage and retrievability of this exemplar information is veridical. If subjects are using strategies and hypotheses during learning, the exemplar information may be incomplete and the salience of information from alternative dimensions may differ considerably.[40] (Medin and Schaffer 1978: 209–210)

Exemplar theories do not deny that we may have other forms of knowledge in long-term memory (e.g., Medin and Schaffer 1978: 211), but they propose that exemplars are used by default in the processes underlying the higher cognitive competences.

Specific exemplar theories of concepts develop differently the idea of a body of knowledge about an individual. Like prototype models, exemplar models can be featural (e.g., Medin and Schaffer 1978) or dimensional

---

[37] Nosofsky 1986, 1988, 1992; Estes 1986; Hintzman 1986; Kruschke 1992; Ashby and Maddox 1993; for a review, see Murphy 2002: ch. 4.

[38] Some psychologists assume that we store in long-term memory an exemplar for each *encounter* with an individual instead of an exemplar for each *individual*. To put it differently, whenever I meet Fido, I store a different exemplar (instead of having a unique exemplar for Fido). This seems to be Nosofsky's views (Nosofsky 1988). I overlook this complication in what follows.

[39] To some extent, Berkeley had anticipated this idea. In the paragraph 16 of the introduction of the revised version of *A Treatise concerning the Principles of Human Knowledge*, he writes ([1734] 1998): "though the idea I have in view whilst I make the demonstration, be, for instance, that of an isosceles rectangular triangle, whose sides are of a determinate length, I may nevertheless be certain it extends to all other rectilinear triangles, of what sort or bigness soever. And that, because neither the right angle, nor the equality, nor determinate length of the sides, are at all concerned in the demonstration."

[40] See also Nosofsky 1986: 39; Nosofsky, Palmeri, and McKinley 1994: 53; Palmeri and Gauthier 2004: 294.

(e.g., Nosofsky 1986). Like prototype theorists, exemplar theorists are also confronted with the selection problem. Given that individuals have an infinite number of properties, they need to explain why exemplars represent such and such properties, instead of others. Unfortunately, this problem, which has been noted time and again (e.g., Smith and Medin 1981), is typically dodged by exemplar theories of concepts.

The exemplar paradigm and the prototype paradigm make very different assumptions with regard to our memory. According to exemplar theorists, we form memories of many encountered category members, and we use by default these memories in the processes underlying the higher cognitive competences. On the contrary, according to prototype theorists, we store in long-term memory some knowledge about some parameters that characterize categories, and we use by default this knowledge in the processes underlying the higher cognitive competences.

4.3.2 An Example: The Context Model

I now describe a well-known exemplar model of concepts, Medin and Schaffer's (1978) Context Model. In Medin and Schaffer's model (1978: 210), each exemplar represents the object it refers to as having a color, a shape, a size, and a position. It is assumed that each of these four properties (also called "dimensions") consists of two possible values. For example, color can have the values *red* or *blue*. Since there are only two values per type of property, values are represented by 0 and 1. Some values may not be specified because people may have selectively attended to some properties of the encountered category members:

> The subject's representation of exemplar information may be something like this:
>
> $$111?\text{-}A(A_1) \qquad 10?0\text{-}A(A_2)$$
> $$00?1\text{-}B(B_1) \qquad 110?\text{-}B(B_2),$$
>
> where the question marks indicate that information that would differentiate value 1 and value 0 on that dimension either has not been stored or cannot be accessed. (Medin and Schaffer 1978: 210)

In the Context Model, exemplars could thus be represented by figure 4.5.

This example brings to the fore an important difference in the methodologies commonly used by prototype theorists, on the one hand, and by exemplar theorists, on the other. To characterize this difference properly, I need to explain first what artificial categories are. Although this distinction is not always explicit in the literature, there are two types of artificial category. First, a category is artificial if it is made of particulars that are abstract figures (figure 4.1). Second, a category is artificial if it cross-cuts the distinctions

Category A	
Object A$_1$	
Dimension 1	Value 1
Dimension 2	Value 1
Dimension 3	Value 1
Dimension 4	Unknown value

Category A	
Object A$_2$	
Dimension 1	Value 1
Dimension 2	Value 0
Dimension 3	Unknown Value
Dimension 4	Value 0

Figure 4.5 Two Exemplars in the Context Model

between categories spontaneously made by people. For instance, a category that would include camels, ostriches, crocodiles, mice, sharks, and eels would cross-cut the distinctions between categories that most of us make.[41] In contrast to these two types of artificial category, natural categories are made of real objects and intuitively make sense to people (Osherson 1978).

In their seminal work on prototypes, Rosch and Mervis (1975) used both artificial and natural categories. As seen previously, Hampton (1979) relied on the property listing task to determine the knowledge stored in concepts of natural categories. Thus, prototype theories have been regularly applied to concepts of natural categories as well as to concepts of

---

[41] However, these animals belong to the same category of unclean animals in the Leviticus (for discussion, see Murphy and Medin 1985).

artificial categories. By contrast, exemplar theorists have relied almost exclusively on experiments done with the first type of artificial category (figure 4.5). This is probably the result of their interest in detailed formal models of concept learning and of categorization because testing such models is easier with artificial categories. Artificial categories can be specifically designed to test competing formal theories of concept learning. Moreover, psychologists typically assume that different subjects form identical concepts of artificial categories. Because the categories are artificial, subjects' diverse background knowledge does not influence concept learning. Finally, psychologists assume that the exemplars formed by subjects can be inferred from the stimuli subjects are presented with. If subjects are successively presented with a red circle and a blue square, exemplar theorists typically assume that subjects have formed a first exemplar that represents one object as being a red circle and a second exemplar that represents the other object as being a blue square.

4.3.3 Exemplar-Based Models of Cognitive Processes

Exemplar-based models of cognitive processes have been used to explain the properties of several cognitive competences, including categorization, typicality estimation, identification—that is, the capacity to make judgments such as the judgment that this is John (Nosofsky 1986)—recognition, reasoning under uncertainty (Juslin and Persson 2002), and problem solving (Hammond 1989 on case-based reasoning). Psychological phenomena such as expertise (Brooks, Norman, and Allen 1991) and automaticity (Logan 1988; Palmeri 1997) have also been explained by means of exemplar-based models.

Exemplar-based models assume that cognitive processes involve the computation of the similarity between exemplars and other representations.[42] To use a toy example, when I categorize Fido as a dog, one or several exemplars of dogs are retrieved from long-term memory (together, maybe, with exemplars of other categories, such as some exemplars of cats); this exemplar (or these exemplars) is (are) matched with the representation of Fido; the similarity between these representations is computed; the judgment that Fido is a dog results from the high degree of similarity between the retrieved exemplar(s) of dog(s) and the representation of Fido. Figure 4.4 needs to be only slightly modified to capture these processes (figure 4.6).

Importantly, exemplar-based models of categorization assume that the same bodies of knowledge are involved in identification and in categorization (Nosofsky 1986). This contrasts with the prototype models of categorization, which assume that different kinds of bodies of knowledge are involved in the cognitive processes underlying these two competences.

---

[42] Medin and Schaffer 1978: 211–212; Nosofsky 1986.

Three Fundamental Kinds of Concept: Prototypes, Exemplars, Theories 97

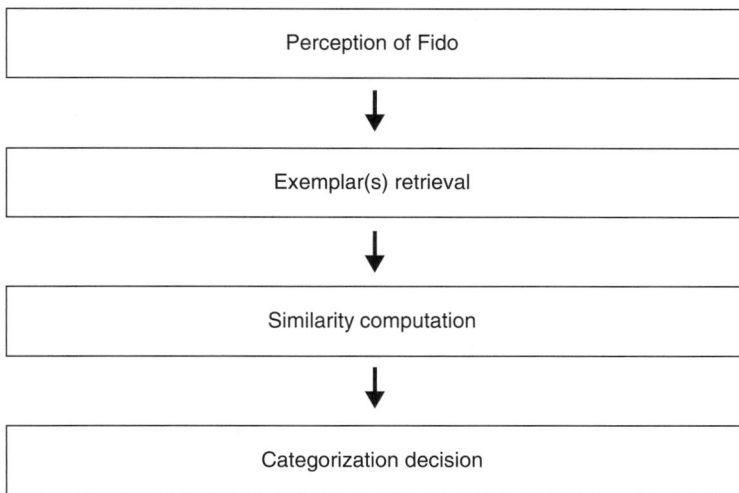

Figure 4.6 Successive Psychological Processes during Categorization

The second central property of exemplar-based models of cognitive processes is that the similarity measure is usually supposed to be non-linear. In non-linear measures, how much a property that is shared by the target and by an exemplar increases the similarity between the target and this exemplar depends on which other properties they share. Suppose that the pet of my neighbors, Fido, has a property (say, *barking*) that is represented by one of my exemplars of dogs (say, the representation of my own dog, Rover). How much the similarity between the representation of Fido and the exemplar of Rover is thereby increased depends on whether Fido and Rover share other properties, such as *chasing cats*. Thus, by contrast to linear measures, the degree of similarity in non-linear measures is supposed to be a function of the configuration of cues: properties are dependent cues for categorization.

Several non-linear measures can be found in the literature. Medin and Schaffer (1978: 212) have proposed a multiplicative function. Consider, for instance, a blue circle and a yellow square. Suppose that when an object is a square and another one is a circle, their degree of similarity is represented by a parameter c_1. Suppose also that when an object is blue and another one is yellow, their degree of similarity is represented by a parameter f_1. Then, the similarity between a blue circle and a yellow square according to Medin and Schaffer's multiplicative function is $f_1 c_1$, instead of $f_1 + c_1$ according to an additive measure (Medin and Schaffer 1978: 211–212). The similarity between a blue circle and a yellow circle could be $f_1 c_2$, with $c_2 > c_1$. Other measures, such as Nosofsky's exponential measure of similarity (1986; see section 4.3.4 below), are qualitatively similar. In fact, Medin and Schaffer's multiplicative rule is a special case of Nosofsky's exponential measure of similarity (Nosofsky 1986: 42).

Non-linear measures of similarity distinguish exemplar-based models of cognitive processes from prototype-based models of cognitive processes. In principle, as noted previously, prototype-based models could be associated with non-linear measures. Similarly, exemplar-based models could be associated with linear measures. However, linear measures and non-linear measures of similarity fit, respectively, the gist of prototype-based models and the gist of exemplar-based models of cognitive processes. Exemplar-based models were devised, among other things, to account for the effect of memories of particular objects on our cognitive competences, particularly, on the acquisition of concepts and on categorization (Medin and Schaffer 1978; see chapter 6 below). For instance, an object that is extremely similar to a specific known category member, but only moderately similar to others is more likely to be categorized as a category member than an object that is moderately similar to most known category members. Combining exemplar theories of concepts with non-linear measures of similarity allows exemplar theorists to explain this phenomenon:

> The multiplicative rule implies that a pattern will be classified more efficiently if it is highly similar to one pattern (differing in only one dimension) and has low similarity to a second (differing in three dimensions) than if it has medium similarity (differing in two dimensions to two patterns in its category). (Medin and Schaffer 1978: 212)

On the contrary, prototype-based models were devised, among other things, to account for the effect of the properties that are typical of category members on our higher cognitive competences, particularly, on categorization (Posner and Keele 1968; Rosch and Mervis 1975; see chapter 6 below). For instance, an object is more likely to be categorized as a category member if it possesses the properties that are typical of category members. Combining prototype-based models of concepts with linear measures of similarity allows prototype theorists to explain this phenomenon.

4.3.4 An Example: The Generalized Context Model

To conclude this review of the exemplar paradigm, I briefly describe the most celebrated exemplar-based model of a cognitive process, Nosofsky's (1986, 1992) Generalized Context Model of categorization. This model is an extension of Medin and Schaffer's (1978) Context Model. The Generalized Context Model consists of an exemplar model of concepts, a similarity measure, and a decision rule. According to this exemplar model, each exemplar represents its referent as a point in a multidimensional space. Each dimension represents a continuous property. Thus, an exemplar represents its referent as having specific values with respect to the dimensions that constitute the multidimensional space.

I now turn to the similarity measure. In the Generalized Context Model, each target is compared to all the exemplars that constitute a concept. For instance, a dog, Fido, may be compared to all the exemplars of dogs that constitute someone's concept of dog as well as to all the exemplars of wolves that constitute someone's concept of wolf. The similarity between Fido and an exemplar, for instance, an exemplar of a dog, is a function of the psychological distance between Fido and this exemplar. This psychological distance depends on the extent to which Fido and the exemplar match on each of the relevant dimensions for categorizing Fido: the more different Fido and the exemplar are on a given dimension, say, k, the further apart they are on this dimension. Formally, for a given dimension, the distance between the target Fido and the exemplar is:

$$|x_{tk} - x_{Ek}| \qquad (4)$$

where x_{tk} is the value of the target, Fido, on dimension k and x_{Ek} is the value of the exemplar on this dimension.

Each psychological dimension is weighted: the weight of dimension k, w_k, measures the attention paid to k. Greater values of this weight capture the idea that mismatch along dimension k increases more the dissimilarity between the exemplar of a dog and Fido, thus decreasing more the likelihood that Fido will be classified as a dog, than mismatch along other dimensions. This parameter is assumed by Nosofsky to be context-dependent. Dimension weights sum to one: this captures the idea that decreasing the attention to one dimension entails increasing the attention to other dimensions. The psychological distance between Fido and the exemplar of a dog depends on whether the relevant dimensions are analyzable (Shepard 1964; Ashby and Maddox 1990). Analyzable (or separable) dimensions can be attended independently of one another. Size and weight are analyzable dimensions of objects. We can attend to the size of an object, independently of its weight. By contrast, non-analyzable (or integral) dimensions cannot be attended independently of one another. For example, hue, brightness, and saturation are non-analyzable dimensions. When dimensions are non-analyzable, the psychological distance is computed with a Euclidean metric:

$$d_{tE} = \sqrt{\sum_{k=1}^{n} w_k (x_{tk} - x_{Ek})^2} \qquad (5)$$

When the dimensions are analyzable, the psychological distance is computed with a city-block metric:

$$d_{tE} = \sum_{k=1}^{n} w_k |x_{tk} - x_{Ek}| \qquad (6)$$

More generally, the distance between the target and the exemplar for n dimensions is calculated as follows:

$$d_{tE} = c \left(\sum_{k=1}^{n} w_k (x_{tk} - x_{Ek})^r \right)^{\frac{1}{r}} \qquad (7)$$

where r depends on whether the dimensions are analyzable, and c is a sensitivity parameter—it measures how much the overall psychological distance between a target and an exemplar affects their similarity.

The similarity between t and E is an exponential function of the psychological distance between the target and the exemplar:

$$S_{tE} = e^{-d_{tE}} \qquad (8)$$

Thus, the greater the psychological distance between the target, Fido, and the exemplar of dog, the smaller their similarity.

The overall similarity of the target, Fido, to the concept of dog, that is, to the set of exemplars of dogs, is the sum of its similarities to each exemplar of a dog. Formally,

$$S_{tC} = \sum_{E \in C} S_{tE} \qquad (9)$$

The decision rule is non-deterministic. If two concepts, say, DOG and WOLF, have been retrieved from long-term memory, the probability of classifying Fido as a dog is a function of the overall similarity of Fido to the concept of dog divided by the sum of the overall similarities to the concepts of dog and of wolf. Formally,

$$P(t \in A) = \frac{S_{tA}}{S_{tA} + S_{tB}} \qquad (10)$$

where A and B are the two relevant concepts.

Nosofsky's Generalized Context Model of categorization illustrates the core ideas of exemplar-based models of cognitive processes: the process of categorization involves matching the representations of targets with exemplars and computing, in a non-linear manner, their similarity.

4.4 The Theory Paradigm of Concepts

4.4.1 Causal, Nomological, and Functional Knowledge

The theory paradigm of concepts was developed independently in the 1980s by Murphy and Medin (1985) and by Carey (1985).[43] Like earlier work on prototypes and exemplars, Murphy and Medin's work belongs to the psychology of categorization and concept learning. By contrast, Carey is a developmental psychologist. The contribution of developmental psychologists to the development of the theory paradigm of concepts distinguishes it from the paradigms of concepts discussed earlier. The theory paradigm has become influential in both fields and is particularly prominent among developmental psychologists.[44]

---

[43] See also Keil 1989; Rips 1989; Gopnik and Meltzoff 1997; Ahn 1998; Keil and Wilson 2000; Murphy 2002: ch. 6; Rehder 2003a, b; Ahn and Luhman 2004; Sloman 2005; Gopnik and Schulz 2007.

[44] Gelman 1990, 2004; Spelke et al. 1992; Carey and Spelke 1994; Gopnik and Wellman 1994; Spelke 1994; Bloom 2000; Gopnik and Schulz 2004; Gopnik et al. 2004.

The core tenets of the theory paradigm are considerably vaguer than the core tenets of the prototype and exemplar paradigms despite a few groundbreaking theoretical articles (Murphy and Medin 1985; Gopnik and Wellman 1994; Gopnik et al. 2004). This may be due to the fact that this paradigm is used in several fields within psychology.

In the psychological literature, the theory paradigm is characterized in two different ways. Some psychologists propose that concepts are theories (e.g., Rips 1995; Rehder 2003a, b), while others propose that concepts are elements of theories (e.g., Gopnik and Meltzoff 1997). Some psychologists move from one idea to the other in the course of the same article (e.g., Murphy and Medin 1985: 298). I spell out these two ideas in turn (see also Prinz 2002: 81–82).

Let us consider first the idea that concepts are theories. This is often taken to mean that the knowledge that is stored in a concept is similar to the knowledge that constitutes a scientific theory. However, this, in itself, is not very informative. Because scientific theories are extremely diverse, it is unclear whether they all contain the same type of knowledge. Some scientific theories are mechanistic, focusing on the mechanisms that bring about phenomena (Machamer, Darden, and Craver 2000). Neurobiology is replete with theories of this type. Other scientific theories provide laws that connect variables with each other. Newtonian physics and thermodynamics are arguably of this kind.

Psychologists have circumvented this problem by focusing on the function of scientific theories. Scientific theories are assumed to explain phenomena, instead of merely describing them. Hence, theoretical knowledge is essentially used in explaining phenomena.[45] Intuitively, this type of knowledge enables us to tell why something happens. Applying this idea to the psychological notion of theory, we get the following: according to theory theorists, a concept of a category stores some knowledge that can explain the properties of the category members. Such concepts are called theories or, sometimes, mini-theories (Rips 1995; Prinz 2002).

What type of knowledge is used to explain? Psychologists assume that laws, causal propositions, functional propositions (for instance, the proposition that birds have wings to fly), and generic propositions (for instance, the proposition that dogs bark) explain why things happen. Thus, a theoretical concept is supposed to store some nomological, causal, functional, and/or generic knowledge about the members of its extension. For instance, a theoretical concept of dog stores some nomological, causal, functional, and/or generic knowledge about dogs.

Clearly, much hangs on the notion of explanation in this account of the notion of theory. Because, the distinction between explanation and description is familiar in the philosophy of science, it might seem that psychologists

---

[45] For instance, Murphy and Medin 1985; Keil 1989, 1991; Gopnik and Meltzoff 1997; Keil and Wilson 2000.

are entitled to use this distinction. Matters are not so straightforward, however. While theory theorists typically draw on an analogy with scientific theories to clarify the psychological notion of theory, when it comes to the notion of explanation, they pay little attention to the analysis of scientific explanation by philosophers of science. Moreover, the philosophical accounts of scientific explanation would probably be useless for spelling out the psychological notion of theory. First, the accounts of scientific explanation disagree on what type of knowledge is involved in scientific explanations (for an introduction, see Salmon 1989 and Woodward 2003b). For instance, in Hempel and Oppenheim's (1948) deductive/nomological model, but not in Salmon's (1971) causal/mechanical model, explanations rest on laws. As a result, appealing to the accounts of scientific explanation provided by philosophers of science may be of little use to explain what type of knowledge psychological theories consist of. Second, some accounts of scientific explanation would blur the distinction between theories and other theoretical entities in psychology, such as prototypes. Particularly, in Salmon's statistical relevance model, explanations are based on statistical relations between events. If this model of explanation is used to spell out the psychological notion of theory, then theories will be made of statistical knowledge, blurring, at least prima facie, the difference with prototypes.

Instead of drawing on the accounts of scientific explanation provided by philosophers, psychologists rely on a folk understanding of explanation. It thus seems that pace those psychologists who have strongly highlighted the analogy with scientific theories, including Carey and Gopnik, this analogy is not the backbone of the psychological notion of theory. Rather, what matters is the folk notion of explanation—the fact that some propositions tell us why things happen.

I turn to the second idea: concepts are parts of theories. Psychologists use different slogans to express this idea: concepts are "embedded in knowledge that embodies a theory about the world" (Murphy and Medin 1985: 298), "concepts are organized by theories" (ibid. 290), theories "structure" concepts (ibid. 301), "people's concepts are tied to their theories about the world" (ibid.), and so on.

Focusing on Carey's theory of concepts (1985, 1988), Margolis (1995) has proposed that these slogans express a commitment to a specific semantic theory: the semantic properties of a concept depend on its functional role in a theory. Although this is probably a dimension of the analogy with scientific theories for some psychologists, this is neither the only one nor, probably, the most important one (section 2.2).

More important for many theory theorists, such as Murphy and Medin (1985), Gelman (1990), and Gopnik (Gopnik and Wellman 1994), is the idea that concepts are organized by domains. Despite its common use in psychology and in the philosophy of psychology, the notion of domain remains vague.[46] As

---

[46] See, particularly, Hirschfeld and Gelman 1994; Boyer and Barrett 2005.

a first approximation, domains are sets of entities, including categories, properties, and processes, that are treated similarly by the mind. That is, we reason in a similar way about the categories, processes, and properties that constitute a domain; we have similar expectations; we draw similar inductions. For instance, non-human animal species constitute a domain if, with the exception of humans, animal species are treated similarly by the mind. They form the folk biological domain (Carey 1985; Medin and Atran 1999).

Theory theorists propose that the concepts of categories, properties, and processes that belong to a given domain (e.g., the folk biological domain or the folk psychological domain) store a similar type of knowledge. For example, some psychologists have proposed that the intention of the artifact maker is central to artifact concepts such as TABLE, CHAIR, and SCREWDRIVER (Bloom 1996).[47] If this is correct, all artifact concepts store the same kind of knowledge. By contrast, concepts of animal species do not store this kind of knowledge. Rather, many psychologists propose that concepts of animals include a belief in an unknown essence within the animals that is causally responsible for the development of species-specific properties (e.g., Gelman and Wellman 1991).

Similarities between concepts within a single domain are typically explained as follows (e.g., Murphy and Medin 1985). We possess some general knowledge about a domain. For instance, folk biology is the knowledge about animals and plants in general together with the knowledge about biological events, such as birth and death. The general knowledge about a domain influences the knowledge that is stored in a concept of an element of this domain. This may be because it determines what we pay attention to when we acquire the concepts relevant to this domain. I call this knowledge about a domain a "framework theory."

To summarize, the theory paradigm is based on two core ideas. Concepts are bodies of knowledge that underlie explanations, where the notion of explanation is explained by means of folk examples of explanation. Second, concepts are organized by domains, that is, concepts form classes such that within a given class, concepts store a similar type of knowledge. Theory theorists typically assume that mini-theories and framework theories are related as follows. Framework theories influence which causal, functional, and nomological knowledge is stored in the mini-theories.

Although the notions of mini-theory and framework theory have not been neatly distinguished, they are in fact independent. Pace Murphy and Medin (1985: 290), a prototype or an exemplar theorist could in fact endorse the notions of domain and framework theory.[48] A prototype theorist could argue that the prototypes of non-human animals (instead

---

[47] For discussion, see, e.g., Malt and Johnson 1992; Gelman and Bloom 2000; Sloman and Malt 2003; Malt and Sloman 2007.

[48] Hampton 1993: 86–88. Heit (1997, 2001) has proposed a similar idea under the name "the weighting account of background knowledge."

of the mini-theories) store the same kind of knowledge because folk biology determines which knowledge prototype learners typically acquire.

Like the prototype and exemplar paradigms, the theory paradigm can be developed in various ways. Gopnik has pushed the analogy between psychological theories and scientific theories as far as possible, arguing that people's concepts, including infants' and children's, possess some of the essential properties of scientific theories.[49] Gopnik and colleagues focus on three properties of scientific theories. Scientific theories introduce theoretical entities that are related in a systematic set of laws; they are used to predict and to explain; and they change in response to evidence. Gopnik and colleagues propose that these three properties characterize what I have called our framework theories:

> We want to claim that infants and young children have cognitive structures like those we have just been describing.... Children's theories should involve appeal to abstract theoretical entities, with coherent causal relations among them. Their theories should lead to characteristic patterns of predictions.... Finally, their theories should invoke characteristic explanations phrased in terms of these abstract entities and laws.... We will also propose that the dynamic features we have described should be apparent in children's transitions from one theory to a later one. (Gopnik and Meltzoff 1997: 41–42)

By contrast, other psychologists, such as Murphy and Medin (1985; see also Keil 2003), have emphasized the differences between concepts and scientific theories:

> We use *theory* to mean any of a host of mental 'explanations,' rather than a complete, organized, scientific account. For example, causal knowledge certainly embodies a theory of certain phenomena; scripts may contain an implicit theory of the entailment relations between mundane events; knowledge of rules embodies a theory of the relations between rule constituents; and book-learned, scientific knowledge certainly contains theories. Although it may seem to be glorifying some of these cases to call them theories, the term denotes a complex set of relations between concepts, usually with a causal basis. Furthermore, these examples are similar to theories used in scientific explanation. (Murphy and Medin 1985: 290)

4.4.2 Example

Theory theorists have rarely developed models of the knowledge stored in concepts. Instead, they have attempted to determine what theoretical knowledge is stored in specific concepts at specific ages, with a special focus on infants' and children's concepts. Frank Keil's work on children's concepts of disease and contamination is a good example of this approach (Keil et al. 1999). Keil and colleagues have attempted to determine

---

[49] Gopnik and Wellman 1994; Gopnik and Meltzoff 1997: ch. 2; Gopnik and Schulz 2004; for a criticism, see Faucher et al. 2002.

whether young children possess some causal or mechanistic knowledge about diseases. They propose that children have some abstract knowledge of what kind of mechanism causes people to fall sick, without having any knowledge about specific mechanisms. Their abstract knowledge guides the protracted acquisition of their knowledge about specific mechanisms.

Recently, however, several psychologists have converged in proposing similar frameworks for describing the knowledge that is stored in theoretical concepts.[50] Particularly, Gopnik and colleagues have proposed that causal Bayes nets represent accurately the causal knowledge possessed by both children and adults:

> [The authors] propose that children use specialized cognitive systems that allow them to recover an accurate 'causal map' of the world: an abstract, coherent, learned representation of the causal relations among events. This kind of knowledge can be perspicuously understood in terms of the formalism of directed graphical causal models or Bayes nets. Children's causal learning and inference may involve computations similar to those for learning causal Bayes nets and for predicting with them. (Gopnik et al. 2004: 3)

In substance, a causal Bayes net represents the causal relations among a set of variables (e.g., Spirtes et al. 2001; Glymour 2001; Woodward 2003a). The variable v is causally related to the variable w ($v \rightarrow w$) in the sense that, once the values for all the variables other than w have been fixed (thereby fixing the probability distribution of w), there is a modification of the value of v (an "intervention") that modifies the probability distribution of w. Bayes nets are associated with algorithms that determine the effects of interventions and with learning algorithms that can infer causal relations from correlations.

Thus, the proposal under consideration is that children's and adults' causal knowledge can be described as causal Bayes nets and that some types of causal reasoning can be described by means of the algorithms associated with causal Bayes nets (Gopnik et al. 2004). Consider a toy example. Because John goes to parties, he smokes; because he smokes, his clothes stink; because his clothes stink, his dry cleaning bills increase. These four events constitute a simple Bayes net (figure 4.7).

In substance, according to Gopnik and colleagues' proposal, this toy causal Bayes net could be John's mini-theory of party or, at least, part thereof. That is, John could think of parties as those events that are causally linked to other events. The causal inferences that would involve his concept of party could be characterized by means of the inferences that are allowed by the toy causal Bayes net represented in figure 4.7.

---

[50] Rehder 2003a, b; Gopnik and Schultz 2004, 2007; Gopnik et al. 2004; Griffiths and Tenenbaum 2007; Griffiths, Steyvers, and Tenenbaum 2007; Tenenbaum, Griffiths, and Niyogi 2007.

Parties ⟶ Smoking ⟶ Stinky clothes ⟶ Dry cleaning bills

Figure 4.7 A Toy Causal Bayes Net

4.4.3 Theory-Based Models of Cognitive Processes

Compared with prototype theorists and, *a fortiori*, with exemplar theorists, theory theorists have had little to say about the cognitive processes that use theories. For a long time, their main contribution was mostly negative. The main effort of theory theorists was to find evidence against prototype and exemplar theorists' claim that cognitive processes involve a similarity computation.[51]

Their positive contribution to understanding the nature of theory-based cognitive processes has been more elusive. Theory theorists have repeatedly proposed that cognitive processes are similar to the reasoning processes that are used in science. They have often compared our reasoning processes to explanations (Keil and Wilson 2000) or to inferences to the best explanation (Murphy and Medin 1985). Murphy and Medin (1985: 295) provided the following toy example. If at a party, a guest jumps in the swimming pool with her clothes on, we may conclude that she is drunk. This categorization judgment does not result from matching the concept of drunken people with a representation of this guest. On the contrary, we infer that the most plausible explanation of the behavior of this guest is that she is drunk.

The causal Bayes net framework described above has allowed theory theorists to develop some models of our cognitive processes. Particularly, Gopnik and colleagues (2004) have suggested that the algorithms associated with causal Bayes nets, either for learning causal relations from correlations or for predicting the effects of interventions, might be to some extent similar to the thought processes involved in causal learning and in prediction. They contrast these algorithms to various learning procedures that merely learn the correlations between events or variables (for a brief review of Gopnik and colleagues' experiments, see section 6.4).

4.4.4 Example

To illustrate this recent work on the theory-based models of cognitive processes, I describe in some detail Bob Rehder's (2003a) model of categorization, which assumes that categorization is based on causal knowledge (for consistent evidence, see section 6.4):

> People's causal models of categories influence their classification behavior by leading them to expect certain distributions of features in category members. Specifically, a to-be-classified object is considered a category member to the extent that its features were likely to have been *generated* by the category's causal laws, such that combinations of features that are likely to be produced

---

[51] Gelman and Markman 1986, 1987; Rips 1989; see chapters 6 and 7 below.

by a category's causal mechanisms are viewed as good category members and those unlikely to be produced by those mechanisms are viewed as poor category members. (Rehder 2003a: 712)

Rehder's model of categorization is, in substance, the following. Suppose that two properties, C and E, characterize the members of a category, A. Suppose also that C and E are causally related: the presence of C causes the presence of E. Rehder proposes that our concept of A stores three pieces of knowledge about the relation between C and E. These three pieces of knowledge are represented by three parameters in his model, m, b, and c (Rehder 2003a: 724). Parameter m measures the probability that the causal mechanism that links C and E works. Parameter e measures the probability that E is present, when C is not present. Parameter c measures the probability that C is present. These three parameters determine the probability of various combinations of C and E (table 4.1).

Suppose now that two categories, A and B, are characterized by the same properties, P, Q, R, and S. The causal relations between these properties are different for each category. For instance, P could be the common cause of Q, R, and S for category A, while S could be the common effect of P, Q, and R for category B. Because these causal relations are different, the likelihood that a given combination of properties, say, P~Q~R~S,[52] is produced by the pattern of causal relations for A is different from the likelihood that P~Q~R~S is produced by the pattern of causal relations for B. Suppose that you have to categorize a target T, characterized by a given combination of properties, say, P~Q~R~S, either as an A or as a B. Rehder proposes the following non-deterministic decision rule for the categorization decision (2003a: 728):

$$P(T \in A) = \frac{L_A(T)}{L_A(T) + L_B(T)} \tag{11}$$

Table 4.1 Probability That Different Configurations of Properties Have Been Generated by the Causal Relation between C and E (inspired by Rehder 2003a: 724)

Neither C nor E (~C~E)	(1-c)(1-e)
Not C, but E (~CE)	(1-c)e
C, but not E (C~E)	c(1-m)(1-e)
C and E (CE)	c(m + e − mb)

[52] That is, P is instantiated, while Q, R, and S are not.

where $P(T \in A)$ is the probability of deciding that T belongs to A and $L_A(T)$ is the likelihood that the combination of properties that characterize T has been generated by the pattern of causal relations that characterizes A.

The contrast between this model and the models of categorization based on prototypes and on exemplars is striking. Rehder's model does not involve computing the similarity between a representation and a target. Instead, we are supposed to know how likely it is that a given configuration of properties has been generated by the causal networks that characterize the candidate categories. This knowledge determines the categorization decision: if based on my causal knowledge, I expect a configuration to be rare among the members of a category A, but common among the members of category B, then I am likely to categorize a target characterized by this configuration as a B.

4.5 Alternative Views of Concepts

I now turn to two other views of concepts. The first one can be characterized as a resurgence of the empiricist approach to concepts in the context of experimental psychology and neuropsychology. It has been most convincingly developed by Barsalou (Barsalou 1999, 2008; Barsalou et al. 2003, 2005; see the discussion in Machery 2006b, 2007a) and by Prinz (2002).[53] It has almost gained the status of a paradigm: it has been elaborated in different theories that share a few core tenets (e.g., Damasio 1994; Glenberg 1997; Barsalou 1999; Prinz 2002), and it underlies a striving experimental research program. The second view, considered more briefly, proposes that concepts are ideals—representations of the perfect instances of a class. This view was proposed by Barsalou in the 1980s (1983, 1985). Despite a few interesting applications, this view has not become a major approach in the psychology of concepts.

4.5.1 Core Tenets of Neo-Empiricism

There are many substantial differences between neo-empiricist theories. However, one can single out two central theses that are endorsed by most neo-empiricists. To spell out these two central theses, I rely mostly on Barsalou's sophisticated theory of concepts, "the perceptual symbol hypothesis," developed in his 1999 target article in *Behavioral and Brain Sciences*, and on Prinz's proxytype theory (2002).[54] These theses are the following:

---

[53] See also Damasio 1989, 1994; Mandler 1992; Stein 1995; Glenberg 1997; Lakoff and Johnson 1999; Martin and Chao 2001; Zwaan, Stanfield, and Yaxley 2002; Thompson-Schill 2003; Poirier and Hardy-Vallée 2005; Kiefer et al. 2007.

[54] For the record, Barsalou (personal communication) is reluctant to accept the label "empiricist" because of the anti-nativism of traditional empiricists like Locke and Hume.

1. The knowledge that is stored in a concept is encoded in several perceptual representational formats.
2. Conceptual processing involves reenacting some perceptual states and manipulating these perceptual states.

Thesis 1 is about the vehicles of concepts (Prinz 2002: 109). In agreement with most psychologists and neuropsychologists of perception, neo-empiricists assume that each perceptual system, as well as our motor and emotional systems, relies on a specific representational format. Thesis 1 claims that our conceptual knowledge is encoded in these perceptual, motor, and emotional representational formats. By contrast, amodal theorists contend that our conceptual knowledge is encoded in a representational format that is distinct from our perceptual representational formats (Barsalou et al. 2003: 85). This distinct representational format is usually thought of as being language-like. To take a simple example, according to neo-empiricists, Marie's conceptual knowledge about apples consists of the visual, olfactive, tactile, somatosensory, and gustative representations of apples that are stored in her long-term memory. These representations are a subset of the perceptual representations of apples Marie has entertained in her life (Barsalou 1999: 577–578; Barsalou et al. 2003: 85–86). According to amodal theorists, Marie's concept of apple stores some perceptual (visual, tactile, gustatory, etc.) as well as some non-perceptual information about apples in a single, distinct representational format. These ideas are well put by Barsalou:

> Once a perceptual state arises, a subset of it is extracted via selective attention and stored permanently in long-term memory. On later retrievals, this perceptual memory can function symbolically, standing for referents in the world, and entering into symbol manipulation. As collections of perceptual symbols develop, they constitute the representations that underlie cognition. (Barsalou 1999: 577–578)

Similarly, Prinz proposes, "Concepts are couched in representational codes that are specific to our perceptual systems" (2002: 119).

Thesis 1 is inspired by a central tenet of classical empiricism. Hume claimed that ideas are qualitatively similar to percepts, although they typically differ from percepts by their intensity ([1748] 1975: section 2; see also Berkeley [1734] 1998: Introduction). Like Hume ([1748] 1975: 19), neo-empiricists such as Prinz (2002: 120 et seq.) and Barsalou (1999) characterize the senses broadly: the senses include proprioception, the emotions, and the motor systems. Prinz goes a bit further, characterizing words in inner speech as perceptual representations (2002: 150).

Despite its apparent clarity, the notion of perceptual representation needs further explanation. Contrary to traditional empiricists, neo-empiricists cannot rely on introspection to illustrate this notion, for they propose that we should not think of perceptual representations on the model of our conscious perceptual experiences (Barsalou 1999: 582). Furthermore, neo-empiricists do not endorse the pictorialism of traditional empiricists. Berkeley and Hume thought about perceptual representations, particularly about visual representations, by analogy with pictures (e.g., Hume [1748] 1975: 151). On the contrary, for most empiricists, pictures are an inappropriate model for thinking about perceptual states (Barsalou 1999: 582; Prinz 2002: ch. 6).

There are two remaining strategies to explain the notion of perceptual representation. The first strategy has been endorsed by Barsalou. He proposes that amodal representations are linguistic, while modal representations are analogical (Barsalou 1999: 578). This strategy is not without problems. Analogical representations are usually thought to be such that some properties of their vehicles covary with what is represented. Maps and mercury thermometers are good examples. Evidence shows that there are some analogical representations in the brain—retinocentric maps, for instance. However, there is no evidence that analogical representations, so understood, are pervasive in the brain. Moreover, there is evidence that some representations are analogical and do not belong to any perceptual system (Machery 2006b). Thus, it seems inadequate to contrast amodal and perceptual representations by means of the notion of analogical representation.

As an alternative, Prinz has proposed that perceptual representations are whatever psychologists of perception say perception involves (2002: 113 et seq.). This proposal is not without problems either. If psychologists of perception propose that perceptual representations are similar to traditional amodal symbols, for instance, if perceptual representations form linguistic representational systems (Pylyshyn 2003), neo-empiricism would propose that our conceptual knowledge is stored in several linguistic systems. In this case, the distinction between neo-empiricism and the amodal approach would be rather thin.

I turn to Thesis 2. It concerns the nature of the cognitive processes underlying categorization, induction, deduction, analogy-making, planning, or linguistic comprehension. The central insight is the following (Stein 1995; Barsalou 1999: 586; Prinz 2002: 148): these cognitive processes involve tokening and manipulating perceptual representations. Retrieving a concept from long-term memory during reasoning or categorization consists of tokening some perceptual representations. For example, retrieving the concept of dog consists of tokening some visual, auditory, etc., representations of dogs. This process is called "simulation" or "reenactment."[55] Thus, Prinz writes, "Tokening a proxytype is generally tantamount to entering a perceptual state of the kind one would be in if one were to experience the thing it represents" (2002: 150; see also

---

[55] Reenacted percepts and the products of perceptual imagery, for instance visual images, are assumed to be the same kind of representation (Barsalou et al. 2003: 85).

Barsalou 1999: 578; Barsalou et al. 2003: 85).[56] Neo-empiricists also propose that reenacted percepts are typically not identical to past actual percepts (e.g., Barsalou 1999: 584). For instance, following Hume ([1748] 1975: 19), they contend that we combine reenacted percepts to create new perceptual representations (Barsalou 2003).

Cognitive processes consist in the manipulation of these reenacted percepts (e.g., Barsalou 1999: 578). This idea is well illustrated by Barsalou's description of the process of verifying whether some object has a given part, for example, whether lions have a mane. We produce a visual representation of a lion and another of a mane, and we match these two representations. If both representations match, we decide that lions have a mane (Solomon and Barsalou 2001: 135–136). Thesis 2 can be seen as a modern development of Berkeley's insight that reasoning consists in manipulating mental states that are similar to percepts (Berkeley [1734] 1998: Introduction).

Noticeably, most neo-empiricists often deny endorsing Hume's associationism (Hume [1748] 1975: section 3). Neo-empiricists are usually committed to computational theories of cognitive processes. Nonetheless, association by contiguity plays a significant role in some neo-empiricist accounts. For instance, Barsalou contends that we store together and we retrieve simultaneously percepts that are experienced simultaneously or successively (e.g., Barsalou et al. 2003: 85). I retrieve simultaneously the auditory percept of Fido's barking and the visual percept of Fido's running because I have often experienced these two percepts together.

Finally, besides rejecting pictorialism and associationism, neo-empiricists differ from traditional empiricists in an important regard. Neo-empiricists are not necessarily committed to anti-nativism (Barsalou 1999; Prinz 2002: ch. 8). Because perceptual representations, such as the perceptual representations of snake-like stimuli (Mineka et al. 1984), can be innate, neo-empiricists can endorse some degree of representational nativism.

4.5.2 Main Problems of Neo-Empiricism

Contrary to its philosophical antecedents, neo-empiricism is not a mere theory of concepts and higher cognition. It also inspires a thriving experimental research program.[57] Barsalou has even claimed that while there is little empirical evidence for amodal theories of concepts, there is a growing body of evidence for neo-empiricism. Hence, if theoretical arguments do not weigh disproportionately in favor of amodal theories of concepts—and Barsalou believes they do not—we should prefer empiricist theories of concepts to their competitors:

---

[56] Roughly, Prinz uses the word "proxytype" to refer to context-sensitive, reenacted perceptual representations.

[57] Introspective psychologists at the beginning of the twentieth century tried also to gather evidence for empiricism (e.g., Fisher 1916).

Amodal theories have been attractive theoretically because they implement important conceptual functions, such as the type-token distinction, categorical inference, productivity and propositions.... Conversely, indirect empirical evidence has accumulated for modality-specific representations in working memory, long-term memory, language and thought. (Barsalou et al. 2003: 85–86)

In spite of Barsalou's and others' important and puzzling findings, I have argued elsewhere that we should be cautious in taking the neo-empiricist findings at face value (Machery 2006b, 2007a). There are two main problems. First, many findings are only inconsistent with specific amodal models of the cognitive processes assumed to be involved in the experimental tasks, while being accommodated by other amodal models of these same cognitive processes. Hence, these findings are not evidence for the neo-empiricist approach to concepts. Rather, they are evidence against some specific amodal models. I have called this problem "Anderson's problem," since in his famous discussion of the mental imagery debate (Anderson 1978), psychologist John Anderson emphasized that experimental findings bear only on specific propositional and specific imagistic models (Machery 2007a).

Consider, for instance, one of Barsalou's experiments. As we saw above, property listing is an important tool in the psychology of concepts. Subjects are presented with a word, for instance, "dog," and are asked to list the properties that are typically true of the denoted objects. Psychologists of concepts assume that in this task, subjects retrieve their concepts from their long-term memory and use the knowledge stored in the concept to solve the task. Because they believe that retrieving a concept consists in reenacting a percept, Barsalou and his former graduate student, psychologist Ling-Ling Wu, propose that property listing involves entertaining some perceptual representations (Wu 1995; Barsalou, Solomon, and Wu 1999; Prinz 2002: 27).

I focus on Barsalou and Wu's first experiment, called "instructional equivalence" (Barsalou, Solomon, and Wu 1999). Barsalou and Wu want to show that explicitly asking subjects to adopt a perceptual strategy when they complete the property listing task, namely, asking subjects to form an image and to describe it, does not affect their performances. This would be evidence that subjects spontaneously use this perceptual strategy, consistent with Thesis 2. Wu and Barsalou compare two conditions. In the neutral condition, subjects are asked to list the properties of the denoted objects, period. In the imagery condition, they are asked to construct an image of the objects denoted by the concept and to describe this image. Listed properties are organized into 34 different types, for instance, internal components, external perceived properties, locations, and so forth (for more detail, see Wu 1995; Barsalou, Solomon, and Wu 1999). The dependent measure is the average number of properties per type, across subjects and concepts. The correlation between each condition is calculated. The high correlation between the two conditions is taken to confirm Wu and Barsalou's prediction (table 4.2).[58]

---

[58] This high correlation means that for each feature type, the same number of features is listed in both conditions, not that the same features are listed.

Table 4.2 Correlation between Neutral and Imagery
Conditions for Nouns and Noun Phrases across
Feature Frequencies (adapted from
Barsalou, Solomon, and Wu 1999)

	Nouns	Noun Phrases
Features	0.89	0.96

Barsalou and colleagues claim (1) that this result is predicted by their neo-empiricist theory, but (2) not by any amodal theory of concepts and conceptual processing. But are those two claims true? I now show that (1) might not be true and that (2) is false. First, let us consider (1). Barsalou and Wu's result is predicted by neo-empiricist theories of concepts only if it is assumed that a conscious, intentional perceptual strategy, "Construct a visual image and describe it," and the hypothesized unconscious manipulation of perceptual representations are identical. Although this assumption is not absurd, neither is it obviously true. Indeed, for many cognitive functions, conscious, intentional processing—that is, the intentional application of a pre-defined strategy in order to solve a task—is known to differ from non-conscious, automatic processing (e.g., Sloman 1998 on deductive reasoning; Stanovich and West 2003 on probabilistic reasoning). For sure, these results are based on a specific type of intentional strategy—applying a formal rule. The intentional strategy assigned to subjects in the imagery condition does not consist in applying a formal rule. However, it remains that instructional equivalence does not fall out directly from neo-empiricism.[59]

What about (2)? A standard amodal theory of perceptual imagery—Fodor's (1975) theory—accommodates this result. It is very natural for proponents of amodal views of concepts to assume that perceptual images are associated with concepts (Fodor 1975: 177). The reason is that in the absence of concepts, images do not have any specific reference. An image of Fido can refer to Fido, to dogs, or even to danger if the visualizer is afraid of dogs. Suppose now, for the sake of argument, that concepts are amodal and that Fodor's theory of imagery is true. In the neutral condition, subjects hear the word "dog," retrieve the concept of dog from their long-term memory, and use this concept to list the properties of dogs. In the imagery condition, subjects hear the word "dog," construct an image of a dog, retrieve the concept of dog from their long-term memory, and use the image together with the concept to list the properties of dogs. Then, in both conditions,

---

[59] Indeed, in another task, called "property verification," subjects did not perform identically in the neutral condition and in the imagery condition (Solomon and Barsalou 2004: 245, 251).

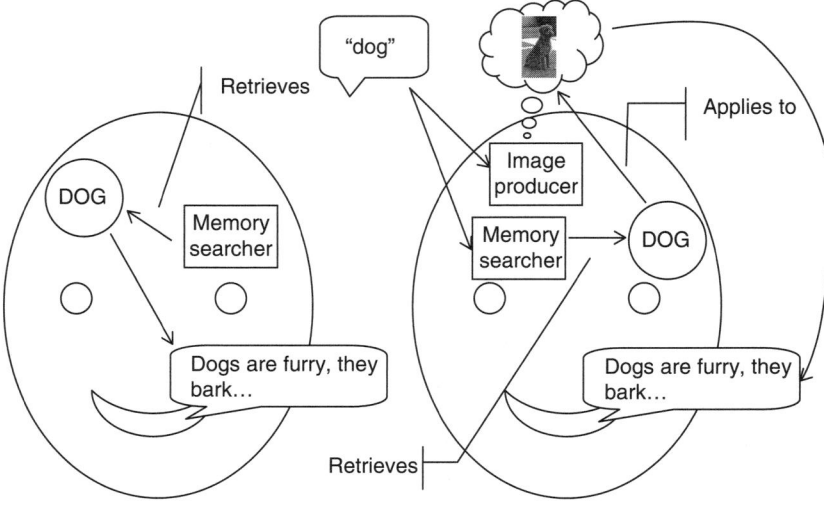

Figure 4.8 Amodal Description of Subjects' Performances in the Neutral and Imagery Conditions

when we are asked to describe a dog, the same amodal concept of dog is retrieved from long-term memory and used to solve the task (figure 4.8).

As a result, Fodor's theory predicts that subjects should behave similarly, though not identically, in the two conditions. Which is indeed what Wu and Barsalou found. Thus, a standard amodal theory of concepts and visual imagery—namely, Fodor's theory—naturally accommodates Wu and Barsalou's results. Upshot: Wu and Barsalou's findings are not evidence for neo-empiricism. Instead, they are evidence against those amodal theories of perceptual imagery that postulate that entirely different types of knowledge are used when we rely on imagery and when we do not.

Anderson's problem affects other findings assumed to be evidence for neo-empiricism (Machery 2007a). Of course, this does not diminish the interest of Wu and Barsalou's and others' results. At the very least, they are consistent with neo-empiricist predictions, and they falsify some amodal predictions. But they do not constitute evidence for neo-empiricism over the amodal approach in general. Since standard amodal models of the cognitive processes involved in Wu and Barsalou's as well as in others' tasks make the same predictions as neo-empiricism, it remains unclear whether people use perceptual representations in these tasks.

The second problem is the following. Typically, neo-empiricists fail to acknowledge that amodal theorists recognize the importance of perceptual imagery (Barsalou 1999; Barsalou et al. 2003). In fact, most proponents of amodal theories acknowledge that perceptual imagery, particularly visual imagery, is often used to solve tasks that tap into higher cognition (e.g., Fodor 1975: 174–194). For instance, Fodor writes, "Of course, nothing

I have said denies that images exist or that images play an important role in many cognitive processes. Indeed, such empirical evidence as is available tends to support both claims" (1975: 184). Simon goes further, asserting that imagery is a necessary component of human cognition (1995: 32–33). What proponents of amodal theorists usually insist on is that not all tasks are solved through imagery. In some situations, we retrieve from long-term memory and we manipulate some knowledge that is stored in a specific, non-modal representational format.

This has an important methodological consequence. If amodal theorists expect people to rely on imagery to solve a given task that is assumed to tap into higher cognition, evidence that perceptual simulation is used to solve this task does not support neo-empiricism over amodal theories. To illustrate this claim, we know introspectively that when we are asked to count the number of windows in our house or in our apartment, we visualize successively each room. In other words, visual imagery is used to solve this task. However, this is not evidence against an amodal approach to concepts and higher cognition because amodal theorists expect people to rely on perceptual imagery in this task. I have called this problem "the problem from imagery" (Machery 2007a).

The problem from imagery affects several neo-empiricist experiments. Consider Solomon and Barsalou (2004). In the research on mental imagery, evidence shows that some perceptual variables—that is, variables that affect perception—affect subjects' performances in some tasks. For instance, when people are asked to determine whether two drawings of three-dimensional objects represent the same object viewed from two different angles, the time needed to complete the task is a linear function of the angular difference (Shepard and Metzler 1971). Solomon and Barsalou claim that retrieving a concept consists in reenacting a perceptual representation of its referent and that deciding that an object has a property consists in matching two perceptual representations. As a result, following the research on visual imagery, they predict that some perceptual variables will affect subjects' performances in a property verification task (also called "feature verification task"; for more detail, see Solomon and Barsalou 2004). In such a task, subjects are asked to decide whether a property is typically possessed by the members of some category. This task has been extensively used in the psychology of concepts. In Solomon and Barsalou's version, subjects were asked to decide whether parts, say, sleeves, typically belong to the members of some category, say, blouses. The question of interest is what are the factors that cause some decisions to be made more quickly than others. Solomon and Barsalou's results are striking:

> P_area [the ratio between the volume of a part and the whole object] was primarily responsible for the importance of perceptual predictors. As properties became larger they took longer to verify. One interpretation of this effect is that subjects must simulate a property before they can search for it in an image, with large properties taking longer to simulate than small ones. (Solomon and Barsalou 2004: 252)

Solomon and Barsalou cogently argue that modulo some plausible auxiliary assumptions, this result is predicted by the neo-empiricist view of property verification. Moreover, they correctly claim that it is not predicted by amodal theories of concepts and conceptual processing. Thus, this result does suggest that to solve at least some property verification tasks, people rely on perceptual simulation: people imagine seeing the object, say, the blouse, and find out whether the object has the relevant part, say, sleeves (see also the convergent neuropsychological evidence in Kan et al. 2003).

Remember, however, the issue singled out earlier—the problem from imagery. Most proponents of amodal theories of concepts and higher cognition recognize that people rely on perceptual simulation to solve some tasks that tap into higher cognition. If amodal theorists expect people to rely on imagery to solve a given task, evidence that people use imagery in this task does not constitute evidence for neo-empiricism. Now, the present task is arguably such a task. Indeed, to decide whether something is a part of something else, a reliable strategy is to visualize it. Relying on imagery is a reliable strategy to solve the part–whole property verification task because, in visual imagery, we access some knowledge about the physical structure of the object. This is even the best strategy when the part–whole relation (say, wheels–car) is not part of the concept of the whole (say, of car). If amodal theorists do expect subjects to rely on imagery in the part–whole property verification task, this task is not ideally suited for distinguishing neo-empiricism and amodal theories of concepts.

Thus, Solomon and Barsalou provide convincing behavioral and neuropsychological evidence that visual imagery is involved in a task consisting in deciding whether a part belongs to the objects of a given type. What is unclear, however, is whether their findings provide evidence for neo-empiricism over amodal theories of concepts and higher cognition.

Let us take stock. Anderson's problem and the problem from imagery loom large in the experimental literature for neo-empiricism. Obviously, they do not diminish its interest. But, in my opinion, they show that there is no strong evidence that concepts (or some concepts) are in fact similar to perceptual representations. For this reason, in the remainder of this book, I will have little to say about the neo-empiricist approach to concepts. Nonetheless, if strong evidence for neo-empiricism were to accumulate, it would be worth considering the possibility that perceptual representations make for one of the fundamental kinds of concept.

4.5.3 Ideals

Ideals were introduced by Barsalou in contrast to prototypes (Barsalou 1983, 1985).[60] A prototype of x is a body of statistical knowledge about

---

[60] Prototypes and ideals are sometimes identified (e.g., Chaplin, John, and Goldberg 1988; Prinz 2002). Since the knowledge stored in ideals is not statistical, this identification is unjustified.

the properties possessed by the *x*'s. By contrast, an ideal of *x* is a body of knowledge about the properties that the *x*'s should possess. For instance, if the concept of table is an ideal, TABLE does not store any knowledge about the typical properties of tables, nor about the cue-valid properties of tables, but about the properties that tables should possess.

There has been little work on models of ideals or on ideal-based models of cognitive processes. Instead, the ideal approach has inspired some experimental work on specific concepts or on specific kinds of concept. Of particular interest are the so-called representations of ad hoc categories (Barsalou 1983, 1985). As we saw in section 1.4, these bodies of knowledge are not permanently stored in long-term memory and represent categories that are related to goals, such as the category of things to take out of home during a fire.[61] Representations of ad hoc categories seem to be ideals. Indeed, the typicality of the members of an ad hoc category is not based on whether they possess the properties that are common among members of this category. Instead, it is determined by the extent to which they possess the properties that members of this ad hoc category should possess. For instance, the typicality of a thing to take on a camping trip is a function of whether it possesses the properties that things to take on camping should have, not a function of the properties that they typically have.

Ideals are not limited to representations of ad hoc categories. They also include goal-derived concepts, such as FISHING EQUIPMENT. Like representations of ad hoc categories, goal-derived concepts are related to specific goals. Contrary to representations of ad hoc categories, they are stored in long-term memory. There is also some tentative evidence that other concepts are ideals too. This is the case of concepts of personality traits (Bornkeneau 1990; Read, Jones, and Miller 1990). To give a toy example, the concept of a bully might not represent the typical bully, but the perfect bully. Lynch and colleagues (2000) have also argued that among tree experts, TREE is an ideal, where the perfect tree is characterized by its height and its weediness. Among experts, typicality with respect to the class of trees is not determined by the possession of common properties, but by the possession of the properties that a tree should possess: a tree should be tall and should not be weedy. Finally, similar findings among the Itza Mayas (Indians living in Guatemala) suggest that in some cultures, at least some concepts of plants might be ideals (Bailenson et al. 2002).

This is at least suggestive evidence for the existence of ideals. Ideals may even be a fundamental kind of concept. That is, it may be that for most categories in most domains, besides prototypes, exemplars, and

---

[61] In the psychological literature, the representations of ad hoc categories are called "concepts." Since they are not stored in long-term memory, this usage is at odds with the characterization of the notion of concept proposed in chapter 1 (see C). However, for the sake of simplicity, I will sometimes follow the terminology used in the literature.

theories, we also possess an ideal. Two issues remain, however. First, it is unclear whether most ideals qualify as concepts. Even if we have some knowledge about what an ideal table would be, this knowledge may be part of our background knowledge about tables instead of being a concept of table. Second, because there has been insufficient work inspired by Barsalou's seminal proposal about ideals, there is very little evidence about which categories in which domains are represented by ideals. For these two reasons, in the remainder of this book, I will pass over ideals.

4.6 Three Theoretical Entities That Have Little in Common

In the last section of this chapter, I briefly argue that the three theoretical constructs introduced by the three main paradigms of concept—prototypes, exemplars, and theories—have little in common.

4.6.1 Criterion

First, I need to explain how one evaluates the extent to which several kinds of concept are different. Clearly, prototypes, exemplars, and theories have plenty of irrelevant properties in common, for example, *not being cups of tea*. What matters, however, are those properties that psychologists take to be important when they characterize concepts. As we saw repeatedly, psychologists focus primarily on what knowledge is stored in concepts and on how concepts are used in cognitive processes. If exemplars, prototypes, and theories store different types of knowledge and are used in different cognitive processes, this would suggest that they have little in common.

This is the appropriate occasion to reiterate that my proposal is not that there are differences between these three kinds of concept. This would be utterly trivial and would bear little theoretical weight. There are many differences between breeds of dogs, but this says little about the utility of the class of dogs for biologists. The reason, obviously, is that above and beyond these differences, there are many similarities between dogs. Similarly, showing that there are differences between prototypes, exemplars, and theories is trivial. Instead, the claim is that there are few relevant similarities between these three theoretical constructs, where "relevant" is spelled out by reference to the properties of concepts psychologists are interested in.

4.6.2 Kinds of Knowledge

Prototypes, exemplars, and theories are assumed to encode three different types of knowledge. This follows directly from the way these three theoretical constructs are characterized. According to prototype theorists, concepts are bodies of statistical knowledge about the properties that characterize classes of individuals. According to exemplar theorists, concepts are bodies of knowledge about the properties of specific individuals. According to theory theorists, concepts are bodies of modal, nomological, causal, and/or functional knowledge about classes of individuals.

Clearly, the three main paradigms of concepts assume that concepts store different types of knowledge. To put it differently, these three paradigms assume that when we reason, categorize, and draw analogies, we have by default in mind three different kinds of knowledge.

For most categories, it is possible to store some knowledge about the typical properties of their members, some modal, nomological, and causal knowledge about their members, and some knowledge about the properties possessed by some of their members. Hence, consistent with the Heterogeneity Hypothesis, most categories could be represented by a prototype, a theory, and a set of exemplars.

4.6.3 Kinds of Cognitive Process

Prototypes, exemplars, and theories are assumed to be used in three different kinds of cognitive process. This also falls out from the way these three theoretical constructs are characterized. Exemplar theorists and prototype theorists suppose that the cognitive processes that underlie the higher cognitive competences involve the computation of the similarity between some representations and, respectively, sets of exemplars and prototypes. Proponents of the prototype paradigm and of the exemplar paradigm assume different ways of computing the similarity between a represented object and, respectively, prototypes and sets of exemplars. The theory paradigm of concepts assumes that the cognitive processes that underlie the higher cognitive competences do not rely on similarity. On the contrary, they are supposed to be similar to the reasoning processes that are used in science—namely, inferences to the best explanation or causal reasoning.

Clearly, the three main paradigms of concepts assume that concepts are used in different kinds of cognitive process. To put it differently, these three paradigms assume that when we reason, categorize, and draw analogies, we use three different kinds of cognitive process.

4.7 Conclusion

In this chapter, I have introduced the three main paradigms of concepts. I have briefly described the classical theory of concepts, and I have criticized the recent revival of this approach to concepts. Then, I have spelled out the three main paradigms of concepts in the contemporary psychology of concepts, namely, the prototype paradigm, the exemplar paradigm, and the theory paradigm. I have particularly focused on what kind of knowledge is stored in concepts and on how concepts are used in cognitive processes according to these three paradigms. I have systematically illustrated these approaches with some real models of concepts and of cognitive processes. Finally, I have briefly reviewed the two most interesting contemporary alternatives to the main paradigms of concepts—the neo-empiricist approach and the ideal approach to concepts.

This discussion of the main paradigms of concepts is a crucial step in this book. Prototypes, exemplars, and theories are assumed to store different types of knowledge and to be used in different kinds of cognitive process. Hence, given the properties that are relevant to characterize concepts, the main psychological paradigms of concepts assume three kinds of concept that have little in common. In chapters 6 and 7, I will argue that prototypes, exemplars, and theories all exist and are used by default in the processes underlying the higher cognitive competences.

5

Multi-Process Theories

In this chapter, I focus on the fourth tenet of the Heterogeneity Hypothesis: it is often the case that a given cognitive competence is underwritten by several cognitive processes, each of which accesses a specific kind of concept. I call theories that make such an assumption "multi-process theories." This view of the mind is at odds with an important tradition in cognitive science, which I call "the Unified View of Cognition"—the view that each cognitive competence is underwritten by a single cognitive process. The goal of this chapter is to investigate, in a somewhat speculative manner, the contours of multi-process theories, highlighting the research issues of interest. The hope is that the issues discussed in this chapter will be further investigated, empirically and theoretically, by psychologists interested in concepts and in higher cognition.

In section 5.1, I contrast multi-process theories and the Unified View of Cognition. In section 5.2, I illustrate this contrast by describing three psychological theories, which have challenged, each in its own way, the Unified View of Cognition.

5.1 Multi-Process Theories

5.1.1 Cognitive Competence, Cognitive Process, Task

In order to contrast multi-process theories with the Unified View of Cognition, it is necessary to clarify the notions of cognitive competence, cognitive process, and task (see also section 1.1). A cognitive competence is characterized by what it is a competence for—what it brings about, its function. Recognizing faces visually, being able to estimate the cardinality of classes visually or to estimate the cardinality of sequences of sounds, being able to classify physical objects into classes, being able to determine the syntactic structure of sentences, distinguishing phonemes, identifying shadows in the visual field are cognitive competences. Cognitive competences are typically nested. That is, typically, having a cognitive competence involves having subcompetences. For instance, the capacity to distinguish three-dimensional objects in our visual field involves being able to identify the shadows projected by these objects.

A cognitive process is a specific way of bringing about what a cognitive competence is a competence for. I say that cognitive processes underwrite or underlie cognitive competences. Describing a cognitive process involves characterizing the steps by virtue of which it brings about what the cognitive competence is a competence for on the basis of its inputs. Comparing the representation of an object to a prototype in order to decide whether the object belongs to the category represented by the prototype is a cognitive process that is assumed by prototype theorists to underwrite categorization.

An analogy between cognitive competences and skills might cast some light on the distinction between competences and processes. While knowing how to hit a backhand in tennis is a skill, there are many ways of performing this skill. One can use two hands or a single hand. Being able to hit a backhand corresponds to a cognitive competence, while a specific way of hitting a backhand corresponds to a cognitive process.

A task is an experimental situation in which subjects are expected to perform some action. The discrimination of tactile sensations that vary in intensity is a task in psychophysics. The pairwise comparison with respect to a criterion, such as the comparison of two cities with respect to their size, is a task in the psychology of reasoning under uncertainty (e.g., Gigerenzer and Goldstein 1996). Tasks are assumed to tap into specific cognitive competences. That is, it is assumed that fulfilling a given task involves using one or several cognitive competences. Subjects' performances in this task can thus be used to test hypotheses about the cognitive processes assumed to underwrite the relevant cognitive competences.

Now that cognitive competences, cognitive processes, and tasks have been characterized, I should address the question of how they are individuated. First, how are cognitive competences individuated? That is, when do we have a single competence instead of several competences? To make this a bit more concrete, consider two different types of categorization, categorization under time pressure and categorization without time pressure. In the first case, but not in the second case, one has to decide quickly whether an object belongs to a given class. Are these two types of categorization two different cognitive competences? Or, rather, is categorization a unique cognitive competence, which is expressed in two different contexts?

To make some progress on this issue, it is helpful to consider again the analogy between skills and cognitive competences. Does playing tennis on grass involve the same skill as playing tennis on clay? Or, rather, do they involve two different skills? There is little doubt that playing tennis on clay is somewhat different from playing on grass. Tennis balls are faster and rebound lower on grass than on clay. In spite of these differences, playing tennis on grass and playing tennis on clay involve a single skill expressed in two different contexts because the capacity to play tennis acquired on one of these two surfaces transfers to the other one. If someone learns to play tennis on grass, she will thereby be able to play tennis on clay, and vice-versa. By contrast, typing and handwriting are two different skills because being able to type does not confer a capacity to handwrite and vice-versa. There are, of course, more complex cases, where learning a skill in a context transfers to a limited extent to another context. Consider playing tennis and playing badminton. Certainly, someone who has learned to play tennis is thereby able to play badminton, at least poorly. So, do playing tennis and playing badminton involve a single skill? Becoming proficient at playing badminton involves refraining from relying on many automatisms acquired during learning how to play tennis. Someone who would play badminton in the same way she plays tennis would be a very unskilled badminton player. One can propose that to the extent that becoming proficient in context 2 supposes refraining from relying on the skill acquired in context 1, then, two different skills are involved in these two contexts. According to this proposal, playing tennis and playing badminton involve two different skills, despite the fact that someone who has learned to play tennis would thereby be able to play badminton. Someone who has learned to play tennis on grass will have to refrain from relying on some automatisms when she plays on clay. But since she can rely on most automatisms acquired on grass when she plays on clay, one might say that a single skill is involved.

The analogy with skills suggests the following individuation principles for cognitive competences:

1. *A sufficient condition for identifying competences.* When two contexts are such that when one is able to bring about x in one context, one is thereby able to bring about x in the other context, bringing about x involves a single cognitive competence in these two contexts. If someone who can categorize when there is no time constraint can thereby categorize under time pressure, and vice-versa, categorization under time pressure and categorization without time pressure constitute a single cognitive competence.
2. *A sufficient condition for distinguishing competences.* When two contexts are such that when one is able to bring about x in one context, one is not thereby able to bring about x in the other context, bringing about x involves two different cognitive competences in these two contexts. There will often be a grey area where being able to bring about x in one context will transfer to some extent to a different context. In these cases, it is unclear

whether or not a single cognitive competence is involved. I propose that bringing about *x* in two contexts involves two competences to the extent that one needs to refrain from relying on the way one brings about *x* in one context in order to become proficient in bringing about *x* in the other context.

The issue of individuation crops up for cognitive processes and for tasks too. Let us focus first on the individuation of cognitive processes. Consider a cognitive competence, categorization. When is categorization underwritten by two distinct processes instead of a single process? Suppose that we can categorize either by comparing the targets to a prototype or to exemplars (chapters 4 and 6). In the former case, we retrieve a prototype from long-term memory, compare the target to this prototype, and decide whether the object belongs to the category represented by this prototype on the basis of this comparison. In the latter case, we retrieve a set of exemplars from long-term memory, compare the target to these exemplars, and decide whether the object belongs to the category represented by this set of exemplars on the basis of this comparison. Do we have a single categorization process that can use different kinds of concept (viz. prototypes and exemplars) or two categorization processes, each of which accesses a distinct kind of concept? Like the individuation of cognitive competences, this is a tricky issue without an obvious answer.

Following Ashby and Ell (2002), I propose three criteria such that, when satisfied, it is likely that we are dealing with two systems rather than one. None of these criteria is a sufficient condition, for one can conceive of situations where they are satisfied, although we are intuitively dealing with a single system. First, prototype-based categorization and exemplar-based categorization are likely to involve two different processes, if prototype-based categorization and exemplar-based categorization involve two doubly dissociable neural systems. Second, prototype-based categorization and exemplar-based categorization are likely to involve two distinct processes if these two types of categorization are characterized by different input-output functions. This would be the case if we do not categorize the same items by means of prototypes and by means of exemplars. This would also be the case if, while we do categorize the same items by means of prototypes and by means of exemplars, some items are categorized differently when they are categorized on the basis of prototypes or on the basis of exemplars. Third, prototype-based categorization and exemplar-based categorization are likely to involve two distinct processes if they involve two different algorithms, even though these two types of categorization are characterized by the same input-output function.

Finally, let us focus on the individuation of tasks. Consider, for instance, pairwise comparison with respect to a criterion. Are comparisons involving different criteria different tasks? For instance, are comparing cities with respect to their size and comparing cities with respect to their latitude two different tasks? Are comparisons of different classes of entities with respect to the same criterion different tasks? Are comparing cities with respect to their size and comparing sports teams (e.g., soccer team with rugby team, etc.) with respect to their size different tasks? For this matter, are comparing cities with respect to their size in the morning and comparing cities with respect to their size in the afternoon the same task? I wish I knew how to answer such questions in a principled manner. Unfortunately, it is unclear whether non-trivial principled criteria for the individuation of tasks can be formulated.

5.1.2 The Unified View of Cognition

According to the Unified View of Cognition, the default situation is that a cognitive competence is underwritten by a single cognitive process. This has been a very influential idea in cognitive science and in neuropsychology. It is implicitly built in the prominent methodology recommended by psychologist David Marr (1977, 1982). Marr distinguishes two types of theories:

> Devising suitable algorithms will [not] be easy, but ... before one can devise them, one has to know what exactly it is that they are supposed to be doing, and this information is captured by the computational theory. When a problem decomposes in this way, I shall refer to it as having a *Type-1 theory*....
> While many problems of biological information-processing have a Type-1 theory, there is no reason why they should all have. This can happen when a problem is solved by the simultaneous action of a considerable number of processes, *whose interaction is its own simplest description*, and I shall refer to such a situation as a *Type-2* theory. (Marr 1977: 38–39)

A Type-1 theory determines what the function defining a cognitive competence is and how it can be fulfilled. It explains in a principled manner in which conditions a given set of mechanisms can fulfill this function and when it cannot. Marr gives the example of Horn's (1975) theory for obtaining shape from shading. Horn proposed the first theory explaining how it is possible to discover the shape of three-dimensional objects from the variation in shading in a two-dimensional image. By contrast, a Type-2 theory of a cognitive competence proposes a set of mechanisms that fulfills the function defining the cognitive competence. Essentially, a Type-2 theory simulates the possession of the cognitive competence. One might not understand why or in which conditions this set of mechanisms fulfills the function defining the relevant cognitive competence. One might just know that under some conditions, the proposed mechanisms do fulfill this function. Marr gives the example of the simulation of the unfolding of proteins. He also contends that most research in artificial intelligence, including the research done by Simon and colleagues on problem solving, consists of Type-2 theories.

Although Marr concedes that many cognitive competences might only be explainable by Type-2 theories, he argues that cognitive scientists should first look for Type-1 theories. Developing a Type-2 theory of a given cognitive competence might prevent the development of a Type-1 theory of this competence. And Marr takes Type-1 theories to be preferable to Type-2 theories because Type-2 theories do not explain how and when the function defining a competence can be fulfilled. As Marr puts it (1977: 39), the "only possible virtue [of a candidate Type-2 theory] might be that it works."

Marr's methodological views nicely fit the Unified View of Cognition because Marr invites psychologists to develop theories that explain how a single process (described by an algorithm) can fulfill the function that defines a given cognitive competence (as characterized by a Type-1 theory). Maybe because of Marr's influence, the Unified View of Cognition is the default position for many psychologists. In the psychological literature, the burden of proof typically bears on those psychologists who argue that several cognitive processes underwrite a specific cognitive competence.

One might justify the default status of the Unified View of Cognition on grounds of parsimony (e.g., Dunn 2003: 178). Everything being equal, we should prefer theories that assume that a given cognitive competence is underwritten by a single cognitive process rather than by several. However, this argument from parsimony is not compelling. In general, parsimony can support a given theory over another in a given scientific area only if in this scientific area, parsimonious scientific theories are more likely to be empirically supported than less parsimonious theories. And one can take parsimonious theories as more likely to be empirically supported than less parsimonious theories if and only if in the past, parsimonious theories have been better supported than less parsimonious theories. To use a fictional example, it might be the case that parsimonious theories of the structure of matter have regularly been better supported than less parsimonious theories. If this were the case, then we would be justified in using parsimony to evaluate new scientific theories about the structure of matter. The epistemological role of parsimony in this scientific area would be derived from an induction about the relative empirical support of past parsimonious theories. Thus, the claim that everything being equal, the Unified View of Cognition is superior to multi-process theories supposes that parsimonious cognitive theories have been better supported than less parsimonious cognitive theories. However, it is unclear whether this is the case. A growing number of successful theories challenge the Unified View of Cognition (section 5.2). Thus, it is dubious whether parsimony can have any bite in the debate between multi-process theories and the Unified View of Cognition.

Finally, it is worth noting that the Unified View of Cognition is in principle consistent with the idea that the class of concepts divides into several fundamental kinds of concept. These different kinds of concept might all be the inputs to a single cognitive process for each cognitive competence. For instance, categorization might be underwritten by a single categorization process, which would take as inputs several concepts (figure 5.1).

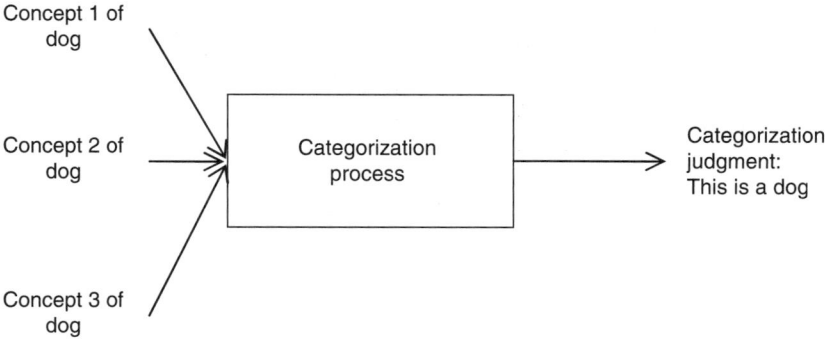

Figure 5.1 A Single Cognitive Process Using Several Kinds of Concepts

Instead, the Heterogeneity Hypothesis proposes that, like many other higher cognitive competences, categorization is underwritten by several cognitive processes.

5.1.3 Multi-Processes Theories

The Unified View of Cognition strongly contrasts with multi-process theories of cognitive competences. To repeat, according to the latter, a cognitive competence is underwritten by several cognitive processes rather than by a single cognitive process.

On one reading, multi-process theories are trivially true. As noted above, cognitive competences often involve numerous subcompetences. Consider, for instance, vision. Vision can be loosely characterized as the production of three-dimensional representations of the objects in the visual field from the patterns of activation of the photoreceptors on the retinas. Vision involves numerous subcompetences, which in turn involve other subcompetences. Seeing involves being able to distinguish the volumes in our environment, which in turn involves being able to identify surfaces, and identifying surfaces involves being able to identify edges. These subcompetences are underwritten by distinct processes (e.g., Felleman and van Essen 1991). In that sense, it is trivial that most cognitive competences are underwritten by several processes (figure 5.2). Importantly, if each of these processes is necessary for having the relevant competence (e.g., seeing), none of them is by itself sufficient.

What singles out multi-process theories is the idea that a cognitive competence is underwritten by several cognitive processes, each of which is sufficient for having this competence (figure 5.3). For each of these processes, if all the other processes were somehow knocked off, the organism would still be in possession of the relevant cognitive competence. The outputs of these cognitive processes are precisely what the cognitive competence is supposed to be a capacity for. By contrast, in figure 5.2, none of the processes that constitute the process producing x (e.g., categorization

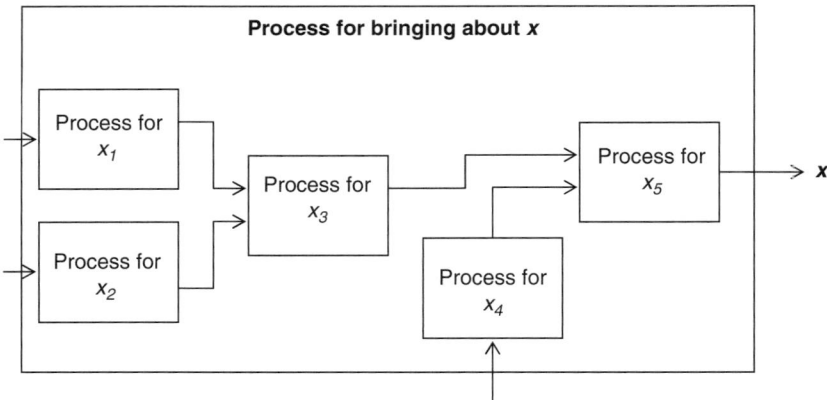

Figure 5.2 A Process and Its Subprocesses

judgments) is sufficient for having the relevant cognitive competence. For each of these processes, if all the other processes were knocked off, the organism would lose the relevant cognitive competence.

It is useful to illustrate multi-process theories with some recent work in moral psychology. Neuropsychologist Joshua Greene has developed a dual-process theory of moral judgments.[1] In substance, Greene proposes that two processes underwrite our capacity to judge the moral value of actions. On the one hand, emotions triggered by the description or perception of actions are supposed to cause people to make moral judgments about these actions. For instance, seeing or hearing of someone killing an innocent individual in order to save several other innocent individuals might trigger a negatively valenced emotion. This emotion might cause people to judge that this action is morally wrong. On the other hand, people endorse some explicit moral principles, particularly, some utilitarian principles. On the basis of these principles, people might judge that killing an innocent individual in order to save several other innocent individuals is morally permissible. Thus, Greene and Haidt write:

> On the one hand, moral thinking is driven largely by social-emotional dispositions built on those we inherited from our primate ancestors. At the same time, humans have a unique capacity for sophisticated abstract reasoning that can be applied to any subject matter. One might suppose, then, that human moral thinking is not one kind of process, but rather a complex interplay between (at least) two distinct types of processes: domain-specific, social-emotional responses and domain-neutral reasoning processes applied in moral contexts. (Greene and Haidt 2002: 519)

Greene's theory illustrates the gist of multi-process theories. Each of the two processes hypothesized by Greene is sufficient for producing a moral

---

[1] Greene et al. 2001, 2004, 2008; Greene and Haidt 2002.

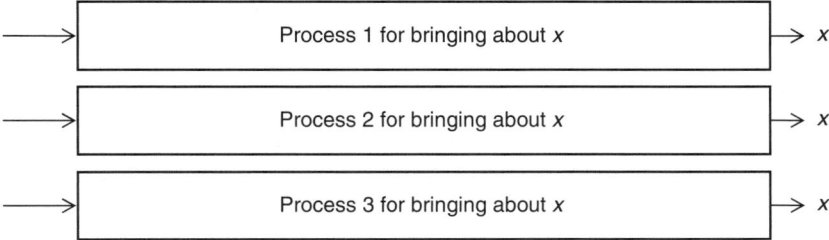

Figure 5.3 Multi-Process Theories

judgment. If one of them were somehow knocked off, we would still be able to make moral judgments about actions, even though our moral judgments might then differ from the moral judgments we would make if the two processes were up and running.

5.1.4 A Variety of Multi-Process Theories

There are, of course, numerous ways of developing a multi-process theory for a given cognitive competence. Two main issues (A and B) distinguish different types of multi-process theory. The first issue (A) bears on the conditions in which the hypothesized processes are triggered:

   A. In which conditions are the hypothesized processes triggered?

There are at least three possible answers to issue A:

1. Each process is triggered in its own range of conditions.
2. For each process, this process is triggered in its own range of conditions, but, in many conditions, all the processes (or several of them) are triggered.
3. In all conditions, all the processes are triggered.

Consider, for instance, a multi-process theory of categorization. Such a theory could propose that each categorization process is triggered in its own range of conditions. Tasks A, B, and C could trigger process 1, while tasks Φ, Γ, and Λ could trigger process 2. Alternatively, the theory could propose that in some conditions, a single process is triggered, while in others, all the processes are triggered. Task A could trigger only process 1 and task Φ only process 2, while tasks B, C, Γ, and Λ could trigger processes 1 and 2. Alternatively, the theory could propose that in all conditions, the different processes are triggered. Tasks A, B, C, Φ, Γ, and Λ could trigger both processes 1 and 2.[2]

---

[2] One might wonder whether the idea that concepts are used by default when one reasons and categorizes (etc.) is consistent with the idea that the cognitive processes that underlie reasoning, categorization (etc.) are triggered in different conditions. To illustrate the

When different processes are triggered in different conditions (1 and 2 above), a multi-process theory should determine what causes these processes to be triggered in these conditions. The activation of distinct cognitive processes in different conditions might be bottom-up. Particularly, it might be that different processes are triggered by different types of stimulus. For instance, a multi-process theory of categorization could propose that categorizing events, categorizing animals, and categorizing artifacts involve different processes. Alternatively, the activation of distinct cognitive processes in different conditions might be top-down: these processes might be intentionally triggered or inhibited. For instance, when I shop at a fruit market abroad, I might intentionally inhibit the prototype-based categorization process (if there is such a process) because I know or have learned that in these conditions such a process is unreliable. Or I might intentionally trigger the theory-based process (if there is such a process) because in these conditions such a process is reliable. Additionally, if the activation of distinct cognitive processes in different conditions is bottom-up, a multi-process theory should determine whether learning determines which process is triggered in which condition or, rather, whether experience has no or little effect on the triggering conditions of these processes.

Providing an answer to issue A is particularly important for testing multi-process theories. A multi-process theory of a given cognitive competence, for instance, categorization, will make different predictions if it contends that different categorization processes are triggered in different conditions or if it contends that they are simultaneously triggered. In the former case, but not in the latter, it will often be possible to identify experimental categorization tasks that tap into a single categorization process. In the latter case, performances in the categorization task will typically result from the interaction of several categorization processes (see issue B).

Because a multi-process theory can propose that some conditions simultaneously trigger several cognitive processes (see 2 and 3 above), a second issue distinguishes different types of multi-process theory:

> B. When several cognitive processes are simultaneously triggered, what happens to the outputs of these cognitive processes?

Or, to put the same point differently, what is the nature of the mechanism that takes as inputs the outputs of the hypothesized cognitive processes and produces a single final output? Although many classifications of such

---

issue, if a prototype-based process of categorization is triggered only in a specific range of conditions, prototypes do not seem to be used by default when one categorizes. Thus, they do not seem to satisfy the characterization of concepts proposed in chapter 1 (see C). In reply, I note that in this specific range of conditions prototypes would be retrieved by default because in these conditions the knowledge stored in these prototypes would be preferentially available when we reason about their extension or categorize objects as members of their extension. Prototypes would thus stand in contrast with the background knowledge in long-term memory, which would not be retrieved by default in these conditions.

mechanisms are conceivable, I highlight an important distinction between integrative and non-integrative mechanisms. Non-integrative mechanisms select one of the outputs of the hypothesized cognitive processes. The non-selected outputs are overridden. By contrast, integrative mechanisms do not select the output of one of the simultaneously triggered cognitive processes. Rather, their outputs reflect the outputs of all these processes.

Some examples might cast some light on the distinction at hand. I first describe two integrative mechanisms. The majority rule is a simple form of integration. Suppose that the task is to decide whether the target is an F (by producing a judgment that p) or not (judging that not p). If the mechanism that takes as inputs the outputs of the categorization processes follows the majority rule, then, the final output—namely, the decision to categorize or not the target—will be the judgment that p if the majority of the outputs of the categorization processes are judgments that p. If among the outputs of these categorization processes, there is an equal number of judgments that p and judgments that not p, the mechanism that is in charge of making a final judgment might choose randomly.

Alternatively, the outputs of the processes underwriting a cognitive competence might be (at least partly) quantitative. For instance, the processes underwriting categorization might associate categorization judgments with a degree of confidence. A second type of integrative mechanism would then produce a quantitative value that is a weighted function of the values produced by the distinct processes underwriting the cognitive competence at hand. For instance, the degree of confidence attached to the final categorization judgment might be a weighed function of the degrees of confidence produced by each process. Suppose that each cognitive process produces a value v_i (e.g., a degree of confidence). Then, the integrative system i^* produces a value v_{i^*}:

$$v_{i^*} = \sum_{i=1}^{n} u_i v_i \qquad (1)$$

where u_i is the weight ascribed to process i (with $\sum_{i=1}^{n} u_i = 1$).

This integration rule might be context-dependent. The integrative mechanism might weigh the outputs of the integrated processes differently in different contexts. That is, the weights u_i might vary across contexts.

There are also several non-integrative mechanisms. For instance, one could hypothesize that a random choice takes place between the outputs of the processes underwriting a cognitive competence. If there are n categorization processes, then

$$P(p) = \frac{\sum_{i=1}^{n} P_i(p)}{n} \qquad (2)$$

where i corresponds to i^{th} process, $P_i(p)$ to the probability that process i produces the categorization judgment p, and $P(p)$ to the probability that the final categorization judgment is p.

The fastest-take-all rule is a second non-integrative mechanism. On this model, as soon as an output is produced, the other processes might be inhibited. One can speculate that given the importance of speed for many cognitive competences like categorization and induction, such a system might have evolved. The most-confident-take-all rule is a third non-integrative mechanism. Suppose that the outputs of the processes that underwrite a cognitive competence are associated with a confidence degree. The output with the strongest confidence degree might override the other outputs.

5.1.5 Three Types of Evidence for Multi-Process Theories

I now turn to a methodological question: what kind of finding can be evidence for a multi-process theory? Since multi-process theories tend to be controversial, it is particularly important to investigate this issue. I consider three types of evidence.

It might be that different tasks selectively trigger different processes. This is to be expected if, as some multi-process theories might have it, different processes are triggered in different conditions. This might also be the case even if in non-experimental conditions, all or several processes are triggered simultaneously, as other multi-process theories might have it. Artificial experimental tasks might be designed that trigger a single process, even though in real-world situations, several processes are typically triggered simultaneously. I note that this consideration might justify the use of artificial, ecologically invalid experimental situations.

If different experimental tasks selectively trigger different processes, each task should result in a specific performance profile. Suppose that different tasks elicit different performance profiles. Suppose also that each performance profile corresponds to the performance profile that would be predicted if it were the case that only one of the processes postulated by a multi-process theory is triggered by this task. This would be evidence that the postulated processes underwrite the relevant cognitive competence.[3] To make this clearer, consider the multi-process theory of categorization defended in the next chapter. I argue that humans possess at least three categorization processes, one involving prototypes, one involving exemplars, one involving theories. I will show that some tasks elicit a performance profile that would be predicted if they triggered a prototype-based categorization process. Other tasks elicit a performance profile that would be predicted if they triggered an exemplar-based categorization process. Other tasks elicit a performance profile that would be predicted if they triggered a theory-based categorization process. I take this to be evidence

---

[3] Merely finding that different tasks elicit different performance profiles is no evidence for a multi-process theory because different tasks always elicit different performances. What is needed is evidence that different tasks elicit the performance profiles that are predicted by a multi-process theory.

for the hypothesized multi-process theory of categorization (sections 6.3 to 6.5).

This type of finding provides evidence for the existence of several processes underwriting a given cognitive competence. It also provides evidence about the nature of these different processes, for instance, about the fact that categorization is underwritten by a process involving prototypes, by a process involving exemplars, and by a process involving theories. However, it is unclear whether this type of finding tells much about the organization of these processes, particularly if the experimental tasks are ecologically invalid. Evidence that different experimental tasks trigger different processes does not entail that in ecologically valid conditions, these processes are not triggered simultaneously.

In the next chapter, I will heavily rely on this type of evidence. Different experimental categorization tasks seem to selectively trigger different categorization processes, providing evidence for a multi-process theory of categorization. The same conclusion is supported by the literature on induction, as we shall see in Chapter 7.

As we saw, some multi-process theories contend that in some conditions, several processes are simultaneously triggered. These theories predict that different performance profiles will be observed when the hypothesized processes produce the same output and when these processes produce different outputs because, in the latter case, but not in the former, a conflict has to be resolved. This idea has been used by Greene to support the dual-process theory of moral judgment presented above. Greene and colleagues (2001) showed that people are slower to make a moral judgment when Greene's dual-process theory predicts that the two hypothesized processes produce conflicting outputs than when his theory predicts that the two processes produce congruent outputs. Greene and colleagues took this finding to be evidence that different processes underlie our moral judgments and that these processes are triggered simultaneously in at least some conditions. Besides reaction time, other dependent variables, such as between-subjects agreement and within-subjects agreement in different occasions (test-retest reliability), might be used to find out whether performances are similar when the multi-process theory being tested predicts that the hypothesized processes concur and when it predicts that they conflict.

The finding that the performance profiles differ when a multi-process theory predicts that the hypothesized processes produce the same output by comparison to when the theory predicts that the processes produce conflicting outputs is evidence for the multi-process theory under consideration. This finding provides evidence about the existence of different processes underwriting a single competence. It also provides evidence about the relation between the hypothesized processes. It supports the view that in at least some conditions, the processes are simultaneously triggered.

In the next chapter, I will mention evidence of this kind, establishing that different categorization processes, relying on different kinds of concept, are simultaneously triggered.

Dissociations might provide a third type of evidence for multi-process theories. I first focus on dissociations in experimental psychology, which are sometimes called "functional dissociations" (e.g., Dunn and Kirsner 1988, 2003). One speaks of a dissociation if subjects' performances in two different tasks is differently affected by different variables.[4] In experimental psychology, a single dissociation is found when and only when a variable affects differently subjects' performances in two tasks. According to this definition, a variable might affect subjects' performances in both tasks, but a dissociation has been found if it affects them differently. The expression "weak dissociation" is sometimes used to refer to this case. A stricter definition (e.g., Dunn and Kirsner 2003) would be that performances in one task are not affected, while performances in the other task are affected (as illustrated in figure 5.4). The expression "strong dissociation" is sometimes used to refer to this case. In figure 5.4, a variable is modified in condition 2, by comparison to condition 1. Performances are affected in task 1, but not in task 2.

In a double dissociation, two variables affect differently subjects' performances in two tasks. According to a stricter definition, a first variable affects subjects' performances in one task, but not in the other, while a second variable affects subjects' performances in the latter task, but not in the former. In figure 5.5, a variable is modified in condition 2, by compar-

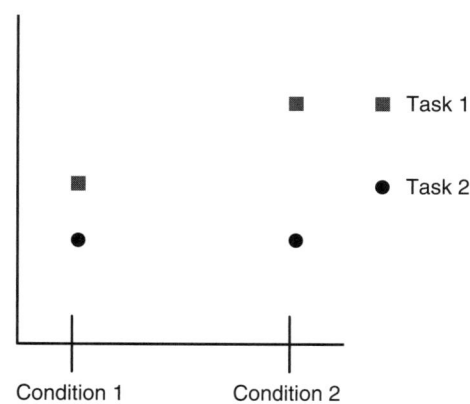

Figure 5.4 Strong Single Dissociation

---

[4] There are several, cross-cutting classifications of dissociation (Dunn and Kirsner 1988, 2003; Shallice 1988).

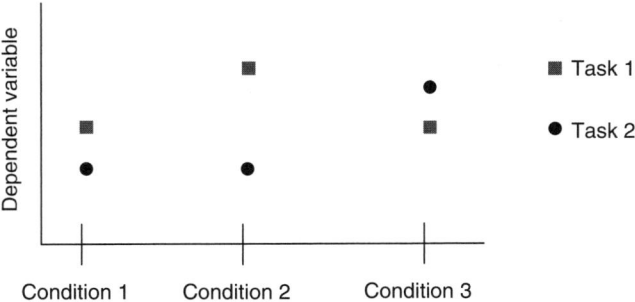

Figure 5.5 Strong Double Dissociation

ison to condition 1. Performances are affected in task 1, but not in task 2. Another variable is modified in condition 3, by comparison to condition 1. Performances are affected in task 2, but not in task 1.

In neuropsychology, one speaks of a single dissociation when a brain lesion affects differently two tasks, by comparison to a control group of unimpaired participants (figure 5.6). In some cases, a lesion might entirely knock off patients' capacity to complete one of these two tasks.

A double dissociation happens when one brain lesion affects the performances of a first group of patients in a first task, by comparison to a control group of unimpaired participants, while another brain lesion affects the performances of a second group of patients in a second task, by comparison to a control group of unimpaired participants (figure 5.7).

In humans, brain lesions are typically accidental, although a technique called "transcranial manipulation" or "TMS" has been developed to simulate brain lesions by temporarily suppressing activity in targeted brain regions.

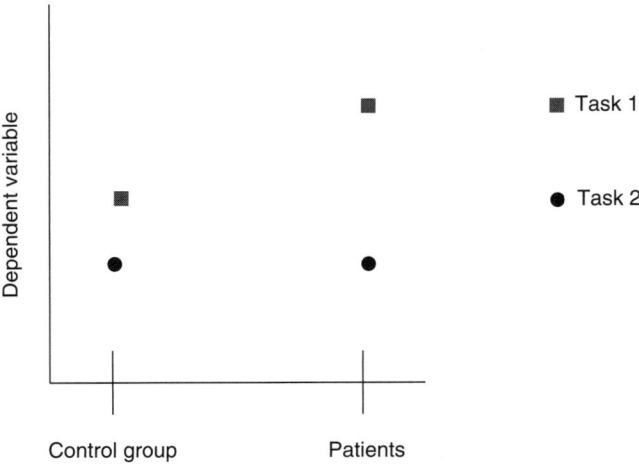

Figure 5.6 Single Dissociation in Neuropsychology

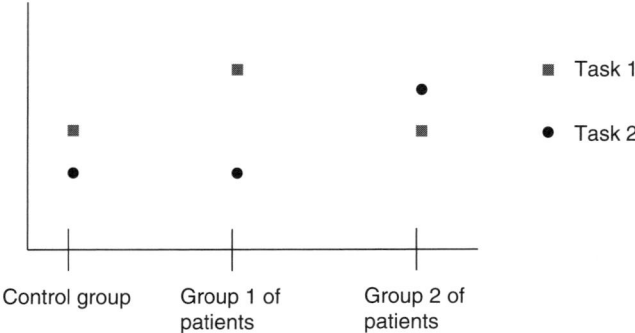

Figure 5.7 Double Dissociation in Neuropsychology

Brain lesions are also intentionally produced on model species, such as rats or macaques. Neuropsychological dissociations are a specific case of dissociation, where the variable of interest is an intact or lesioned brain area.

Psychologists and neuropsychologists have used both functional and neuropsychological dissociations to isolate different processes involved in different tasks. If a variable differently affects subjects' performances in two tasks, two different processes are likely to be involved in these tasks— or so the idea goes. In addition, neuropsychological dissociations, but not functional dissociations, are also used to localize cognitive processes in the brain. Since I am interested in what type of evidence can support multi-process theories, I focus on how dissociations can contribute to the distinction of processes, not to their localization in the brain.

There is little agreement on whether and how dissociations can be used to determine the nature of our cognitive processes.[5] What I want to do here is to criticize psychologists' and neuropsychologists' conception of what is required of dissociations if they are to support multi-process theories. The proponents of a multi-process theory for a given competence often attempt to falsify the hypothesis that this competence is underwritten by a single process by finding a dissociation that is taken to be inconsistent with the single-process hypothesis. In response, opponents of these multi-process theories often argue that this dissociation is consistent with the single-process hypothesis, typically by showing that the dissociation at hand can be simulated by means of a computational model that involves a single process (e.g., Plaut 1995). Both sides thereby assume that dissociations provide evidence about the number of cognitive processes underwriting a given cognitive competence only by being inconsistent with the hypothesis that the cognitive competence is underwritten by a single cognitive process. If the dissociation is not inconsistent with a

---

[5] Teuber 1955; Caramazza 1986; Dunn and Kirsner 1988, 2003; Shallice 1988; Glymour 1994; Plaut 1995; Young, Hilgetag, and Scannell 2000; Van Orden, Pennington, and Stone 2001; Ashby and Ell 2002; McCloskey 2003; see also the special issue of *Cortex* 2003 (volume 39, issue 1).

theory positing a single process, it is viewed as having no evidential value. That is, psychologists and neuropsychologists often assume that to count as evidence for a multi-process theory, a dissociation has to be a crucial experiment—that is, an experiment that decisively distinguishes between the competing scientific hypotheses.

Let us consider an example. According to some proponents of dual-process models of reading, such as neuropsychologist Max Coltheart (e.g., Coltheart et al. 1993, 2001), several dissociations provide evidence for a dual-process model of reading.[6] A striking example is a preserved capacity to read pseudo-words, such as "bint," but a lost or impaired capacity to read real words whose pronunciation is irregular, such as "pint" (deep dyslexia), and vice-versa (surface dyslexia). To simplify, Coltheart and colleagues conclude that two processes underlie reading. A first process involves applying phonetic rules to written words, while a second process involves mapping directly written words to their pronunciation (for further detail, see Coltheart et al. 2001). In deep dyslexia, the latter process is disrupted, while in surface dyslexia, the former process is disrupted. Critics of Coltheart's dual-process model of reading have argued that these dissociations are consistent with single-process models and have concluded that these dissociations do not undermine the single-process hypothesis (Plaut 1995; Van Orden, Pennington, and Stone 2001). For present purposes, what matters is that these critics assume that by showing that the dissociation at hand is not a crucial experiment—namely that it is not inconsistent with the single-process hypothesis—they have established that the dissociation has no evidential value against the single-process hypothesis.[7]

The issue with this kind of controversy is that crucial experiments play as little role in cognitive science as in science in general. The typical situation in cognitive science is that experimental findings can be accommodated by the relevant competing hypotheses modulo some appropriate auxiliary hypotheses. This situation is illustrated by the controversies between the propositional and imagistic theories of cognition (e.g., Anderson 1978), between egoistic and altruistic theories of motivation (e.g., Batson 1991), or between neo-empiricist and amodal theories of concepts (Machery 2007a). In these and other controversies, experimental findings are consistent with all the competing hypotheses, modulo the appropriate auxiliary hypotheses.

Fortunately, to have some evidential value, dissociations do not have to be crucial experiments. Dissociations constitute data that are to be accounted for by multi-process models and by single-process models of the relevant cognitive competences. They support multi-process models

---

[6] Coltheart does not think that dissociations falsify single-model hypotheses (Coltheart and Davies 2003).

[7] Similarly, in a celebrated article, Dunn and Kirsner (1988) attempt to define the conditions in which a dissociation is inconsistent with a single-process hypothesis.

over single-process models to the extent that to account for them, the latter are compelled to appeal to increasingly dubious auxiliary assumptions. This is how I propose to view the dissociations that have been used to support multi-process theories of the higher cognitive competences (section 7.3).[8]

5.1.6 Two Objections

One might object to the distinction between multi-process theories and the Unified View of Cognition. Suppose that evidence seems to show that a cognitive competence is underwritten by two cognitive processes. A critic of multi-process theories could make the following proposal: rather than supporting a multi-process theory, the evidence shows that we were mistaken in assuming that we were dealing with a single cognitive competence. Rather, we are in fact dealing with two different cognitive competences. According to this proposal, each cognitive process underwrites a single cognitive competence. If this reply can be generalized whenever findings apparently support a multi-process theory, multi-process theories seem to collapse into the Unified View of Cognition.

Consider the case of memory. Typically, psychologists and neuropsychologists interested in memory do not propose that a single cognitive competence—storing knowledge about the past—is underwritten by several cognitive processes (e.g., a process for storing knowledge about past personal events, a process for storing factual knowledge about non-personal events and matters of fact, a process for storing skills, and a process for storing temporarily the knowledge used during cognitive processing). Rather, they typically propose that what was once believed to be a single cognitive competence—memory—consists in fact of several cognitive competences—episodic memory, semantic memory, procedural memory, and working memory—each of which is underwritten by a single cognitive process involving specific brain structures.[9] By analogy, one could object to multi-process theories of categorization (or of other cognitive competences) that, like memory, categorization consists in fact of several cognitive competences, each of which is underwritten by a single cognitive process.

There are at least three things to be said in reply. First, this objection concedes to the proponents of multi-process theories that what current psychological or neuropsychological theories take to be a single cognitive competence—namely, categorization—turns out not to be underwritten by a single cognitive process, be it a prototype-based process or an exemplar-based process, but rather by several processes. But this is tantamount to conceding what is really at stake here: instead of having a single categorization process, we have several categorization processes.

---

[8] See, particularly, Squire and Knowlton 1995; Knowlton 1997, 1999; Ashby et al. 1998; Reed et al. 1999.

[9] But see Baddeley (1986) on the distinct processes that underlie working memory.

Moreover, even if, by redefining our cognitive competences, one were to establish a one-to-one correspondence between competences and processes, it would still be the case that different kinds of concept (prototypes, exemplars, and theories) would be used in distinct processes. For example, suppose that we replace categorization with three competences—prototype-based categorization, exemplar-based categorization, and theory-based categorization. Each of these three competences might be underwritten by a single categorization process—a prototype-involving categorization process, an exemplar-involving categorization process, and a theory-involving categorization process. In such a case, it would still be the case that prototypes, exemplars, and theories are used in different types of cognitive process, which is what the Heterogeneity Hypothesis proposes.

Finally, the individuation principles of cognitive competences developed in section 5.1.1 put a limit on how the higher cognitive competences can be redefined. We saw that when one is able to do x in context 1 by virtue of being able to do x in context 2 (and vice-versa), doing x in contexts 1 and 2 involves a single cognitive competence. If the distinct processes that underwrite the capacity to categorize can produce categorization judgments in the same conditions, then categorization is a single cognitive competence and should not be divided into distinct competences corresponding to the categorization processes.

The second objection goes as follows. One might doubt that our mind includes several cognitive processes that underwrite the same cognitive competence because no artificial system would be built in such a way. For instance, if one had to build a categorization system, one would probably build a single categorization process, which would use as much information as possible about the classes in which objects should be categorized.

One could reply that engineering considerations are poor guides for speculating about the architecture of cognition because neither evolution nor development work like engineers. Biologists and philosophers of biology often emphasize that adaptations are more similar to Rube Goldberg's inventions than to well-engineered artifacts. However, I do not want to push further this line of reply because engineering considerations are often useful discovery heuristics in psychology (Pinker 1997; Machery and Barrett 2006).

Rather, I propose that multi-process theories make some engineering sense. Processes that take into account all the available information are often not more efficient than processes that take into account a subset of the available information (Gigerenzer, Todd, and the ABC Research Group 1999; section 5.2.3 below). Categorizing an object as a tomato based only on this object possessing many typical properties of tomatoes is a reliable strategy in many environments, for instance, at a local farmers' market. In these environments, a process that would integrate my knowledge about the typical properties of tomatoes with my biological knowledge about tomatoes would not be more reliable. Additionally, the time and effort needed to gather and integrate all the available information might make the processes that take into account all the available information less efficient than the processes that access only a subset of the available information.

This argument explains why different processes might be triggered in different circumstances. But it does not explain why several processes might be simultaneously triggered, particularly when their outputs are not integrated, as non-integrative multi-process theories might propose. So, first, does simultaneously triggering several processes make any engineering sense? The answer is, "Yes": triggering the processes that underlie a cognitive competence in the same circumstances circumvents the need to decide which process is triggered in which circumstance.

Second, if several processes are simultaneously triggered, does it make any engineering sense to select the output of one of these processes instead of integrating all the outputs? The answer is, again, "Yes, at least in some circumstances." Integrative mechanisms are slower than those non-integrative mechanisms that follow the fastest-take-all rule because they need to be fed the outputs of all the simultaneously triggered processes. If response speed is important, selecting the first output produced by the processes that are simultaneously triggered might be the best way of producing a single final output. Moreover, suppose that the outputs of the simultaneously triggered cognitive processes are associated with a degree of confidence. Suppose also that the degree of confidence is (even imperfectly) correlated with the likelihood of the output being correct. Then, selecting the output associated with the highest degree of confidence is the best way of producing a correct final output.

5.2 Examples of Multi-Process Theories

Multi-process theories have been developed in various areas of psychology and neuropsychology—reading (e.g., Coltheart et al. 1993), moral judgments (e.g., Haidt 2001; Greene and Haidt 2002), decision under uncertainty (e.g., Gigerenzer, Todd, and the ABC Research Group 1999; Kahneman and Frederick 2002), reasoning (e.g., Evans and Over 1996; Chaiken and Trope 1999; Stanovich 1999; Stanovich and West 2000, 2003), induction (e.g., Sloman 1996, 1998), and choice (e.g., Wilson 2002). All these theories challenge the Unified View of Cognition one way or another. In this section, I discuss some of the most interesting multi-process theories in order to illustrate the types of multi-process theory distinguished in section 5.1.4. The first two theories propose that at least in some conditions, several processes underwriting the same competence are simultaneously triggered. By contrast, the third theory proposes that the processes underwriting the same competence are always triggered in different conditions. The first two theories are both non-integrative, but they characterize differently the manner in which the final output is selected. Furthermore, the multi-process theories discussed in this section constitute positive or negative examples for the development of future multi-process theories.

5.2.1 Explicit versus Implicit Cognition

The first multi-process theory considered in this section draws on a distinction between two types of cognitive process—*implicit* versus *explicit* cognitive processes. Although similar distinctions are often found in psychology and neuropsychology, there is some confusion about what is distinguished.[10] While some have distinguished two types of process (e.g., Ashby et al. 1998), others have focused on two types of knowledge (e.g., Knowlton 1999). In both cases, the terminology is not entirely fixed. For example, some contrast our "declarative" and our "non-declarative" knowledge about categories (e.g., Knowlton 1999), others our "explicit" and our "implicit" knowledge (e.g., Goschke 1997; Knowlton 1999) or, in artificial intelligence, our procedural knowledge and our declarative knowledge (see the review in Knowlton 1997). It is also unclear whether all psychologists conceive of this distinction in a similar manner, even when they use the same terminology. In what follows, I briefly focus on the distinction drawn by neuropsychologists Larry Squire and Barbara Knowlton between declarative and non-declarative knowledge (e.g., Knowlton 1999) and, at greater length, on the distinction drawn by neuropsychologist Gregory Ashby between implicit and explicit processes of concept learning (e.g., Ashby et al. 1998).

Squire and Knowlton define declarative knowledge as any knowledge that is consciously accessible (e.g., Knowlton 1997; section 7.3). They propose a broad definition of "consciously accessible." Some knowledge is said to be consciously accessible if the knower is aware that she acquired this knowledge, even when she is not aware of the content of this knowledge. According to this definition, I know declaratively that Paris is in France. In this case, I am aware both of the fact that I have some knowledge about Paris and of the content of this knowledge. I also know declaratively what distinguishes a sculpture by Bourdelle and a sculpture by Rodin, although I am not aware of the content of my knowledge and although, as a result, I am not able to verbalize this knowledge. This knowledge is declarative because I am aware that I acquired it when I learned the history of nineteenth-century French sculpture. Squire and Knowlton propose that we have these two types of knowledge about categories. These two types of knowledge are acquired by different processes, are stored in different memory systems, and are used in different categorization processes.

---

[10] Knowlton and Squire 1993; Squire and Knowlton 1995; Goschke 1997; Knowlton 1997, 1999; Shanks 1997; Ashby et al. 1998; Reber, Stark, and Squire 1998; Ashby and Waldron 2000; Ashby and Valentin 2005.

Ashby and colleagues (1998) draw a distinction that is somewhat similar to Squire and Knowlton's distinction.[11] There are a few differences, however. First, Ashby and colleagues draw a distinction between the processes of knowledge acquisition rather than between types of knowledge. They distinguish explicit learning from implicit learning. Second, their implicit/explicit distinction differs from Squire and Knowlton's distinction between declarative and non-declarative knowledge (e.g., Ashby et al. 1998: 442). Learning about a category is implicit if learners are not aware of the content of their acquired knowledge, although they might be aware that they acquired some knowledge. Under this definition, my knowledge about what distinguishes Bourdelle's sculptures from Rodin's sculptures has been implicitly acquired. I know that I acquired some knowledge about what distinguishes the former from the latter, but I am not aware of the content of this knowledge, and I am unable to verbalize it. Ashby and colleagues rightly note that this narrower definition is needed to study experimentally implicit learning. In experiments that study implicit learning, subjects are asked to learn to classify new stimuli into categories. Because their performances improve, subjects realize that they are learning something, although they are unable to articulate what they are learning.

Ashby and colleagues have developed a sophisticated multi-process theory of category learning, that is, a theory of how we learn to classify category members when we are presented with items, attempt to classify them, and (sometimes) receive some positive or negative feedback about the correctness of our classification decisions (more on category learning in chapter 6). Ashby and colleagues' theory is called "COVIS" for COmpetition between Verbal and Implicit Systems (e.g., Ashby et al. 1998; Ashby and Waldron 2000). It involves several neurobiological and formal models of the processes involved in category learning. Ashby and colleagues distinguish two main processes, although they recognize that there may be others. A first learning process is involved in the explicit acquisition of knowledge about categories. According to Ashby and colleagues, this process is responsible for our capacity to learn simple verbalizable rules about category membership. This process is supposed to involve the prefrontal cortex and the anterior cingulate, which is implicated in focusing our attention on candidate rules, and the head of the basal ganglia, which is implicated in switching between candidate rules. The second process is supposed to be responsible for our capacity to acquire implicitly some associative knowledge between simple behavioral responses, including linguistic responses, and the perception of category members. Ashby and colleagues propose that this implicit process of category learning leads to the acquisition of some kind of procedural knowledge, similar to the knowledge that underlies our physical skills. This process involves the tail

---

[11] For a more recent review, see Ashby and Valentin 2005; Ashby and Ennis 2006.

of the caudate nucleus in the basal ganglia, which is implicated in associating motor responses in the premotor cortex with activations in the visual cortex, such as the inferotemporal cortex.

Thus, contra the Unified View of Cognition, Ashby and colleagues propose a dual-process theory of category learning. As we saw in section 5.1.4, we first want to know in which conditions these two processes are triggered (issue A). Ashby and colleagues distinguish two types of situation. They hold that the process of implicit category learning is triggered only when the learner is given some feedback about whether she is correctly learning to categorize the stimuli. Thus, when there is no feedback, only the process of explicit learning is triggered. By contrast, when the learner is given some feedback about her performances, Ashby and colleagues propose that the two processes of category learning are simultaneously involved when people learn to categorize the stimuli into their correct category.

As we also saw in section 5.1.4, the second thing we want to know is what happens to the outputs of the two processes of category learning when these are triggered simultaneously (issue B). Ashby and colleagues propose that they are not integrated. When, during or after learning, the two processes result in two different categorization judgments, "the system producing the strongest response wins out" (Ashby et al. 1998: 452; see also the formal model p. 460). The strength of an output measures the degree of confidence that characterizes this output. If a stimulus is categorized as being clearly a member by one of the two processes, this process produces a strong output. If a stimulus is categorized as an ambiguous category member by one of the two processes, this process produces a weak output. Ashby and colleagues (1998) recognize that there is little neurobiological evidence for this hypothesis, but they speculate that lateral inhibition in the striatum might be involved. The idea is that when the head of the caudate nucleus is more strongly activated than the tail of the nucleus, it inhibits the tail—and vice-versa.

What determines the strength of the outputs of each system? Ashby and colleagues (1998) propose that the system of explicit learning dominates early learning, in that, at the beginning of a learning episode, the categorization decisions made by the learner are likely to correspond to its outputs. We are then supposed to learn which of the two systems is the most accurate, given the specifics of the categories. Learning leads to some tasks loading more heavily on the most accurate system. That is, after learning, the categorization decisions made by the organism in these tasks are likely to correspond to the outputs of the most accurate system. Ashby and Waldron summarize this proposal as follows: "The theory postulates separate, competing explicit and implicit category-learning systems that are simultaneously active at all times. Depending on the relationship between the categories to be learned, however, one system may dominate the other" (2000: 12). Categories that can be defined by what Ashby and colleagues call an "explicit rule" end up loading on the explicit process of category learning, while categories that cannot be so defined end up loading on the implicit process of category learning. A category is defined by an explicit rule if category membership is defined by the possession of a few properties that are easily verbalized:

> More important, a number of studies have found qualitative differences in the way people learn categories that are best separated by an explicit rule (hereafter called explicit tasks) as opposed to how they learn categories that cannot be separated successfully by a salient explicit rule (i.e., implicit tasks). First, learning is often sudden (e.g., insightful) in explicit categorization tasks and gradual (i.e., incremental) in implicit tasks. Second, in the absence of trial-by-trial feedback, people can learn some explicit categorization rules, but there is no evidence that it is possible to learn implicit rules without feedback. (Ashby and Waldron 2000: 12)

Ashby and colleagues' theory is an exemplary psychological theory. It integrates different types of data—behavioral measures, neuropathological findings, brain images, and neurobiological data. It also includes several models of the hypothesized processes, including a neurobiological model and several computational models. It is also an exemplary multi-process theory. The hypothesized processes of category learning are specified in detail and so is the relation between these processes. Indeed, Ashby and colleagues have mathematically characterized this relation. As a result, clear predictions can be derived from this multi-process theory. In these respects, it should be emulated by multi-process theorists.

Unfortunately, as a theory of concept learning, Ashby and colleagues' theory is not without problems. First, the distinction drawn between the two processes of category learning is somewhat unclear. To draw this distinction, Ashby and colleagues appeal to four different distinctions: verbal vs. non-verbal, explicit vs. implicit, unidimensional vs. multidimensional, and rule-based vs. similarity-based. Category learning is verbal if and only if subjects are able to verbalize how they classify the stimuli during and after learning. If subjects follow a rule that the experimenter, but not the subjects, is able to verbalize, learning does not count as verbal. Ashby and colleagues propose that subjects can verbalize how they classify stimuli, when they pick out properties that can be attended selectively (analyzable properties) and that are denoted by words in their vocabularies. Category learning is explicit if and only if the learner is aware of the grounds by which she distinguishes category members from other stimuli. A sufficient, but not necessary, condition is that subjects be able to articulate the principles they use to classify stimuli. For instance, subjects might be aware of the learned rule "Members of category A are red." Category learning is unidimensional if and only if subjects use a single property (or having a value superior to a given criterion on a single dimension) to distinguish category members from other stimuli. For example, learners might distinguish category members from other stimuli because category members are triangular. Category learning involves a rule if and only if it involves finding necessary and sufficient conditions of membership in the relevant categories.

The problem is that these distinctions need not be aligned. The rule "Members of category A are red and triangular" is multidimensional, but subjects might be aware of this rule and might be able to verbalize it. Some principles of classification might be unidimensional, but might not be easily verbalized by subjects, because the relevant property is not denoted by any word in the subjects' vocabulary or because it is not salient.

Ashby and colleagues are aware of this issue. However, they "argue that rules of this type ["Members of category A are red and triangular"], although possible to verbalize, have very low saliency. As a result, the verbal categorization system will almost never spontaneously select such a rule. In fact, in this article, [they] assume that rules of this type are never selected by the verbal system" (1998: 446).

This reply is unconvincing. Experiments on category learning before the development of the prototype approach to concepts show that people are able to learn explicitly some rules of category membership defined by the conjunction of properties (e.g., Conant and Trabasso 1964). If subjects were unlikely to do so in the experiments discussed by Ashby and colleagues (1998), this might be due to the complexity of the multidimensional rules that they would have had to learn rather than to their multidimensionality per se. Moreover, the real-world concepts that are the best candidates for having been learned by the process of explicit category learning, such as UNCLE or BACHELOR, are all multidimensional.

Let us turn to the second problem. One might question whether the two main systems identified by Ashby and colleagues have any relevance to the acquisition of knowledge about categories outside the lab. It is unclear whether any real-world concept is a unidimensional, easily verbalized rule. This is certainly not the case of the concepts DOG, TABLE, or LOVE AFFAIR. One might thus suspect that the neural network involving the prefrontal cortex, the anterior cingulate, and the head of the caudate nucleus is not involved in acquiring concepts of real-world categories, although it is certainly involved in acquiring some knowledge about the artificial categories used in Ashby and colleagues' experiments.

It is also dubious whether any concept of real-world categories consists of associative links between specific behaviors, including verbal responses, and the perception of the members of these categories. The members of a few categories might trigger some phobic, stereotypical behavioral reactions. I, for one, tend to smash spiders (that is, small spiders). But, for most categories, it is unclear what the behavioral reaction associated with the perception of their members is supposed to be. The best candidate might be a linguistic reaction—for instance, uttering a word. This is reminiscent of behaviorists' idea that learning a concept consists of associating a verbal response to the perception of the members of the denoted category (Machery 2007b). This is not a very promising idea, however. People do not go around naming things, showing that categorization does not consist in producing a verbal behavior. And, in many cultures, children are not invited to name category members, showing that category learning does not consist in associating a verbal behavior with the perception of category members. To conclude, it seems that Ashby and colleagues are engaged in a thorough study of the psychology of category learning in experimental tasks, not in the real world.

5.2.2 Dual-Process Theories of Cognition

The second type of multi-process theory considered in section 5.2 are the dual-process theories, developed, among others, by psychologists Jonathan Evans (Evans and Over 1996), Steven Sloman (Sloman 1996), Keith Stanovich (e.g., Stanovich 1999; Stanovich and West 2000), Timothy Wilson (2002), and Daniel Kahneman (Kahneman and Frederick 2002). For the sake of simplicity, I focus on Stanovich's distinction between System 1 and System 2 (for a comparison of several dual-process theories, see Stanovich and West 2000: 659).

System 1 refers to a set of automatic, typically unconscious, and computationally undemanding cognitive processes. Because they are computationally undemanding, Stanovich and West (2000: 658) view them as heuristics. Stanovich and West (2000, 2003) also propose that many of these processes are the product of evolution by natural selection. They are geared toward producing outcomes that have been fitness-conducive in the past, not toward producing rational behavior nor adaptive behavior in present environments. By contrast, System 2 consists of conscious, intentionally triggered, computationally demanding cognitive processes:

> System 2 conjoins the various characteristics that have been viewed as typifying controlled processing. System 2 encompasses the processes of analytic intelligence that have traditionally been studied by information processing theorists trying to uncover the computational components underlying intelligence. (Stanovich and West 2000: 658)

It is the source of non-stereotypical behavior and cognitive performances. System 2 is often believed to solve problems by following formal rules, such as reasoning rules derived from logic or probability theory.[12]

Stanovich's dual-process theory stands in contrast to the Unified Theory of Cognition. System 1 and System 2 can be brought to bear on the same tasks, for instance, on tasks involving our capacity to reason deductively. As a result, this theory asserts that many cognitive competences are underwritten by several processes.

Although Stanovich characterizes his two systems very sketchily, he has a few things to say about their organization (see issue A in section

---

[12] Haidt (2001) and Wilson (2002) have developed a rather different picture of System 2. This system is supposed to provide conscious justifications or explications, which might be erroneous, of the outputs produced by the automatic processes that compose System 1.

5.1.4). According to Stanovich, the processes that constitute System 1 are automatically triggered. Thus, whenever we have to solve a problem, the relevant process in System 1 is triggered. For instance, Stanovich and West (2000: 659) claim that in the deontic version of the Wason Selection Task, the process that yields the answer P and not-Q belongs to System 1 and is automatically triggered (be it the cheater detection module, as Cosmides [1989] would have it, or a pragmatic schema, as Cheng and Holyoak [1985] have proposed). This explains why most subjects give this pattern of answers in deontic versions of the Wason Selection Task. By contrast, if I understand Stanovich correctly, System 2 is intentionally triggered. Its triggering is "controlled," in contrast to being "automatic." That is, when we have to solve a problem, the relevant process in System 2 might or might not be triggered, depending on people's intentional control. For example, the knowledge of the truth-conditions of indicative conditionals is supposed to belong to System 2 and, thus, to be only intentionally used. This explains why few subjects give the pattern of answers P and not-Q in non-deontic versions of the Wason Selection Task. Unfortunately, Stanovich says little about what determines the intentional triggering of the processes that constitute System 2. He seems to contend that people's disposition to rely on System 2 is a function of their general intelligence.

When both kinds of process are simultaneously triggered, what happens to their outputs (see issue B in section 5.1.4)? The question is pressing because, following Evans (Evans and Over 1996), Stanovich claims that these systems can produce conflicting outputs. For instance, they propose that in the non-deontic versions of the Wason Selection Task, System 1 produces the P and Q answer or the P answer, while System 2 produces the P and not-Q answer. Unfortunately, Stanovich has very little to say about what happens to the outputs of the System 1 and System 2 processes when these are simultaneously triggered. The view that is most in keeping with his approach would be along the following lines. When a process in System 2 is intentionally triggered, the output of the relevant process in System 1 is overridden by the output of the System 2 process:

> One of the functions of System 2 is to serve as an override system ... for some of the automatic and obligatory computational results provided by System 1. This override function might only be needed in a tiny minority of information processing situations (in most cases, the two Systems will interact in concert), but they may be unusually important ones. (Stanovich and West 2000: 662)

Like many dual-process theories, Stanovich's dual-process theory is somewhat unsatisfying. The cognitive processes that are assumed to constitute System 1 and System 2 are not described in any detail. Their triggering conditions and the nature of the integrative or non-integrative mechanisms are left pretty much unspecified. As a result, it is difficult to derive any clear predictions from his theory, which is better suited to provide post-hoc explanations. Thus, in spite of the real interest of

Stanovich's work, his dual-process theory illustrates the pitfalls to be avoided in building a multi-process theory.

5.2.3 A Toolbox of Simple Heuristics

The last multi-process theory considered in this section is the "fast and frugal heuristics" research program developed by Gerd Gigerenzer, Peter Todd, and their colleagues (Gigerenzer, Todd, and the ABC Research Group 1999).[13] These psychologists study the rules that underlie our judgments, inferences, and choices. A first working hypothesis is that these rules, called "heuristics," are simple. Their simplicity partly results from their frugality: they do not take into account all the cues that could be relevant for making a judgment or taking a decision. On the contrary, these rules often use a limited number of cues, sometimes a single cue (in which case they are called "one-reason decision rules"). As an example of a simple and frugal process, consider the recognition heuristic (Gigerenzer and Goldstein 1996; Goldstein and Gigerenzer 2002). It is a decision rule that applies to choices between two (or more) options. These options are ranked according to some criterion, and people have to find the option that has the highest value or the lowest value with respect to this criterion. For choices among two options, the heuristic can be described as follows: "Recognition heuristic: If one of two objects is recognized and the other is not, then infer that the recognized object has the higher value with respect to the criterion" (Goldstein and Gigerenzer 2002: 76). Suppose that a European has to decide whether San Antonio or San Diego has the larger population. San Antonio and San Diego are the two options, and city size is the criterion. Suppose also that she only recognizes San Diego. If she were to apply the recognition heuristic, she would conclude that San Diego is bigger than San Antonio. And her judgment would be correct. The recognition heuristic is a simple and frugal one-reason decision rule, since it takes into account a single cue—whether or not the options (e.g., San Diego or San Antonio) are recognized.

A second working hypothesis is that these rules are paired with specific environments in which they perform as well, and sometimes better, than more complex rules. These rules are said to be ecologically rational in these environments. Consider again the recognition heuristic. It works well when recognition is correlated with the criterion. For German subjects, but not for American subjects, there is a correlation between the recognition of an American city and its size. Thus, the recognition heuristic is ecologically rational for German subjects when they are asked to decide which of two American cities is the larger.

A third working hypothesis, the most relevant one for present purposes, is that we possess numerous rules for making judgments, for

---

[13] See also Gigerenzer and Goldstein 1996; Todd and Gigerenzer 2000.

making choices, and for drawing inferences. For instance, proponents of the fast and frugal heuristics research program propose that besides the recognition heuristics, there are other heuristics that can be used to decide which of two (or more) options has the highest value with respect to a criterion, for instance, which of two cities has the larger population. Take-the-Best is one of them. Take-the-Best is supposed to be used to choose between two options that are ranked with respect to a criterion on the basis of cues that are more or less valid. The validity of a cue is defined as the relative frequency with which options with a positive cue have a higher value with respect to the criterion than options with a negative cue. Take-the-Best is a one-reason decision rule. We look for the most valid cue that discriminates between the two options, and we decide on the basis of this cue, neglecting thereby less valid cues. For example, Take-the-Best may be used to decide whether Bonn or Dresden has the larger population. The fact that a city has a soccer team in the Bundesliga is a cue for making this decision. The validity of this cue is defined as the relative frequency with which cities with a soccer team in the Bundesliga are larger than cities without a soccer team in the Bundesliga. The validity of this cue is imperfect because it happens that the smaller of two cities has a soccer team in the Bundesliga while the larger does not. If having a soccer team is the most valid cue, and if Bonn has a soccer team while Dresden does not, we decide that Bonn has the larger population. If both Bonn and Dresden have a team in the Bundesliga or if none does, we move to the next cue. Take-the-Best is ecologically rational in many environments, for instance, in environments where the cues are not compensatory. Cues are not compensatory when the validity of the most valid cue is higher than the added validities of the other cues, the validity of the second cue is higher than the added validities of the remaining cues, and so on. If Take-the-Best is used in such an environment, it is optimal despite its simplicity. Taking into account other cues would not improve people's performances. In other environments, Take-the-Best might not be optimal, but it can result in satisfactory results. For example, if there are only a few cues, Take-the-Best often performs as well as decision rules that take into account all the possible cues.

As Gigerenzer, Todd, and their colleagues put it, our cognitive processes form a toolbox of simple heuristics. Most psychologists assume that for a given task, such as pairwise comparison with respect to a criterion, we possess a single cognitive process. Gigerenzer, Todd, and their colleagues propose instead that in this task, we can use several heuristics. If we do not recognize one of the options, we might use the recognition heuristic. If we do recognize both options, we might use Take-the-Best or other heuristics in the toolbox. Thus, judgments under uncertainty might result from one of many cognitive processes. This challenges the Unified View of Cognition.

As we saw in section 5.1, proponents of multi-process theories need to answer two central issues—"When are the hypothesized processes triggered?" and "When several cognitive processes are simultaneously triggered, what happens to the outputs of these cognitive processes?" Gigerenzer and colleagues propose that in any given circumstance, a single heuristic is triggered. For example, in a given pairwise comparison, such as the size of German cities, it is assumed that either the recognition heuristic or Take-the-Best is triggered, but not both. Because the hypothesized heuristics are not triggered together, no mechanism is needed to produce a final output.

Since a single heuristic is assumed to be used in a given circumstance, one might want to know what determines which heuristic is used in which circumstance. Gigerenzer's emphasis on the ecological rationality of these heuristics makes this issue particularly pressing. Since these heuristics are supposed to be efficient in specific environments, one would like to know what ensures that they are typically, if not always, used in the appropriate environments. In some simple cases, the condition for the application of a given heuristic is simply not met. For instance, in a pairwise comparison, if both options are recognized, the recognition heuristic cannot be applied. Not all cases are so straightforward, however. For example, if Take-the-Best is to be a useful decision rule, it should not be used, even though it could, when there are numerous cues and when the cues are compensatory. Similarly, the recognition heuristic is not useful when recognition is not correlated with a high value with respect to the criterion. How do we decide to use a given heuristic in a given circumstance? This complex issue has yet to be solved (but see Todd and Dieckmann 2005; Rieskamp and Otto 2006).

Gigerenzer and colleagues' multi-process theory has numerous virtues. Models are clearly described and algorithmically specified. Simulations and behavioral experiments are used to provide evidence. In spite of these virtues, this type of theory is probably not appropriate for characterizing the use of concepts in the processes underwriting many competences. As we shall see in the next two chapters, evidence suggests that at least sometimes, we simultaneously use several processes instead of using a single process at a time, as Gigerenzer and colleagues would have it.

5.3 Conclusion

In this chapter, I have focused on the fourth tenet of the Heterogeneity Hypothesis: it is often the case that a given cognitive competence is underwritten by several cognitive processes, each of which uses a specific fundamental kind of concept. Theories that assume that a cognitive competence is underwritten by several processes are called "multi-process theories." This chapter has investigated the outline of such theories, which contrast with the default position in psychology and neuropsychology, the Unified View of Cognition.

6

Categorization and Concept Learning

In Chapter 4, I described three theoretical entities—prototypes, exemplars, and theories—and I proposed that the class of concepts includes these three entities. In Chapter 5, I contended that these theoretical entities are typically used in distinct processes. So far, no evidence has been given to support these claims. Chapters 6 and 7 fill this gap: I review the evidence that bears on the existence of these three theoretical entities and on the nature of the cognitive processes that use them. In this chapter, I focus on categorization and concept learning. I argue that the research on categorization and concept learning since the 1970s shows that the capacity to categorize and the capacity to learn concepts are both underwritten by several cognitive processes, each of which involves its own kind of concept—prototypes, exemplars, or theories. I call this proposal "the heterogeneity of categorization and of concept learning."

Two kinds of evidence are discussed in this chapter (see section 5.1.5). First, for each theoretical entity under consideration, there is a large body of experimental findings about categorization and concept learning that is well explained by means of this theoretical entity, but poorly explained by means of the others. Many findings about categorization are well explained by prototype-based theories of categorization, but poorly explained by exemplar-based and theory-based theories of categorization. Other findings are best explained, respectively, by exemplar-based and theory-based theories of categorization. This situation has led some leading psychologists to question the adequacy of the main paradigms of concepts. I propose a different conclusion. Different findings about categorization and concept learning are best explained by different theories of categorization and of concept learning because each of these two cognitive competences is underwritten by several cognitive processes.

What about the second type of evidence? As we saw in Chapter 5, some multi-process theories of categorization predict that subjects' performances will differ when the hypothesized categorization processes are supposed to produce conflicting outputs, by comparison to the situations where the hypothesized categorization processes are supposed to concur. This is evidence that the processes underwriting categorization are triggered simultaneously (rather than being triggered one at a time, in different conditions). I discuss some evidence that the cognitive processes that underwrite categorization sometimes yield conflicting outputs.

In section 6.1, I explain what categorization and concept learning are. In section 6.2, I consider some key aspects of the methodology used in the psychology of categorization and concept learning. In sections 6.3 to 6.5, I examine the evidence for the heterogeneity of categorization and concept learning. I review the findings that are best explained if one assumes that prototypes (section 6.3), exemplars (section 6.4), and theories (section 6.5) exist. Finally, in section 6.6, I discuss the organization of the hypothesized categorization processes and of the hypothesized processes of concept learning.

6.1 *Categorization and Concept Learning*

Categorization and concept learning are the two sides of the same psychological phenomenon—our disposition to put individual objects into equivalence classes. As psychologists of categorization are keen to point out, this is an important phenomenon.[1] If we were unable to create equivalence classes, each object would be unique (provided, of course, that the capacity to treat objects as individuals does not depend on the capacity to create equivalence classes). We would be unable to generalize our knowledge from one individual to the other. Our knowledge would only be about individuals, rather than about categories, and our mind would be overwhelmed by the quantity of information we would have to deal with. In this section, I characterize these two competences in more detail.

6.1.1 *What Is Categorization?*

It is hard to overestimate the importance of categorization in the experimental psychology of concepts. Most theories of concepts have been closely associated with theories of categorization. Theories of concepts have also been constantly tested in categorization tasks, and their evidential value has been measured according to their capacity to account for

---

[1] See, e.g., Mervis and Rosch 1981; Smith and Medin 1981: 1.

subjects' categorization performances in controlled experiments. Categorization is thus a key cognitive competence for evaluating the Heterogeneity Hypothesis.

Although psychologists rarely explain what categorization is, this notion can be characterized as follows.[2] The capacity to categorize is the capacity to produce judgments that an item belongs to a class, for example, the judgment that Fido is a dog—what I call "membership judgments." Judgments are occurrent mental states, which can, but need not, be expressed linguistically. Membership judgments are about distal stimuli—objects, events, or substances—in contrast to the proximal stimuli of our perceptual systems—the excitation of the cones and rods, for example. Psychologists agree that membership judgments are typically the inputs to other cognitive processes, particularly to the processes that underlie induction. Once we have classified an object as a dog, we typically infer some of its properties, including its likely behavior. Thus, Smith and Medin write, "Concepts also allow us to go beyond the information given; for once we have assigned an entity to a class on the basis of its perceptible attributes, we can then infer some of its nonperceptible attributes" (1981: 1; see also Hampton and Dubois 1993: 13).

Surprisingly, categorization experiments often ask subjects to make a different type of judgment—inclusion judgments, that is, judgments that a class is included in another (e.g., Rosch and Mervis 1975: experiment 2). The judgments that dogs are mammals and that poodles are dogs illustrate this second type of judgment.

One might wonder why the capacity to make membership judgments and the capacities to make inclusion judgments are viewed as a single capacity —namely, categorization. After all, although these two types of judgment are expressed similarly in many languages, they could be psychologically different. The reason is that most psychologists believe that membership and inclusion judgments are produced by a single cognitive process, as is shown by the fact that the categorization models developed by psychologists are meant to account for both types of judgment. For this reason, they conclude that the capacity to make membership judgments and the capacity to make inclusion judgments constitute a single cognitive competence (on how to individuate cognitive competences, see section 5.1).

What are the inputs of the process(es) underwriting categorization? To answer this question, we can examine the stimuli used in experiments on categorization because these experiments would be pointless if it were not assumed that the experimental stimuli are to some extent similar to the everyday inputs of the categorization process(es).

The diversity of the stimuli used in categorization experiments is striking. Many experiments rely on artificial objects (i.e., meaningless

---

[2] As noted in chapter 4, I focus for the most part on the concepts of categories of physical objects. Nonetheless, the discussion in this chapter and in the next one applies, *mutatis mutandis*, to the concepts of substances, events, and so on.

items such as abstract figures or strings of letters) that are visually presented. Thus, in experiments 5 and 6 of their famous article (1975), Rosch and Mervis used strings of letters and numbers as stimuli (e.g., "HPNWD", "R7QUM", etc.).

These artificial objects are often characterized only by their perceptual properties. Medin and Schaffer's (1978) stimuli consisted of forms varying along four binary dimensions, shape (triangle or circle), size (small or large), color (red or green), and position (centered on the right side or on the left side of a card). Other experiments rely on unfamiliar, but meaningful objects that are presented visually, such as computer-generated pictures of fictional creatures. Some experiments also rely on familiar objects that are also presented visually. For example, Malt and colleagues (1999) used photos of bottles and containers as stimuli.

In other experiments, subjects are presented with verbal descriptions of objects. Murphy and Allopenna (1994) tested the acquisition of the concepts of two categories of vehicles. The members of both categories were verbally described. For instance, the descriptions of the members of category 1 were created by selecting some of the following properties, *made in Africa, lightly insulated, green, drives in jungle, has wheels*, and by adding a few filler properties.[3] Verbal descriptions in categorization experiments vary in length and content.

Finally, when subjects are asked to produce inclusion judgments, they are often merely presented with the name of the class to be categorized. For instance, they might be shown on a computer screen or they might be told the word "pigeon" when they have to judge that pigeons are birds (e.g., Rosch and Mervis 1975). These names are assumed to trigger the retrieval of the relevant concepts—PIGEON in the present case—from long-term memory.

It is clear that for psychologists, the inputs of the process(es) of categorization do not belong to any specific modality, even though many categorization experiments have used visual stimuli. Moreover, inputs do not have to be perceptual, since linguistic descriptions and even single words are also used in categorization experiments. Thus, our categorization processes are assumed not to take the proximal stimuli of our perceptual systems, but rather representations of distal stimuli, as inputs. To put it differently, according to most psychologists, the inputs of the process (es) of categorization consist of the representations that are produced by our perceptual systems when we perceive or by our linguistic systems when we understand sentences or words. Figure 6.1 summarizes this idea.

Categorization should be clearly distinguished from other cognitive competences, such as discrimination and rote learning. Discrimination consists of deciding whether two stimuli, for instance, two colored patches or two sounds, are identical or different. It does not involve judging that an object belongs to a class. Rote learning consists of learning the

---

[3] See also, e.g., Keil 1989; Rips 1989; Smith and Sloman 1994.

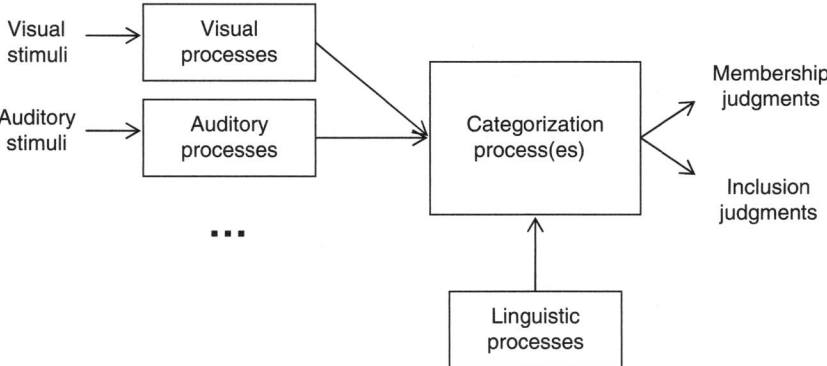

Figure 6.1 Inputs and Outputs of the Categorization Process(es)

association between each member of a category and its category. Rote learning does not allow any membership judgment about new objects.

To summarize, categorization is the capacity to produce membership judgments and inclusion judgments. The inputs of the categorization process(es) are either the outputs of our perceptual systems (perceptual representations) or of our linguistic systems. The psychology of categorization sets out to characterize these processes.

Categorization decisions take many different forms. We categorize different kinds of entities, from three-dimensional objects to substances to events. Categorization decisions also range from being quasi-instantaneous (e.g., Thorpe, Delorme, and VanRullen 2001) to being protracted. Some categorization decisions are stimuli-driven, while others are under our intentional control. The confidence associated with the resulting judgments and the goal of our categorization decisions also vary. We sometimes categorize in order to increase our knowledge, while in other occasions, we categorize during the course of an action.

Although psychologists interested in categorization do not necessarily assume that all categorization judgments are produced by a single cognitive process, they have typically assumed that most of them result from a single process. They account for the diversity of categorization judgments by assuming that many factors, including attention and intentional control, affect the functioning of this process rather than by proposing that categorization judgments result from several distinct cognitive processes.

6.1.2 What Is Concept Learning?

Concept learning, widely defined, is the capacity to acquire concepts.[4] Concept learning, narrowly defined, is the capacity to acquire concepts from

---

[4] I have nothing to say about the argument that primitive concepts cannot be learned (Fodor 1981, 1998). As explained in chapters 1 and 2, "concept" is used differently by philosophers such as Fodor and by cognitive psychologists. Concepts in psychology are bodies of

encountering some members of their extension. For instance, traveling abroad, one could acquire the concept of a new type of fruit from encountering this fruit in grocery stores. This would be an example of concept learning narrowly defined. By contrast, one could acquire the concept of this fruit by being told about it. This would be an example of concept learning widely defined.

The distinction between concept learning widely and narrowly defined is required because the study of what has been called "concept learning," "category learning," or "concept abstraction" in experimental psychology and, more recently, in neuropsychology has focused almost exclusively on the acquisition of concepts from encountering category members. Thus, when Clark Hull attempts to describe how a concept is typically learned in an early work on concept learning, he describes a child encountering some members of its extension:

> A young child finds himself in a certain situation ... and hears it called 'dog.' After an indeterminate intervening period he finds himself in a somewhat different situation, and hears that called 'dog.' ... Thus, the process continues. The 'dog' experiences appear at irregular intervals. The appearances are thus unanticipated. They appear with no obvious label as to their essential nature. This precipitates at each new appearance a more or less acute problem as to the proper reaction. ... Meanwhile the intervals between the 'dog' experiences are filled with all sorts of other absorbing experiences which are contributing to the formation of other concepts. At length the time arrives when the child has a 'meaning' for the word dog. Upon examination this meaning is found to be actually a characteristic more or less common to all dogs and not common to cats, dolls and 'teddy bears.' But to the child the process of arriving at this meaning or concept has been largely unconscious. (Hull 1920: 5–6)

To distinguish the two meanings of the expression "concept learning," I will call widely conceived concept learning "concept acquisition," and I will reserve the expression "concept learning" for narrowly conceived concept learning. So defined, concept learning is the capacity to form the concept of a class of entities from encountering some members of this class (figure 6.2).

Throughout the twentieth century, a specific experimental paradigm, which I have called "the concept-learning design," has been the cornerstone of the experimental study of concept learning (Machery 2007b).[5] The concept-learning design includes a learning phase. During this phase, subjects are presented with some members of the category(ies) whose concept (s) have to be learned (what are called the "learning items" or "old items"). The task is to find out what distinguishes category members from those items that do not belong to the category. Several presentation conditions have

---

knowledge used in the processes underlying the higher cognitive competences, not capacities to think about classes, properties, and so on. Experimental studies of concept learning bear on the former, not the latter. By contrast, Fodor's argument bears on the latter, not the former.

[5] See, for instance, Fisher 1916; Hull 1920; Bruner, Goodnow, and Austin 1956; Rosch and Mervis 1975; Medin and Schaffer 1978; Nosofsky 1986.

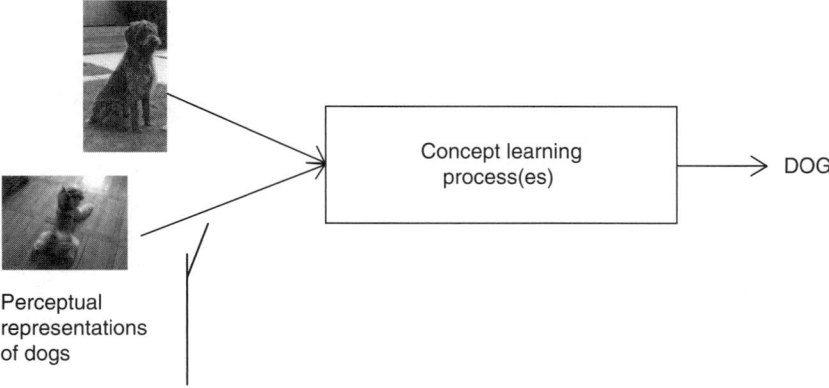

Figure 6.2 Inputs and Outputs of the Concept-Learning Process(es)

been used. In some experiments, subjects have to learn the concept of a single category, while in others, subjects have to learn the concepts of several categories. When a single category is used, negative evidence (i.e., items that do not belong to the relevant category) can be presented. Feedback is given in some experiments, but not in others. Learning items can be presented a fixed number of times or up to a perfect performance. They can also be presented successively or simultaneously. If they are presented successively, subjects can control the transition between items or the transition can be automatic. Usually, some properties of the learning phase are measured as dependent measures. Rate of learning is the most common dependent measure. It can be operationalized in various ways, for instance, as the time needed to find out what characterizes a category.

Often, a test phase follows the learning phase. The test phase consists of ascribing the learning items or some new items (also called "test items" or "transfer items") to the category(ies) that were presented during the learning phase. Various dependent measures can be measured. The most common are reaction time and the number of errors. Psychologists use the word "transfer" to refer to the capacity to use the knowledge gained in the learning phase to categorize the new items presented in the test phase.

Since Hull (1920), concept learning has been operationalized in the same way in the concept-learning design (Machery 2007b). While introspective psychologists, such as Fisher (1916), operationalized concept learning by reference to subjects' explicit knowledge of the membership conditions in the relevant category(ies), Hull and most psychologists after him have operationalized this notion by reference to subjects' categorization performances: subjects are said to have learned the concept under consideration if and only if they are able to categorize correctly the learning items or a prespecified list of new items. Divergence from perfect categorization measures the imperfection of concept learning. The modification of the operationalization of concept learning at the end of the 1910s probably resulted from the increasing role of behavioral measures in the various fields of psychology as well as from a growing distrust toward introspection at the beginning of the twentieth century.

I emphasized above that categorization decisions take many different forms. The same is true of concept acquisition and concept learning proper. Concept acquisition can be supervised, for instance, when parents draw distinctions for their children. But it need not be: children seem to acquire many concepts without supervision. Concept acquisition can result from encountering the members of some category (concept learning proper), but it also often results from a mere linguistic description of the category, for instance, when one learns the meaning of a new word in a dictionary. Concept acquisition takes place at different ages—from childhood to adulthood. The circumstances of acquisition vary dramatically across these ages. The time course of concept acquisition also varies. Reading the definition of a new word in a dictionary takes a couple of seconds. There is also some evidence that children acquire some concepts on the first exposure to the members of their extension (Carey and Bartlett 1978; see the discussion in Bloom 2000). On the other hand, the acquisition of some technical concepts, for example, of mathematical concepts, may take months, if not years.

Psychologists are not committed to the claim that all these forms of concept acquisition are underwritten by a single cognitive process. What they seem typically committed to is that the acquisition of a concept from encountering the members of a given category—concept learning—is underwritten by a single cognitive process (see, e.g., Nosofsky and Zaki 1998; Nosofsky and Johansen 2000).

6.2 Studying Categorization and Concept Learning

In this section, I discuss critically the methodology of the experimental psychology of categorization and concept learning.

6.2.1 Artificial Categories

As explained in section 6.1, categorization and concept learning in psychology and neuropsychology are not supposed to be low-level visual processes. The processes underlying these two cognitive competences are supposed to involve representations of distal objects. Their outputs—namely, learned concepts or membership and inclusion judgments—are assumed to feed into other higher cognitive processes. For this reason, the experimental study of these two competences should satisfy a first constraint:

1. Experiments should be designed in such a way as to tap into higher cognitive competences.

A very different constraint on experimental designs derives from the need to control for the variables that affect concept learning and categorization. Subjects come to the experimental settings with a large number of concepts. Acquaintance with specific concepts varies across subjects. Formula 1 fans are presumably better acquainted with cars than National Geographic aficionados. Formula 1 fans' categorization performances would differ from National Geographic aficionados' performances if the experimental tasks were to involve concepts of cars. Although random assignment could probably control for this factor, it may be harder to control for other related factors. The concepts that subjects possess are likely to affect categorization and concept learning if these concepts are related to the concepts involved in the experiments. To give a toy example, suppose that in an experiment on category learning, subjects are asked to learn the concepts of subspecies of dogs they were previously unfamiliar with. Subjects are likely to bring their concept of dog as well as their concepts of known subspecies of dogs, such as POODLE, to bear on the task. Random assignment will not control for this variable, for what is at issue is not a difference between subjects, but the fact that some concepts that are probably possessed by all subjects might affect the process of concept learning. To put it a bit differently, the issue consists of distinguishing the process of concept learning from the additional effects that known concepts have on concept learning. This is the second constraint:

2. Experiments on concept learning and categorization need to distinguish the properties of the processes involved in concept learning and in categorization from the effects of the concepts previously possessed by subjects.

A third constraint derives from the need to distinguish between the different theories of categorization and concept learning. In many conditions, these theories predict the same performance profiles. Thus, specific conditions need to be carefully designed so that different theories of concepts, together with the relevant theories of categorization and of concept learning, yield distinct predictions.

3. Experiments on concept learning and categorization need to distinguish between the competing theories.

Constraints 2 and 3 have led psychologists to rely on artificial categories—that is, to repeat, categories made of meaningless items, such as abstract figures or strings of letters (see section 4.3.2 on the notion of artificial category). Artificial categories can be specifically designed to test competing theories of concept learning. Moreover, since these categories are meaningless, experiments that involve these categories are not affected by the concepts previously possessed by subjects.

Numerous experiments on concept learning and categorization have used artificial categories. I illustrate this experimental strategy with the experimental design developed by Posner and Keele (1968, 1970). This design, sometimes called "the dot-distortion category task," has been extensively used in the psychology of concepts, including in recent studies, as well as in the neuropsychology of concepts.[6] The basic structure of the design follows the concept-learning design presented in section 6.1.2. The experiment consists of two phases, a learning phase and a test phase. In Posner and Keele's (1968) experiment, during the learning phase, subjects are presented with the members of four artificial categories and are asked to classify these members correctly. Feedback is given, and the learning phase is stopped when subjects have classified all the items correctly. In the test phase of Posner and Keele's (1968) experiment, subjects are presented with new items. They are asked to categorize them in the categories introduced during the learning phase. The originality of Posner and Keele's design comes from the fact that the stimuli consist of patterns of points (figure 6.3). These patterns of points are obtained by systematically deforming four original patterns of points. Since these deformations are random, the original patterns constitute the most typical members of the four categories used in Posner and Keele's experiments.

For present purposes, what matters is the nature of the stimuli used in Posner and Keele's experiment and in subsequent experiments. These stimuli are meaningless entities that are only characterized by their perceptual properties. This enables psychologists to satisfy Constraints 2 and 3. Known concepts are unlikely to affect the manner in which subjects learn the representations of categories of patterns of points (Constraint 2). Moreover, categories made of patterns of points can be so designed that the different models of concept learning and of categorization make different predictions (Constraint 3). However, the cost is obvious. It is unclear whether experiments that rely on the experimental design created by Posner and Keele have much to say about higher cognition. That is, it is unclear whether they satisfy Constraint 1. More generally, artificial categories enable psychologists to satisfy Constraints 2 and 3, but at the cost of failing to satisfy Constraint 1. This problem looms large in the psychology of concept learning and categorization.

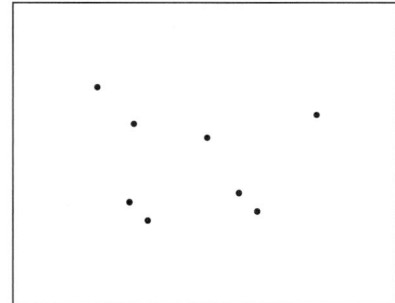

Figure 6.3 Kind of Stimuli Used in the Dot-Distortion Category Task

---

[6] See, e.g., Knowlton and Squire 1993; Squire and Knowlton 1995; Palmeri and Flanery 1999; Smith and Minda 2001; Smith 2002.

It could be replied that experiments on concept learning and categorization that involve artificial categories are not supposed to test hypotheses about higher cognitive competences (e.g., Ashby and Maddox 2005: 151). Instead, these experiments could be supposed to bear on the nature of low-level visual processes. However, this reply is problematic. Most experiments on categorization and concept learning have been designed to test theories of concepts—for instance, to provide evidence for and against prototype theories and exemplar theories. To illustrate, Hampton (1979, 1981) takes Rosch and Mervis's (1975) experiments, including their experiments involving artificial stimuli (experiments 5 and 6), to bear on the nature of lexical concepts, such as DOG and SCIENCE. Similarly, in the abstract of an experiment using Posner and Keele's experimental design, Squire and Knowlton write, "A fundamental question about memory and cognition concerns how information is acquired about categories and concepts as the result of encounters with specific instances" (1995: 12470).

Thus, the issue remains: what are we to conclude from the tension between Constraint 1, on the one hand, and Constraints 2 and 3, on the other? Particularly, are the experiments relying on artificial stimuli of any use for studying higher cognitive competences? Several psychologists committed to the theory paradigm have answered negatively to this second question. These psychologists often disagree with the idea that experiments on concept learning should eliminate the effects of subjects' previously possessed concepts (Murphy and Medin 1985; Ahn and Luhmann 2004). For being already in possession of some concepts is part and parcel of any real-world situation of concept learning. Moreover, they have criticized the categorization experiments that rely on stimuli that are only characterized by perceptual properties, such as abstract forms or drawings. For categorization involves paying attention to numerous properties that are not perceptual, such as the causal properties of objects (e.g., Rehder 2003a, b; Gopnik et al. 2004). Typically, the categorization and concept-learning experiments run by proponents of the theory view of concepts do not rely on artificial categories. Rather, the categories used in these experiments often make sense to subjects: they are related to the categories subjects are acquainted with. In one of Wattenmaker and colleagues' (1986) experiments, three types of people were described to subjects. In Wisniewski and Medin (1994), subjects were shown drawings and were told that these drawing were made by different kinds of children (e.g., creative vs. non-creative children). Sometimes, subjects are given some causal information. For instance, in one of Nazzi and Gopnik's (2003) experiments, children are shown the interactions between two objects.

The worries about the use of artificial, perceptual stimuli in categorization and concept-learning experiments are justified. If the findings made with such stimuli were not congruent with the results of experiments involving other types of stimuli, one would probably conclude that these findings are experimental artifacts. However, the striking fact is that many findings made in experiments using artificial stimuli are replicated in experiments involving other types of stimuli. But, I emphasize, these replications are essential. Phenomena in categorization or concept-learning experiments involving artificial stimuli that are not replicated in other kinds of experiments are subject to caution.

6.2.2 Ecological Validity of Concept-Learning Experiments

Experiments on concept learning face an additional problem: the experimental set-ups are very different from the real-world circumstances of concept acquisition, for both adults and children.

We can, and sometimes do, acquire concepts from encountering some members of their extension. Consider the concept POSTMODERN ARCHITECTURE. If a friend of mine does not possess such a concept, I could certainly describe to her the typical properties of postmodern architecture. Or I could describe a famous postmodern building, such as Philip Johnson's AT&T Headquarters in New York or Charles Moore's Piazza d'Italia in New Orleans. Or I could briefly summarize the history of and main ideas behind postmodern architecture. But I could also open a book about the history of architecture in the twentieth century and show her several postmodern buildings as well as several buildings that are not postmodern. My friend might quickly identify what the main properties of postmodern buildings are or she might be impressed by one of these buildings and use it as a yardstick for postmodern architecture in general.

Nevertheless, concept-learning experiments are often very different from the real-world conditions in which we acquire concepts, even when we learn a concept from encountering some members of its extension. In many cultures, caregivers do not bother showing objects to children and telling them the names of these objects. When children are shown objects, it is rare that they are successively shown several members of the extension of the relevant concept. Rather, children (and adults) are shown a single object and they are told the name of the class this object belongs to. Children and adults are also rarely given negative evidence, and children and adults are not presented again and again with the same objects up to a perfect categorization of these objects.

Worries about the ecological validity of concept-learning experiments are not new. At the end of the second decade of the twentieth century, commenting on previous research on concept learning, Hull was already writing:

> It will be convenient at this point to consider the methods followed by the three experimenters who have attacked the problem of generalizing abstraction [Moore, Grünbaum, Fisher]. According to our preceding analysis, all of them fall considerably short of fulfilling the conditions for the evolution of concepts, as it usually takes place in ordinary life. (Hull 1920: 6)

Over the years, little has been done to improve the concept-learning design, and the ecological validity of most concept-learning experiments remains unclear. One might conclude that psychologists interested in concept learning have failed to study how people really acquire concepts. Rather, they have focused on how people solve some artificial tasks. I would like to resist this radical conclusion. More moderately, I propose that experimental psychologists have only studied one type of concept acquisition. Besides the processes underlying this type of concept acquisition, people probably have other processes for acquiring concepts. The moderate conclusion is plausible because, as noted above, we sometimes acquire concepts in situations that are similar to the set-ups of concept-learning experiments.

6.3 Evidence for the Existence of Prototypes

In this section, I review the evidence for the existence of prototypes and of prototype-based processes of categorization and of concept learning. Since the experimental study of categorization and concept learning is a huge field, it is impossible to review most experiments, results, and controversies in this field from the 1970s onward (for a good overview of the field, see Murphy 2002). Instead, I focus on the most striking findings.

6.3.1 Typicality Effects

The prototype approach to concepts, remember, proposes that concepts are bodies of statistical knowledge. In several versions of the prototype approach, a concept represents the typical properties of a category or, in other versions, the cue-valid properties of a category. When we decide whether an object belongs to a category C, we compare the representation of this object to the prototype of C, and we measure the similarity of this object to the prototype. Roughly, the likelihood that a target will be categorized as a C is a function of how many properties this target possesses among the typical (or cue-valid, etc.) properties that are represented by a prototype of C (see chapter 4 for further detail).

If this view of our cognitive processes is correct, people should judge that objects vary with respect to how much they instantiate the properties that are believed to be characteristic (i.e., typical or cue-valid) of a given category. This dimension has been called "typicality" or, sometimes, "prototypicality," "representativeness," or "goodness-of-example."[7] As Hampton and Dubois put it, "Where the exemplars of a category vary in how well they appear to fit the category, then they are said to vary in typicality" (1993: 14).[8] To illustrate, Tina Turner is a less typical

---

[7] The existence of this dimension is consistent with the classical approach to concepts. Proponents of this approach need not deny that we have some beliefs about the typical (or cue-valid, etc.) properties of a category. However, the classical approach did not predict that typicality would affect subjects' performances in a wide range of experimental tasks.

[8] In this quotation, "exemplar" means category member.

grandmother than my own grandmother. Typicality also characterizes subclasses with respect to their superclasses. Pigeons are a typical bird, while penguins are an atypical bird. Prototype theorists in the 1970s were the first to show that people distinguish objects with respect to their typicality, and they were the first to establish that typicality affects categorization and concept learning as well as other cognitive competences (for review, see Hampton 1993; Murphy 2002).

Psychologists have sometimes confused typicality and degree of membership. That is, the fact that people can evaluate how typical an object is with respect to a given class has been taken as evidence that people believe that objects belong more or less to categories.[9] For example, the fact that people judge that pigeons are a more typical bird than penguins has been taken as evidence that people believe that pigeons are birds to a fuller extent than penguins. The two ideas ought to be distinguished, however. It may be that for some categories, such as bullies, people believe in degree of membership (Osherson and Smith 1997). However, even if for other categories, people believe that membership is not graded, they could still judge that objects or subclasses vary with respect to their typicality. To illustrate, even if people believe that penguins and pigeons are equally birds, it still makes sense to judge that pigeons are more typical birds than penguins. Notice also that an item's probability of being categorized in a category C should not be confused with a degree of membership in C. Someone might not be sure that a weirdly shaped object is a chair. As a result, the probability that she categorizes this object as a chair might be less than one. At the same time, she might believe that all chairs are chairs to the same degree.

Typicality is usually measured by asking subjects to evaluate the typicality of objects by means of a scale (rankings are also sometimes used). For instance, in Armstrong and colleagues (1983), which follows Rosch (1975), subjects were given the following instructions:

> This study has to do with what we have in mind when we use words which refer to categories. Think of dogs. You all have some notion of what a 'real dog', a 'doggy dog' is. To me a retriever or a German Shepherd is a very doggy dog while a Pekinese is a less doggy dog. Notice that this kind of judgment has nothing to do with how well you like the thing. You may prefer to own a Pekinese without thinking that it is the breed that best represents what people mean by dogginess. On this form you are asked to judge how good an example of a category various instances of the category are. You are to rate how good an example of the category each member is on a 7 point scale. A 1 means that you feel the member is a very good example of your idea of what the category is. A 7 means you feel the member fits very poorly with your idea or image of the category (or is not a member at all). A 4 means you feel the member fits moderately well. Use the other numbers of the 7 point scale to indicate

---

[9] See, e.g., Hampton and Dubois 1993: 14 and the critical discussion in Armstrong, Gleitman, and Gleitman 1983.

intermediate judgments. Don't worry about why you feel that something is or isn't a good example of the category. And don't worry about whether it's just you or people in-general who feel that way. Just mark it the way you see it.

There is robust evidence that people have no difficulty evaluating the typicality of an object.[10] For instance, Rosch (1973) asked subjects to indicate how good an example of the category of fruits subclasses such as figs, apples, or olives were. People judged without difficulty that apples were a good example of fruits, while olives were a bad example of fruits. In the first studies, typicality evaluation was found to be substantially correlated across subjects (Rosch 1975; Hampton 1979; Armstrong, Gleitman, and Gleitman 1983). For example, Rosch (1975) used split-group correlation: she correlated the mean ratings between two randomly chosen halves of the subjects and found that for the categories used in her study, split-group correlation was above .97. Armstrong and colleagues (1983) replicated this finding. The within-subjects stability of typicality evaluation has however been questioned. Barsalou (1987) reports that subjects were given the same list of categories and instances one month apart. The categories were either ad hoc categories (see section 4.5) or "taxonomic categories," meaning probably categories that are denoted by an English word. The mean correlation for taxonomic categories was .82 (1987: 111). Unsurprisingly, the typicality judgments for highly typical and highly atypical items were stable. By contrast, the typicality judgments for those items that were not highly typical varied across occasions. Barsalou concludes, "In general these experiments show that there is substantial instability in the graded structures of particular subjects" (1987: 112). This conclusion is erroneous. In fact, 0.8 is already a high correlation. Moreover, as suggested by Barsalou himself, the correlation would even be higher without the items that are neither atypical nor typical. The right conclusion is that there is instability in our judgments about the typicality of some items, namely those items that are neither typical nor atypical. Consider the following analogy. Ask subjects to categorize items as heaps or not heaps on two occasions. It is likely that the correlation of categorization judgments across two occasions will not be much higher than .8. For, besides the items that are clearly heaps and the items that clearly not heaps, subjects will be presented with items whose membership in the class of heaps is indeterminate. The classification of these items as heaps might vary across the two occasions. But it would be a mistake to conclude that our judgments about whether something is a heap are in general unstable. Rather, some judgments about heaps are unstable.

As we saw, the typicality of an object is the extent to which this object instantiates the properties that are deemed to characterize a class. This predicts that the evaluation of an object's typicality with respect to a given

---

[10] See, e.g., Rosch 1973, 1975; Rosch and Mervis 1975; Hampton 1979, 1981; Armstrong, Gleitman, and Gleitman 1983; Smith et al. 1988.

category should be correlated with the number of properties this object possesses among the properties that are represented by the concept of this category. Evidence strongly supports this prediction. Hampton (1979) used property listing as a means to tap into the properties represented by the concepts of several natural categories (for discussion of the property-listing task, see section 4.2). The typicality of the target objects with respect to these categories was correlated to the number of properties these objects possessed. Using both artificial and natural categories, Rosch and Mervis (1975) have found similar results.

It is known that typicality evaluation—that is, subjects' judgments of typicality—is not only influenced by the extent to which an object instantiates the properties deemed to characterize a category. Barsalou (1985) has shown that other factors influence typicality evaluation—including frequency (the subjective estimate of how often an object has been encountered) and similarity with ideals (on ideals, see section 4.5). For this reason, the typicality of an object should not be confused with its evaluation on a given scale. Like any measure, typicality evaluation may be noisy. It may be affected by other variables besides the dimension it is supposed to measure.

Typicality is important because it affects many cognitive competences (Murphy 2002: ch. 2). Let us start with categorization. Typical objects and subclasses are categorized more quickly and more accurately than less typical objects and subclasses.[11] We are faster and more accurate at deciding that pigeons are birds than at deciding that penguins are birds. This has been well established in property verification tasks with verbal stimuli. In these tasks, subjects are presented with a sentence, such as "a robin is a bird," and have to decide whether the sentence is true. Lance Rips and colleagues (1973) found that typical category members are classified more quickly than atypical category members (see also Smith, Shoben, and Rips 1974): subjects respond more quickly to "a robin is a bird" than to "an ostrich is a bird." Similar results are obtained when the stimuli are presented visually, for instance, when subjects are shown a picture or a drawing of the object to be categorized, such as a drawing of a robin (Murphy and Brownell 1985). Similar findings are also found with artificial categories (Rosch and Mervis 1975: experiments 5 and 6).

Moreover, typicality with respect to a category predicts the likelihood of being considered a member of this category (Hampton 1979). A similar result has been found in linguistics. Labov (1973) has shown that in American English, artifacts are called "mug" or "bowl" to the extent that they are similar to a prototypical shape.

Typicality also affects concept learning. Using artificial stimuli, Posner and Keele (1968, 1970) have shown that following the acquisition of a

---

[11] See, e.g., Smith, Shoben, and Rips 1974; Rosch 1975; Rosch and Mervis 1975; Hampton 1979; for a summary, see Murphy 2002.

concept, the most typical member of the category is sometimes more likely to be classified as a category member than the category members seen during training, although this most typical member has not been seen during training.[12] The basic design of Posner and Keele (1968, 1970) has been described in section 6.2. For memory, in the training phase, subjects were asked to learn to categorize patterns of points into different categories. They were not presented with the most typical patterns of points for the relevant categories. In the test phase, they were presented with new items, including the most typical items for each category, and some of the previously seen patterns of points. When the test phase immediately followed the training phase, subjects classified the unseen, most typical items more accurately than the other unseen patterns of points, but somewhat less accurately than the patterns seen during training (Posner and Keele 1968). When the test phase was delayed, subjects classified the unseen, most typical items more accurately than the patterns seen during training (Posner and Keele 1970). Similar findings have been found with other stimuli, such as images of real faces (e.g., Cabeza et al. 1999). This is tentative evidence that when people are shown some members of a category, they abstract a prototype of this category.

Moreover, in experiments with artificial categories, subjects learn the category membership of typical items faster than the category membership of atypical items (Rosch and Mervis 1975; Rosch et al. 1976). Subjects also learn to classify items in a category more easily if they are trained with typical items than if they are trained with atypical items.

The findings reviewed so far are consistent with the prototype paradigm of concepts. Since the representation of a target is supposed to be matched with a prototype during categorization, theories of prototype-based categorization expect typicality to affect categorization. Because concept learning consists of forming a prototype, prototype theories also expect typicality to affect concept learning.

However, the prototype paradigm of concepts needs to be supplemented with specific models of the processes of categorization and concept learning if it is to yield specific predictions. For instance, a process model of categorization is needed to accommodate the fact that typical objects or subclasses are categorized faster than atypical ones. Such process models are easily designed and are germane to the prototype paradigm of concepts. Suppose, for example, that when we categorize, we try to serially match each property represented by the concept of the category C with the properties represented by the representation of the target T. Suppose also that we increase a similarity measure M whenever there is a match. Finally, suppose that we decide to categorize T as a member of C if M is above some threshold (figure 6.4). This type of model does not predict the latency of a specific categorization decision. However, it predicts the

---

[12] For a critique of Posner and Keele's experimental paradigm, see Palmeri and Flanery 1999 and the discussion in section 7.3.

relative latency of categorization decisions. According to this model, typical category members or subclasses should be classified faster than atypical ones.

Typicality effects have been found for many types of concept. Concepts of three-dimensional objects, including artifacts, animals, fruits, and plants, constitute the bulk of the research on typicality effects. Typicality effects have also been found for other concepts. Some abstract concepts (e.g., ART, SCIENCE, WORK, and CRIME) but not all (e.g., neither RULE nor INSTINCT) give rise to typicality effects (Hampton 1981). Typicality effects have also been found for concepts of character traits, psychiatric conditions (Cantor and Mischel 1979; Cantor et al. 1980), and emotions (Shaver, Shelley, and Schwartz 1992), as well as for concepts of everyday situations (Cantor,

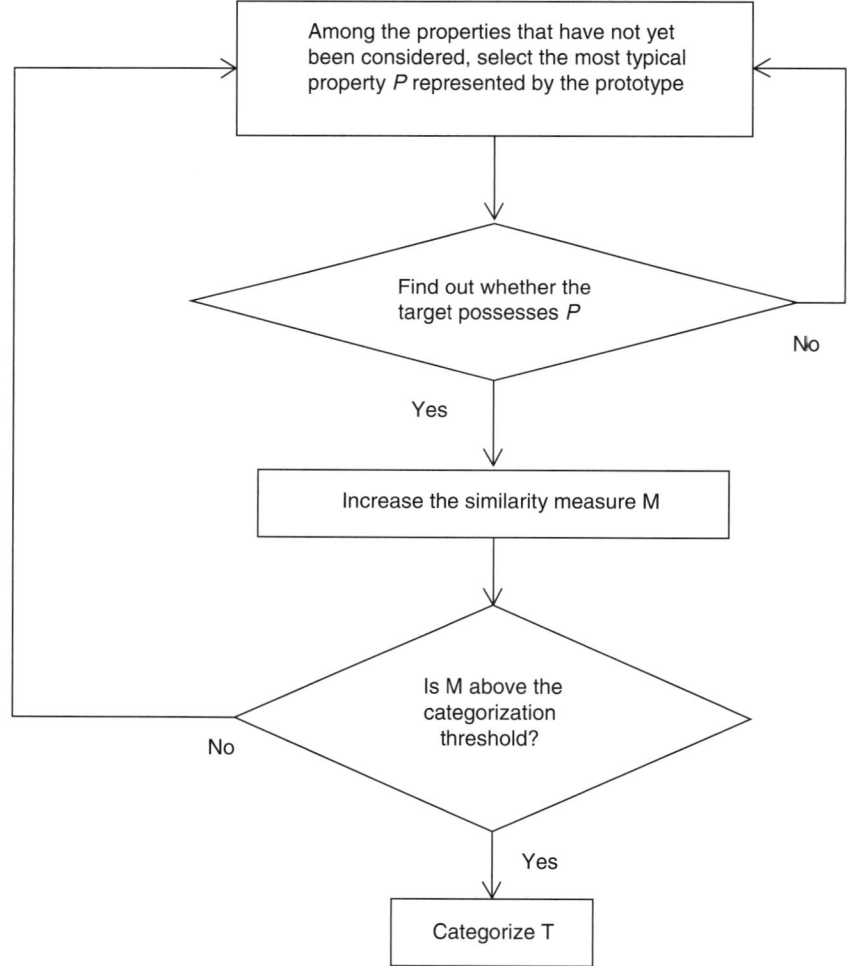

Figure 6.4 A Serial Process of Categorization

Mischel, and Schwartz 1982) and actions (Coleman and Kay 1981). This suggests that we possess prototypes for abstract entities, classes of three-dimensional objects, properties such as character traits, and situations.

6.3.2 Three Critiques of the Typicality Effects

The inference from the typicality effects to the prototypicality of concepts has been challenged. In a famous article, Sharon Armstrong, Lila Gleitman, and Henry Gleitman (1983) have argued that typicality effects show nothing about the nature of concepts. They cleverly designed an experimental task where typicality effects were found for concepts that are unlikely to be prototypes. Consider the concept of an even number. Contrary to most concepts (section 4.1), adults are often able to define what even numbers are. This suggests that EVEN NUMBER is among the few concepts that satisfy the classical theory of concepts: we know the necessary and sufficient conditions for being an even number, and this knowledge is used when we reason about even numbers. Armstrong and colleagues' surprising finding is that this and other concepts give rise to typicality effects. Some even numbers, such as 2, are rated as being better even numbers than others, such as 726. Subjects did agree on their typicality evaluation. Typical even numbers are also more quickly categorized than atypical even numbers. For instance, subjects were faster at verifying that 2 is even than at verifying that 18 is even (table 6.1). Armstrong and colleagues drew the following conclusion:

> We hold that *fruit* and *odd number* have different structures, and yet we obtain the same experimental outcome for both. But if the same result is achieved regardless of the concept structure, then the experimental design is not pertinent to the determination of concept structure. (Armstrong, Gleitman, and Gleitman 1983: 284–285)

Armstrong and colleagues' experiments have been justly celebrated. However, I now argue that they have failed to establish that typicality effects show nothing about the nature of concepts. Two of the concepts used by Armstrong and colleagues as examples of well-defined concepts are inappropriate. The concept FEMALE was used as a well-defined concept. This is a very dubious choice. FEMALE seems to be a good candidate for being a prototype. Although people may believe that there are some necessary and sufficient conditions for being a female, people do not know how to define the class of females. Armstrong and colleagues' findings in their third experiment provide further evidence for the claim that FEMALE is not a definition. Armstrong and colleagues first asked subjects whether it made sense to belong to some degree to specific categories, such as fruits, odd numbers, and females. Then, they asked subjects to evaluate the typicality of objects or subclasses with respect to these categories. When subjects responded that it did not make sense to belong to some degree to a well-defined category, all the category members

Table 6.1 Mean Reaction Times for Good and Poor Instances of Prototype and Well-Defined Categories in Milliseconds (inspired by Armstrong, Gleitman, and Gleitman 1983: 282)

	Good exemplars	Poor exemplars
Prototype categories		
Fruit	903	1125
Sport	892	941
Vegetable	1127	1211
Vehicle	989	1228
Well-defined categories		
Even number	1073	1132
Odd number	1088	1090
Female	1032	1156
Plane geometry figure	1104	1375

were judged to be equally typical—save for the category of females (see table 6 in Armstrong, Gleitman, and Gleitman 1983: 288–289). The typicality of the least typical even number, namely 106, was 3.9 in the first experiment, but only 1.7 in the third experiment. By contrast, the typicality of comediennes with respect to the category of females was 4.5 in the first experiment and 3.1 in the second experiment—a much smaller relative reduction. This is evidence that FEMALE is different from ODD NUMBER, suggesting that, contrary to ODD NUMBER, FEMALE is not a definition. "Plane geometry figure" was also assumed to express a well-defined concept. The body of knowledge about plane geometry figures is not permanently stored in long-term memory. The properties of this type of body of knowledge are likely to be different from the properties of concepts permanently stored in memory, such as DOG. Thus, the concept expressed by "plane geometry figure" is inadequate to test whether concepts are prototypes.

When FEMALE and PLANE GEOMETRY FIGURE are excluded, there is no substantial difference between how quickly subjects categorized atypical and typical members of the extensions of well-defined concepts (see table 6.1). For instance, mean verification time for typical even numbers is 1088 ms, while mean verification time for atypical uneven numbers is 1090 ms. That is, categorization decisions are not affected by the typicality of even numbers.

What should we conclude? We do distinguish typical from atypical numbers as we do distinguish typical fruits from atypical fruits. But the typicality of objects or subclasses with respect to concepts such as FRUIT and VEHICLE should be distinguished from the typicality with respect to concepts such as EVEN NUMBER and ODD NUMBER. Typicality with respect to FRUIT and VEHICLE affects how we categorize, while typicality with respect to EVEN NUMBER and ODD NUMBER does not. Hence, pace Armstrong and colleagues (1983), although the mere fact that some category members are judged to be more typical than others is not evidence that the concept of the relevant category is a prototype, the fact that typicality affects our cognitive competences—the typicality effects—remains relevant for determining the nature of concepts.

I now turn to Barsalou's critique of the inference from the typicality effects to the prototypicality of concepts (Barsalou 1990). Barsalou proposed that instead of extracting a prototype from encountering category members during concept learning and using this prototype to categorize, we might store exemplars and produce a prototype on the fly, when necessary (1990: 72–73). He concludes that prototype and exemplar models are empirically undistinguishable: "Exemplars and abstracted representations [i.e., prototypes] in principle are informationally equivalent. Because of this equivalence, we cannot determine whether people use exemplars or abstracted representations" (1990: 61). Barsalou's argument is intriguing, but ultimately unconvincing. For a model in which people store all exemplars and abstract, when necessary, a prototype provides an ad hoc account of the findings predicted by prototype theories. What would rescue this proposal from being ad hoc is an a priori account of the conditions in which a prototype is abstracted from the hypothesized set of exemplars. Alternatively, independent evidence might be found that people do indeed produce prototypes on the fly, although it is unclear to me what this evidence would look like. Barring such an account or such evidence, there is little reason to take this hypothesis seriously. Moreover, the hypothesis proposed by Barsalou seems to be a very inefficient categorization strategy. Instead of regularly producing a prototype out of the exemplars stored in long-term memory, as is proposed in Barsalou's hypothesis, it seems more efficient to extract a prototype from category members during concept learning and to use this prototype when needed.

Finally, exemplar theorists have argued that typicality phenomena fall out from exemplar models of concepts and categorization (Medin and Schaffer 1978; Hintzman 1986). Consider Posner and Keele's (1968, 1970) findings. According to exemplar theories, during the test phase, the patterns of points are compared with the exemplars of the patterns of points seen during training. During testing, subjects are presented with the most typical pattern of points, which was not seen during training, and with some patterns of points seen during training. The most typical pattern of points is similar to many exemplars of patterns of points. By contrast, each pattern of points seen during training is highly similar to its own exemplar (that is, the exemplar formed when subjects were presented with this pattern), but dissimilar to the other exemplars, because the patterns of points seen during training were obtained by randomly deforming the original pattern of points. As a result, the overall degree of similarity between the most typical pattern of points and all the exemplars might be equal to or higher than the overall degree of similarity between a given pattern of points seen during training and all the exemplars (Medin and Schaffer 1978: 214; on the computation of similarity in exemplar theories, see section 4.3). Thus, exemplar theories predict that in spite of not having been seen during the learning phase, the typical patterns of points might be sometimes categorized more quickly and more accurately than the known, but less typical patterns. Thus, the typicality phenomena do not favor prototype theories over exemplar theories—or so exemplar theorists concluded. This came to be the common wisdom among psychologists of concepts in the 1980s and 1990s.

6.3.3 Prototypes Upheld

Recent work, however, suggests a different picture. Psychologist J. D. Smith (2002) has shown that exemplar theories and prototype theories have a different categorization profile as a function of typicality (also known as "typicality gradient"). Imagine a category of patterns of points created by the random distortion of an original pattern of points. The training items are patterns of points that are obtained by distorting the original pattern moderately and equally. Consider now four test items that vary according to their typicality—particularly two low-level distortion patterns of points (items 3 and 4 in figure 6.5) and two high-level distortion patterns of points (items 1 and 2 in figure 6.5). Exemplar and prototype theories of categorization make similar predictions about how the high-level distortion patterns of points (1 and 2) will be categorized. However, their prediction differs for the low-level distortion patterns (3 and 4). Exemplar theories predict that the probability of classifying low-level distortion patterns of points should not increase with increasing typicality or, equivalently, decreasing distortion. That is, exemplar theories predict that the probability of classifying 4 as a category member should be equal to the probability of classifying 3. The reason is that for low-level distortion patterns of points, any change in typicality will increase the similarity with some exemplars of patterns of points, but decrease the similarity with others, leaving the overall similarity to the set of exemplars unmodified. By contrast, prototype theories predict that the probability of classifying low-level distortion patterns of points should increase with increasing typicality or, equivalently, decreasing distortion. That is, prototype theories predict that the probability of classifying 4 as a category member should be greater than the probability of classifying 3 (figure 6.5; inspired by Smith 2002: 439).

Using existing data sets, Smith (2002) has shown that prototype models of categorization fit better subjects' categorization performances. Smith's (2002) findings show that typicality can be used to distinguish between different models of concept, categorization, and concept learning (see also Smith and Minda 2001). Moreover, these findings are evidence that in at least some tasks, a prototype-based concept-learning process and a prototype-based categorization process are activated.

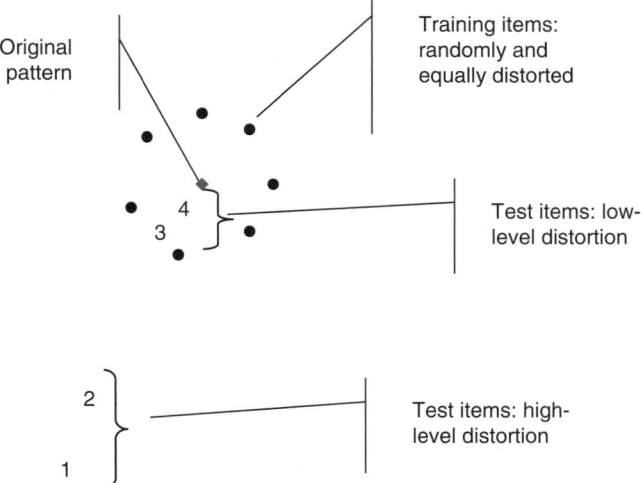

Figure 6.5 Test and Training Patterns of Points (inspired by Smith 2002: 439)

6.4 Evidence for the Existence of Exemplars

6.4.1 Exemplar Effects

The exemplar paradigm of concepts, remember, proposes that concepts are sets of representations of specific category members. In substance, in most models of the exemplar-based categorization process, people retrieve one or several exemplars from their long-term memory when they categorize. The target is compared to these exemplars and if their similarity is above some threshold, people classify the target in the class represented by these exemplars.

The exemplar paradigm is supported by the exemplar effects: in some cases, categorization fluency (measured in terms of reaction time and accuracy) and learnability (measured as the time needed to learn that an item belongs to a category) are not predicted by the similarity to the hypothetical prototype of the category, as prototype models would have it, but rather by the similarity to known members of the category.

Two phenomena need to be distinguished. First, let us consider the old-items advantage. Subjects are asked to learn the category membership of the artificial stimuli that compose two categories. They are then asked to categorize new items as well as the items seen during training. The finding is that the old items are usually more easily categorized than new items that are equally typical (for a review, see Nosofsky 1992; Smith and Minda 1998). To give a toy example, it is easier to classify my pet Fido as a dog than an unknown dog that is an equally typical dog. This effect is not predicted by prototype theories of concepts. Prototype theorists assume that people abstract a prototype from the stimuli they are presented with in the learning phase and categorize stimuli, old as well as new, by comparing them to the prototype. What matters for categorization is the typicality degree of the items, not whether they have already been seen. By contrast, the old-items advantage falls out from the exemplar paradigm. The similarity of an old item that belongs to a given category A to the set of exemplars of members of A is greater than the similarity of a new item to this same set because the set of exemplars includes a representation of the old item, but no representation of the new item.

The second phenomenon is the following. A less typical category member can be categorized more quickly and more accurately than a more typical category member, and its category membership can be learned more quickly than the category membership of a more typical category member if this category member is similar to previously encountered category members (e.g., Medin and Schaffer 1978). To give a toy example, it may be easier for me to categorize a three-legged dog as a dog than a four-legged dog because my own pet dog lost a leg. Medin and Schaffer (1978) establish this finding as follows. They single out two items among the training items, A_1 and A_2. These two items belong to the same category, A. The critical point is that A_1 is more similar than A_2 to the prototype that subjects would plausibly abstract if the prototype paradigm were correct. Thus, the prototype paradigm predicts that subjects will learn more quickly the category membership of A_1 than the membership of A_2. Because A_2 is highly similar to two other members of A and to no member of the alternative category, B, while A_1 is highly similar to only one member of A and to two members of B, Medin and Schaffer's Context Model (section 4.3) makes the opposite prediction. Medin and Schaffer found evidence that supports their prediction.

These findings are problematic for the prototype paradigm of concepts, while being consistent with the exemplar paradigm, since the prototype paradigm of concepts makes the strong prediction that typical members should be easier to categorize than atypical members. Moreover, learning the category membership of typical members should be easier than learning the category membership of atypical members. The exemplar approach, on the contrary, can account for the influence of encountered category members in subsequent learning or categorization, since concepts are assumed to be sets of representations of specific category members. Thus, there seems to be strong evidence for the exemplar paradigm.

6.4.2 Critique of the Exemplar Effects

In an important article, Smith and Minda (2000) have cast some doubts on the strength of the evidence for the exemplar approach to concepts, categorization, and concept learning (but see Nosofsky 2000). Many experiments that support the exemplar paradigm of concepts against the prototype paradigm have used the same category structure. A category structure is an abstract characterization of the categories used in a categorization or in a concept-learning experiment. Four properties of these categories matter:

- How many categories are used in the experiment?
- For each category, how many members belong to it?
- How many properties or dimensions characterize the items used in the experiment?
- For each property, does each category member possess it?

Importantly, the nature of the properties is not specified, so that the same category structure can be implemented with different stimuli. The category structure singled out by Smith and Minda, called the "5-4 category structure," consists of two categories. Category A consists of five elements, category B of four elements. Seven items are also used in the test phase of the experiments on concept learning. Four binary dimensions distinguish these sixteen items. Each item has a value 1 or 0 along each of these four dimensions. Table 6.2 summarizes the 5-4 category structure (inspired by Smith and Minda 2000: 4).

Table 6.2 The 5-4 Category Structure (inspired by Smith and Minda 2000: 4)

	Dimension			
	D1	D2	D3	D4
Category A				
A1	1	1	1	0
A2	1	0	1	0
A3	1	0	1	1
A4	1	1	0	1
A5	0	1	1	1
Category B				
B1	1	1	0	0
B2	0	1	1	0
B3	0	0	0	1
B4	0	0	0	0
Transfer stimuli				
T1	1	0	0	1
T2	1	0	0	0
T3	1	1	1	1
T4	0	0	1	0
T5	0	1	0	1
T6	0	0	1	1
T7	0	1	0	0

A prototype 1111 could be abstracted from category A, while category B would correspond to a prototype 0000. Four members of category A share three features with the hypothesized prototype of A, while one member shares two features with it. As emphasized by Smith and Minda (2000: 3), category A has no "exceptional" member, that is, a member "sharing more features in common with the opposing prototype," but it has an "ambiguous" member, which shares "features equally with both prototypes." Two members of category B share two features with the hypothesized prototype of B, while a third one shares three and a fourth one four features with it. Thus, category B contains two ambiguous members and no exceptional member. The average typicality of the members of A and of the members of B is the same. This category structure has been implemented in many different stimuli, including geometric figures, line-drawn rocket ships, and Brunswick faces (for further detail, see Smith and Minda 2000).

Smith and Minda (2000) develop three main objections. First, the explanatory scope of the exemplar paradigm of concepts is questionable, since many experiments have relied on the 5-4 category structure. Second, the ecological validity of the 5-4 category structure is unclear. Real categories are more different from each other than the two categories in the 5-4 category structure. Furthermore, in contrast to these two categories, real categories are not restricted to a few members. Thus, results found with the 5-4 category structure (and similar category structures) may say little about how we learn concepts and categorize in real-world situations.

Finally, Smith and Minda argue that the 5-4 category structure primes subjects to form exemplars as well as to use them to categorize. Thus, the findings that seem to support the exemplar paradigm might be experimental artifacts. They highlight some properties of the 5-4 category structure:

> This low index of category differentiation correctly reflects that the individual features are only 70% diagnostic, that exemplars are nearly as similar across categories (sharing 1.6 features) as within categories (sharing 1.9 features if one excludes self-identities), and that three of the nine items are ambiguous because they share features equally with both prototypes. Thus the two categories within themselves are poor assemblages with a weak family resemblance, and they are poorly differentiated from each other. (Smith and Minda 2000: 4)

Because the categories are poorly differentiated, because subjects may find it hard to perceive any unity in each category, and because there are few category members (4 and 5), subjects may attempt to memorize the category membership of each category member. If you were told that a dog, a frying pan, and the moon belong to category A, and that a cat, a knife and the sun belongs to category B, you would not even look for properties that might be common to the members of each category. Rather, you would attempt to remember each category member together with its category membership.

In addition to these three objections, Smith and Minda (2000) note that subjects' performances in experiments that use the 5-4 category structure do not support the exemplar paradigm as clearly as exemplar theorists would have it. They examined thirty data sets obtained with the 5-4 category structure. They confirm that standard prototype models of categorization, which rely on an additive computation of the similarity between targets and prototypes (section 4.2), do not fit the data sets very well. By contrast, the Generalized Context Model (section 4.3) successfully fits the data sets (see also Nosofsky 1992).

However, Smith and Minda show that the poor fit of additive prototype models of categorization results from the categorization of the items seen during training, that is, the old items: "By assuming that all items (old and new) are referred to the category prototypes, it [the prototype model] assumes that all items will equivalently obey the typicality gradients in the task. It has no way to treat training exemplars specially by according them any processing fluency or performance advantage" (2000: 8). By contrast, additive prototype models fit well the categorization of new items.

Smith and Minda show that prototype models can be extended in various ways to fit the categorization of old items. It can be assumed that the comparison of an item to a prototype and the decision to categorize it are faster and smoother for old items than for new items. More plausibly, it can also be assumed that we have individual memories of old items (exemplars) and that these memories are used to categorize the old items, while the new items are categorized by comparing them to the prototype. Two models based on these alternative ideas fitted the data sets as well as the Generalized Context Model. Smith and Minda conclude:

> Performance in the 5-4 task, whether on the new, transfer items or the old, training items, really has *no particular representational or process implications.* All three models, whether they assume prototype or exemplar representations, explain new-item performance equivalently well and easily. All three confront the selective training boost to old items and incorporate a mechanism that reproduces that boost. But the boost—whether it is modeled in a way that is grounded in prototypes or exemplars, and whether it is attributed to memorization, skilled prototype assimilation, or high sensitivity—only acknowledges that participants perform better on old items. It does not confirm the purely exemplar-based categories of exemplar theory. It does not confirm the systematic exemplar-to-exemplar comparisons of the context model. (Smith and Minda 2000: 17; my emphasis)

Smith and Minda have also cast doubts on whether the category membership of an item that is similar to previously learned items is easier to learn than the category membership of an item that is more typical, but less similar to previously learned items (Medin and Schaffer 1978). Focusing on twelve data sets, which are supposed to be the most congenial for Medin and Schaffer's hypothesis, they argue that this hypothesis is not supported: "The result is not consistent, robust, present overall, or even present within the 12 data sets that should most favor exemplar theory" (2000: 19).

Smith and Minda's (2000) critiques are devastating for the claim that the exemplar paradigm is supported by an overwhelming body of evidence. However, for the sake of fairness, it is important to note that many criticisms raised by Smith and Minda against the experiments that support the exemplar paradigm carry over against the experiments that support the prototype paradigm. The ecological validity of the stimuli used in the latter experiments (e.g., Smith 2002) is as questionable as the validity of the stimuli used in the former experiments. Moreover, it remains that in some experiments, if not in all, the category membership of less typical items is more quickly learned than the membership of more typical items.

6.4.3 Linear Separability

As explained in section 4.2, in most prototype models, the properties that are common to the prototype and the target are independent cues for categorizing the target. That is, the contribution of a property possessed by an object to the similarity between this object and the prototype does not depend on the other properties possessed by this object. Thus, if concepts are prototypes, people should find it difficult to form a concept of a non-linearly discriminable category (Medin and Schwanenflugel 1981; Murphy 2002: ch. 4). That is, subjects should learn more quickly to categorize the members of two categories when these two categories are linearly discriminable than when they are not. A category is linearly discriminable (or separable) if and only if one can determine whether an item belongs to this category by summing the evidence offered by each property of this item. For example, suppose that two categories are characterized by two dimensions. These categories are linearly discriminable if and only if one can determine the category membership of each item by summing its value along the *x*- and *y*-axes, that is, if a line can be drawn between the members of each category (figure 6.6).

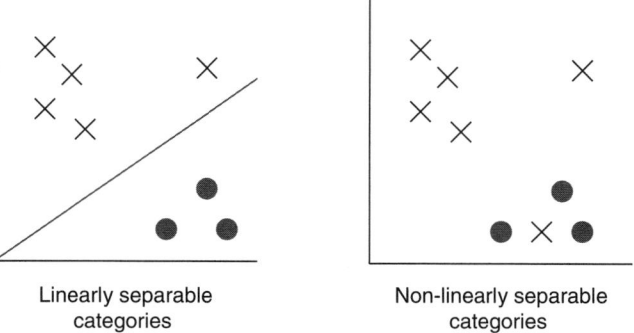

Linearly separable categories

Non-linearly separable categories

Figure 6.6 Linear Separability

Exemplar theories of concepts do not predict that subjects should learn more easily to categorize the members of linearly discriminable categories than the members of categories that are not linearly separable.

Evidence does not support the claim that membership in linearly discriminable categories is easier to learn (Medin and Schwanenflugel 1981; Wattenmaker et al. 1986). In the first condition of Medin and Schwanenflugel (1981), subjects were successively presented with eight items divided in two linearly discriminable categories. In the second condition, subjects were successively presented with eight items divided into two non-linearly discriminable categories. In each condition, subjects were asked to categorize the items into their correct categories. Subjects were presented with the items sixteen times. The proportion of subjects being able to categorize the items correctly at the end of this learning phase was the dependent variable. Controlling for various factors, Medin and Schwanenflugel (1981) found that the two types of category were equally difficult to learn. This finding was viewed as strong evidence for the exemplar models of concept learning.

Murphy has raised some doubts about this body of evidence for the exemplar paradigm (2002: 103–106). His objections against the research on non-linearly discriminable categories are similar to the objections developed by Smith and Minda (1998, 2000; see above). Contrary to real categories, the categories used in Medin and Schwanenflugel's (1981) experiments included very few members, which could have invited subjects to memorize the category membership of each item instead of attempting to abstract a prototype. Moreover, contrary to most real-world categories, these categories did not show any clear central tendency. This might also have invited subjects to memorize the category membership of each item. Thus, the fact that no difference was found between the linearly discriminable categories and the non-linearly discriminable categories might be an artifact of the stimuli used by exemplar theorists.

6.4.4 Prototypes and Exemplars

In the last pages, we have seen that the evidence for the exemplar paradigm of concepts was judged to be extremely strong in the 1980s and 1990s. Exemplar theories of concept learning were also thought to be able to account for most findings once taken to support the prototype paradigm of concepts. As a result, the exemplar paradigm came to be the dominant paradigm in the experimental study of categorization and concept learning. The tide has now turned. The evidence drawn from the research on concept learning with non-linearly separable categories is at least suspect. The evidence drawn from the research on categorization and concept learning suffers from its reliance on a narrow range of category structures whose ecological validity is questionable. Prototype theorists, such as J. D. Smith, are also collecting a growing body of evidence for the prototype paradigm of concepts that, at least prima facie, cannot be explained by exemplar theories of concept learning and categorization.

So, should we conclude that the available evidence supports the existence of prototypes and of prototype-based processes of categorization and concept learning, while there is at best weak evidence for the existence of exemplars and of exemplar-based processes of categorization and concept learning? It seems fair to say that the evidence reviewed above fails to clearly support the exemplar paradigm.

However, another body of research shows that people can use either exemplars or prototypes to solve categorization tasks.[13] The evidence consists in individual differences in the strategies used to solve these tasks. These individual differences could be interpreted as showing that some people have acquired prototypes and use them in categorization tasks, while other people have acquired exemplars and use them in these tasks. Another interpretation is that everybody can use either prototypes or exemplars in these categorization tasks. Consistent with this latter interpretation, some subjects switch from using prototypes to using exemplars. Together with the evidence for the exemplar paradigm and the evidence for the prototype paradigm that has been reviewed above, this supports the claim that we possess both exemplars and prototypes.

Let us consider Malt (1989) in some detail. Malt was keenly aware that it was difficult to distinguish exemplar-based models of categorization and of concept learning from the prototype-based models of these competences on the basis of behavioral measures such as categorization probability and reaction time. To solve this problem, she proposed a new experimental design. The key insight is the following. When a representation is retrieved from memory, subjects' performances in a subsequent task that involves this representation are primed. This principle can be used to test whether subjects use exemplars when they categorize. Suppose subjects use exemplars to categorize animals into the class of dogs. Because the exemplars of dogs will have been retrieved from long-term memory, subjects' performances in a subsequent task that is known to involve exemplars of dogs should be primed. By contrast, suppose that subjects use a prototype to categorize animals into the class of dogs. Subjects' performances in a subsequent task that is known to involve exemplars of dogs should not be primed.

Malt's first experiment tested this key insight. Pairs of animals were created. Animals within a pair were physically similar. For instance, a pair might have included a jaguar and a lion. The pairs were divided into two categories, A and B. Suppose that the pair (lion, jaguar) belonged to category A. During the learning phase, subjects were presented with a member of each pair (say, the jaguar). They were asked to classify it into A or B. For example, when shown the jaguar, subjects had to answer that it belonged to A. In the test phase, subjects had to categorize all the animals, including the animals used during training, such as the jaguar. Members of

---

[13] Malt 1989; Smith, Murray, and Minda 1997; Smith and Minda 1998.

a given pair were categorized successively, the animal not used during training being presented first. For instance, subjects had to categorize the lion and then the jaguar. Subjects were asked to categorize the new animal (the lion) by thinking about the animal that was most similar to the new animal and by classifying the new animal in the category of this animal. It was expected that subjects would retrieve a memory of the jaguar when they were asked to classify the lion and that they would classify the lion as an A. In effect, subjects were explicitly told to use exemplars to categorize new items. If subjects did this, the subsequent categorization of the jaguar should have been primed. To identify this priming effect, a control condition was defined: instead of classifying a new animal (e.g., the lion), subjects were asked to decide whether the new animal was larger than a cocker spaniel. Then, subjects were asked to categorize the animals used during training (e.g., the jaguar). The reaction time for the classification of the animals used during training was compared across the control condition and the main condition. Finally, subjects were given a recognition task: they had to decide whether some animals had been presented during the learning phase.

The results show that Malt's key insight is correct. Subjects recognized the animals seen during training almost perfectly. This shows that subjects did encode representations of the members of the two categories, A and B. Most important, a priming effect was found: subjects were significantly faster in the main condition than in the control condition. This is evidence that Malt's experimental design is sensitive to the use of exemplars in categorization tasks.

Thus, this design can be used to find out whether subjects spontaneously retrieve exemplars in categorization tasks. Experiment 3 bears on this issue. The design is identical to the design of experiment 1, except that subjects were not told to categorize the new items, such as the lion, by thinking about the most similar animal. In effect, they were not told to use exemplars as a categorization strategy. Subjects were also asked to describe their categorization strategy.

Malt found a small, but non-significant priming effect.[14] She interprets the non-significance of this effect as a sign that not all subjects retrieved exemplars to categorize. Some used exemplars; a few relied on the prototypes of the two categories, A and B; and others appealed both to exemplars and to prototypes. A protocol analysis of subjects' description of their categorization strategy confirms this interpretation. Malt writes:

> 3 said they used only general features of the category in classifying the new exemplars. Nine said they used only similarity to old exemplars, and 8 said that they used a mixture of category features and similarity to old exemplars. If reports accurately reflect the strategies used, then the data are composed of responses involving several different decision processes. The mixture of

---

[14] This result is replicated in experiment 6 with different stimuli.

strategies will, of course, reduce the amount of priming overall compared with Experiment 1, where subjects were presumably all using an exemplar retrieval strategy. (Malt 1989: 546–547)

This is evidence that people can use either prototypes or exemplars to solve Malt's categorization task.

These findings are consistent with Smith and colleagues' (1997) and Smith and Minda's (1998) findings with artificial stimuli. Instead of fitting prototype-based and exemplar-based models of categorization on aggregated data, Smith and colleagues (1997) fitted the models on each subject's data. They found that the performances of half of the subjects were best fitted by a prototype-based model, while the performances of the other half were best fitted by an exemplar-based model. This is evidence that people can learn at least two different types of concepts—prototypes and exemplars—and that they can follow at least two strategies of categorization. Smith and Minda (1998) replicated these findings. Additionally, they found that during learning, subjects' performances were best fitted by different models, suggesting that when learning to categorize artificial stimuli, subjects can switch from a strategy involving prototypes to a strategy involving exemplars. They also found that the learning path is influenced by the properties of the categories subjects are presented with. Categories with few, dissimilar members promoted the use of exemplar-based categorization strategies.[15]

Thus, we do not rely on a single categorization strategy involving a single kind of knowledge (knowledge about the typical properties of category members or knowledge of individual category members). Rather, evidence suggests that we have at least two different mechanisms for categorizing objects, events, and substances. These mechanisms rely on different kinds of concept—prototypes and exemplars. We categorize objects in a category by comparing them to a prototype of this category or by comparing them to individual memories of category members. We also have different processes for learning concepts from encountering members of their extension. We learn what properties are typical (or cue-valid, etc.) of the whole category or we form a set of memories of individual members of the category.

Before turning to the evidence for the theory paradigm, it is worth paying attention to three shortcomings of the body of evidence discussed so far. Most experiments described in this section involve extremely artificial experimental conditions. This artificiality might be necessary for distinguishing between different theories of concepts and different models of concept learning and of categorization, and it might also be needed to find conditions where exemplar-based processes of concept learning and categorization, but

---

[15] For additional evidence about people's flexible use of prototypes and exemplars in categorization, see Ross, Perkins, and Tenpenny 1990; Spalding and Ross 1994; Ross and Makin 1999.

not prototype-based processes, are triggered (and vice-versa). But one worries that rather than tapping into the categorization processes used during real-world categorization, these experiments tap into ad hoc strategies only used by subjects to deal with abnormal learning and categorization conditions. Moreover, even if this worry were assuaged, this body of evidence says little about the organization of the prototype-based and the exemplar-based processes of categorization and concept learning. It merely shows that we have prototypes and exemplars, without providing much evidence about how the prototype-based and exemplar-based categorization processes or concept-learning processes are organized (see section 6.6). Finally, there are numerous prototype-based models of categorization and of concept learning as well as numerous exemplar-based models of categorization and concept learning. I have not tried to determine which of these theories best fits the evidence. Although this is a crucial psychological question, I feel that it is best left to psychologists.

6.5 Evidence for the Existence of Theories

In this section, I discuss the most striking pieces of evidence for the existence of theories. These findings cannot be easily accounted for either by exemplar or by prototype theories.

6.5.1 Does Categorization Depend on Similarity?

For a long time, the research inspired by the theory paradigm of concepts has been mostly negative. Most exemplar-based and prototype-based models of categorization predict that the probability of being categorized as an x is a function of the similarity of the target either to a prototype of the category of x's or to the representations of some members of the category of x's. By contrast, theory theorists deny that categorization depends on similarity. They often propose that categorization involves some kind of inference to the best explanation (Chapter 4). Rips writes:

> In most situations that call for categorizing, we confront some representation of an instance with our knowledge of the various categories it might belong to. *If the assumption that the instance is in one of these categories provides a reasonable explanation of the information we have about it and if this explanation is better than that provided by other candidate categories*, then we will infer that that instance is a member of the first category. (Rips 1989: 52; my emphasis)

To support the theory paradigm of concepts against the prototype and exemplar paradigms, theory theorists have looked for evidence that categorization is unrelated to similarity.

One of the most famous experiments—the pizza experiment—was done by Rips (1989). Subjects were asked to imagine a round object whose diameter was intermediate between the diameter of a quarter and the diameter of the smallest pizza they had ever seen (figure 6.7). No other

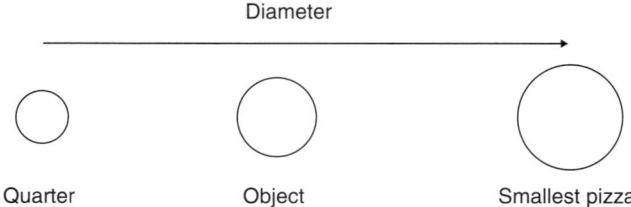

Figure 6.7 Rips's (1989) Pizza Experiment

information about this object was given. Subjects were asked to decide (1) whether the object was more similar to a quarter or to a pizza, and (2) whether the object was more likely to be a quarter or a pizza.

Unsurprisingly, subjects gave random answers to the first question. Half of the subjects said that the object was more similar to the quarter than to the smallest pizza, and half of them gave the reverse answer. By contrast, most subjects judged that the object was more likely to be a pizza than a quarter. Rips argues that in this task, subjects took into account the variability of the diameter of quarters and pizzas. Because the diameter of quarters is fixed by law, while the diameter of pizzas varies, the object is more likely to be a pizza than a quarter. Rips concludes that contrary to what exemplar-based and prototype-based models of categorization assert, in this case, categorization is not determined by similarity.

The pizza experiment has been widely discussed. The most interesting discussion is due to Smith and Sloman (1994).[16] They argue that Rips's (1989) findings result from two properties of the experimental design: (1) A single property of the object to be categorized (the target), that is, its diameter, is described, and (2) subjects are instructed to talk aloud during the experiment. In Smith and Sloman's (1994) experiment 1, besides being told its diameter, half of the subjects were also told that the object was silver-colored, that is, that it had the typical (but not necessary) color of quarters.[17] Half of the subjects were only told the diameter of the object. Subjects were not instructed to talk aloud. In both conditions, subjects' judgments about similarity did predict subjects' categorization judgments. Most subjects judged that a silver object whose diameter is intermediate between a quarter and the smallest pizza was more similar to a quarter than to a pizza and, most surprisingly, that it was more likely to be a quarter than a pizza. Moreover, contrary to Rips's findings, subjects who were only told the diameter of this object gave random answers for both the similarity and the categorization questions.

In experiment 2, subjects were instructed to reason aloud. Most subjects who were only told the diameter of the target object judged that it was more likely to be a pizza than a quarter, but answered randomly

---

[16] For a different interpretation of Rips's findings, see Hampton 1998, 2001.
[17] Other stimuli were also used, but for the sake of simplicity, I focus on the pizza case.

to the similarity question, which replicates Rips's findings. However, most subjects who were told the diameter and the color of the target object still judged that it was more likely to be a quarter than a pizza and found it more similar to a quarter. The protocol analysis revealed some interesting facts. Subjects who were only told the diameter typically mentioned the fact that having a specific diameter is a necessary property of quarters when they commented on their categorization decision. They did not mention the variability of the diameter of pizzas. Subjects who were told the diameter and the color of the target typically mentioned the color—that is, the typical property of quarters—or the color and the diameter when they commented on the similarity decision and when they commented on the categorization decision.

These are striking findings. Rips's findings and Smith and Sloman's experiment 2 provide strong evidence that in some conditions, people's categorization judgments are not driven by similarity—which is inconsistent with prototype- and exemplar-based models of categorization. Smith and Sloman's findings also show that verbal reasoning promotes, but does not necessitate, categorization judgments that are not driven by similarity. Moreover, the protocol analysis suggests that when subjects are not categorizing by similarity, they are relying on what properties objects can and cannot have—that is, on some modal knowledge. Theories, but not prototypes or exemplars, are supposed to store this type of knowledge.

Additionally, Smith and Sloman's findings show that besides a categorization process that is not driven by similarity, possibly a theory-driven categorization process, people also possess a categorization process that depends on similarity. In most conditions, similarity evaluation predicted categorization probability. Surprisingly, in Smith and Sloman's experimental conditions, this process often trumped the theory-based categorization process.

To summarize, the body of evidence under discussion suggests the existence of at least two categorization processes, a process that is not based on similarity—possibly a process involving theories—and a similarity-based process, whose nature is unspecified. This is in fact the conclusion drawn by Smith and Sloman themselves:

> The most parsimonious and principled account of the current findings, as well as results from other comparables studies (e.g., Keil 1989; Rips 1989), is that two distinct processes can be used to categorize common objects. One of these processes is deliberative, analytic, and capable of providing justification for a categorization decision; we have treated this process as rule-based, and we have noted that it is clearly relevant to theory-driven categorization. The other process is more automatic and holistic, and it cannot be used to supply convincing justifications for categorization decisions. We have treated this process as similarity-, or matching-, based. (Smith and Sloman 1994: 385)

Like Smith and Sloman, I believe that this body of evidence suggests the existence of several categorization processes. However, I do not endorse a dual-process theory of categorization (see section 5.2 on dual-process theories). Rather, evidence suggests that there are at least three categorization processes. Moreover, it is theoretically misguided to contrast linguistic, non-automatic, slow, theory-based processes and non-linguistic, automatic, fast processes. These properties do not form two natural clusters (Gigerenzer and Regier 1996). For instance, a theory-based categorization process can be fast (Luhmann, Ahn, and Palmeri 2006), and linguistic processes can be automatic (for instance, we automatically understand the sentences that we hear).

Rips's experiments were based on stimuli whose ecological validity is questionable. We rarely have to decide whether an item, most of whose properties are unknown, belongs to categories as different as quarters and pizzas. However, in his celebrated book *Concepts, Kinds and Conceptual Development* (1989), Keil reports converging evidence that categorization is sometimes independent of similarity, using stimuli that are ecologically more valid. Children and adults were given two types of scenarios—the transformation scenarios and the discovery scenarios. In a transformation scenario, various properties of the perceptual appearance of an object, whose category membership is explicitly stated (the initial category), are modified. As a result, the object looks like the members of another category (the target category). Subjects are asked whether the change in perceptual appearance entails a change in category membership. For instance, subjects were given the following scenario—the zebra scenario:

> The doctors took a horse and did an operation that put black and white stripes all over its body. They cut off its mane and braided its tail. They trained it to stop neighing like a horse, and they trained it to eat wild grass instead of oats and hay. They also trained it to live in the wilds in Africa instead of in a stable. When they were all done, the animal looked just like this. When they were finished, was this animal a horse or a zebra? (Keil 1989: 307)

Keil focuses on four main independent variables—subjects' age, whether the changes are superficial, whether the objects are artifacts or animals, and the ontological distance between the initial and the target categories. To illustrate, changing the appearance of an object by means of a costume is more superficial than changing its appearance by surgery. Furthermore, from an ontological point of view, a species of animal and a species of plant are further apart than two species of animal.

In the discovery scenario, scientists find out that an object that looks like the members of a category (the original category) has some hidden properties that characterize another category (the target category). For example, an animal that looks like a cat may have the internal organs of dogs. Subjects are asked to decide whether the object belongs to the target category or to the original category. For instance, subjects were given the following scenario—the horse/cow scenario:

> These are animals that live on a farm. They go 'neigh' and people put saddles on their backs and ride them, and these animals like to eat oats and hay and

everybody calls them horses. But some scientists went up to this farm and decided to study them really carefully. They did blood tests and X-rays and looked way deep inside with microscopes and found out these animals weren't like most horses. These animals had the inside parts of cows. They had the blood of cows, the bones of cows; and when they looked to see where they came from, they found out their parents were cows. And, when they had babies, their babies were cows. What do you think these animals really are: horses or cows? (Keil 1989: 162)

I focus on the transformation scenarios. (Subjects' answers to the discovery scenarios were qualitatively similar.) Adults treat artifacts and animals differently. When the perceptual appearance of artifacts is modified, subjects tend to judge that their category membership has changed. Not so for animals: for all modifications, adults judge that when the appearance of animals is modified, their category membership has not changed. Children progressively come to make similar judgments. More superficial modifications (e.g., using a costume) are judged not to affect the category membership of animals earlier than less superficial modifications (e.g., surgery). Moreover, the greater the ontological distance between the initial category and the target category, the earlier children judge that a change in appearance does not affect category membership.

Keil takes this impressive body of evidence to show that people's categorization judgments are not driven by similarity.[18] An object might be similar to the members of a given category, but nonetheless not belong to this category. Keil rightly draws attention to the fact that even 6-year-old children's categorization judgments are not driven by similarity. When the initial category is an animal species and the target category is a kind of artifact (for instance, the initial category is a real bird and the target category is a toy bird), 6-year-old children judge that changing the appearance of an animal does not affect its category membership. Keil proposes that categorization judgments in children and in adults are not driven by similarity, but rather by increasingly more complex theories about which changes can affect the category membership of animals and artifacts. What distinguishes children's and adults' categorization judgments are different theories about which changes affect category membership. What distinguishes categorization judgments about animals and artifacts are different theories about what changes can affect the category membership of animals and of artifacts.

6.5.2 Causal Effects

I call "causal effects" the phenomena found in many tasks that are best explained if one supposes that subjects bring some causal knowledge to bear on these tasks. Since neither prototypes nor exemplars store causal knowledge, the cognitive processes that are triggered by these tasks use

---

[18] See also Rips 1989; but see Hampton 1995.

neither prototypes nor exemplars. This is evidence that besides prototypes and exemplars, we possess a third kind of concept, namely, theories.

Psychologist Woo-Kyoung Ahn has developed a version of the theory paradigm of concepts called "the causal status hypothesis" (for review, see Ahn and Luhmann 2004). She defines the causal status hypothesis as follows: "The causal status hypothesis states that people regard cause features as more important and essential than effect features in their conceptual representation" (Ahn and Luhmann 2004: 278). In substance, she proposes that the concept of a category of objects stores some knowledge about the causal relations between the properties that characterize the denoted category. Acquiring a concept involves learning these causal relations. Moreover, when we decide whether an item belongs to a category, the properties that are causally more central are more important than the properties that are causally less central. A property is causally more central to the extent that the instantiation of many properties depends on its instantiation and less central to the extent that its instantiation depends on the instantiation of many other properties.

Ahn has gathered an impressive body of evidence consistent with the causal status hypothesis, using both experiments where subjects have to acquire new concepts and experiments that probe their real-world concepts. Ahn (1998: experiment 1) asked subjects to evaluate how important a property is to decide whether an object is a member of a category. Subjects were given the question "Would an x be still x if it were in all ways like an x except that it did not have y?", where x is the category of interest and y the property of interest. For example, subjects were asked whether a goat would still be a goat if it were in all ways like a goat except that it did not give milk. Three properties were used for each category—a "functional" property (typically, something the members of the relevant category do, such as *giving milk* for goats), a "molecular" property (the substance an artifact is made of or the genetic code of animals), and a "physical" property (a part of the object, its shape or its weight). Subjects were also asked to describe the causal relations between these three properties. For each ordered pair of properties (A, B) made out of these three properties, subjects were asked to evaluate whether the category members had A because they had B. For instance, subjects were asked whether they agreed with the claim that records are round because they are made of plastic. They were also asked whether they agreed with the claim that records are made of plastic because they are round. Ahn found that the importance of a property for categorization was significantly correlated with whether it caused the instantiation of the two other properties. That is, causally central properties were judged to be more important for categorization.

Additional evidence comes from Ahn, Kim, and colleagues (2000). During the learning phase of the first experiment, subjects were verbally given some general knowledge about three properties of an imaginary species of animals, the "roobans." For half of the subjects (causal group), this knowledge was causal: one of the properties (the most central property) causes the instantiation of the second property (the intermediate property), which causes the instantiation of the third property (the less central property). For instance, they were told that eating fruits causes the roobans to have sticky feet, which allow them to build nest in trees. Half of the subjects (control group) were simply told that the roobans have these three properties. In the test phase, all subjects were presented with three items, described verbally, which possessed two of the three properties. Subjects were asked to rate how likely it was that these three items were roobans.

The findings show that the causal centrality of properties (*eating fruits, having sticky feet, building nest in trees*) affects people's categorization judgments. In the control group, there was no significant difference between subjects' evaluation of the membership likelihood of the three items. By contrast, in the causal group, subjects rated the item without the most central property (*eating fruits*) as less likely to be a member of the category than the item without the intermediate property (*having sticky feet*). In turn, this item was judged to be less likely to be a member of the category than the item without the less central property (*building nest in trees*).[19] Similar findings were found with 7- to 9-year-old children (Ahn, Gelman, et al. 2000).

There is room for nitpicking. In the training phase, subjects in the causal group were given some causal information about roobans. Then, they were asked to successively categorize three items. Subjects might have assumed that the information provided in the training phase was relevant for what they were asked to do in the test phase. Thus, subjects in the causal group might have inferred that the test items should be categorized differently depending on the causal status of the missing property. If this interpretation is correct, then Ahn, Kim, and colleagues' (2000) findings do not show that real-world concepts store some causal knowledge and that this causal knowledge is used during real-world categorization. Rather, the findings may be an artifact, due to subjects' pragmatic understanding of the experimental situation. This is a serious worry, but it should be resisted. Causal knowledge affects our categorization decisions both when it is taught during the experiment (e.g., Ahn, Kim, et al. 2000; Rehder 2003a, b) and when its retrieval from long-term memory is somehow primed (e.g., Wisniewski 1995). In the latter case, subjects are not taught any knowledge that they might take to be relevant for the subsequent categorization task.

Rehder also found some evidence that adults' causal knowledge about a category influences their categorization decisions (2003a, b; Rehder and Kim 2006; see also section 4.4). Our beliefs about the causal relations among the properties that characterize a category determine which

---

[19] Similar findings were found with another experimental design (free sorting) in experiment 2.

properties we expect to be associated among category members. When an object does not possess the properties we expect to be associated, we judge it less likely to belong to the relevant category. To illustrate, a winged animal that does not fly and builds nests in trees is judged to be less likely to be a bird than a winged animal that does not fly and builds nests on the ground (Rehder 2003a: 711). A plausible explanation is that the combination of properties of the former animal does not match our causal knowledge about birds: since birds build trees in nests because they fly, *building nests in trees* and *flying* should be associated.

Suppose Rehder's theory is correct. Then, different causal structures, particularly common cause structure—the instantiation of a property causing the instantiation of several other properties—and common effect structure—the instantiation of a property being caused by the instantiation of several other properties—should result in different expectations about which properties should be correlated. In Rehder 2003a, subjects were told some information about six categories, including Lake Victoria Shrimps or Neptune Personal Computers, each characterized by four properties (A, B, C, D). In the common-cause condition, a property (A) causes the instantiation of the three others (B, C, D). In the common-effect condition, three properties (A, B, C) independently cause the instantiation of the fourth one (D). Subjects were asked to rate the category membership of targets on a 21-point scale, ranging from "definitively not an X" to "definitively an X." Each target was characterized by a combination of these four properties. Targets were classified differently across conditions. Particularly, a target that instantiates B, C, and D, but not A was judged to be significantly less likely to be a category member in the common-cause condition than in the common-effect condition. Inversely, a target that instantiates D, but not A, B, and C, was judged to be significantly less likely to be a category member in the common-effect condition than in the common-cause condition. This is evidence that our knowledge of the causal relations among the properties that characterize a category leads us to expect a specific combination of properties among category members.

Rehder (2003a) also analyzed the weight of the four properties in categorization decisions (A, B, C, and D). He showed that in the common-cause condition, the cause, that is, A, is weighted more heavily than the effects (B, C, D). That is, in the common-cause condition, the presence or absence of A affected more strongly the category membership ratings than the presence or absence of B, C, and D. A similar effect was found for the common effect (D) in the common-effect condition (see also Rehder and Hastie 2004). That is, in the common-effect condition, the presence or absence of D affected more strongly the category membership ratings than the presence or absence of A, B, and C. This finding provides further evidence for the importance of causal knowledge in categorization decisions.

Remarkably, this finding is also inconsistent with Ahn's causal status hypothesis. According to Ahn, effects are less important than causes for categorization. This predicts that in the common-effect condition, D should be less important than A, or B, or C—contrary to what Rehder found. I will not try to adjudicate this disagreement between these two versions of the theory paradigm of concepts, categorization, and concept learning (see, e.g., Rehder and Kim 2006). For, in this book, I am mainly interested in providing evidence for the existence of theories and of theory-based processes. However, Rehder's finding shows that once it is granted that some of our concepts are theories, much work remains to be done by psychologists, namely, specifying exactly the nature of theories and of the theory-based processes.

6.5.3 Developmental Evidence

Convergent evidence that a type of concept learning involves learning the causal relations between the properties that characterize a category of objects and that a type of categorization appeals to our causal knowledge comes from the work of Gopnik and colleagues (for a review, see Gopnik et al. 2004; Gopnik and Schulz 2007). Gopnik and colleagues have provided some startling evidence that toddlers (some as young as 30 months old) can learn concepts that consist of some causal knowledge about their extensions. The design is the following. A box ("a blicket detector") plays music when the experimenter puts some specific objects (called "blickets") on it (figure 6.8). Children are told that "blickets make the machine go." In effect, psychologists introduce a new concept, BLICKET, by means of what amounts to be a causal definition. Moreover, in a learning phase, children see some objects placed upon the detector. Whenever the detector plays music, the experimenter tells children that the object is a blicket.

In the experiments run by Gopnik and colleagues, children are presented with different patterns of contingency between several objects that are put on the blicket detector (say, a red cube and a green pyramid) and the music played by the blicket detector. For instance, the blicket detector

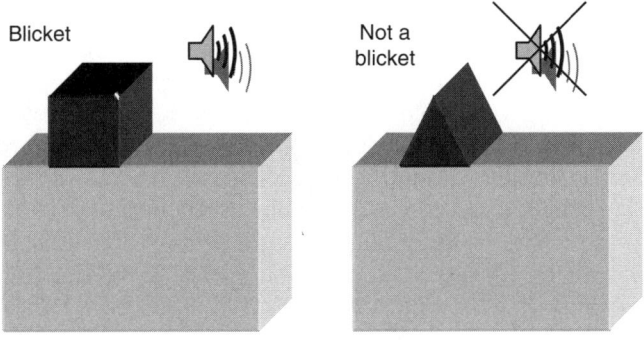

Figure 6.8 The Blicket Detector

might play music when the red cube is placed on it, but not when the green pyramid is placed on it. Because children are asked to categorize the objects used in the experiment (the red cube or the green pyramid) as blickets, they have to decide whether the patterns of contingency they are presented with are evidence of a causal relation between these objects and the blicket detector. By varying the patterns of contingency, Gopnik and colleagues can investigate (1) whether children understand causal relations at all and (2), if they do, how they understand causal relations.

For present purposes, what matters is that these experiments bear on what kind of concept children can acquire and how they categorize. If children are able to classify the objects used in the experiment into the class of blickets based on a causal understanding of the patterns of contingency between an object that is placed on the detector and the music played by the detector, then their concept of blicket truly stores some causal knowledge—rather than some knowledge about the association between the blickets being placed upon the detector and the detector playing music. Moreover, they use this causal knowledge to decide whether the objects used in the experiment are blickets.

Consider Sobel and colleagues' (2004) third experiment. Three- and 4-year-old children saw two objects, A and B, placed twice simultaneously on the blicket detector. The detector played music in both cases. In the control condition, when A was placed upon the detector a third time, the detector did not play music. By contrast, in the backward blocking condition, the detector played music when A was placed on it a third time. In both conditions, children were asked whether A and B were blickets. Of particular interest are children's answers about B: are they more likely to conclude that B is not a blicket in the backward blocking condition than in the control condition? If children were merely keeping track of how strongly B and the music are associated, as most prototype theories would have it, they should give the same positive answer in both conditions. For, in both conditions, whenever the child saw B on the detector, it played music. If children are less likely to judge that B is a blicket in the backward-looking condition than in the control condition, this would be evidence that they use their knowledge about the contingency between A being put on the detector and the detector playing music in order to draw a conclusion about the causal powers of B. It was indeed found that children, including 4-year-old children, classified B significantly less often as a blicket in the backward blocking condition than in the control condition. Similar results were found when children were asked to place one of the two objects upon the detector to make it play music.

More generally, children display a sophisticated understanding of which patterns of contingency instantiate causal relations. Gopnik and colleagues' findings are strong evidence that when they are verbally taught some causal knowledge and when their visual experience is consistent with this knowledge, even young children are able to form concepts that store some causal knowledge about categories. They also use this knowledge in categorization tasks.

To conclude, evidence strongly supports the claim that from an early age on, we form some theories and use these theories to categorize objects. Together with the evidence reviewed in sections 6.4 and 6.5, this strongly supports the Heterogeneity Hypothesis. Before considering how the processes that underwrite categorization and concept learning are organized, it is worth paying attention to a shortcoming of the present discussion. As we have seen, there are several versions of the theory paradigm and several theory-based models of categorization and of concept learning. I have not tried to determine which of these theories and models best fits the evidence, leaving this important question to psychologists.

6.6 Organization of the Categorization Processes and of the Concept-Learning Processes

There is strong evidence for the existence of three kinds of concept acquired by distinct processes and deployed in distinct categorization processes. By contrast, as we will see in this section, the evidence that bears on the organization of these processes is scant.

6.6.1 The Heterogeneity of Categorization and of Concept Learning

An important aspect of the Heterogeneity Hypothesis is the claim that instead of being the inputs to a single categorization process, prototypes, exemplars, and theories are often used in distinct processes. The evidence reviewed above supports this claim.

Two exceptions should be noted. Analyzing subjects' verbal reports, Malt (1989; section 6.3.3) found that some subjects claimed to use some knowledge about individual members and some generalizations about the categories at hand. Similarly, when Smith and Minda (1998; section 6.3.3) fitted several models to different stages of subjects' learning, they found that some stages were best fitted by a model of a process that used both exemplars and prototypes.

It might be that in some conditions, prototypes and exemplars are the inputs to a single categorization process. However, another interpretation of these findings is possible. Suppose that in some conditions, our categorization decisions result from integrating the categorization judgments produced by the three categorization processes identified in this chapter (the prototype-based process, the exemplar-based process, and the theory-based process). This process of integrating the outputs of several categorization processes might explain Malt's (1989) and Smith and Minda's (1998) findings.

In Malt's experiment, subjects report that they are taking into consideration two kinds of knowledge. They might make such a report because they are weighing the judgments they would make if they were to rely on their knowledge about individual category members and the judgments they would make if they were to rely on their statistical generalizations about the categories at hand. That is, they might make such a report because they are trying to integrate the outputs of two distinct processes, each of which uses a single kind of concept. The strength of their final judgment might be a function of the strength of each output.

For what it is worth, introspection suggests that integrating several categorization judgments is a plausible way of using different kinds of knowledge. Consider the following toy example. Imagine an animal that does not look like nor behave like a typical dog, but that looks like and behaves like your pet dog (you own an atypical pet dog). You might decide that the strange animal is a dog by weighing the judgment you would make on the basis of its similarity with your pet dog and the judgment you would make on the basis of its dissimilarity with typical dogs. The strength of your final judgment might be a function of the strength of these two judgments.

In Smith and Minda's (1998) experiment, the model of a process that takes both prototypes and exemplars as inputs fits subjects' performances better than the models of processes that take only prototypes or only exemplars as inputs. Now, this model might be indistinguishable from a model in which the outputs of several distinct processes are integrated. If this is the case, like Malt's protocol analysis, Smith and Minda's model fitting does not show that prototypes and exemplars are the inputs to a single cognitive process. Rather, it suggests that the outputs of the categorization processes are at least sometimes integrated.

6.6.2 Selective Triggering of the Categorization Processes and of the Concept-Learning Processes

As we saw in Chapter 5, when a cognitive competence is underwritten by several processes, one needs to determine whether each of these processes is triggered in its own specific set of conditions or, rather, whether these processes are simultaneously triggered. The evidence discussed above suggests that in experimental conditions, the three hypothesized categorization processes and the three hypothesized concept-learning processes can be triggered selectively. What remains unclear is whether the same is true when we categorize or acquire new concepts in the real world.

What causes the hypothesized categorization processes and concept-learning processes to be selectively triggered in experimental conditions? Some experimental stimuli seem to inhibit some processes of concept learning and of categorization. Particularly, the process for forming theories and the theory-based categorization process are apparently not triggered by visual, meaningless stimuli, such as patterns of dots or sequences of letters and numerals (section 6.3.1). The structure of the categories seems also to prime some processes of concept learning and of categorization. When a category has no central tendency and few members, the process for forming sets of exemplars and the exemplar-based categorization process are primed (section 6.3.2), while the theory-based categorization process is primed when people are told some causal information about a category (sections 6.5.2–6.5.3). Finally, Rips's (1989) and Smith and Sloman's (1994) experiments suggest that talking aloud promotes, but does not necessitate, the use of a theory-based categorization process (section 6.5.1).

The experimental conditions that inhibit or that prime the processes of concept learning and categorization might have real-world counterparts. For example, when we are thinking aloud, we might tend to use the theory-based categorization process to categorize. When we have encountered only a few members of a category and have no additional knowledge about this category, the prototype-based categorization process might be inhibited, and the exemplar-based process might be primed. More research is needed in this area.

6.6.3 Simultaneous Triggering of the Categorization Processes and of the Concept-Learning Processes

During categorization, several processes are simultaneously triggered in at least some conditions. As we saw in section 6.6.1, in some conditions, the outputs of different categorization processes might be integrated. This supposes that several processes have been simultaneously triggered.

Moreover, evidence cogently shows that several processes for forming concepts are at least sometimes simultaneously triggered. In an important article, cognitive psychologists Scott Allen and Lee Brooks (1991: experiment 1) asked subjects to learn the concepts of two categories, A and B. Each category was defined by a disjunctive rule: an object belonged to the category if and only if it possessed a sufficient number of properties. Half of the subjects were told the rule (rule condition), half were not (no-rule condition). During the test phase, subjects were asked to categorize old and new items. Some new items (called "negative matches") were such that they satisfied the rule of a given category, say, A, but were very similar to a member of B seen during training.[20]

Of interest was how subjects would categorize the negative matches. In the rule condition, negative matches were more likely to be misclassified as members of B than the new items that satisfied the rule for belonging to A and that were similar to a member of A seen during training (called "positive matches"). This is evidence that in the rule condition, subjects formed two coreferential concepts—a set of exemplars and a disjunctive rule. These two concepts were also used during categorization by those subjects in the rule condition.

---

[20] A limit of this experiment is that it pits exemplars against rules—i.e., definitions. As argued in section 4.1, it is unclear whether many real-world concepts are definitions.

Moreover, in the rule condition, subjects were significantly slower when they had to classify the negative matches compared to the positive matches. A plausible interpretation of this finding is that when subjects had to categorize the negative matches, they had to resolve a conflict between two different categorization judgments (Allen and Brooks 1991: 7). This is evidence that in Allen and Brooks's experiment, the exemplars and the rule were not the inputs to a single cognitive process, but rather the inputs to two distinct processes yielding conflicting categorization judgments. Thus, Allen and Brooks (1991) provide evidence that at least two categorization processes were simultaneously triggered. Smith and colleagues (1998) have replicated these behavioral findings. They have also shown that different brain areas are involved when subjects' categorization is driven by the similarity between a negative match and an exemplar and when it is driven by the negative match satisfying the rule. This provides further evidence for the idea that several distinct processes underwrite categorization (see section 5.1 on the individuation of cognitive processes).

6.6.4 Limits of Our Current Knowledge

Much remains to be found about the organization of the categorization processes and of the concept-learning processes. While evidence suggests that they are sometimes triggered simultaneously and sometimes one at a time, what determines their simultaneous or selective triggering remains largely unclear. Furthermore, when these processes are simultaneously triggered, we do not know whether and how the outputs of the categorization processes are integrated.

6.7 Conclusion

In this chapter, I have gathered a large body of evidence drawn from the research on concept learning and on categorization. This body of evidence supports the Heterogeneity Hypothesis. It shows that we possess several kinds of concept, specifically, prototypes, exemplars, and theories. We possess several distinct processes for learning these concepts and several distinct processes for categorizing.

This chapter leaves many questions unanswered. I have not tried to determine which version of the prototype paradigm, which version of the exemplar paradigm, and which version of the theory paradigm is correct. This is a project that is beyond the scope of this book and that is best left to psychologists. Moreover, it remains unclear how the processes for forming concepts and the categorization processes are organized. Future research should certainly focus on these issues.

7

Induction, Concept Combination, and Neuropsychology

In the previous chapter, I discussed at length the behavioral experiments on concept learning and on categorization because these two competences have been central to the psychology of concepts. In this chapter, I turn more briefly to two other cognitive competences, induction and concept combination. In sections 7.1 and 7.2, I argue that research on these two competences provides converging evidence for the Heterogeneity Hypothesis. Finally, in section 7.3, I discuss some recent work in neuropsychology that bears on the Heterogeneity Hypothesis.

7.1 Induction

7.1.1 What Is Induction in Psychology?

The term "induction" is used in various ways in psychology.[1] Typically, psychologists use "induction" or, sometimes, "categorical induction" and "category-based induction" to refer to the capacity to generalize a property from a category (the source category) to another category (the target category). Suppose we know that a property, for instance, *having a liver*, is possessed, or typically possessed, or generically possessed, by the members of a category. We might conclude that this property—namely, *having a*

---

[1] This section owes much to several reviews of the psychological literature on induction. See, particularly, Heit 2000; Murphy 2002: ch. 8; Sloman and Lagnado 2005; Feeney and Heit 2007.

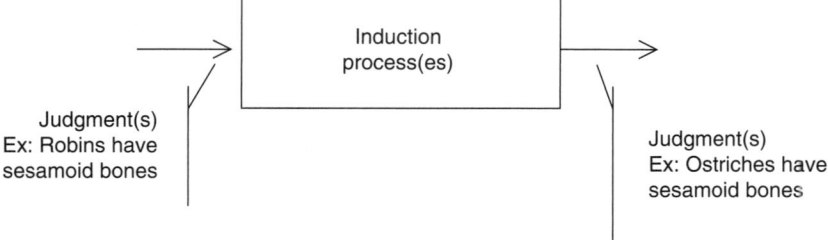

Figure 7.1 Categorical Induction

liver—is also (typically, generically . . .) possessed by the members of other categories (figure 7.1). For instance, because we believe that dogs have a liver, we might conclude that cats have a liver. Not only do we often generalize properties from one category to another category, we also take such generalizations to be more or less likely. For instance, we might conclude that it is more likely that cats have a liver than that earthworms have a liver from our belief that dogs have a liver. Equivalently, we might come to believe more strongly that cats have a liver than that earthworms have a liver from our belief that dogs have a liver. (That is, I take for granted that the strength of our beliefs is a function of how likely we take their content to be true.) The nature of the target category varies: it can include the source category (e.g., mammals could be the target category and dogs the source category); it can be a disjoint category (e.g., cats could be the target category and dogs the source category); or it can be a subclass of the source category (e.g., poodles could be the target category and dogs the source category).

Psychologists have focused on identifying the factors that determine the strength of our categorical inductions. For instance, they try to explain why induction (1) is taken to be stronger than induction (2):

(1) <u>Robins have sesamoid bones</u>
Hence, sparrows have sesamoid bones.
(2) <u>Robins have sesamoid bones</u>
Hence, ostriches have sesamoid bones.

Additionally, the word "induction" in psychology (e.g., Rehder and Hastie 2004; Rehder 2007) is sometimes used to refer to what is called "ampliative induction" in philosophy, namely, the act of inferring that all or most members of a category possess a property from the fact that some of its members have this property (see (3)).

(3) <u>All encountered ravens are black</u>
Hence, all ravens are black

This kind of induction could naturally be seen as a type of categorical induction. A property is generalized from a class, for instance, the class that includes all encountered ravens, to another class, for instance, the class that includes all ravens. However, there is a difference between this type of induction and categorical induction. In the latter case, psychologists typically assume that the source category and the target category are both represented by a concept permanently stored in memory, for instance, ROBIN and SPARROW. By contrast, the class that includes all encountered ravens is not represented by a concept permanently stored in memory.

"Induction" is also occasionally used to refer to the act of ascribing a property to an individual from some knowledge about other properties of this individual. For instance, if you know that John is a graduate student at the Harvard Law School, you might infer that John is likely to be ambitious. This cognitive competence is also studied under the name "reasoning under uncertainty."

In what follows, I focus mostly on categorical induction. I use "induction" to refer to this competence.

7.1.2 The Blank Predicate Design

Rips's (1975) seminal article introduced an experimental design that came to be widely used in psychology: the blank predicate design. In this design, subjects are presented with one or several premises. Premises are either generics (4) or universally quantified sentences (5).

(4) Dogs have a liver
(5) All dogs have a liver

Rips asked subjects to evaluate how many members of other categories possessed the property described in the premises:

> Subjects were told that scientists had recently discovered that all the members of this species [the original category] had a new type of contagious disease. Finally, subjects were asked to estimate, for each of the seven Target instances [target categories], the proportion of animals that had the disease. These estimates were made on a scale from 0 to 100%, with the stipulation that the percentage judgments should not all be equal. (Rips 1975: 667)

In other experiments, subjects are presented with another sentence (the conclusion), for instance (6):

(6) Rats have a liver

They are asked to evaluate on a scale how likely the conclusion is to be true, given that the premises are true (Osherson et al. 1990). Again, conclusions can either be generics or universally quantified sentences.

It is unfortunate that typically, psychologists do not distinguish generics from universally quantified sentences (but see Gelman and Bloom 2007), for these two types of sentence have different logical properties. Universally quantified sentences, such as (5), but not generics, such as (4), are inconsistent with negative existentials, such as (7).

(7) A dog does not have a liver

Reasoning inductively with generics and reasoning inductively with universally quantified sentences might thus be different. In future research on induction, these two types of sentences ought to be better distinguished.

Importantly, the premises and the conclusion presented to subjects include what are called "blank predicates."[2] A blank predicate is a (typically invented) predicate that subjects are not familiar with. For instance, the predicate "have sesamoid bones" in the inductive arguments (1) and (2) is blank. Psychologists use blank predicates because they want to understand specifically how the nature of our knowledge about the source categories and the target category influences the strength of the conclusion. Because the predicate is not familiar, the strength of the conclusion is not affected by subjects' knowledge about the property expressed by the predicate.

It has often been noted that predicates are never entirely blank. Subjects can easily identify the type of property blank predicates refer to. For example, the predicate "have sesamoid bones" refers to the possession of a specific kind of bone, that is, to a biological property. Thus, subjects' knowledge about biological properties such as bones is likely to affect their judgments about the strength of the conclusion involving this predicate. This difficulty is unavoidable. Using an entirely blank predicate, such as "has property X," would make subjects reluctant to evaluate the strength of the inductive conclusion. Blank predicates, such as "have sesamoid bones," strike a satisfactory balance: they minimize the influence of subjects' knowledge about the predicates without making subjects reluctant to project them.

Additionally, blank predicates used in psychological experiments often sound scientific. For instance, the predicates "have sesamoid bones," "have a high potassium concentration in their blood," "require vitamin K," or "have an ulnar artery" (Murphy 2002) are similar to the predicates one might find in a physiological description of an organism. This might affect subjects' inductive dispositions. People might be disposed to project differently predicates that refer to properties presumably discovered by scientists and predicates that refer to properties with which the folk are supposed to be familiar.

Finally, in the blank predicate design, the experimental study of induction boils down to the study of what factors affect subjects' judgments about the strength of inductive arguments. One could question whether studying the latter is tantamount to studying the former. The processes we use to evaluate an argument, be it inductive or deductive, might differ from the processes we use when we induce or deduce. It is unfortunate that to my knowledge, psychologists have not shown that the findings concerning subjects' judgments about the strength of inductive arguments converge with findings about subjects' inductive reasoning.

---

[2] For a critique of the use of blank predicates, see Heit and Rubinstein (1994) and Heit (2000).

7.1.3 Similarity-Based Induction

Several findings that bear on the Heterogeneity Hypothesis have emerged from the research using the blank predicate design.[3] The first finding is called "the similarity effect." A conclusion that is inferred from a single premise is judged to be stronger to the extent that the source category is judged to be more similar to the target category (Rips 1975; Osherson et al. 1990). The similarity effect is illustrated by the inductive arguments (1) and (2) above.

The second finding is "the typicality effect" (Rips 1975). A conclusion that is inferred from a single premise is judged to be stronger to the extent that the source category is typical of the target category (if the target category includes the source category) or of the category that includes both the target category and the source category (if the target category does not include the source category). Consider for instance (8) and (9).

(8) Robins have sesamoid bones
    Hence, birds have sesamoid bones
(9) Penguins have sesamoid bones
    Hence, birds have sesamoid bones

Sentence (8) is judged to be stronger than (9) because robins are a more typical kind of bird than penguins. Lopez and colleagues (1992) found convergent findings with 5-year-old children. Typicality was even a stronger determinant of the strength of the inductive conclusion for them than for adults.

The fact that typicality affects induction suggests that at least in some cases, prototypes or exemplars are retrieved from memory when we evaluate the strength of inductive arguments. Two well-known models of the processes involved in induction explain these and other effects by assuming that we retrieve from memory the prototypes of the source categories and of the target category. In Osherson and colleagues' (1990, 1991) similarity-coverage model, the strength of the induction is a function of the average similarity between the source categories and the target category and of the coverage of the source categories, defined as the average similarity between the source categories and either the typical subclasses of the target category (when the target category includes the source categories) or the typical subclasses of the lowest-level category that includes both the source and target categories (when the target category does not include the source categories). Similarity is determined by matching the relevant prototypes. The similarity effect falls out from the similarity component of Osherson and colleagues' model. The typicality effect is a consequence of the coverage component of their model because the typicality of a category x, such as robins, with respect to a more inclusive

---

[3] For additional findings on induction, see the reviews mentioned above.

category *y*, such as birds, is correlated with the similarity between the prototype of *x* and the prototypes of the typical subclasses of *y*.

In Sloman's (1993) feature-based model, the strength of the conclusion increases to the extent that the properties that are represented by the prototype of the target category are also represented by the prototypes of the source categories.[4] The similarity effect falls out from this model because categories that are judged to be similar are represented by prototypes that share many properties. Furthermore, the prototype of a source category shares more properties with the prototype of the target category to the extent that it (the source category) is typical of the target category (or of the category that includes both the target category and the source category). As a result, the typicality effect is also predicted by Sloman's model.

7.1.4 Theory-Based Induction

The recent history of the research on induction shares many features with the recent history of the research on categorization. Proponents of the theory paradigm of concepts challenged prototypes theorists' claim that similarity was central to the categorization process (section 6.5). Similarly, proponents of the theory paradigm of concepts have challenged prototypes theorists' claim that similarity is central to the induction process.

Proffitt and colleagues (2000) investigated the judgments made by tree experts (landscapers, taxonomists, and parks maintenance personnel) about the strength of inductive conclusions about trees. In the first experiment, tree experts were told that disease A affects a species of tree, *x*, while disease B affects another species, *y*. They were then asked: "Which disease do you think would affect more of the other kinds of trees found around here?" Blank predicates were used. Subjects were also asked to justify their judgments.

Proffitt and colleagues found that typicality often did not affect experts' judgments about whether other trees would be affected by the disease. Rather than relying on the typicality of the two species of trees, *x* and *y* (as predicted, for instance, by Osherson and colleagues' similarity-coverage model), the pattern of answers and the justifications provided suggest that experts often based their judgments on hypothetical causal mechanisms that could explain the spread of the disease. Particularly, they judged that a disease would likely be present in many trees, if the species under consideration were ecologically related to many trees. Proffitt and colleagues reported the following explanation: "For example, one expert mentioned that oaks are likely to spread disease through their roots and that their extensive root system made oaks a stronger base for induction" (Proffitt, Coley, and Medin 2000: 818). López and colleagues (1997) have

---

[4] For a comparison of these two models, see Sloman and Lagnado 2005.

similarly shown that ecological relations are also often used by Itza Mayas to evaluate the strength of inductive arguments involving animals.[5]

To construct hypothetical explanations of the spread of a disease from trees to trees or animals to animals, tree experts and Itza Mayas used some causal knowledge about the relevant species of tree and of animal as well as some causal knowledge about diseases in general. Prototypes and exemplars are not supposed to store this kind of knowledge. Thus, López and colleagues' (1997) and Proffitt and colleagues' (2000) findings provide evidence for the existence of theories of trees and of animals and for the use of these theories in induction.

The use of causal knowledge is not restricted to experts as can be shown, for example, by the causal asymmetry effect (Medin et al. 2003; Sloman and Lagnado 2005). The causal asymmetry effect is the following: when there is an intuitive causal explanation of why the target category would have a property if the source category had it, switching the premise and the conclusion weakens the strength of the induction. Thus, induction (10) is stronger than induction (11) (Sloman and Lagnado 2005: 112–113):

(10) <u>Gazelles contain retinum</u>
 Lions contain retinum
(11) <u>Lions contain retinum</u>
 Gazelles contain retinum

Additionally, induction is sensitive to the causal centrality of the properties of a category. The causal centrality of a property in the source categories affects its generalizability (Hadjichristidis et al. 2004). Suppose that John, but not Ted, believes that having a specific gene explains many properties of dogs. Having this gene is a causally central property of dogs for John, but not for Ted. As a result, John should be more likely than Ted to draw the inductive conclusion that cats also have this gene. The causal centrality of a property in the target category also affects its generalizability (Hadjichristidis et al. 2004). A property P will be more likely to be projected from the category x to the category y than from x to the category z, if P is viewed as more causally central in y than in z.

Similarity-based models of induction cannot account for the large body of evidence just reviewed, which involves both real-world concepts and concepts that are learned during experiments and which clearly shows that people bring to bear some causal knowledge in the inductive tasks designed by psychologists.[6] Theories are supposed to store this type of knowledge. These findings provide strong evidence for the existence of theories and for their use in induction.

---

[5] Typicality effects were however also found by López et al. 1997.
[6] For additional findings on the role of causal knowledge in induction, see Sloman 1994; Heit 2000; Rips 2001; Bailenson et al. 2002; Kemp and Tenenbaum 2003; Medin et al. 2003; Tenenbaum, Griffiths, and Kemp 2006. For some consistent work on ampliative induction, see Rehder and Hastie 2004; Rehder 2007.

7.1.5 A Multi-Process Theory of Induction

There is evidence that typicality affects some inductions, providing evidence either for prototype- or for exemplar-based models of induction. On the other hand, there is evidence that subjects engage in causal reasoning to evaluate the strength of inductive conclusions, recruiting some theories about categories and properties. How to account for these prima facie inconsistent findings? There is an emerging consensus that people have several induction processes (Proffitt, Coley, and Medin 2000; Murphy 2002; Sloman and Lagnado 2005; Rehder 2007):

> We believe that the bag of tricks describes most completely how people go about making inductive leaps. People seem to use a number of different sources of information for making inductive inferences, including the availability of featural information and knowledge about feature overlap, linguistic cues about the distribution of features, the relative centrality of features to one another, the relative probability of premises, and objects' roles in causal systems. (Sloman and Lagnado 2005: 112)

To put the same point differently, several psychologists have recently converged on a multi-process theory of induction.

A multi-process theory of a cognitive competence needs to state whether the hypothesized processes are all triggered in the same conditions or whether different processes are triggered in different conditions (sections 5.1 and 6.6). Most psychologists propose that one induction process is triggered at a time. For instance, Proffitt and colleagues write:

> We believe that both experts and novices have a variety of reasoning strategies at their disposal. Typicality and diversity, as described by Osherson and colleagues (1990), are two strategies that are powerful because they may be used in a wide range of situations. To some extent, they are domain general; however, they do depend on knowledge about the similarity relationships among categories. ... The causal-ecological strategies exhibited by the experts are even more dependent on an elaborated knowledge base, however, and for that reason may be applicable only in certain domains. (Proffitt, Coley, and Medin 2000: 826)

That is, what process underlies our inductions depends on the quality and nature of the knowledge that people might bring to bear on the inductive tasks. When people have some developed causal knowledge about the categories and the properties involved in induction, Proffitt and colleagues propose that they base their inductive judgments on their capacity to explain causally why a property possessed by the members of a given category would be possessed by the members of another category— whence the lack of typicality effects among experts. When our causal knowledge about the categories and properties involved in induction is sketchy, we might instead rely on the similarity between categories— whence the typicality effects in some conditions.

In an important article on ampliative induction, Rehder (2006) has provided some important evidence concerning the interaction between a similarity-based process and a theory-based process of induction.[7] In the learning phase of the first experiment, subjects were told that the members of an imaginary category, for instance, a category of artifacts called "Romanian Rogos," possess four properties. These properties were described as occurring in 75 percent of Romanian Rogos. In the test phase, subjects were presented with a new Rogo that possesses a novel property. Rehder did two manipulations. Half of the subjects were given a causal explanation for the possession of this property: they were told that this property was an effect of one of the characteristic properties of Rogos. For instance, in the learning phase, Rogos were said to have a hot engine, and the Rogo in the test phase was said to have melted wiring because of its hot engine. By contrast, half of the subjects were not given this causal explanation. Second, the typicality of the Rogo in the test phase was manipulated: it possessed one, two, three, or the four characteristic properties of the class of Rogos. Subjects were asked to evaluate on a scale the proportion of Rogos that would have the novel property. Of interest was how typicality and the presence of a causal explanation would interact.

The results are the following. When no causal explanation was given, typicality affected subjects' performances: the proportion of category members judged to possess the novel property was a function of the typicality of the item presented during the test. The influence of typicality was reduced when a causal explanation was given. This might be taken to suggest that prototypes (or exemplars) and causal knowledge affected induction simultaneously. This result can be interpreted in one of two ways. First, this could be evidence that a single process takes prototypes (or exemplars) and causal knowledge as inputs. This would be inconsistent with the emerging consensus that induction is underwritten by several processes. Alternatively, this could be evidence that the outputs of two induction processes—a process taking prototypes (or exemplars) as inputs and a process taking theories as inputs—are integrated (on integrating the outputs of different processes, see section 5.1). This would be consistent with the idea that there are several induction processes, but inconsistent with the idea that these processes are triggered in different conditions.

A more detailed analysis of subjects' judgments shows that these two interpretations are incorrect. Rehder (2006) has shown that subjects divided into two subgroups. For the first subgroup, typicality affected induction when no causal explanation was given, but did not affect induction when a causal explanation was given. For the second subgroup, subjects' judgments were not affected by the presence of a causal explanation. Typicality affected their judgments whether or not a causal explanation was given.

---

[7] I assume that findings about this form of induction are relevant for category-based induction. However, these two forms of induction might recruit different cognitive processes.

These findings suggest that consistent with psychologists' emerging consensus, people have several induction processes. They also show that prototypes (or exemplars) and the presence of a causal explanation were not integrated. When the presence of a causal explanation affected induction, typicality did not, and vice-versa. On the basis of these findings, Rehder proposes that an induction process that involves building causal explanations on the basis of theories inhibits a similarity-based induction process:

> The results of Experiments 1–3 supported the claim that when a causal explanation for a novel property is available, it often supplants similarity as the basis for the generalization of that property.... Apparently, when people note the presence of a causal explanation for a novel property, it often draws attention away from the exemplars' other features, making their similarity (or typicality or diversity) largely irrelevant to the inductive judgment. (Rehder 2006: 13–14)

Importantly, Rehder's conclusion can be interpreted in two ways. On a first interpretation, a single induction process is triggered at a time—either a theory-based process or a similarity-based process. It determines people's inductive judgments. This is in-line with the emerging consensus between psychologists working on induction. However, on a second interpretation, several induction processes are simultaneously triggered and a non-integrative process selects one of the outputs of these processes (on non-integrative processes, see section 5.1). As a result, a single process determines people's inductive judgments. In both interpretations, prototypes (or exemplars) and our causal knowledge are not integrated.

How can we distinguish between these two interpretations? Allen and Brooks's (1991) article on categorization suggests the following line of research (see sections 5.1 and 6.6). If several hypothesized induction processes are simultaneously triggered, subjects should be slower in making inductive judgments when these hypothesized processes yield conflicting outputs than when they yield consistent outputs. If induction processes are triggered one at a time, as suggested, for example, by Proffitt and colleagues (2000), subjects should not be slower in making inductive judgments when these hypothesized processes yield conflicting outputs than when they yield consistent outputs. To my knowledge, no evidence bears on this issue.

Finally, it is worth noting that there are several theories of prototype-based induction and several theories of theory-based induction.[8] I have not tried to distinguish between these theories. This task is better left to psychologists.[9]

---

[8] On the former, see, e.g., Osherson et al. 1990; Sloman 1993. On the latter, see Heit 2000; Rehder 2006.

[9] For a comparison of the models of theory-based induction, see Rehder 2007; for a comparison of two prototype-based models, see Sloman and Lagnado 2005.

7.2 Concept Combination

Since Osherson and Smith's seminal study (1981), concept combination has been intensively studied by psychologists of concepts.[10] Their results suggest that concept combination requires the kinds of knowledge that exemplars, prototypes, and theories are assumed to store. This is evidence for the Heterogeneity Hypothesis.

7.2.1 What Is Concept Combination?

Concept combination is the capacity to form new bodies of knowledge about classes for which we have no concept permanently stored in long-term memory. Those bodies of knowledge traditionally called "complex concepts" (e.g., GRANDMOTHER SPY) are formed on the basis of the bodies of knowledge stored in long-term memory (e.g., GRANDMOTHER and SPY). There is a finite stock of concepts stored in long-term memory because we are finite creatures. Thus, to fulfill various cognitive purposes (e.g., language comprehension, reasoning, etc.), complex concepts need to be produced on the fly. Psychologists attempt to characterize the processes that underlie the creation of new bodies of knowledge out of the bodies of knowledge that are stored in long-term memory. The claim defended in this section is that in order to explain the properties of concept combination, one has to assume the storage of prototypes, exemplars, and theories in long-term memory.

7.2.2 Prototypes and Property Inheritance

When subjects are given two expressions, say, "Harvard graduate" and "carpenter," and are asked to list the properties that are typical of Harvard graduates who are carpenters, they often find the task meaningful and easy.[11] In some experiments, they are also asked to determine which properties are typical of the two original categories—Harvard graduates and carpenters.[12] Hampton (1987) has shown that there is a correlation between the properties that are judged to be typical of the members of the original categories (Harvard graduates and carpenters) and the properties that are judged to be typical of the members of the resulting category (Harvard graduates who are carpenters).

This correlation suggests that the creation of a complex concept involves determining which properties are typical of the denoted category, Harvard graduates who are carpenters, on the basis of the typical properties of the original categories, Harvard graduates and carpenters. Now, prototypes are supposed to store the knowledge about typical properties.

---

[10] For reviews, see Hampton 1997a; Murphy 2002: ch. 12; Hampton and Jönsson, forthcoming; Machery and Lederer, forthcoming; Wisniewski and Wu, forthcoming.
[11] Hampton 1987; Kunda, Miller, and Claire 1990; Johnson and Keil 2000.
[12] Hampton 1987; Johnson and Keil 2000.

Thus, it is plausible that when we produce a complex concept on the fly, we retrieve the prototypes of the original categories from long-term memory, and we use them to determine the typical properties of the category represented by the complex concept. This is known as "property inheritance" (Hampton 1997a; figure 7.2). The inheritance of properties by the complex concept is (partly, as we shall see) driven by the assumption that the typical properties of the categories denoted by the compounded concepts are also typical of the category denoted by the complex concept.[13] Notice that I am not claiming that complex concepts are prototypes. Although complex concepts do store some knowledge about the typical properties of the denoted categories, as do prototypes, they may also store some modal and some causal knowledge (see below).

Evidence suggests that the bodies of knowledge constructed on the fly are used in various cognitive processes. Particularly, subjects are able to evaluate the typicality of individuals qua Harvard graduates who are carpenters (e.g., Medin and Shoben 1988). That is, when subjects are given the description of an individual, they are able to determine whether this individual is a typical Harvard graduate who is a carpenter. This suggests that people use their beliefs about which properties are typical of Harvard graduates who are carpenters to evaluate the typicality of individuals.

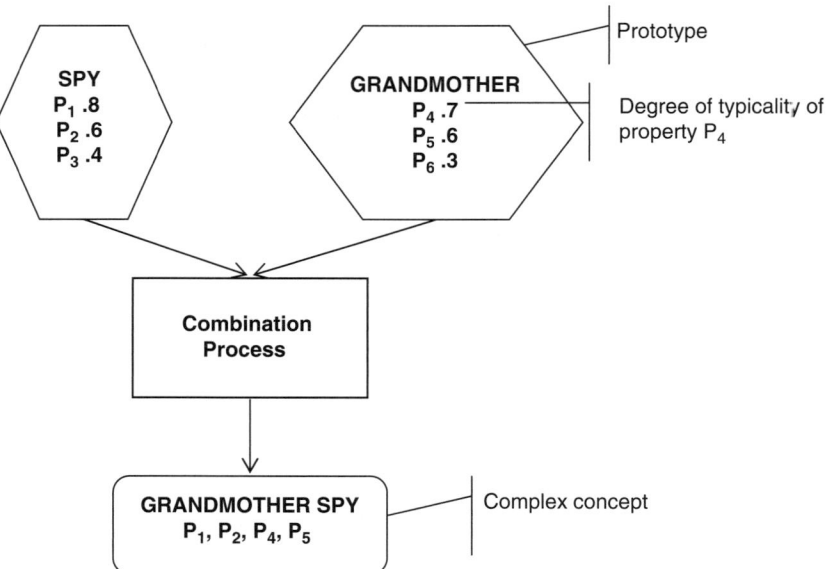

Figure 7.2 The Role of Prototypes in Concept Combination

---

[13] For discussion, see Connolly et al. 2007; Jönsson and Hampton 2007; Gleitman, Connolly, and Armstrong, forthcoming; Machery and Lederer, forthcoming.

One might reply that these typicality judgments are based on the typicality of these individuals qua Harvard graduates and on their typicality qua carpenters (Huttenlocher and Hedges 1994). That is, we may judge that an individual is a typical Harvard graduate who is a carpenter if we judge that she is a typical Harvard graduate and a typical carpenter. Hence, these judgments may not rely on a complex concept that represents the typical properties of Harvard graduates who are carpenters. In other words, to judge whether an individual is a typical Harvard graduate who is a carpenter, we may not need to produce a complex concept, HARVARD GRADUATE WHO IS A CARPENTER.

This objection fails, however. For the typicality of items with respect to a complex concept (HARVARD GRADUATE WHO IS A CARPENTER) is often not a function of their typicality with respect to the combined concepts (HARVARD GRADUATE and CARPENTER). The former is a function of the latter only when the membership in one category (Harvard graduates) is believed to be independent from the membership in the other (carpenters) (Hampton 1987: 57; Huttenlocher and Hedges 1994). Hence, the best explanation of the typicality judgments under consideration is that people do produce a complex concept that represents typical properties, and that they use this complex concept to make typicality judgments. Together with other phenomena (Hampton 1982, 1987, 1988, 1996), this discussion suggests that we produce complex concepts by retrieving prototypes from long-term memory, and that we use them to reason.

7.2.3 Theories and Property Inheritance

The story is, however, more complex, for psychologists have shown that the typicality of a property is not the only factor that determines whether it is represented by the complex concept. To illustrate, whether the property *being ambitious* is typical of Harvard graduates and of carpenters is not the only factor that determines whether it is represented by the complex concept HARVARD GRADUATE WHO IS A CARPENTER. Property inheritance is also influenced by our theoretical knowledge about the categories that are combined.[14]

Concept combination uses some modal information about the properties of the members of the original categories, for example, about the properties of grandmothers and of spies. Which properties are represented by the complex concept, GRANDMOTHER SPY, is a function of their modal force. Studies show that if the input concepts represent so-called "impossible properties" (properties that are typically possessed by the members of one category, say, *male* for spies, but that are believed to be impossible for the members of the other category, say, grandmothers), these are never represented by the complex concept; if the input concepts represent

---

[14] Medin and Shoben 1988; Murphy 1988, 1990; Rips 1995; Johnson and Keil 2000; Costello and Keane 2000, 2005.

so-called "necessary properties" (properties that are believed to be necessarily possessed by the members of one category, say, *being the mother of a parent* for grandmothers), these properties are always represented by the complex concept (Hampton 1987).

Moreover, concept combination requires some causal information about the properties of the original categories.[15] Causally central properties are preferentially represented by complex concepts.

These results show that during concept combination, we access some modal and causal knowledge (figure 7.3). Now, prototypes do not represent any modal nor any causal knowledge, but only some statistical knowledge. Consequently, during concept combination, we access some knowledge that is not stored in prototypes. Theories are supposed to store this type of knowledge. Thus, to account for concept combination, we need to posit a second type of concept (i.e., theories) besides prototypes.

One could object that the evidence does not show that we have some theoretical concepts, that is, bodies of theoretical knowledge that are used by default in a large number of cognitive competences. We may simply rely on some background modal and causal knowledge about the categories that are combined. This is indeed how Hampton himself thinks of the use of modal knowledge in concept combination (Hampton 1997a). Being a prototype theorist, he believes that this modal knowledge is specifically extracted for the purpose of building complex concepts. Hence, this

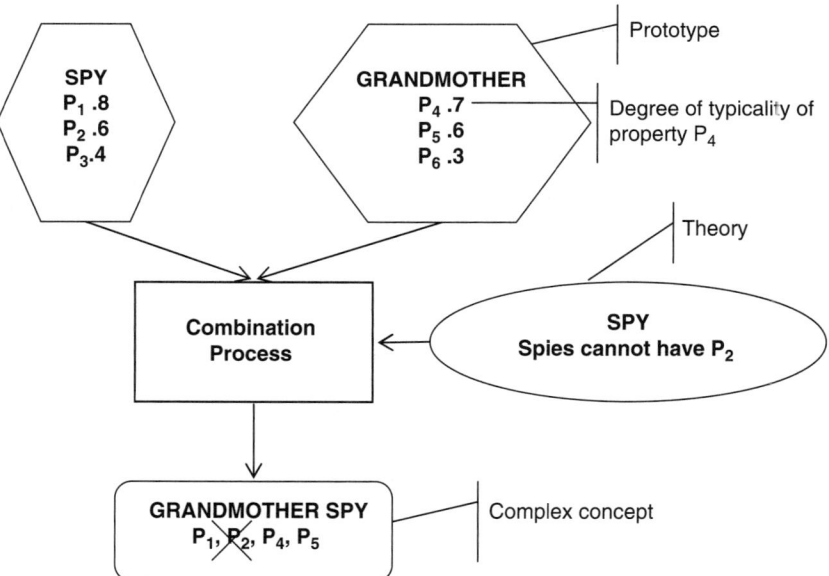

Figure 7.3 The Role of Theories in Concept Combination

---

[15] Medin and Shoben 1988; Murphy 1988, 1990; Johnson and Keil 2000.

modal knowledge is not used by default in the processes underlying the higher cognitive competences. At this stage of the book, it should be clear that I disagree with this interpretation of the evidence. As we have repeatedly seen, we routinely use this very same causal and modal knowledge in the processes underlying other higher cognitive competences (see chapter 6 on categorization and section 6.1 on induction). Thus, the bodies of knowledge that store this knowledge are genuine concepts.

7.2.4 Exemplars and Property Emergence

Not all properties that are represented by a complex concept are represented by the original prototypes. The properties not represented by the original prototypes are said to be emergent, and this phenomenon is known as "property emergence."[16] For example, Harvard graduates who are carpenters may be judged to have an artistic character, while neither Harvard graduates nor carpenters are judged to have an artistic character (Kunda, Miller, and Claire 1990). Several explanations of property emergence have been suggested. They are not mutually exclusive. For the sake of argument, I focus on the explanation that relies on exemplars.

Some properties derive from our knowledge of specific members of the complex category (Hampton 1987; Medin and Shoben 1988: 183 et seq.). For example, if a young liberal has to produce on the fly a complex concept like PRESIDENT FROM TEXAS, he may look in her long-term memory

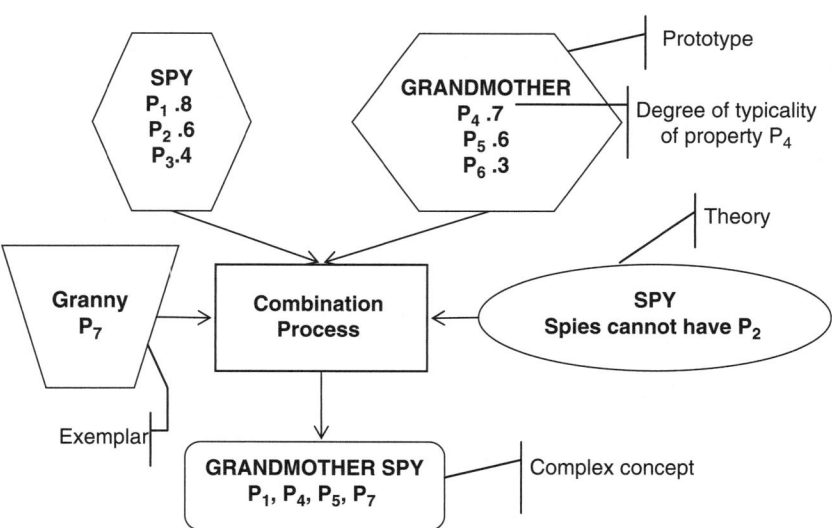

Figure 7.4 The Role of Exemplars in Concept Combination

---

[16] Hampton 1987, 1997a; Kunda, Miller, and Claire 1990; Costello and Keane 2000, 2005; Johnson and Keil 2000.

for someone who is president and who comes from Texas. Plausibly, she would retrieve the representation of G. W. Bush, and she would transmit to the complex concept the properties that are represented by this singular memory. She would thus represent presidents from Texas as being dull. Hence, concept combination accesses some representations of particular individuals. To use another example, suppose that my grandmother is a spy, her properties might be transmitted to the bodies of knowledge about grandmother spies that I might form on the fly (figure 7.4).

7.2.5 *Upshot*

The research on concept combination provides further support for the Heterogeneity Hypothesis—it provides evidence for the existence of prototypes, exemplars, and theories that are retrieved from long-term memory to create complex concepts. It is worth emphasizing that contrary to the models of the processes involved in categorization, concept learning, and induction proposed so far, the model of the process involved in concept combination is not a multi-process theory. Following Hampton, I have proposed that a single process, taking different kinds of concept as inputs, underlies the creation of complex concepts.

7.3 *Neuropsychology*

The psychology of concepts has mostly been behavioral, relying on behavioral measures—such as reaction time, probability of mistaken answers, or type of mistaken answers—to provide evidence for and against theories of concepts and for and against models of concept-involving cognitive processes. Recently, neuropsychologists have turned their attention to the study of concepts. It is fair to say that the field is still inchoate. Controversies abound, and robust conclusions are yet to emerge. Nonetheless, it is important to find out whether the neuropsychology of concepts casts some light on the Heterogeneity Hypothesis. As I explained in section 5.1, dissociations might provide some telling evidence for the existence of several processes underwriting a given cognitive competence. I now argue that although some recent neuropsychological work on concepts seems to support the Heterogeneity Hypothesis, a closer look at these findings leads to a more disappointing conclusion.

7.3.1 *Neuropsychology and the Classical Theory of Concepts*

As noted in section 4.1, much of the recent neuropsychological work on concepts amounts to a revival of the classical theory of concepts.[17]

---

[17] See, e.g., Smith, Patalano, and Jonides 1998; Seger et al. 2000; Grossman et al. 2002; Filoteo et al. 2005.

Grossman and colleagues' (2002) work is a good example. Grossman and colleagues' hypothesis is consistent with the Heterogeneity Hypothesis. They contend that categorization is underwritten by several cognitive processes. Particularly, they contrast those categorizations that are based on the application of a rule with those categorizations that are based on similarity. Although they refer to Murphy and Medin's (1985) article on theories, Grossman and colleagues' characterization of rule-based categorization is in fact in line with the classical theory of concepts: objects are categorized in a category if and only if they are believed to satisfy its definition. To characterize similarity-based categorization, Grossman and colleagues refer indiscriminately to exemplar-based and prototype-based models.

Based on previous studies, Grossman and colleagues predicted that the dorsolateral prefrontal cortex and the anterior cingulate would be involved with the first kind of categorization, the inferior parietal cortex with the second kind of categorization. To test this prediction, Grossman and colleagues used the design of Rips's pizza experiment (section 6.5.1). Subjects were given different instructions in order to prime either a rule-based categorization process or a similarity-based categorization process. Brain images were compared across the two conditions. Neuropsychological findings confirmed Grossman and colleagues' prediction: "In sum, the finding of partially distinct activation patterns for rule-based and similarity-based categorization is consistent with the claim that there are multiple approaches to categorization" (Grossman et al. 2002: 1558).

These findings seem to provide some telling neuropsychological evidence for the view that we have several distinct categorization processes. This would of course be consistent with the Heterogeneity Hypothesis. Unfortunately, it is very unclear whether these findings (as well as similar findings) really support the Heterogeneity Hypothesis. The first issue is specific to Grossman and colleagues' study. The instructions that were supposed to prime the hypothesized similarity-based categorization system do not in fact ask subjects to categorize objects. Rather, subjects were asked to evaluate the similarity of the targets to two categories. But evaluating the similarity of an object to a category is not categorizing this object in this category. Instead of priming two different ways of categorizing, the two sets of instruction defined two tasks—a categorization task and a similarity judgment task. Finding that different brain areas are activated in these two tasks provides no evidence whatsoever for the idea that categorization is underwritten by several systems.

The second issue bears on numerous studies besides Grossman and colleagues (2002). The experiment is supposed to pit a rule-based categorization process against a similarity-based categorization process. The problem is that even though people are certainly able to follow a rule in categorizing objects, I doubt that they often do so during real-world categorizations. As argued in section 4.1, neuropsychologists systematically fail to address the main objection against the classical theory: even though people are able to learn and use definitions of categories, there is no reason to believe that they do so for real-world categories. Studies that look for a rule-based process may say very little about how we categorize outside the lab.

7.3.2 A Dissociation between Prototypes and Exemplars?

Squire and Knowlton (1995) studied a profound anterograde and retrograde amnesic patient, E.P., whose medial temporal lobes are severely injured in both hemispheres.[18] The declarative memory of amnesic patients, often characterized as "the capacity for conscious recollections about facts and events" (ibid. 12470), is often only partially impaired.[19] By contrast, E.P.'s declarative memory is entirely impaired. He is unable to recognize previously seen items, which suggests that he is unable to form new memories of singular objects. Squire and Knowlton (1995) report that after more than thirty visits, E.P. was still unable to recognize the experimenter.

Squire and Knowlton found that in spite of this impairment, E.P.'s categorization performances in some experimental conditions were similar to normal subjects' performances. Squire and Knowlton relied on Posner and Keele's (1968, 1970) dot-distortion category task (see section 6.1). In one experiment, E.P. was presented with dot patterns in the training phase and was told that all these dot patterns belonged to the same category. In the test phase, he was presented with new dot patterns and was asked to decide whether they belonged to this category. Like normal subjects, E.P.'s categorization decisions were a function of the typicality of the target: the probability that a target was classified as a category member was a decreasing function of the similarity of this target to the prototype of the category. By contrast, E.P. was unable to recognize a training item that had been presented forty times during the training phase. His performance was at chance, while normal subjects were 95 percent correct.

These findings suggest that not all categorization judgments result from an exemplar-based categorization process. Because of his amnesia, E.P. was unable to form representations of the patterns of dots seen during training. As a result, he was unable to recognize training items. However, he classified new items as normal subjects do. Squire and Knowlton conclude:

> These findings demonstrate that the ability to classify novel items, after experience with other items in the same category, is a separate and parallel memory function of the brain, independent of the limbic and diencephalic structures essential for remembering individual stimulus items (declarative memory). (Squire and Knowlton 1995: 12470)

[18] Knowlton and Squire (1993) studied less profoundly impaired amnesic patients. See also Knowlton 1997, 1999; Reed et al. 1999.

[19] It is dubious that declarative memory is a single competence. It underlies our feeling of familiarity ("this person looks familiar," "this place looks familiar"), the identification of individuals ("this is G. W. Bush"), and our conscious recollection of facts and events.

A plausible explanation of E.P.'s normal classification performances is that during training, he abstracted a prototype of the category of dot patterns and used this prototype to classify new patterns during the test phase.

This single dissociation between categorization and declarative memory could be interpreted as providing some support for the Heterogeneity Hypothesis. If one is convinced by the behavioral evidence that there is an exemplar-based categorization process, Squire and Knowlton's findings show that this is not the unique categorization process.

Knowlton and Squire's work with amnesic patients has been under heavy fire.[20] Several alternative explanations of the performances of amnesic patients in classification and recognition tasks have been proposed. Endorsing a single-process approach to categorization, Nosofsky and Zaki (1998) have argued that exemplar-based models of categorization and of recognition can simulate the dissociation between categorization and recognition found by Knowlton and Squire. If this is correct and if the relevant models are plausible (see section 5.1.5), this dissociation does not provide support for the Heterogeneity Hypothesis.

The key aspect of their explanation is that amnesic patients have poorer memory discrimination than normal subjects. That is, the memories, or exemplars, of the dot patterns seen during training are less distinct from one another for amnesic patients than for normal subjects. Similarly, a normal subject's memory discrimination of a set of dot patterns is poorer a week after having seen them than right after seeing them. In substance, Nosofsky and Zaki (1998) propose that a poor memory discrimination is sufficient for categorization, but not for recognition.

Let us look more closely at Nosofsky and Zaki's (1998) model. They make the following assumption:

$$S(i,j) = [\text{rating}(i,j)]^p \tag{12}$$

where $S(i,j)$ is the similarity between two patterns of points i and j and rating (i,j) is the mean value of the similarity judgments made by subjects when they are presented with i and j.

Nosofsky and Zaki propose that the value of p in equation 12 is higher for normal subjects than for amnesic patients ($p_N > p_A$). This entails that the similarity of a given target to two different exemplars of patterns of dots differs less for amnesic patients than for normal subjects:

$$|S_A(t, E_1) - S_A(t, E_2)| < |S_N(t, E_1) - S_N(t, E_2)| \tag{13}$$

where $S_A(t, E_1)$ is the similarity of the target and exemplar 1 for an amnesic patient and $S_N(t, E_1)$ is the similarity of the target and exemplar 1 for a normal subject (*mutatis mutandis* for exemplar 2). This captures amnesiacs' poorer memory discrimination.

---

[20] Nosofsky and Zaki 1998; Palmeri and Flanery 1999; Smith and Minda 2001; Zaki and Nosofsky 2001; Zaki et al. 2003.

The probability to categorize a target as a category member and the probability to recognize it are two increasing functions of the similarity of the target to the representations of the dot patterns seen during training. Both functions have the form:

$$\frac{ax}{ax+k} \qquad (14)$$

where k, called either the "classification criterion" or the "recognition criterion," is a constant that varies across categorization and recognition and across normal subjects and amnesic patients, x is the average similarity between the target and the exemplars in long-term memory, and a is the number of dot patterns seen during training.

Because $p_N > p_A$, the average similarity between the target and the exemplars (x in 14) is higher for normal subjects than for amnesic patients. Hence, the probability of categorizing and recognizing tends to be higher for a normal subject compared to an amnesic patient. However, because many dot patterns are seen during the training phase of the categorization task, the higher value of p_N by comparison with p_A does not lead to markedly better categorization performances for normal subjects than for amnesic patients. By contrast, because few dot patterns are seen during the training phase of the recognition task, the higher value of p_N by comparison with p_A leads to much better recognition performances for normal subjects.

Thus, amnesic patients' poorer memory discrimination accounts for the dissociation found by Knowlton and Squire. Since Nosofsky and Zaki's model assumes that both tasks are solved by retrieving exemplars from long-term memory, Knowlton and Squire's findings are not evidence that at least some categorization judgments do not result from an exemplar-based process—or so Nosofsky and Zaki conclude.

Nosofsky and Zaki's model is well-known. However, it is not completely satisfying. First, it does not account for all of Knowlton and Squire's findings. As noted by Knowlton (1999), this model cannot be easily applied to E.P.'s categorization performances, since it assumes that amnesic patients' declarative memory is not entirely impaired.

Moreover, an aspect of Nosofsky and Zaki's models of categorization and recognition is puzzling. The values of the classification criterion (k_c) and recognition criterion (k_R) vary across normal subjects and amnesic patients (Nosofsky and Zaki 1998: 252, table 3). Thus, in their models, the similarity between a target and the hypothesized exemplars of dot patterns differently affects the probability of classification and the probability of recognition for normal subjects and for patients. It is unclear how one can make sense of the variation of these criteria across normal subjects and amnesic patients. Unfortunately, Nosofsky and Zaki (1998) do not comment on these aspects of their models.

Finally, Palmeri and Flanery (1999) have proposed an explanation of Knowlton and Squire's findings that differ both from Squire and

Knowlton's own account and from Nosofsky and Zaki's (1998) account. They experimentally show that subjects can perform well in Squire and Knowlton's version of the dot-distortion category task, even when they have not been trained to distinguish category members from non-category members. How can people correctly classify dot patterns without having been previously exposed to members of the relevant categories? Palmeri and Flanery (1999) propose that subjects use the similarities among test items to decide how to classify them. As they put it, "Even without memory for the training stimuli, participants might quickly realize that the similar patterns are most likely to be members of one category" (1999: 526).

Palmeri and Flanery's findings show that neither storing in memory exemplars of category members (pace Nosofsky and colleagues) nor extracting a prototype during a training phase (pace Knowlton and Squire) is necessary for performing well in the dot-distortion category task. Since amnesiacs do possess the short-term memory needed to compare the test items during the test phase, their performances in the dot-distortion category task might say very little about how concepts are learned and about how objects are categorized.

Strictly speaking, Palmeri and Flanery's startling findings do not show that subjects, including E.P., are not using some knowledge acquired during the training phase to classify the training items (either a prototype or a set of exemplars). It would be useful to compare E.P.'s classifications of the first test items with the classifications of these items made by Palmeri and Flanery's subjects. If these subjects are really focusing on the similarities between the test items, their first classifications should be random. If E.P.'s classifications are driven by some knowledge acquired during the training phase, his first classifications should not be random. Presently, however, Palmeri and Flanery's findings cast some serious doubts on any conclusion that one would want to draw from E.P.'s and other amnesiacs' performances in Squire and Knowlton's version of the dot-distortion category task.

Another issue with Knowlton and Squire's research is worth stressing. Knowlton and Squire's findings seem to be at odds with what is known about visual categorization. Very little is uncontroversial about the brain areas involved in categorizing visually presented objects. However, there is converging evidence and substantial agreement that the left temporal lobe is an important area for this function (e.g., Tanaka 2004). E.P. has severely impaired bilateral medial temporal lobes. This suggests that E.P.'s preserved capacity to classify dot patterns says little about how we categorize real-world objects.

7.3.3 Upshot

Recent findings in the neuropsychology of concepts initially seem to support the Heterogeneity Hypothesis. However, a closer look at this field leads to a disappointing conclusion for the hypothesis developed in this book: none of these neuropsychological findings provide robust evidence for the Heterogeneity Hypothesis.

7.4 Conclusion

The empirical study of induction provides evidence for the existence of at least two distinct induction processes—a process involving matching concepts and measuring their similarity and a process involving building causal explanations. The similarity-based induction process could involve either prototypes (as assumed by most psychologists) or exemplars. In fact, we could have several similarity-based induction processes. Psychologists assume that the explanation-based induction process involves theories. Thus, although the literature on induction does not support the full-blown Heterogeneity Hypothesis—since it does not show that we have prototypes, exemplars, and theories—it is by and large consistent with it. The empirical study of concept combination provides further support for the Heterogeneity Hypothesis. Prototypes, exemplars, and theories are used when we produce complex concepts. It is noteworthy that I did not propose a multi-process theory of concept combination. Rather, I proposed that a single process takes different kinds of concept as inputs. Finally, the neuropsychological research on concept has the potential to provide evidence for or against the Heterogeneity Hypothesis. However, much of the current research in this field is problematic. Many studies are mistakenly committed to the classical theory of concepts. And there are strong reasons to doubt that the well-known findings by Squire and Knowlton have much to say about categorization.

8

Concept Eliminativism

In previous chapters, I have argued that in psychology, concepts are taken to be the bodies of knowledge that are used by default in the processes underlying the higher cognitive competences (chapter 1). Reviewing the theoretical literature on concepts, I have shown that psychologists have developed several theories about the nature of concepts, positing several theoretical entities that have little in common (chapter 4). Although other theoretical entities, such as ideals and perceptual symbols, have been proposed, I have focused on prototypes, exemplars, and theories because there is clear evidence for their existence. In chapters 6 and 7, I have reviewed the empirical literature on categorization, induction, and concept combination—three important higher cognitive competences—and I have argued that prototypes, exemplars, and theories all exist and are often used in distinct cognitive processes.

Thus, the discussion so far strongly supports the first four tenets of the Heterogeneity Hypothesis (chapter 3):

1. The best available evidence suggests that for each category (for each substance, event ...), an individual typically has several concepts, that is, several bodies of knowledge that are by default retrieved from long-term memory and used when he or she categorizes, reasons inductively or deductively, or makes analogies.
2. Coreferential concepts have very few properties in common. Thus, coreferential concepts belong to very heterogeneous kinds of concept.

3. Evidence strongly suggests that prototypes, exemplars, and theories are among these heterogeneous kinds of concept.
4. Prototypes, exemplars, and theories are often used in distinct cognitive processes.

The last chapter of this book focuses on the fifth tenet of the Heterogeneity Hypothesis.

5. The notion of concept ought to be eliminated from the theoretical vocabulary of psychology because it might prevent psychologists from correctly characterizing the nature of the knowledge in long-term memory and its use in cognitive processes.

In section 8.1, I review and discard two previous arguments against the notion of concept. In section 8.2, I describe a new type of eliminativist argument—showing that the extension of a scientific notion is not a natural kind. In section 8.3, I apply this argument to concepts. In section 8.4, I reply to a few objections against the elimination of "concept." I conclude that concepts are not a natural kind and that the notion of concept ought to be eliminated from the theoretical vocabulary of psychology and replaced by the notions of prototype, exemplar, and theory.

8.1 Two Inconclusive Arguments against the Notion of Concept

Despite its prominence in psychology, the notion of concept has not gone unchallenged. In this first section, I present the two main arguments that have been put forward against this notion, and I show that they are not conclusive.

8.1.1 Anti-Representationalism in Cognitive Science

Hard-liners among proponents of the dynamical-systems approach in cognitive science (e.g., Thelen and Smith 1994) and among advocates of embodied robotics (e.g., Brooks [1991] 1999) argue that the mind does not store or manipulate representations.[1] I call this view the anti-representationalist tenet.[2] Since concepts are assumed to be representations, this tenet entails that we have no concepts.

Proponents of embodied robotics and of dynamical systems offer the same type of argument for the anti-representationalist tenet. They focus

---

[1] Not all proponents of the dynamical-systems approach to cognition eschew representations (Van Gelder 1995).

[2] In some places, Brooks hedges his bets by conceding that some aspects of cognition might require representations ([1991] 1999: 81; my emphasis): "Representation is the wrong unit of abstraction in building *the bulkiest parts* of intelligent systems."

on some phenomena that proponents of representation-based approaches to cognition explain (or would explain) by means of representations and representation-based processes. Proponents of embodied robotics and of dynamical systems explain these phenomena without positing any cognitive process that manipulates representations. Then, they propose the following inductive leap. If it is possible to explain these phenomena without representations, it is plausible that most, and maybe all, phenomena can be explained without representations.

Rodney Brooks's well-know article ([1991] 1999) illustrates this argumentative strategy. Brooks focuses on three basic behaviors, moving in a real, changing environment without bumping into objects, avoiding moving objects, and reaching specific points in the environment. He describes several robots that move in real, cluttered environments, avoid moving objects, and reach some points in their environment without having states that can be naturally characterized as representing their environment. These robots stand in sharp contrast with the few robots that were built in the 1970s, like Shakey at the Stanford Research Institute. Shakey displayed the three behaviors discussed by Brooks: moving, avoiding, and reaching a pre-specified point. It was representation-hungry: on the basis of its input systems, it produced a map of its environment, which was used to elaborate a plan for reaching a pre-specified point in its environment. Contrary to Brooks's robots, Shakey was unable to move in real, cluttered environments. Instead, its movements were limited to an artificial, specially designed room. Brooks and colleagues have thus shown that some behaviors that were previously presumed to be produced by representation-based processes can result from processes that do not manipulate representations. These remarkable successes are used as the inductive basis for the anti-representationalist tenet. If these behaviors do not result from representation-based processes, maybe no, or only few, behaviors result from such processes.

However, this inductive inference is dubious. First, anti-representationalists such as Brooks make the same mistake as behaviorists like Skinner. They explain some simple behaviors without assuming representation-based processes, and they propose that this type of explanation generalizes to all (or, at least, most) behaviors. Thereby, they make a strong empirical hypothesis about the complexity of the causal mechanisms that underlie behavior in general. They assume that the mechanisms that underlie all (or most) behaviors are similar to the mechanisms that explain the simple behaviors they have focused on. The truth of this hypothesis is clearly an empirical question. But it is fair to say that anti-representationalists have not provided any reason to believe in this empirical hypothesis. On the contrary, half a century of representationalist cognitive science gives us plenty of reasons to resist it. Additionally, the dynamical-systems models of complex psychological phenomena, such as decision making, typically assume the existence of representations (e.g., Busemeyer and Townsend 1993).

Second, one can question the inductive basis of the induction made by anti-representationalists. There is evidence that in mammals at least, the type of behavior that has been studied by the proponents of embodied robotics or of dynamical systems results from representation-based processes. Grush (2003) has argued that physical actions are often guided by representations of the feedback that is to be expected from our muscles. Proprioceptive feedback from our muscles is used to fine-tune our actions—for instance, to specify the exact strength needed to lift a heavy object. Because it takes time for this proprioceptive feedback to reach our brain, in some circumstances, we cannot afford to wait for actual feedback. In these circumstances, the brain needs to guide movement without actual proprioceptive feedback. Grush speculates that in these cases, the relevant brain systems are fed representations of the proprioceptive feedback that would be received if we had enough time. To put it simply, the brain simulates the feedback it would receive. Grush (2004) reviews a large body of neuropsychological evidence that supports these theoretical speculations. Thus, if Grush is correct, even simple actions cannot be explained without positing some representations.

There is presently very little reason to endorse the anti-representationalist argument made by the radical proponents of embodied robotics and of dynamical systems. Thus, the notion of concept is not threatened by the concerns about representations voiced by these radicals.

8.1.2. *The Argument from Context-Sensitivity*

L. Smith has proposed a more specific argument against the notion of concept (Smith and Samuelson 1997).[3] She writes:

> Theories of concepts have concentrated on the stability of categories—on the fact that people treat quite diverse entities as equivalent and that they do so in globally similar ways across contexts and tasks. However, the evidence suggests that on closer inspection categories are variable as well as stable. Further, people appear able to create categories on the spot. Category variability and in task category creation are facts not well explained by the idea of a concept. (Smith and Samuelson 1997: 170)

And, following James (1890),[4] she draws the following conclusion, "A successful theory of categories...might require that we give up timeless abstractions such as concepts" (Smith and Samuelson 1997: 190). I propose to reconstruct this argument as follows:

1. "Concept" is meant to refer to "stable" bodies of knowledge about categories (substances, events...) in long-term memory: that is, the same bodies of knowledge are used across contexts.

---

[3] Other psychologists have come close to endorsing this argument (e.g., Barsalou et al. 2003: 84).

[4] James wrote ([1890] 1950: 246): "I shall avoid the use of the expression 'concept' altogether."

2. Empirical evidence shows that the bodies of knowledge that we use when we reason, categorize, or understand a language are "variable": that is, they vary across contexts.
3. Hence, "concept" does not refer to anything.
4. Hence, there are no concepts.

There are several reasons to resist this argument. First, Premise 1 should not be misunderstood. As stated in Premise 1, the notion of concept does suppose that when people categorize or reason inductively about, say, dogs, the same body(ies) of knowledge about dogs—that is, the body(ies) of knowledge that is(are) constitutive of our concept(s) of dog—is(are) retrieved from long-term memory. However, this is consistent with some amount of context-sensitivity of the knowledge used when people categorize or reason inductively—thus, with some amount of context sensitivity of subjects' performances in categorization and induction tasks. As we saw in section 1.4, when people categorize or reason inductively, the concepts retrieved from long-term memory may be adapted to the relevant contexts. Once the whole body of knowledge that is constitutive of a concept is retrieved from memory, a specific subset of this knowledge might be used in a context-sensitive manner. Additionally, in some contexts, some knowledge about a category x (or a substance x...) will be retrieved from long-term memory in addition to the knowledge about x stored in our concept(s) of x. These two processes might explain a certain amount of context-sensitivity of subjects' performances in categorization or in induction tasks.

What would be problematic for the notion of concept used in psychology is an extreme variability in subjects' performances across contexts (in contrast to some variability of their performances). For instance, evidence that categorization in the class of dogs varies tremendously across contexts would suggest that people do not retrieve from long-term memory a stable body of knowledge about dogs (or several stable bodies of knowledge about dogs). But, as we shall see below, there is no evidence for such an extreme variability in subjects' performances across contexts (see also section 1.4).

To support Premise 2, Smith and Samuelson refer to Barsalou's work on ad hoc categories (see sections 1.4 and 4.5) and the variability across occasions of people's performances in several experimental tasks (see section 1.4), such as feature production (Barsalou 1993), typicality judgments (Barsalou 1993), and categorization judgments (McCloskey and Glucksberg 1978). As noted in Chapter 1, however, Barsalou's work on ad hoc categories says nothing about the nature of concepts in long-term memory. Bodies of knowledge about ad hoc categories are created on the fly, not retrieved from long-term memory. McCloskey and Glucksberg's (1978) findings on people's variability in categorization judgments across contexts are also a red herring. McCloskey and Glucksberg found that across occasions, subjects make inconsistent categorization judgments for some entities. For instance, people are likely to make inconsistent categorization decisions when asked in different occasions whether bacteria are animals, whether elevators are vehicles, or whether carpets are pieces of furniture. That is, people make inconsistent categorization judgments across occasions for those entities whose membership is neither clearly positive nor clearly negative. It is however easy to see that this kind of variability is consistent with standard models of concepts. Suppose that categorizing a lift as a vehicle consists of determining whether elevators possess a sufficient number of typical properties of vehicles. Suppose also that people have two thresholds, a positive threshold and a negative one. If the number of properties shared by elevators and vehicles is above a positive threshold, people give a positive answer; if it is below the negative threshold, people give a negative answer; if it is between these two thresholds, people are unsure about the answer, and if compelled to give an answer, they answer randomly. This simple categorization model would predict McCloskey and Glucksberg's findings.[5] For instance, consider elevators. Because elevators possess a few properties among the typical properties of vehicles, but only a few, the number of properties would be above the negative threshold for being a vehicle, but below the positive threshold. Thus, when compelled to decide whether elevators are vehicles, people would give a random answer. This would explain why people's categorization decisions vary across contexts. Finally, performances in feature production and typicality judgments vary little across contexts (sections 1.4 and 4.3). To sum up, pace Smith and Samuelson, a limited amount of context-sensitivity of people's performances in experimental tasks is consistent with any notion of concept worth arguing for. And the best available evidence shows that the context-sensitivity of our performances in experimental tasks is limited in precisely this way.

8.1.3 Beyond Old-Fashioned Eliminativist Arguments

The two arguments discussed above follow the template of eliminativist arguments. The structure of these arguments is well-known. Consider, for instance, the argument for the elimination of beliefs, desires, and other propositional attitudes (Churchland 1981; Stich 1983, 1996). It is argued that "belief" is defined by the role of the concept of belief in the generalizations about beliefs that we hold explicitly or implicitly. It is then argued that scientific evidence, for example, evidence drawn from neuropsychology (Churchland 1981) or from artificial intelligence (Ramsey et al. 1990), shows that no entities fulfill the role that defines "belief." It is inferred that "belief" fails to refer, hence, that beliefs do not exist.

---

[5] Alternatively, there may be a unique threshold, which may vary slightly across contexts (e.g., Hampton 1995).

The similarity between this classic argument and the two arguments discussed above should be striking. In the first case, it is argued that by definition, concepts are representations. It is then argued there are no concepts because, as a matter of fact, there are no representations. The second case is even clearer. It is argued that concepts are by definition stable representations in long-term memory. It is then argued that there are no concepts because there are no stable representations in long-term memory.

Many things can be said about this type of eliminativist argument (for a careful discussion, see Stich 1996: ch. 1). One can debate about which generalizations are constitutive of the definition of the term under consideration, say, "concept" or "belief" (e.g., Clark 1993: ch. 10 discussing Ramsey et al. 1990). One can also debate whether the best available empirical evidence shows that nothing fulfills the role defining the term under consideration. This is precisely what I have done above to rebut the anti-representationalist argument and the argument from context-sensitivity.

But, more fundamentally, there is a strong case to be made that such eliminativist arguments are fundamentally vitiated (Stich 1996; Mallon et al., forthcoming). These arguments rely on assumptions about how words like "concept" or "belief" refer. Two individuals, John and Jim, could agree on which generalizations define a term like "belief." They could also agree that the best empirical evidence from neuropsychology or from artificial intelligence suggests that nothing satisfies the definition of "belief" based on these generalizations. Nonetheless, John and Jim could still disagree on whether or not there are beliefs. If John endorses a descriptivist theory of reference for terms like "belief," he should conclude that there are no beliefs. For, according to this theory of reference, the reference of a term like "belief" is whatever entity (if any) best satisfies its definition. Since the best empirical evidence suggests that the definition is not satisfied, "belief" does not refer. Hence, there are no beliefs.[6] If Jim endorses a causal-historical theory of reference for terms like "belief," he should not conclude that there are no beliefs. Instead, Jim could argue that people may simply be mistaken about the nature of beliefs. For, according to this theory of reference, the reference of a term such as "belief" is not determined by its definition, but by a historical link between this term and a referent in the world. If "belief" was historically associated with a class of mental states, "belief" refers to this class, whether or not the generalizations that define "belief" are true. Similarly, the Greeks and the Romans had a host of false beliefs about the moon. But it does not follow that the Greek and Latin words for "moon" were empty. Instead, these words were historically associated with a specific stellar object; they referred to this object, whether or not the beliefs that defined them were true—or so Jim could argue. This discussion shows that the fate of eliminativist arguments,

---

[6] On this last inference, see, however, Bishop and Stich 1998.

including the two eliminativist arguments against concepts considered above, hangs on which theory of reference is correct.

The next question is obviously, "What is the correct theory of reference for words like 'belief' and 'concept?'" This is where eliminativist arguments become murky. First, there is currently no agreement about the correct theory of reference for "belief," "concept," nor for any other term. And there is no sign of a forthcoming consensus. Second, and most important, there are reasons to be cautious with the use of theories of reference to support metaphysical claims in general and eliminativist conclusions in particular (Machery et al. 2004; Mallon et al., forthcoming).

Arguments for or against a given theory of reference rely on the method of cases. The method of cases consists in confronting one's intuitions about the reference of a given term in an actual situation or in a fictional situation with the reference of this term according to the theory of reference under consideration. The correct theory of reference is the theory of reference that is consistent with most of our intuitions about actual cases and fictional cases. An example may be useful to shed some light on the method of cases. To falsify the descriptivist theory of reference for proper names, philosopher Saul Kripke imagined a counterfactual situation, where a proper name, "Gödel," was associated with a description that was not true of the original bearer of "Gödel." According to Kripke, our pre-theoretical intuitions suggest that "Gödel" refers to the original bearer of this name, while simple descriptivist theories of reference entail that "Gödel" does not refer to the original bearer of this name. Since simple descriptivist theories of reference fail to capture this and other intuitions, they are assumed to be false. On the contrary, the causal-historical theory of reference captures these intuitions and is thus assumed to be correct. Thus, Kripke writes:

> Suppose that Gödel was not in fact the author of [Gödel's] theorem. A man called 'Schmidt'... actually did the work in question. His friend Gödel somehow got hold of the manuscript and it was thereafter attributed to Gödel. On the [descriptivist] view... when our ordinary man uses the name 'Gödel,' he really means to refer to Schmidt, because Schmidt is the unique person satisfying the description 'the man who discovered the incompleteness of arithmetic'.... But it seems we are not. We simply are not. (Kripke [1972] 1980: 83–84)

Ron Mallon, Shaun Nichols, Steve Stich, and I hypothesized that this kind of intuition may vary across cultures. Our hypothesis was suggested by Richard Nisbett's cross-cultural research on Western and Eastern cognitive styles (Nisbett et al. 2001; Nisbett 2003). Nisbett and colleagues have gathered a large body of evidence that different cognitive styles are prevalent in Eastern cultures, primarily, China, Japan, and Korea, and in Western cultures, primarily, the United States. Of particular importance is the fact that causal relations are more salient to Westerners than to Easterners when people explain events and categorize objects. Now, causality is

Table 8.1 Percentages of Subjects who had Causal-Historical Intuitions

	Westerners	Easterners
Gödel case 1	58%	29%
Gödel case 2	55%	32%

an important aspect of the distinction between descriptivist theories and causal-historical theories. Causal-historical theories, but not descriptivist theories, suppose that terms are causally related to their reference. On this basis, we predicted that Westerners would be more likely than Easterners to have intuitions in line with causal-historical theories of reference.

We tested this prediction. Subjects in Hong Kong and in the United States were presented with thought experiments based on Kripke's own Gödel story (see above). The results were consistent with our prediction. American subjects were significantly more likely than Chinese subjects to have intuitions in line with causal-historical theories of reference (table 8.1; for further detail on the experiments, see Machery et al. 2004).

We are not under the illusion that our simple experiment is the last word on the issue. However, we believe that we have found some preliminary evidence that intuitions about the reference of proper names vary across cultures. Furthermore, intuitions about reference vary within each culture.

Now, suppose that this result is robust. Suppose also that other intuitions about reference, including intuitions about the reference of predicates, vary across and within cultures. A natural response to such a variation is to reject the premise that speakers' intuitions about reference provide evidence about reference—that is, to reject the method of cases. To see why, consider the analogy between our intuitions about reference and other linguistic intuitions, such as, for example, our intuitions about grammaticality. We are confident that intuitions about the grammaticality of sentences provide evidence about grammatical properties because variation in these intuitions maps onto variation in languages or in dialects. People who have different intuitions about the grammaticality of sentences tend to speak different languages or different dialects. The same is true of other linguistic intuitions, such as intuitions about synonymy, antonymy, or polysemy. By contrast, we would doubt that intuitions about grammaticality provide reliable evidence about grammatical properties if people who evidently speak the same dialect had different intuitions about the grammaticality of sentences. At the very least, syntacticians would be hard-pressed to justify their reliance on intuitions about grammaticality as a source of evidence. Now, our data show that two individuals can have distinct intuitions about reference despite evidently speaking the same dialect. Faced with this variation, one might be tempted to abandon the assumption that intuitions about reference provide evidence about reference altogether. Instead, one might, for example, propose that a speaker's intuitions about reference result from numerous causes that turn out to have nothing do with reference, including her culture and, maybe, her philosophical commitments (Stich 1996: 85 n. 35).

Suppose that one does indeed conclude that intuitions about reference do not provide evidence about the nature of reference. The issue, then, is that it is unclear how theories of reference are to be supported at all, for, among philosophers of language interested in reference, there is so far no alternative to the method of cases. And without a theory of reference, the kind of eliminativist arguments considered in section 8.1 (what I call "old-fashioned eliminativist arguments") do not go through.

Instead of rejecting the assumption that intuitions about reference provide evidence about the nature of reference, one might bite the bullet and remain committed to the method of cases.[7] One would then assert that, if intuitions about reference really vary across cultures, then proper names, predicates, and maybe other classes of terms, such as mass terms, refer differently in different cultures—descriptively in Eastern cultures and causally-historically in Western cultures. (The same point applies to those individuals who have different intuitions about reference in spite of belonging to the same culture.) Particularly, "belief" would refer descriptively in Eastern cultures and causally-historically in Western cultures. Suppose that this is the case. Suppose that the description associated with "belief" is massively erroneous. Because "belief" refers descriptively when used by East Asians, when an East Asian says "Beliefs do not exist," what this East Asian says is true. However, because "belief" refers causally-historically when used by a Westerner, when a Westerner says "Beliefs do exist," what this Westerner says is also true. The obvious issue is that these two conclusions apparently flatly contradict one another. How can it be that "Beliefs do not exist" and "Beliefs do exist" are both true? Combined with the cross-cultural diversity of intuitions about reference, eliminativist arguments that hang on theories of reference appear to result in contradictions.

It may be tempting to deny that if predicates refer differently in different cultures, eliminativist arguments entail contradictory propositions, such as the proposition that beliefs exist and do not exist. Consider the following situation. John and Jean are talking to each other by phone. John is in New York, while Jean is in Paris. It is noon in New York and 6 p.m. in Paris. John says, truly, "It's noon," while Jean says, truly, "It's not noon." It is raining in New York, but not in Paris. John says, truly, "It's raining," while Jean says, truly, "It's not raining." John and Jean are not contradicting each other, and it is clear to them that they are not. For the truth of what John and Jean say is relativized to some context of use of these two sentences. And the context of use is not the same for Jean's

---

[7] In Mallon et al. (forthcoming), we consider various objections against the argument summarized here. The reader is referred to this article.

utterances and for John's utterances. The context of use for Jean's utterance of "It's not noon" and "It's not raining" involves the weather and the time in Paris when the phone conversation takes place, while the context of use for John's utterance of "It's noon" and "It's raining" involves the weather and the time in New York when the phone conversation takes place. This type of situation is extremely common in natural languages.

One might argue that a similar phenomenon is going on when an East Asian says, truly, "Beliefs do not exist," while a Westerner says, also truly, "Beliefs do exist." The context of use of the East Asian's utterance of "Beliefs do not exist" and the context of use of the Westerner's utterance of "Beliefs do exist" are not the same. When the East Asian says "Beliefs do not exist," the context of use includes how terms such as "belief" refer when they are used by East Asians, which itself depends on what kind of intuitions about reference East Asians have. When a Westerner says "Beliefs do exist," the context of use includes how terms such as "belief" refer when they are used by Westerners, which itself depends on what kind of intuitions about reference Westerners have. That is, ultimately, the truth of what a speaker says when he or she utters "Beliefs do exist" or "Beliefs do not exist" is relativized to the kind of intuitions about reference this speaker has.

This reply is implausible, however. It is committed to the absurd view that the overwhelming agreement between East Asian speakers and American speakers about what beliefs are is illusory. Although both East Asian speakers and American speakers assent to dozens of sentences such as "Beliefs are mental states," "Beliefs interact with desires," or "Beliefs are true or false," they do not in fact agree, according to the reply under consideration. For, if they do not disagree when they say "Beliefs exist" and "Beliefs do not exist," by the same token, they should not agree when they say "Beliefs are mental states."

Let us take stock. The fate of old-fashioned eliminativist arguments, including the argument for the elimination of beliefs and the arguments for the elimination of concepts discussed above, depends on which theory of reference is correct. The method of cases is the central tool for establishing a theory of reference. If intuitions about the reference of proper names and predicates vary across cultures, then either intuitions about reference provide no evidence about the nature of reference or proper names and predicates refer differently in different cultures. In the former case, it is unclear how to identify the correct theory of reference. In the latter case, old-fashioned eliminativist arguments seem to entail contradictions. In both cases, old-fashioned eliminativist arguments ought to be discarded. Evidence does suggest that intuitions about the reference of proper names vary across Western and Eastern cultures. We do not know whether the result reported in Machery et al. (2004) extends to other types of term, particularly to predicates such as "belief" and "concept." However, our result suggests that this is a live possibility. Thus, as long as the empirical status of the cross-cultural variability of intuitions about reference is unclear, we ought to refrain from endorsing eliminativist arguments that rely on a theory of reference. For present purposes, this means that Smith's and others' old-fashioned eliminativist arguments against the notion of concept ought to be rejected because, as explained at the beginning of section 8.1.3, these arguments rely, explicitly or implicitly, on a premise about how the theoretical term "concept" refers. Concept eliminativism should not be hostage to debates about reference.

8.2 Natural Kinds and Scientific Eliminativism

In this section, I introduce in some detail a new type of eliminativist argument. Since this argument does not bear on the elimination of folk notions, but exclusively on the elimination of scientific notions and on their replacement by other theoretical notions, I call this form of eliminativism "scientific eliminativism." Applied to "concept," scientific eliminativism goes in substance as follows. In contrast to old-fashioned eliminativist arguments, the scientific eliminativist does not dispute that "concept" picks out a class of entities: there are bodies of knowledge stored in long-term memory and used by default in the processes underlying the higher cognitive competences. Instead of arguing that "concept" does not refer, the scientific eliminativist makes a case that the class of concepts does not possess the properties that characterize the classes that matter for the empirical sciences. Or, to use a slogan, that this class is not a natural kind. If "concept" does not pick out a natural kind, then it is unlikely to be a useful notion in psychology. It is even likely to stand in the way of progress in psychology, by preventing the development of a more adequate classificatory scheme that would identify the relevant natural kinds. If this is the case, the term "concept" ought to be eliminated from the theoretical vocabulary of psychology and replaced with more adequate theoretical terms. In what follows, I consider this argument in more detail.

8.2.1 What Is a Natural Kind?

In philosophy of science, the notion of natural kind is essentially enmeshed with the problem of induction (Mill 1843; Quine 1969; Hacking 1991).[8]

---

[8] "Natural kind" is used differently in cognitive psychology and in philosophy of science. In cognitive psychology, natural kinds are, by stipulation, those classes of three-dimensional middle-sized physical objects that are not compounded of artifacts and that are denoted by nouns (e.g., Keil 1989; Gelman and Coley 1991: 150–158; Gopnik and Meltzoff 1997: ch. 6). Dogs and trees are paradigmatic natural kinds, so defined. Natural kinds are typically opposed to artifacts. People are assumed to conceptualize differently natural kinds, so defined, and artifacts. In philosophy of science, natural kinds are opposed to nominal classes, classes that do not yield scientific generalizations.

This notion assumes a distinction between two kinds of classes: those about which scientifically relevant inductive generalizations can be formulated and those about which no or few scientifically relevant generalizations can be formulated. Gold is a natural kind because one can formulate many scientifically relevant generalizations that are true of gold, for instance, that its atomic number is 79, that it dissolves in mercury to form liquid alloys, and so on.[9] The same point could be made of the class of gases, the class of electrons, the substance water, the phyla of dogs, mammals, vertebrates, and the ecological category of predators. By contrast, few scientifically relevant generalizations are true of the things that weigh more than 124 kg and of the Aristotelian class of supralunar celestial objects. Thus, the notion of natural kind singles out those classes about which scientifically relevant inductive generalizations can be formulated. Members of a natural kind share a large number of (logically unrelated) scientifically important properties (or relations) besides the properties (or relations) that are used to identify them. Since members of natural kinds have many properties in common, natural kinds are the building blocks of scientific generalizations.[10]

This basic idea has been developed in several ways. Not all accounts are equally suited for my purposes. The suitable account of natural kinds has to satisfy two properties: it has (1) to be applicable to psychological kinds and (2) to be broad, meaning that many classes have to qualify as natural kinds under this account. Otherwise, the claim that concepts are not a natural kind would be trivial.

Many philosophers have characterized natural kinds as those kinds that possess an essence, that is, a set of intrinsic, causally explanatory properties that are necessary and jointly sufficient for belonging to the kind.[11] Chemical substances are natural kinds in this sense. Something is a fragment of gold if and only if it is made of atoms whose atomic number is 79. Being made of atoms whose atomic number is 79 also explains many properties of gold, for instance, that it is oxidized by mercury. I call this notion "the essentialist notion of natural kind."

The essentialist notion is of little use in the present context, for it does not meet the two criteria proposed above. First, it is unlikely that psychological kinds possess essences—at least, if the functionalist view of mental state types is true. For, according to this view, types of mental state, such as desires, beliefs, emotions, or concepts, are not defined by intrinsic properties, but

---

[9] As shown by Quine (1960), substances, like water or gold, can be treated as classes.

[10] The notion of natural kind has been criticized. Particularly, Hacking (1986, 1999) has argued that the notion of natural kind does not fit easily with the social sciences because the kinds studied in the natural sciences differ from the kinds studied in the social sciences: generalizations that are formulated about humans often modify the very properties of humans, leading to their self-validation or to their falsification. For another criticism, see Russell (1948).

[11] Locke ([1690] 1979); Kripke [1972] 1980; Putnam 1975; for a critique, see Mellor 1977.

rather by their causal role, that is, by relational properties. Moreover, this notion of natural kind is excessively restrictive. For example, species would not be natural kinds according to this account (Hull 1978).

One might want to broaden the notion of essence, by including relational properties alongside intrinsic ones. However, the essentialist account of natural kind would remain unsatisfactory. For it would not distinguish the properties that determine membership from the causally explanatory properties. However, for some natural kinds, the properties that determine the membership in these kinds are not identical to those that causally explain why the members of these kinds have many properties in common. Species provide a good example. Membership in species is historical. For instance, an animal is a rhesus macaque if its parents were rhesus macaques. This historical relation explains some properties that are shared by most or all members of a given species. But other properties that are shared by most or all members of a given species are explained by other causal mechanisms, such as common developmental environments or shared environments that prevent the selection of different adaptations in different subgroups of the species.

I turn to a second notion of natural kind—the nomological notion: natural kind terms feature in laws, that is, in generalizations that are temporally and spatially unrestricted and that support counterfactuals (Collier 1996). This nomological notion of natural kind is also of little use in the present context, for it fails to meet the two criteria imposed on the notion of natural kind. Psychological kinds underwrite *ceteris paribus* generalizations—not laws (Fodor 1974). And, again, this notion is too restrictive, for few theoretical terms feature in laws. For instance, it is dubious whether there are laws that are true of species and other phyla.

One could propose to replace the notion of law with the notion of *ceteris paribus* generalization. This would be a step in the right direction, as we shall see. However, an important element would still be missing from this account, namely, the idea that there is at least one causal mechanism that accounts for these generalizations. This is an important aspect of the kinds scientists are interested in for inductive purposes.

Finally, let us consider the notion of natural kind I favor, which is loosely based on Richard Boyd's work on natural kinds (1990, 1991, 1999; see also Griffiths 1997: chs. 6 and 7; Machery 2005):

> A class C of entities is a natural kind if and only if there is a large set of scientifically relevant properties such that C is the maximal class whose members tend to share these properties because of some causal mechanism.

I call this notion the "causal notion of natural kind." The core idea of this definition is the following. A natural kind is a class about which many generalizations can be formulated: its members tend to have many properties in common. These generalizations are not accidental: there is at least one causal mechanism that explains why its members tend to have those properties. Finally, this class is not a subset of a larger class about which the same generalizations could be formulated.[12]

One might object that "large" is too vague. That is, one might suspect that this notion will remain useless as long as I do not explain how many generalizations are needed to have a large number of generalizations. This complaint is unfounded, however. The notion of natural kind, like the notion of heap, is vague. Even if there is no way to sharpen the idea of a large set of properties, it remains that the number of properties that can be projected from one subset of the class to the whole class is one dimension that distinguishes natural kinds from other classes.

Inversely, one might object that a class of entities that would share a few scientifically fundamental properties would be a natural kind. First, one can question whether such classes really exist. These fundamental properties (whatever they might be) would plausibly cause the members of these classes to share other properties. Moreover, if there were such classes, I would argue that they are not natural kinds, for they would be noticeably different from the paradigmatic natural kinds. Instead of stretching the notion of natural kind in order to include them, it would arguably be better to distinguish two types of scientific kinds: the natural kinds whose members share many properties and, say, the basic kinds, whose members share a few fundamental properties.

In the present context, two aspects of the definition of a natural kind are important. First, the properties that characterize a natural kind are not necessarily possessed by all its members. It is only required that members of a natural kind tend to have these properties. Hence, natural kind terms do not have to feature in laws. It is only required that they feature in *ceteris paribus* generalizations. It cannot be emphasized too strongly that the notion of natural kind is independent from the idea of having a property or a set of properties shared by all and only the members of the kind.

Second, essences are only one of the possible causal mechanisms that explain why members of a natural kind share or tend to share many properties. Boyd (1990) has insisted upon the homeostasis of properties: in some natural kinds, the instantiation of a property causes the occurrence of other properties and is caused by their instantiation. Other mechanisms are possible, including common descent and social causes (Griffiths 1997). Common descent is an important causal mechanism that explains why the members of a given species or a given phylum share many properties. For instance, common descent explains the structure of bats' wings. Functional relations also explain the properties of many artifacts. For instance, the fact that cars are made for humans explains their size and the shape of their seats.

---

[12] This is, of course, consistent with the fact that some generalizations are true of the members of a natural kind because they are true of the members of this superset. Dogs are quadrupeds, as are wolves and many other mammals. Thus, some generalizations are true of dogs because dogs are quadrupeds.

The causal notion of natural kind is relevant for my present purposes. It allows psychological kinds to be natural kinds because natural kinds have neither to possess essences nor to underwrite laws. Moreover, this notion has a large extension: substances (e.g., gold), physical entities (e.g., atoms), species (e.g., dogs), and artifacts do qualify as natural kinds. However, the causal notion of natural kind is not vacuous. It implies that nominal kinds, for instance, the class of physical objects that weigh more than 30 kg, are not natural kinds, for their members do not share many (scientifically relevant) properties. Moreover, it implies that many subsets of natural kinds (e.g., white dogs) are not natural kinds either, for the scientifically relevant properties that are true of white dogs are true of all dogs.

One could object that this notion is too broad. According to the causal notion of natural kind, artifacts qualify as natural kinds. But artifacts are precisely the paradigms of classes that are not natural kinds—or so the objection would go. However, this objection should be resisted because some artifacts are the objects of inquiry in the social sciences. Paleoanthropology may be the most telling example. Classifying the artifacts made by our ancestors, particularly their tools and weapons, and describing their properties is an important aspect of this discipline. Controversies abound about the proper classification and description of tools (e.g., Boyd and Silk 2000: 443–445). In paleoanthropology, kinds of tool play the same role as psychological kinds in psychology (concepts, emotions...), ecological kinds in ecology (predators...), species in evolutionary biology, and elements in chemistry. This fact may be overlooked because paradigmatic artifacts are familiar objects, like tables, chairs, and cups. Because of our acquaintance with such artifacts, they are not the objects of inquiry of any science. What could science tells us about dishes that we do not know already? But this is not an essential property of artifacts. Artifacts can be non-familiar and, as a result, they can then become objects of scientific inquiry, as happens in paleoanthropology. Hence, artifacts are bona fide natural kinds.

8.2.2 *Four Characteristics of Natural Kinds*

8.2.2.1 Natural Kinds and Causal Mechanisms

It might often be that several causal mechanisms, rather than a single causal mechanism, explain the co-occurring properties of the members of a given natural kind.[13] At least three cases have to be distinguished. First, different causal mechanisms may explain why different properties are possessed by the members of a given kind. That is, property a is explained by mechanism A, but not by mechanism B, and property b is explained by mechanism B, but not by mechanism A. For many species, different properties are explained by different mechanisms, including common

---

[13] I use liberally the notion of mechanism to refer to any causal process.

descent and selective pressures from a shared environment during the evolution of the species. Dogs provide a good illustration: dogs' body plan is inherited from their mother species, while dogs' social properties result probably from the artificial selection imposed on them by humans (e.g., Hare et al. 2002).

Second, the possession of a given property may be explained by several different mechanisms. These explanations are complementary, and the explanation based on each mechanism is complete. That is, property a may be explained by mechanism A and by mechanism B. Each explanation is complete. One can provide a satisfying explanation of the possession of a by means of A, without referring to B (and vice-versa). The explanation based on mechanism A and the explanation based on mechanism B are not redundant because each of them constitutes an answer to a distinct question about property a. Again, species illustrate this case. At least since Tinbergen (1963), it is a commonplace that a given trait can be explained in several ways. For instance, one can explain developmentally and functionally why female humans have nipples. The developmental explanation is not exclusive of the functional explanation and does not need to be complemented by the functional explanation.

Finally, a given property, a, may be explained by several causal mechanisms, A and B. By contrast to the second case, in itself, each causal mechanism provides an incomplete explanation of the possession of a. That is, to explain in a satisfying way the possession of a, it is necessary to refer both to A and to B. For instance, it is a commonplace that the phenotype is a product of both the environment and the genome. This last case is particularly relevant for concepts. Many properties of the bodies of knowledge used by default in the processes underlying the higher cognitive competences are likely to be co-determined by the structure of our learning mechanisms, the properties of our long-term memory, the environment in which we live, and so on.

8.2.2.2 Nested Hierarchy of Natural Kinds and Cross-Cutting Natural Kinds

Natural kinds are typically nested within other natural kinds: the subsets of natural kinds are often natural kinds themselves. To put it differently, some causally grounded generalizations are specifically true of the members of the superordinate class, while others are specifically true of the members of its subclasses. For instance, dogs as well as the breeds of dogs are natural kinds. Some causally grounded generalizations are true of dogs, while other causally grounded generalizations are specifically true of, say, Chihuahuas. Natural kinds may also cross-cut each other. That is, a subset of a natural kind may be included in another natural kind. Females and males or predators and preys in biology illustrate this point. Hence, neither the fact that the subclasses of the class of concepts are natural kinds nor the fact that its subclasses are included into other natural kinds entail that the class

8.2.2.3 Properties of Natural Kind Members

The properties that are projected in generalizations about natural kinds need not be all of the same type. To illustrate, vision scientists have established functional, computational, and neural generalizations about the visual systems that detect shape (e.g., Ullman 1996).

8.2.2.4 Diversity of Natural Kinds

Finally, natural kinds vary along several dimensions, including the nature of the causal mechanism(s) (essence, homeostasis, historical origins...), the robustness of these causal mechanisms (whether or not they are likely to be disrupted), the number of generalizations, and the nature of these generalizations (*ceteris paribus* generalizations or laws).

It is tempting to introduce the idea of degree of naturalness to characterize the different types of natural kind. The dimensions mentioned previously could all be used to define naturalness. One could propose that a kind is more natural to the extent that its causal mechanism is intrinsic. Thus, essence-based natural kinds would be more natural than origins-based natural kinds. Similarly, a kind could be more natural to the extent that its generalizations are law-like. We could thereby capture the common intuition that not all kinds are equally natural, for instance, that artifacts are less natural than species, which themselves are less natural than chemical elements.

This proposal should be resisted, however. Natural kinds vary along several dimensions. To define a measure of naturalness, one would have to integrate these disparate dimensions. However, it is unclear how one would do this in a non-arbitrary way. If a kind X yields more generalizations than a kind Y, but if the generalizations that are true of members of Y are underwritten by a causal mechanism whose causal efficiency is less likely to be disrupted than the mechanism for the kind X, which of X and Y is more natural? It is unlikely that there is a non-arbitrary answer to this question.

8.2.3 *Splitting Natural Kinds*

Many empirical sciences aim at identifying the natural kinds in their domain in order to develop adequate empirical theories.[14] Taxonomies are modified when it is found that they do not map onto natural kinds. Some taxonomic changes can involve a full conceptual system, as happened to the chemical taxonomy in the eighteenth century. The scope of other

---

[14] The expression in the section title comes from Craver (2004), Piccinini and Scott (2006), and Machery (2006a). For discussion, see Griffiths 1997; Murphy and Stich 1999.

taxonomic changes is more limited. Particularly, a given theoretical term may be found to fail to pick out a natural kind. "Memory" in psychology and neuropsychology is a good example. This term has been replaced by several theoretical terms, such as "working memory," "long-term memory," "declarative memory," "procedural memory," "episodic memory," "implicit memory," and "explicit memory." While "memory" is not believed anymore to pick out a natural kind, each of the replacing theoretical terms is fruitfully used to formulate psychological generalizations.

This second form of taxonomic change is relevant for my present purposes: a given theoretical term is eliminated from a scientific taxonomy because it is found not to map onto a natural kind. I focus now on the conditions for this kind of elimination. I elaborate on a distinction proposed by Dominic Murphy and Steve Stich (1999). Commenting on Griffiths (1997), they distinguish two eliminativist arguments—"vertical arguments" and "horizontal arguments."

Consider first the vertical arguments for scientific eliminativism. Vertical arguments start by noting that a given theoretical term features in generalizations that involve different types of property. Thus, in psychiatry, "depression" is used to formulate behavioral generalizations (the bodily manifestations of depression), psychological generalizations (what beliefs are associated with depression), computational generalizations (what cognitive mechanisms underlie depression), neuropsychological generalizations (what brain areas are involved in depression), and chemical generalizations (what molecules are involved in depression and how). As noted above, such a situation is common because different types of generalization can be true of the members of a given natural kind.

Vertical arguments then note that these distinct types of generalization do not line up with each other. When we focus on the behavioral, contextual, and neurobiological properties that characterize depression, we may ascribe depression to apes as well as to humans. When we focus on the cognitive properties of depression, depression is exclusively ascribed to humans. Thus, different types of generalization about depression result in two different classes of organisms being susceptible to depression. Vertical arguments conclude from this fact that the theoretical term should be eliminated (Murphy and Stich 1999: 24).

I turn now to the horizontal arguments, which are the most relevant for this book. Vertical arguments against a theoretical term ⌜K⌝ do not deny that this theoretical term can be used to formulate scientifically relevant generalizations. But they argue that this theoretical term picks out more than one natural kind. By contrast, horizontal arguments for the elimination of a theoretical term ⌜K⌝ deny that this theoretical term picks out a natural kind.

When does a theoretical term ⌜K⌝ fail to pick out a natural kind? The clearest circumstances are the following:

- There are very few generalizations that are true of the K's, besides the properties that are used to identify the K's. At the same time,

many generalizations are true of the members of subclasses of K—$K_1, \ldots, K_n$.
- The generalizations that were assumed to be specifically true of the K's are in fact true of the members of a superset S of K. Generalizations are true of the K's because the K's belong to this superset.
- The generalizations that were assumed to be causally grounded are in fact accidental.

"Emotion" in psychology and neuropsychology illustrates the first situation. In recent years, it has been repeatedly argued that there are few scientifically relevant properties that are common to all emotions. It has also been proposed that instead of looking for generalizations about emotions, psychologists should focus on specific emotions (e.g., LeDoux 1996) or on groups of emotions (Griffiths 1997). Thus, Joseph LeDoux, a neuropsychologist, writes:

> If we are interested in understanding the various phenomena that we use the term 'emotion' to refer to, we have to focus on specific classes of emotions. We shouldn't mix findings about different emotions all together independent of the emotion that they are findings about. Unfortunately, most work in psychology and brain science has done this. (LeDoux 1996: 16)

What does and what should happen when it is found out that a theoretical term ⌜K⌝ does not pick out a natural kind? That is, are theoretical terms typically eliminated when it is found out that they do not pick out natural kinds? Moreover, should they be eliminated? The first question is descriptive, while the second is normative. These two questions are not entirely disjointed because philosophers of science by and large agree that as a defeasible rule, normative proposals about science should be consistent with scientists' practices or, at least, with those scientific practices that are commonly regarded as successful.

Answering the descriptive question would require a systematic inquiry into the history of science. In order to be systematic, such an inquiry would ideally identify a large number of relevant cases and randomly select a sample of cases. This would control for any confirmation bias, such as a selection of case studies supporting one's own views. Unfortunately, to my knowledge such an inquiry is lacking. Barring a systematic inquiry into the history of science, a definitive answer to the descriptive question is impossible. However, this should not prevent us from considering plausible normative considerations about what should happen when it is found out that a theoretical term does not pick out a natural kind.

The main considerations that bear on the normative issue are pragmatic. A theoretical term that has been found to fail to pick out a natural kind should be kept if it plays a useful role. Not all terms in science are assumed to pick out natural kinds. Terms that do not pick out natural kinds might have several functions. Particularly, after it is found that a term

⌜K⌝ does not pick out a natural kind, ⌜K⌝ might remain a useful shorthand for a descriptive phrase. If "concept" does not pick out a natural kind, it might remain a useful shorthand for the description "bodies of knowledge used by default in the processes underlying most higher cognitive competences." However, by the same token, a theoretical term that has been found to fail to pick out a natural kind should be eliminated if it fails to play a useful role or if it plays a harmful role. I believe that the latter is likely to be the most common case. When evidence emerges that a hypothesized natural kind term fails to pick out a natural kind, keeping this theoretical term is likely to prevent the development of a new classification system that would identify the relevant natural kinds. Keeping this term might invite numerous scientists to discard this body of evidence and to look for evidence that the hypothesized natural kind term picks out a natural kind after all.

In what follows, I focus on one of these horizontal eliminativist arguments. I consider the case where a hypothesized natural kind term ⌜K⌝ is found out to fail to pick out a natural kind because few generalizations are true of the K's, while distinct sets of generalizations are true of subclasses of K. If the term ⌜K⌝ is a hurdle to developing a more appropriate classification, ⌜K⌝ ought to be eliminated.

8.2.4 Pluralism versus Scientific Eliminativism

Suppose that many generalizations are specifically true of the K's. However, these generalizations are underwritten by different causal mechanisms ($M_1, \ldots, M_n$) for $K_1, \ldots, K_n$. Moreover, because of M_1, K_1's have some specific properties (i.e., that are not shared by K_2's, ..., K_n's) besides the properties that are shared by all K's (*mutatis mutandis* for the other subsets). Is K a natural kind? And in this situation, should ⌜K⌝ be eliminated? In this case, two elements of the causal notion of natural kind—whether or not we can formulate generalizations and whether or not they are causally grounded—pull apart. The first element suggests that K is a natural kind, the second element that it is not.

The most common answer in philosophy is that in this case, K is a natural kind and ⌜K⌝ should not be eliminated (Fodor 1974; but see Kim 1992). Instead, K, $K_1, \ldots, K_n$ are nested natural kinds. The present case is indeed similar to a case of multiple realizability. Eliminating ⌜K⌝ would make it impossible to formulate many generalizations. For instance, if our syntactic competence can be described in computational terms, then a machine could be able to parse sentences in exactly the same computational way as humans. However, the causal mechanisms that implement this syntactic competence in the machine and in the human brain would be different. Eliminating the notion of syntactic competence because different mechanisms can underlie this syntactic competence would prevent the formulation of numerous computational generalizations about syntax.

Instead of suggesting the elimination of ⌜K⌝, this case suggests a type of pluralism. Pluralism should not be confused with scientific eliminativism. Pluralism is the view that a natural kind K divides into several natural kinds, $K_1, \ldots, K_n$. Importantly, pluralism is not committed to deny that the kind K is a natural kind. As noted above, natural kinds are typically nested. Thus, K, $K_1, \ldots, K_n$, can all be natural kinds. Pluralism applies, for instance, to the class of elements. The class of elements is a natural kind because generalizations can be made about its members. In turn, the elements, such as gold and oxygen, are themselves natural kinds. Pluralism has one main virtue: it attracts scientists' attention to the properties that are characteristic of kinds ($K_1, \ldots, K_n$) that may be neglected by an exclusive focus on the kind K. In the domain of concepts, pluralism has been recently endorsed by Medin and colleagues precisely for this reason (Medin, Lynch, and Solomon 2000; see also Weiskopf, forthcoming).

8.2.5 An Objection

Suppose that the term ⌜K⌝ is replaced by the terms ⌜K_1⌝ and ⌜K_2⌝ because it is found out that the K's are not a natural kind. One could argue that the notion expressed by ⌜K⌝ has not been eliminated, but, rather, that it is expressed by ⌜K_1⌝ or by ⌜K_2⌝. Although the word ⌜K⌝ has been eliminated, the notion it expressed has not. Suppose that, as has been proposed by Griffiths (1997), "emotion" were to be replaced by "affect program" and "cognitive emotion." One could propose that the notion of emotion has not been eliminated, but that it is expressed by "affect program" or by "cognitive emotion." In such a case, the elimination would be merely apparent. The term "emotion" would have been eliminated, but the notion it expresses would not.

Dealing appropriately with this problem seems to require a theory of the individuation of scientific notions, that is, a theory that explains when two scientific terms express the same notion or a different notion. This is, of course, a vexed issue and a traditional one at that. Unfortunately, neither I nor anybody else has such a theory. For this reason, it seems impossible to evaluate the objection.

Furthermore, the importance of the problem at hand should not be overstated. For simplicity, I will consider the case of "emotion." Suppose that "emotion" is replaced by "affect program" and "cognitive emotion." Suppose also that under the right theory of the individuation of scientific notions, the notion of emotion has not been eliminated. Rather, it is expressed by, say, "affect program." The important point is that, although the notion of emotion has not been eliminated, psychologists' understanding of what this notion refers to would have been fundamentally transformed. Particularly, after the change in classification, but not before, psychologists interested in emotions would argue that affect programs have little to do with cognitive emotions. Before the change in classification, but not after, psychologists would look for properties shared by psychological events as different as an episode of mild, long-lasting guilt and an outburst of fear triggered by the vision of a snake. Eliminating the word "emotion" might have been useful in bringing about these changes. Promoting this type of change is really what the arguments for scientific eliminativism are about.

8.3 The Argument for the Elimination of "Concept"

In the previous section, I have gone at some length over the general structure of scientific eliminativism. Instead of arguing that a scientific term does not refer because nothing satisfies its definition, as old-fashioned eliminativist arguments do (Churchland 1981; Stich 1983), horizontal arguments for scientific eliminativism argue that a scientific term is likely to be useless, if not a hurdle, in a given science because it fails to pick out a natural kind; they conclude that this term should be eliminated from the theoretical apparatus of the relevant science (Griffiths 1997; Machery 2005). In this section, I apply this general argument to "concept."

8.3.1 The Natural Kind Assumption

I use the causal notion of natural kind to specify the hypothesis that concepts form a natural kind—what I call "the Natural Kind Assumption" (Machery 2005). The Natural Kind Assumption claims that the class of bodies of knowledge that are used by default in the processes underlying the higher cognitive competences possesses three characteristics:

- There is a large set of properties that these bodies of knowledge tend to possess.
- These bodies of knowledge possess these properties because of some causal mechanism(s).
- This set of properties is specific to this class of bodies of knowledge.

As seen in section 3.1, psychologists of concepts typically endorse the Natural Kind Assumption.

8.3.2 Denying the Natural Kind Assumption

There are at least three options to rebut the Natural Kind Assumption:

- Very few generalizations are true of all (or most) concepts besides the properties that are used to identify them, while many generalizations are true of some subsets of concepts. The class of concepts is not a natural kind, while these subsets are natural kinds.
- The generalizations that were assumed to be specifically true of concepts are in fact true of the members of a superset of the class of concepts. Generalizations are true of concepts because concepts

belong to this superset. The class of concepts is not a natural kind, while this superset is a natural kind.
- The generalizations about concepts are accidental.

We have seen at length in previous chapters that the available empirical evidence about concepts strongly supports the first option. It is not the case that concepts have in common a large set of properties besides the properties used to identify them. Rather, the class of concepts is divided into several kinds that have little in common—namely prototypes, exemplars, and theories. Prototypes have in common numerous properties; so do exemplars; and so do theories. But the scientifically relevant properties that characterize each of these kinds are different from the properties that characterize the two other kinds.

If very few generalizations are true of concepts besides the generalizations that are used to identify them, then the class of concepts is not a natural kind: the Natural Kind Assumption is false. Rather, the class of concepts divides into three classes—the class of prototypes, the class of exemplars, and the class of theories—that are natural kinds.

8.3.3 Eliminating "Concept"

If "concept" does not pick out a natural kind, should we eliminate "concept" from the theoretical vocabulary of psychology? On pragmatic grounds, I propose that psychologists ought to stop using this term. They should replace it with the terms that do pick out natural kinds—namely "prototype," "exemplar," and "theory."

Despite a growing recognition that there are different kinds of concept used in distinct cognitive processes (e.g., distinct induction processes), numerous psychologists interested in concepts are still looking for generalizations about the whole class of concepts—a useless endeavor if the argument developed in this book is correct. It might be that the use of the term "concept" invites psychologists to think that the class picked out by this term is a natural kind. By dropping the term "concept" from their taxonomy, psychologists who reject the Natural Kind Assumption might curb other psychologists' tendency to assume that concepts form a natural kind.

The psychological research on concepts has often been framed in a polemical manner. Prototype theorists have been looking for evidence that was consistent with the existence of prototypes and that was not predicted by exemplar theories or theory theories (*mutatis mutandis* for exemplar theorists and theory theorists). Now, if prototypes, exemplars, and theories all exist, the prototype, the exemplar, and the theory paradigms of concepts are not inconsistent. Rather, they characterize the main features of three distinct kinds of body of knowledge used in the processes underlying the higher cognitive competences. As a result, many controversies between proponents of the three main paradigms of concepts are empty. Replacing the term "concept" with "prototype," "exemplar," and "theory" would make it clear that findings not predicted by, say, the exemplar paradigm of concepts do not count *ipso facto* against this paradigm (*mutatis mutandis* for the two other paradigms). Thus, the elimination of "concept" would probably help reframing the research on concepts and eliminate the unproductive controversies between proponents of different paradigms.

Even more important, replacing "concept" with "prototype," "exemplar," and "theory" might attract psychologists' attention to the numerous questions raised by the Heterogeneity Hypothesis. If this hypothesis is in the right ballpark, these are among the most important questions a psychological theory of concepts must find answers to.

First, it is one thing to argue that prototypes, exemplars, and theories all exist; it is another thing to determine the exact nature of prototypes, exemplars, and theories and to specify the nature of the processes that use these bodies of knowledge. As we saw, there are several prototype theories, several exemplar theories, and several theory theories. But, so far, the emphasis in the psychological research on concepts has not been put on identifying what the right prototype theory is, what the right exemplar theory is, and what the right theory theory is. Rather, as noted above, prototype theorists have been more interested in looking for evidence against the exemplar and the theory paradigms of concepts (*mutatis mutandis* for exemplar and theory theorists). Putting an end to these unproductive controversies might help turn prototype theorists', exemplar theorists', and theory theorists' attention to the task of identifying the nature of prototypes, of exemplars, and of theories.

Second, multi-process theories of categorization and of induction leave many questions pending. It remains unclear whether the processes that underwrite a given cognitive competence (e.g., categorization) are simultaneously triggered or whether they are triggered in different conditions. In the former case, it is entirely unclear what happens to the outputs of the simultaneously triggered processes. Replacing the term "concept" with the terms "prototype," "exemplar," and "theory" (and other terms, if needed) would bring these questions to the fore.

8.4 Objections and Replies

In this last section, I consider several objections that may have come to the mind of even the most benevolent readers. First, one could object to the eliminativist argument developed so far that whatever concepts are, they share, by definition, several scientifically important properties: they are used to categorize, they are used to reason inductively, they are used to draw analogies, they are involved in linguistic comprehension, and they store some knowledge. Therefore, some scientific generalizations are true of the class of concepts. Hence, concepts are a natural kind.

This objection misconceives the nature of natural kinds. Members of a natural kind have many properties in common besides those properties that are used to identify the kind. This is not the case of concepts, for most of the properties mentioned in this objection are used to identify the class of concepts.

Moreover, psychologists are not interested in the properties mentioned in the objection. What psychologists want to find out is not that concepts store some knowledge about categories, but what kind of knowledge is stored. Similarly, the fact that concepts can be used to reason inductively (or to categorize, or can be learned through experience...) is not a generalization that is of much interest to psychologists. What they want to know is how concepts are used to solve inductive tasks, to categorize, or how they are learned. Now, the class of concepts is inadequate for drawing generalizations concerning what kind of knowledge is by default available in long-term memory, how we solve inductive tasks, and how we categorize. That is, the class of concepts is inadequate for drawing the generalizations psychologists are interested in. Thus, the class of concepts is not a natural kind.

One could also argue that even if few scientific generalizations are true of the class of concepts, rejecting the notion of concept in favor of notions picking out heterogeneous fundamental kinds of concepts prevents us from formulating the few generalizations that are true of all concepts, such as the fact that concepts are used to categorize or to reason inductively (Weiskopf, forthcoming). This reply is dubious. It is easy to reformulate these generalizations. For instance, instead of saying that concepts are used to categorize, one might easily say that prototypes, exemplars, and theories are used to categorize.

Finally, criticizing my eliminativist approach, which he calls "concept nihilism," philosopher Dan Weiskopf argues that there are in fact many generalizations that can be formulated about the class of concepts (Weiskopf, forthcoming). Hence, although he grants that the class of concepts includes several distinct kinds, such as prototypes, exemplars, and theories, he argues that this does not invalidate the scientific value of the notion of concept. In brief, like Medin and colleagues (2000), he is committed to a pluralist view of concepts: the class of concepts is a natural kind and divides into natural kinds.

Weiskopf refers to five kinds of generalization. As we shall see, however, his arguments carry little weight. First, he notes that to the extent that inferences depend on the logical form of mental states, generalizations concerning reasoning are independent from the nature of the concepts that compose these mental states. As he puts it, "these are regularities that operate over concepts *tout court*." This is unconvincing, however. It is unclear whether these putative generalizations about inferences are truly generalizations about concepts.

Second, Weiskopf notes that at least in some cases of conceptual combination, various kinds of concept, such as exemplars and theories, are involved in producing complex bodies of knowledge (Machery 2005; section 7.2 above). This much is correct. It is, however, unclear why this is taken to justify conserving the notion of concept. Evidence suggests that in conceptual combination, prototypes, exemplars, and theories fulfill different functions. For instance, prototypes are supposed to be used to determine which properties are likely to be typical of the classes denoted by the complex bodies of knowledge, while theories are supposed to be used to determine which properties cannot be possessed or are necessarily possessed by the members of these classes. Thus, prototypes, exemplars, and theories are likely to be used by different subprocesses of the process underwriting concept combination.

Third, Weiskopf remarks that some of the fundamental kinds of concept are used in similar processes, for instance, in similarity-based processes (see chapter 4). However, Weiskopf himself undercuts the strength of this point. He correctly notes that exemplars and prototypes are usually assumed to be involved in similarity-based processes, while theories are not. Thus, not all the fundamental kinds of concept are used in the same kind of process. It is thus unclear why Weiskopf takes this third point to support the idea that the class of concepts yields important generalizations. Moreover, he neglects the fact that similarity-based processes that use exemplars and similarity-based processes that use prototypes are usually taken to be different (chapter 4). Pace Weiskopf, it is simply not the case that these two kinds of process are only "slightly different." Similarity is computed differently in these two kinds of process, retrieval from long-term memory is different, since prototypes and exemplars are probably located in different memory systems (Knowlton 1999), matching between prototypes and other representations, on the one hand, and between exemplars and other representations on the other is different, and decisions to categorize are made differently.

The fourth observation suffers from a similar problem. Weiskopf remarks that different kinds of concept, such as prototypes and exemplars, are likely to be acquired by similar processes. But again, this does not generalize to all the fundamental kinds of concepts, as is needed if this point is to support the scientific value of the notion of concept. Moreover, it is unlikely that except at a very coarse grain, the processes involved in the acquisition of prototypes and of exemplars are really similar.

Weiskopf's last point does not fare much better. He notes that concepts of all kinds are stored in long-term memory. Again, this cuts little ice. Prototypes, exemplars, and theories are stored in long-term memory all right, but the rules that govern their storage, permanence, and retrieval are likely to be different. Thus, there is so far no serious evidence that the notion of concept underwrites non-trivial scientific generalizations. I conclude that the case for concept pluralism (Medin et al. 2000; Weiskopf, forthcoming), instead of a robust eliminativist approach, is weak, indeed.

8.5 Conclusion

In this last chapter, I have made a case for the elimination of the theoretical term "concept" from the vocabulary of contemporary psychology. I have shunned old-fashioned eliminativist arguments because they are hostages to debates about reference. Instead, I have developed a new form of eliminativist argument, which I have called "scientific eliminativism." Horizontal arguments for scientific eliminativism starts with the empirical discovery that a hypothesized natural kind term fails to pick out a natural kind. On pragmatic grounds, they conclude that the hypothesized natural kind term should be eliminated. "Concept" fails to pick out a natural kind, although it has been assumed by many psychologists to do so. On pragmatic grounds, I conclude that "concept" ought to be eliminated from psychology.

Conclusion

Conceptual change is an essential component of scientific progress. Scientific terms are routinely redefined, new scientific terms are introduced, and old scientific terms are eliminated. Scientific disciplines or, within disciplines, scientific theories that resist such changes linger and, ultimately, disappear.

The research on concepts in psychology and neuropsychology has reached a point where drastic conceptual changes are required. The theoretical term "concept" should be eliminated from the vocabulary of contemporary psychology and should be replaced with terms that are more appropriate for fulfilling psychologists' goals, such as "prototype," "exemplar," and "theory."

The psychology of concepts has been rejuvenated by new work on prototypes, inventive ideas on causal cognition, the development of neo-empiricist theories of concepts, and the inputs of the budding neuropsychology of concepts. New empirical findings about the nature of concepts and about the higher cognitive competences have been added to the robust phenomena found in the 1970s and 1980s. As a result, we now know of lot about concepts.

But what we know has yet to be organized in a coherent framework. The current theories of concepts—prototype theories, exemplar theories, theory theories, and neo-empiricist theories—fail to explain all the known phenomena. Rather, each of these theories seems to be tailored to explain a subset of these phenomena. It is tempting to conclude, as some psychologists have done, that the current theories of concepts are unsatisfactory.

I have argued that the research on concepts points in fact toward a very different conclusion. The current theories explain some, but only some phenomena about concepts and about the higher cognitive competences because the class of concepts divides into kinds that have little in common—primarily, prototypes, exemplars, and theories. The main approaches in the contemporary psychology of concepts have identified the principal properties of these fundamental kinds of concept.

Because the fundamental kinds of concept have little in common, it is a mistake to attempt to encompass all known phenomena within a single theory of concepts. As proposed by the Heterogeneity Hypothesis, concepts do not have many properties in common: they are not a natural kind.

When it is found out that a class is not a natural kind, the relevant theoretical term need not be eliminated from the vocabulary of the relevant science, for many theoretical terms in science are not natural kind terms. But many factors might justify its elimination. I have argued that pragmatic considerations are crucial in deciding whether a theoretical term that was believed to pick out a natural kind should be eliminated or retained. Keeping this theoretical term might encourage useless theoretical controversies; it might slow down, and maybe prevent, the development of a more adequate classification; it might overshadow the theoretical and empirical issues that are raised by this more adequate classification. In all these cases, the relevant theoretical term should be eliminated.

Exactly for this kind of reason, the term "concept" should be eliminated from the vocabulary of contemporary psychology. It has encouraged psychologists to believe that a single theory of concepts could be developed, leading to continuing controversies between the dominant paradigms of concepts. Psychologists committed to one of these paradigms have spent much of their time, energy, and funding attempting to rebut the competing paradigms. These controversies have largely diverted psychologists' efforts from the most urgent tasks in the field, and keeping the term "concept" in the theoretical vocabulary of contemporary psychology might incite psychologists to carry on with their old habits and might prevent them from turning to these important tasks. I now describe these tasks in more detail.

Psychologists should investigate the factors that determine whether an element of knowledge about x comes to be part of the concept of x rather than being part of the background knowledge about x. As noted in chapter 1, frequency of use is the only factor that has been systematically investigated (Barsalou 1987). Other factors should be considered—including attention and explicit teaching.

Furthermore, as we have seen, each paradigm of concepts is typically developed by distinct and competing theories. There are several prototype theories, several exemplar theories, and several theory theories. While evidence clearly indicates that we have prototypes, exemplars, and theories, it remains however unclear which prototype theory, which exemplar theory, and which theory theory is correct. That is, the exact nature of prototypes, exemplars, and theories remains to be investigated.

Similarly, it is unclear which prototype-based model of categorization (induction, etc.), which exemplar-based model of categorization (induction, etc.), and which theory-based model of categorization (induction, etc.) is correct. Recently, some psychologists have taken up the important task of comparing the models of categorization and of induction developed by prototype theories as well as the models of categorization and of induction developed by theory theorists. For instance, Sloman and Lagnado (2005) compare several competing prototype-based models of induction, and Rehder and Kim (2006) compare several competing theory-based models of categorization. These comparisons are a first step toward moving away from a debate between paradigms of concepts to a debate between distinct theories within each paradigm of concepts. Such efforts should be systematically pursued.

It is also important to determine whether in addition to prototypes, exemplars, and theories, there are other fundamental kinds of concept. Particularly, the neo-empiricist approach to concepts should be further investigated. Although I have expressed doubts about the strength of the current evidence supporting the claims made by neo-empiricists, it might well be that perceptual symbols are a fundamental kind of concept. Similarly, the ideal approach of concepts, briefly considered in chapter 4, should be developed by psychologists in a more systematic manner. Evidence shows that people have some knowledge about ideals. What is now needed is to determine whether these bodies of knowledge qualify as concepts and to develop models of the processes that might use them.

By contrast, psychologists and neuropsychologists are probably mistaken to assume that definitions are one of the fundamental kinds of concept. There is no doubt that people are able to learn the definitions of well-defined categories and to use them to classify objects into these categories. There is also no doubt that learning and using definitions involve some brain areas that can be disrupted in various ways. But all these findings do not show that outside the lab, people learn definitions and use them to categorize, reason, draw analogies, and so on. This objection against the classical theory of concepts, which was originally raised in the 1960s and 1970s, remains as valid today as forty years ago.

Multi-process theories are also another important research area that requires systematic attention. Proponents of the Received View of concepts have typically endorsed the Unified View of Cognition, that is, they have typically assumed that each cognitive competence is underwritten by a single cognitive process. By contrast, the Heterogeneity Hypothesis proposes that a cognitive competence is typically underwritten by several distinct processes that use distinct kinds of concept.

I have sketched a framework for developing multi-process theories of the higher cognitive competences, identifying several key questions that need to be answered by proponents of these theories. Are the distinct cognitive processes that underwrite a single competence triggered simultaneously or one at a time? What causes them to be triggered in such and such conditions? Are these processes triggered in a bottom-up or in a top-down manner? Do learning and experience affect the triggering conditions of these processes? When several processes are simultaneously triggered, are their outputs integrated? If so, how are they integrated? If not, how does the mind produce a single output?

This framework is imperfect, however. It is likely that in addition to these key questions, multi-process theories need to deal with numerous important issues that have not been identified here. Psychologists should identify these issues and develop a more systematic typology of multi-process theories.

Psychologists should also investigate further what kind of evidence can support the hypothesis that a given cognitive competence is underwritten by several distinct processes. In chapter 5, I have described three types of evidence that can support this hypothesis, and I have shown in chapters 6 and 7 that these types of evidence can be successfully used to support multi-process theories. But there are probably other types of evidence that might support multi-process theories. Because the burden of proof currently bears on those psychologists who contend that a given cognitive competence is underwritten by distinct cognitive processes rather than by a single cognitive process, identifying these additional sources of evidence is a crucial task for proponents of multi-process theories.

Psychologists should also develop detailed multi-process theories of those cognitive competences that are the best candidates for being underwritten by several distinct processes. So far, we know very little about how the distinct cognitive processes that underwrite competences such as categorization and induction are organized. We do not really know whether outside the lab, the categorization and induction processes are triggered simultaneously or in distinct conditions. We do not really know what determines their triggering. And we do not know what happens to the outputs of the categorization and induction processes when these processes are simultaneously triggered.

Contemporary psychologists who reject the Unified View of Cognition are often pleased with dual-theories of cognition that pit System 1 processes and System 2 processes against each other. However, psychologists should realize that there are numerous other types of multi-process theory. This is particularly important because, as we saw in chapter 5, dual-process theories are not without problems. Most important, they are typically sketchily described and, as a result, are unable to yield clear predictions instead of mere post hoc accommodations. I have contrasted the current dual-process theories with the multi-process theories developed by Ashby and by Gigerenzer and colleagues. The latter theories include clear, often formal descriptions of the relevant processes together with detailed descriptions of their organization. This type of theory should be emulated by opponents of the Unified View of Cognition.

Finally, most of the experiments discussed in this book use ecologically invalid set-ups. Artificial categories (e.g., classes of patterns of dots or of sequences of numerals and letters) are extremely different from real categories. The learning conditions in concept-learning experiments—repeated presentations of a small number of category members—have little to do with most learning conditions outside the lab. Psychologists should check whether their findings apply to concepts, categorizations, and inductions outside the lab. A first step in this direction would be to systematically replicate the experiments on categorization and concept learning with different kinds of stimulus. Psychologists could also look for properties of real-world concepts (e.g., lexicalized concepts) that are analogous to the properties identified in controlled laboratory experiments. To illustrate the latter idea, Labov's (1973) finding that in American English, the class of bowls is organized around the prototype of a bowl converged with laboratory findings and provided strong support to the prototype paradigm of concepts.

Eliminating "concept" from the vocabulary of psychology is likely to bring these important tasks to the fore. If psychologists were to say that categorization involves prototypes, exemplars, and theories, rather than saying (as they now do) that it involves concepts, it would be clear that psychologists have to describe what prototypes, exemplars, and theories are, rather than describing what concepts are. It would also be clear that they have to explain how the categorization processes that use prototypes, exemplars, and theories are organized. Bringing these tasks to the fore is the main pragmatic reason that justifies the drastic conceptual change proposed in this book—doing psychology without the theoretical term "concept."

References

Abbott, B. 1997. A note on the nature of water. *Mind* 106:311–319.
—— 1999. Water = H$_2$O. *Mind* 108:145–148.
Ahn, W. K. 1998. Why are different features central for natural kinds and artifacts? The role of causal status in determining feature weights. *Cognition* 69:135–178.
Ahn, W. K., and Luhmann, C. C. 2004. Demystifying theory-based categorization. In *Building object categories in developmental time*, ed. L. Gershkoff-Stowe and D. Rakison, 277–300. Mahwah, NJ: Lawrence Erlbaum Associates.
Ahn, W. K., Kim, N. S., Lassaline, M. E., and Dennis, M. J. 2000. Causal status as a determinant of feature centrality. *Cognitive Psychology* 41:361–416.
Ahn, W. K., Gelman, S. A., Amsterlaw, J. A., Hohenstein, J., and Kalish, C. W. 2000. Causal status effect in children's categorization. *Cognition* 76:B35–B43.
Allen, S. W., and Brooks, L. R. 1991. Specializing the operation of an explicit rule. *Journal of Experimental Psychology: General* 120:3–19.
Anderson, J. R. 1978. Arguments concerning representations for mental imagery. *Psychological Review* 85:249–277.
Anderson, J. R., and Betz, J. 2001. A hybrid model of categorization. *Psychonomic Bulletin and Review* 8:629–647.
Armstrong, S. L., Gleitman, L. R., and Gleitman, H. 1983. What some concepts might not be. *Cognition* 13:263–308.
Ashby, F. G., and Ell, S. W. 2001. The neurobiology of category learning. *Trends in Cognitive Sciences* 5:204–210.
—— 2002. Single versus multiple systems of learning and memory. In *Stevens' handbook of experimental psychology*. Vol. 4, *Methodology in experimental psychology*. 3d ed., ed. J. Wixted and H. Pashler, 655–692. New York: Wiley.

Ashby, F. G., and Ennis, J. M. 2006. The role of the basal ganglia in category learning. In *The psychology of learning and motivation*. Vol. 46, ed. B. H. Ross, 1–36. New York: Elsevier.

Ashby, F. G., and Gott, R. E. 1988. Decision rules in the perception and categorization of multidimensional stimuli. *Journal of Experimental Psychology: Learning, Memory, and Cognition* 14:33–53.

Ashby, F. G., and Maddox, W. T. 1990. Integrating information from separable psychological dimensions. *Journal of Experimental Psychology: Human Perception and Performance* 16:598–612.

——— 1993. Relations between exemplar, prototype, and decision bound models of categorization. *Journal of Mathematical Psychology* 37:372–400.

——— 2005. Human category learning. *Annual Review of Psychology* 56:149–178.

Ashby, F. G., and O'Brien, J. B. 2005. Category learning and multiple memory systems. *Trends in Cognitive Science* 2:83–89.

Ashby, F. G., and Valentin, V. V. 2005. Multiple systems of perceptual category learning: Theory and cognitive tests. In *Categorization in cognitive science*, ed. H. Cohen and C. Lefebvre, 548–573. New York: Elsevier.

Ashby, F. G., and Waldron, E. M. 2000. The neuropsychological bases of category learning. *Current Directions in Psychological Science* 9:10–14.

Ashby, F. G., Alfonso-Reese, L. A., Turken, A. U., and Waldron, E. M. 1998. A neuropsychological theory of multiple systems in category learning. *Psychological Review* 105:442–481.

Baddeley, A. 1986. *Working memory.* Oxford: Clarendon Press.

Bailenson, J. B., Shum, M. S., Atran, S., Medin, D., and Coley, J. D. 2002. A bird's eye view: Biological categorization and reasoning within and across cultures. *Cognition* 84:1–53.

Baillargeon, R., Kotovsky, L., and Needham, A. 1995. The acquisition of physical knowledge in infancy. In *Causal cognition: A multidisciplinary debate*, ed. D. Sperber, D. Premack, and A. J. Premack, 79–116. New York: Oxford University Press.

Barclay, J. R., Bransford, J. D., Franks, J. J., McCarrell, N. S., and Nitsch, K. E. 1974. Comprehension and semantic flexibility. *Journal of Verbal Learning and Verbal Behavior* 13:471–481.

Barsalou, L. W. 1983. Ad hoc categories. *Memory & Cognition* 10:82–93.

——— 1985. Ideals, central tendency, and frequency of instantiation as determinants of graded structure in categories. *Journal of Experimental Psychology: Learning, Memory, and Cognition* 11:629–654.

——— 1987. The instability of graded structure: Implications for the nature of concepts. In *Concepts and conceptual development: Ecological and intellectual factors in categorization*, ed. U. Neisser, 101–140. Cambridge: Cambridge University Press.

——— 1989. Intraconcept similarity and its implications for interconcept similarity. In *Similarity and analogical reasoning*, ed. S. Vosniadou and A. Ortony, 76–121. Cambridge: Cambridge University Press.

——— 1990. On the indistinguishability of exemplar memory and abstraction in category representation. In *Advances in social cognition*. Vol. 3, *Content and process specificity in the effects of prior experiences*, ed. T. K. Srull and R. S. Wyer, 61–88. Hillsdale, NJ: Erlbaum.

——— 1993. Flexibility, structure, and linguistic vagary in concepts: Manifestations of a compositional system of perceptual symbols. In *Theories of memory*, ed.

A. C. Collins, S. E. Gathercole, and M. A. Conway, 29–101. London: Lawrence Erlbaum Associates.
—— 1999. Perceptual symbol systems. *Behavioral and Brain Sciences* 22:577–660.
—— 2003. Abstraction in perceptual symbol systems. *Philosophical Transactions of the Royal Society of London: Biological Sciences* 358:1177–1187.
—— 2008. Grounded cognition. *Annual Review of Psychology* 59:617–645.
Barsalou, L. W., Solomon, K. O., and Wu, L. L. 1999. Perceptual simulation in conceptual tasks. In *Cultural, typological, and psychological in cognitive linguistics: The proceedings of the 4th conference of the International Cognitive Linguistics Association*, ed. M. K. Hiraga, C. Sinha, and S. Wilcox, 209–228. Amsterdam: John Benjamins.
Barsalou, L. W., Simmons, W. K., Barbey, A., and Wilson, C. D. 2003. Grounding conceptual knowledge in modality-specific systems. *Trends in Cognitive Sciences* 7:84–91.
Barsalou, L. W., Pecher, D., Zeelenberg, R., Simmons, W. K., and Hamann, S. B. 2005. Multi-modal simulation in conceptual processing. In *Categorization inside and outside the lab: Essays in honor of Douglas L. Medin*, ed. W. Ahn, R. Goldstone, B. Love, A. Markman, and P. Wolff, 249–270. Washington, DC: American Psychological Association.
Batson, C. D. 1991. *The altruism question: Toward a social-psychological answer.* Hillsdale, NJ: Lawrence Erlbaum Associates.
Beer, J. S., Shimamura, A. P., and Knight, R. T. 2004. Frontal lobe contributions to executive control of cognitive and social behavior. In *The Cognitive Neurosciences.* 3d ed., ed. M. S. Gazzaniga, 1091–1104. Cambridge, MA: MIT Press.
Berkeley, G. [1734] 1998. *A treatise concerning the principles of human knowledge,* ed. J. Dancy. Oxford: Oxford University Press.
Berretty, P. M., Todd, P. M., and Martignon, L. 1999. Categorization by elimination. In *Simple heuristics that make us smart,* ed. G. Gigerenzer, P. M. Todd, and the ABC Research Group, 235–254. New York: Oxford University Press.
Binet, A. 1903. *L'Étude expérimentale de l'intelligence.* Paris: Schleicher Frères et Cie.
Bishop, M. A., and Stich, S. P. 1998. The flight to reference, or how not to make progress in the philosophy of science. *Philosophy of Science* 65:33–49.
Bloom, P. 1996. Intention, history, and artifact concepts. *Cognition* 60:1–29.
—— 2000. *How children learn the meanings of words.* Cambridge, MA: MIT Press.
Boghossian, P. 1996. Analyticity reconsidered. *Nous* 30:360–391.
Boring, E. G. 1950. *A history of experimental psychology.* New York: Appleton-Century-Crofts.
Bornkeneau, P. 1990. Traits as ideal-based and goal-derived social categories. *Journal of Personality and Social Psychology* 58:381–396.
Boyd, R. 1990. What realism implies and what it does not. *Dialectica* 43:5–29.
—— 1991. Realism, anti-foundationalism and the enthusiasm for natural kinds. *Philosophical Studies* 61:127–148.
—— 1999. Kinds, complexity and multiple realization. *Philosophical Studies* 95:67–98.
Boyd, R., and Silk, J. A. 2000. *How humans evolved.* New York: W. W. Norton.
Boyer, P., and Barrett, H. C. 2005. Domain specificity and intuitive ontology. In *Handbook of evolutionary psychology,* ed. D. M. Buss, 200–223. Hoboken, NJ: Wiley.

Brigandt, I. 2005. A theory of conceptual advance. Ph.D. diss., University of Pittsburgh.

Brooks, L. R. 1978. Nonanalytic concept formation and memory for instances. In *Cognition and concepts*, ed. E. Rosch and B. B. Lloyd, 169–211. Hillsdale, NJ: Erlbaum.

Brooks, L. R., Norman, G. R., and Allen, S. W. 1991. The role of specific similarity in a medical diagnostic task. *Journal of Experimental Psychology: General* 120:278–287.

Brooks, R. A. [1991] 1999. Intelligence without representation. *Artificial Intelligence* 47:139–159. Reproduced in R. A. Brooks, *Cambrian Intelligence*. Cambridge, MA: MIT Press.

Bruner, J. S., Goodnow, J.-J., and Austin, G. A. 1956. *A study of thinking*. New York: Wiley.

Burge, T. 1979. Individualism and the mental. *Midwest Studies in Philosophy* 4:7–121.

Busemeyer, J., and Townsend, J. T. 1993. Decision field theory: A dynamic-cognitive approach to decision making. *Psychological Review* 100:432–459.

Cabeza, R., Bruce., V., Kato, T., and Oda, M. 1999. The prototype effect in face recognition: Extension and limits. *Memory & Cognition* 27:139–151.

Cantor, N., and Mischel, W. 1979. Prototypes in person perception. In *Advances in experimental social psychology*. Vol. 12, ed. L. Berkowitz, 3–52. New York: Academic Press.

Cantor, N., Mischel, W., and Schwartz, J. C. 1982. A prototype analysis of psychological situations. *Cognitive Psychology* 14:45–77.

Cantor, N., Smith, E. E., French, R., and Mezzich, J. 1980. Psychiatric diagnosis as prototype categorization. *Journal of Abnormal Psychology* 89:181–193.

Caramazza, A. 1986. On drawing inferences about the structure of normal cognitive systems from the analysis of patterns of impaired performance: The case for single-patient studies. *Brain & Cognition* 5:41–66.

Caramazza, A., and Mahon, B. Z. 2003. The organization of conceptual knowledge: Evidence from category-specific semantic deficits. *Trends in Cognitive Sciences* 7:354–361.

—— 2006. The organization of conceptual knowledge in the brain: The future's past and some future directions. *Cognitive Neuropsychology* 23:13–38.

Carey, S. E. 1985. *Conceptual change in childhood*. Cambridge, MA: MIT Press.

—— 1988. Conceptual differences between children and adults. *Mind & Language* 3:167–181.

—— 1991. Knowledge acquisition: enrichment or conceptual change? In *The epigenesis of mind: Essays in biology and cognition*, ed. S. E. Carey and R. Gelman, 257–291. Hillsdale, NJ: Erlbaum.

Carey, S. E., and Bartlett, E. 1978. Acquiring a single new word. *Proceedings of the Stanford Child Language Conference* 15:17–29.

Carey, S. E., and Johnson, S. C. 2000. Metarepresentations and conceptual change: Evidence from Williams syndrome. In *Metarepresentation: A multidisciplinary perspective*, ed. D. Sperber, 225–264. New York: Oxford University Press.

Carey, S. E., and Spelke, E. S. 1994. Domain specific knowledge and conceptual change. In *Mapping the mind: Domain specificity in cognition and culture*, ed. L. A. Hirschfeld and S. A. Gelman, 169–200. Cambridge: Cambridge University Press.

Chaiken, S., and Trope, Y. 1999. *Dual-process theories in social psychology*. New York: Guilford Press.

Chalmers, D. 2006. Two-dimensional semantics. In *Oxford handbook of the philosophy of language*, ed. E. Lepore and B. Smith, 574–606. Oxford: Oxford University Press.

Chaplin, W. F., John, O. P., and Goldberg, L. R. 1988. Conceptions of states and traits: Dimensional attributes with ideals as prototypes. *Journal of Personality and Social Psychology* 54:541–557.

Cheng, P. W., and Holyoak, K. J. 1985. Pragmatic versus syntactic approaches to training deductive reasoning. *Cognitive Psychology* 17:391–416.

Chomsky, N. 1995. Language and nature. *Mind* 104:1–61.

Churchland, P. M. 1981. Eliminative materialism and the propositional attitudes. *Journal of Philosophy* 78:67–90.

Clark, A. 1993. *Associative engines: Connectionism, concepts, and representational change*. Cambridge, MA: MIT Press.

Coleman, L., and Kay, P. 1981. Prototype semantics: The English word *lie*. *Language* 57:26–44.

Collier, J. 1996. On the necessity of natural kinds. In *Natural kinds, laws of nature and scientific reasoning*, ed. P. Riggs, 1–10. Dordrecht: Kluwer.

Coltheart, M., and Davies, M. 2003. Inference and explanation in cognitive neuropsychology. *Cortex* 39:188–191.

Coltheart, M., Curtis, B., Atkins, P., and Haller, M. 1993. Models of reading aloud: Dual-route and parallel-distributed-processing approaches. *Psychological Review* 100:589–608.

Coltheart, M., Rastle, K., Perry, C., Langdon, R., and Ziegler, J. 2001. DRC: A dual route cascaded model of visual word recognition and reading aloud. *Psychological Review* 108:204–256.

Conant, M. B., and Trabasso, T. 1964. Conjunctive and disjunctive concept formation under equal-information conditions. *Journal of Experimental Psychology* 67:250–255.

Connolly, A. C., Fodor, J. A., Gleitman, L. R., and Gleitman, H. 2007. Why stereotypes don't even make good defaults. *Cognition* 103:1–22.

Cosmides, L. 1989. The logic of social exchange: Has natural selection shaped how humans reason? Studies with the Wason selection task. *Cognition* 31:187–276.

Costello, F. J., and Keane, M. T. 2000. Efficient creativity: Constraint-guided conceptual combination. *Cognitive Science* 24:299–349.

—— 2005. Compositionality and the pragmatics of conceptual combination. In *The compositionality of meaning and content*. Vol. 2, *Applications to linguistics, psychology and neuroscience*, ed. E. Machery, M. Werning, and G. Schultz, 203–216. Frankfurt: Ontos.

Craver, C. 2004. Dissociable realization and kind splitting. *Philosophy of Science* 71:960–971.

Damasio, A. R. 1989. Time-locked multiregional retroactivation: A systems-level proposal for the neural substrates of recall and recognition. *Cognition* 33:25–62.

—— 1994. *Descartes' error: Emotion, reason, and the human brain*. New York: Grosset/Putnam.

Danks, D. 2007. Theory unification and graphical models in human categorization. In *Causal learning: Psychology, philosophy, and computation*, ed. A. Gopnik and L. Schulz, 173–189. New York: Oxford University Press.

Davies, R. R., Hodges, J. R., Kril, J. J., Patterson, K., Halliday, G. M., and Xuereb, J. H. 2005. The pathological basis of semantic dementia. *Brain* 128:1984–1995.

Dennett, D. C. 1969. *Content and consciousness.* London: Routledge & Kegan Paul.

—— 1993. Learning and labeling. *Mind & Language* 8:540–548.

—— 1996. *Kinds of minds: Toward an understanding of consciousness.* New York: Basic Books.

Devlin, J. T., Rushworth, M. F. S., and Matthews, P. M. 2005. Category-related activation for written words in the posterior fusiform is task specific. *Neuropsychologia* 43:69–74.

Dias, M., and Harris, P. L. 1990. The influence of the imagination on reasoning by young children. *British Journal of Developmental Psychology* 8:305–318.

Dunn, J. C. 2003. The elusive dissociation. *Cortex* 39:177–179.

Dunn, J. C., and Kirsner, K. 1988. Discovering functionally independent mental processes: The principle of reversed association. *Psychological Review* 95:91–101.

—— 2003. What can we infer from double dissociations? *Cortex* 39:1–7.

Estes, W. K. 1986. Array models of concept learning. *Cognitive Psychology* 18:500–549.

Evans, J. St. B. T., and Over, D. E. 1996. *Rationality and reasoning.* Hove: Psychology Press.

Farah, M. J. 2004. *Visual cognition.* 2d ed. Cambridge, MA: MIT Press.

Faucher, L., Mallon, R., Nichols, S., Nazer, D., Ruby, A., Stich, S. P., and Weinberg, J. 2002. The baby in the labcoat: Why child development is an inadequate model for understanding the development of science. In *The cognitive basis of science*, ed. P. Carruthers, S. P. Stich, and M. Siegal, 335–362. Cambridge: Cambridge University Press.

Feeney, A., and Heit, E., eds. 2007. *Inductive reasoning: Experimental, developmental, and computational approaches.* Cambridge: Cambridge University Press.

Felleman, D. J., and Van Essen, D. C. 1991. Distributed hierarchical processing in primate cerebral cortex. *Cerebral Cortex* 1:1–47.

Filoteo, J. V., Todd Maddox, W., Simmons, A. N., Ing, A. D., Cagigas, X. E., Matthews, S., and Paulus, M. P. 2005. Cortical and subcortical brain regions involved in rule-based category learning. *Neuroreport* 16:111–115.

Fisher, S. C. 1916. The process of generalizing abstraction; and its product, the general concept. *Psychological Monographs*, 21:1–209.

Fodor, J. A. 1974. Special sciences. *Synthese* 28:97–115.

—— 1975. *The language of thought.* New York: Crowell.

—— 1981. The present status of the innateness controversy. In *Representations: Philosophical essays on the foundations of cognitive science*, by J. A. Fodor, 257–316. Cambridge, MA: MIT Press.

—— 1994. Concepts: A potboiler. *Cognition* 50:95–113.

—— 1998. *Concepts: Where cognitive science went wrong.* New York: Oxford University Press.

Fodor, J. A., and Pylyshyn, Z. W. 1988. Connectionism and cognitive architecture: A critical analysis. *Cognition* 28:3–71.

Fodor, J. A., Garret, M. F., Walker, E. C. T., and Parkes, C. H. 1980. Against definitions. *Cognition* 8:263–367.

Gärdenfors, P. 2000. *Conceptual spaces: The geometry of thought.* Cambridge, MA: MIT Press.

Gelman, R. 1990. First principles organize attention to and learning about relevant data: Number and the animate–inanimate distinction as examples. *Cognitive Science* 14:79–106.

——— 2004. Cognitive development. In *Stevens' handbook of experimental psychology.* Vol. 3, *Memory and cognitive processes,* ed. H. Pashler and D. L. Medin, 533–560. New York: Wiley.

Gelman, S. A. 1988. The development of induction within natural kinds and artifacts categories. *Cognitive Psychology* 20:65–95.

——— 2003. *The essential child: Origins of essentialism in everyday thought.* New York: Oxford University Press.

Gelman, S. A., and Bloom, P. 2000. Young children are sensitive to how an object was created when deciding what to name it. *Cognition* 76:91–103.

——— 2007. Developmental changes in the understanding of generics. *Cognition* 105:163–183.

Gelman, S. A., and Coley, J. D. 1991. Language and categorization: The acquisition of natural kind terms. In *Perspectives on language and thought: Interrelations in development,* ed. S. A. Gelman and J. P. Byrnes, 146–196. Cambridge: Cambridge University Press.

Gelman, S. A., and Markman, E. 1986. Categories and induction in young children. *Cognition* 23:183–209.

——— 1987. Young children's inductions from natural kinds: The role of categories and appearances. *Child Development* 58:1532–1541.

Gelman, S. A., and Medin, D. L. 1993. What's so essential about essentialism? Different perspective on the interaction of perception, language, and conceptual knowledge. *Cognitive Development* 8:157–167.

Gelman, S. A., and Wellman, H. M. 1991. Insides and essences: Early understandings of the non-obvious. *Cognition* 38:213–244.

Gengerelli, J. A. 1927. Mutual interference in the evolution of concepts. *American Journal of Psychology* 38:639–646.

Gennari, S. P., Sloman, S., Malt, B., and Fitch, T. 2002. Motion events in language and cognition. *Cognition* 83:49–79.

Gigerenzer, G., and Goldstein, D. G. 1996. Reasoning the fast and frugal way: Models of bounded rationality. *Psychological Review* 103:650–669.

Gigerenzer, G., and Regier, T. P. 1996. How do we tell an association from a rule? *Psychological Bulletin* 119:23–26.

Gigerenzer, G., Todd, P. M., and the ABC Research Group. 1999. *Simple heuristics that make us smart.* New York: Oxford University Press.

Gleitman, L. R., Connolly, A. C., and Armstrong, S. L. Forthcoming. Can prototype representations support composition and decomposition over features and words? In *The Oxford handbook of compositionality,* ed. M. Werning, W. Hinzen, and E. Machery. Oxford: Oxford University Press.

Glenberg, A. M. 1997. What memory is for? *Behavioral and Brain Sciences* 20:1–55.

Glymour, C. 1994. On the methods of cognitive neuropsychology. *British Journal for the Philosophy of Science* 45: 815–835.

——— 2001. *The mind's arrows: Bayes nets and graphical causal models.* Cambridge, MA: MIT Press.

Goldman, A. I. 2006. *Simulating minds: The philosophy, psychology, and neuroscience of mindreading.* New York: Oxford University Press.

Goldstein, D. G., and Gigerenzer, G. 2002. Models of ecological rationality: The recognition heuristic. *Psychological Review* 109:75–90.

Goldstone, R. L., and Kersten, A. W. 2003. Concepts and categorization. In *Handbook of psychology*, ed. I. B. Weiner. Vol. 4, *Experimental psychology*, ed. A. F. Healy and R. W. Proctor, 599–621. New York: Wiley.

Gopnik, A., and Meltzoff, A. N. 1997. *Words, thoughts, and theories*. Cambridge, MA: MIT Press.

Gopnik, A., and Schulz, L. 2004. Mechanisms of theory-formation in young children. *Trends in Cognitive Sciences* 8:371–377.

——— eds. 2007. *Causal learning: Psychology, philosophy, and computation*. New York: Oxford University Press.

Gopnik, A., and Wellman, H. M. 1994. The theory theory. In *Mapping the mind: Domain specificity in cognition and culture*, ed. L. A. Hirschfeld and S. A. Gelman, 257–293. Cambridge: Cambridge University Press.

Gopnik, A., Glymour, C., Sobel, D., Schulz, L., Kushnir, T., and Danks, D. 2004. A theory of causal learning in children: Causal maps and Bayes nets. *Psychological Review* 111:1–31.

Goschke, T. 1997. Implicit learning and unconscious knowledge: Mental representations, computational mechanisms and brain structure. In *Knowledge, concepts, and categories*, ed. K. Lamberts and D. Shanks, 247–334. Cambridge, MA: MIT Press.

Grant, C. M., Riggs, K. J., and Boucher, J. 2004. Counterfactual and mental state reasoning in children with autism. *Journal of Autism and Developmental Disorders* 34:177–188.

Greene, J. D., and Haidt, J. 2002. How and where does moral judgment work? *Trends in Cognitive Sciences* 6:517–523.

Greene, J. D., Nystrom, L. E., Engell, A. D., Darley, J. M., Cohen, J. D. 2004 The neural bases of cognitive conflict and control in moral judgment. *Neuron* 44:389–400.

Greene, J. D., Sommerville, R. B., Nystrom, L. E., Darley, J. M., and Cohen, J. D. 2001. An fMRI investigation of emotional engagement in moral judgment. *Science* 293 (Sept. 14):2105–2108.

Greene, J. D., Morelli, S. A., Lowenberg, K., Nystrom, L. E., and Cohen, J. D. 2008. Cognitive load selectively interferes with utilitarian moral judgment. *Cognition* 107:44–54.

Griffiths, P. E. 1997. *What emotions really are*. Chicago: Chicago University Press.

Griffiths, T. L., and Tenenbaum, J. B. 2007. Two proposals for causal grammar. In *Causal learning: Psychology, philosophy, and computation*, ed. A. Gopnik and L. Schulz, 323–346. New York: Oxford University Press.

Griffiths, T. L., Steyvers, M., and Tenenbaum, J. B. 2007. Topics in semantic representation. *Psychological Review* 114:211–244.

Grossman, M., Koenig, P., DeVita, C., Glosser, G., Alsop, D., Detre, J., and Gee, J. 2002. The neural basis for category-specific knowledge: An fMRI study. *Neuroimage* 15:936–948.

Grünbaum, A. 1908. Über die Abstracktion der Gleichheit. *Archiv für die Geschichte der Psychologie* 7:340–478.

Grush, R. 2003. In defense of some "Cartesian" assumptions concerning the brain and its operation. *Biology & Philosophy* 18:53–93.

——— 2004. The emulation theory of representation: Motor control, imagery, and perception. *Behavioral and Brain Sciences* 27:377–396.

Hacking, I. 1986. Making up people. In *Reconstructing individualism: Autonomy, individuality, and the self in western thought*, ed. T. Heller, M. Sosna, and D. Wellberry, 222–236. Stanford, CA: Stanford University Press.

——— 1991. A tradition of natural kinds. *Philosophical Studies* 61:109–126.

——— 1999. *The social construction of what?* Cambridge, MA: Harvard University Press.

Hadjichristidis, C., Sloman, S. A., Stevenson, R. J., and Over, D. E. 2004. Feature centrality and property induction. *Cognitive Science* 28:45–74.

Hahn, U., and Chater, N. 1998. Similarity and rules: Distinct? exhaustive? empirically distinguishable? *Cognition* 65:197–230.

Hahn, U., and Ramscar, M., eds. 2001. *Similarity and Categorization*. Oxford: Oxford University Press.

Haidt, J. 2001. The emotional dog and its rational tail: A social intuitionist approach to moral judgment. *Psychological Review* 108:814–834.

Hammond, K. 1989. *Case-based planning: Viewing planning as a memory task*. New York: Academic Press.

Hampton, J. A. 1979. Polymorphous concepts in semantic memory. *Journal of Verbal Learning and Verbal Behavior* 18:441–461.

——— 1981. An investigation of the nature of abstract concepts. *Memory & Cognition* 9:149–156.

——— 1982. A demonstration of intransitivity in natural categories. *Cognition* 12:151–164.

——— 1987. Inheritance of attributes in natural concept conjunctions. *Memory & Cognition* 15:55–71.

——— 1988. Overextension of conjunctive concepts: Evidence for a unitary model of concept typicality and class inclusion. *Journal of Experimental Psychology: Learning, Memory, and Cognition* 14:378–383.

——— 1993. Prototype models of concept representation. In *Categories and concepts: Theoretical views and inductive data analysis*, ed. I. Van Mechelen, J. A., Hampton, R. S. Michalski, and P. Theuns, 67–95. London: Academic Press.

——— 1995. Testing the prototypes theory of concepts. *Journal of Memory and Language* 34:686–708.

——— 1996. Conjunctions of visually-based categories: Overextensions and compensation. *Journal of Experimental Psychology: Learning, Memory, and Cognition* 34:686–708.

——— 1997a. Conceptual combination. In *Knowledge, concepts, and categories*, ed. K. Lamberts and D. Shanks, 133–160. Cambridge, MA: MIT Press.

——— 1997b. Conceptual combination: Conjunction and negation of natural concepts. *Memory & Cognition* 25:888–909.

——— 1997c. Psychological representation of concepts. In *Cognitive models of memory*, ed. M. A. Conway, 81–110. Cambridge, MA: MIT Press.

——— 1998. Similarity-based categorization and fuzzyness of natural categories. *Cognition* 65:137–165.

——— 2001. The role of similarity in natural categorization. In *Similarity and categorization*, ed. U. Hahn and M. Ramscar, 13–28. Oxford: Oxford University Press.

——— 2006. Concepts as prototypes. In *The psychology of learning and motivation: Advances in research and theory.* Vol. 46, ed. B. H. Ross, 79–113. New York: Academic Press.

Hampton, J. A. 2007. Typicality, graded membership, and vagueness. *Cognitive Science* 31:355–384.

Hampton, J. A., and Dubois, D. 1993. Psychological models of concepts: Introduction. In *Categories and concepts: Theoretical views and inductive data analysis*, ed. I. Van Mechelen, J. Hampton, R. S. Michalski, and P. Theuns, 11–33. London: Academic Press.

Hampton, J. A., and Jönsson, M. L. Forthcoming. Typicality and compositionality: The logic of combining vague concepts. In *The Oxford handbook of compositionality*, ed. M. Werning, W. Hinzen, and E. Machery. Oxford: Oxford University Press.

Hare, B., Brown, B., Williamson, C., and Tomasello, M. 2002. The domestication of social cognition in dogs. *Science* 298:1634–1636.

Heit, E. 1997. Knowledge and concept learning. In *Knowledge, concepts, and categories*, ed. K. Lamberts and D. Shanks, 7–42. Cambridge, MA: MIT Press.

—— 2000. Properties of inductive reasoning. *Psychonomic Bulletin and Review* 7:569–592.

—— 2001. Background knowledge and models of categorization. In *Similarity and categorization*, ed. U. Hahn and M. Ramscar, 155–178. Oxford: Oxford University Press.

Heit, E., and Rubinstein, J. 1994. Similarity and property effects in inductive reasoning. *Journal of Experimental Psychology: Learning, Memory, and Cognition* 20:411–422.

Hempel, C. G., and Oppenheim, P. 1948. Studies in the logic of explanation. *Philosophy of Science* 15:135–175.

Hewson, C. 1994. Empirical evidence regarding the folk psychological concept of belief. In *Proceedings of the sixteenth annual conference of the Cognitive Science Society*, ed. A. Ram and K. Eiselt, 403–406. Hillsdale, NJ: Erlbaum.

Hintzman, D. L. 1986. Schema abstraction in a multiple-trace memory model. *Psychological Review* 93:411–428.

Hirschfeld, L. A., and Gelman, S. A., eds. 1994. *Mapping the mind: Domain-specificity in cognition and culture*. Cambridge: Cambridge University Press.

Homa, D., Sterling, S., and Trepel, L. 1981. Limitations of exemplar-based generalization and the abstraction of categorical information. *Journal of Experimental Psychology: Human Learning and Memory* 7:418–439.

Horn, B. K. P. 1975. Obtaining shape from shading information. In *The psychology of computer vision*, ed. P. H. Winston, 115–155. New York: McGraw-Hill.

Hull, C. L. 1920. Quantitative aspects of the evolution of concepts. *Psychological Monographs*, 28:1–86.

Hull, D. 1978. A matter of individuality. *Philosophy of Science* 45:335–360.

Hume, D. [1748] 1975. *Enquiries concerning human understanding and concerning the principles of morals*. Ed. P. H. Nidditch. Oxford: Oxford University Press.

Huttenlocher, J., and Hedges, L. V. 1994. Combining graded categories: Membership and typicality. *Psychological Review* 101:157–165.

Inagaki, K., and Hatano, G. 2006. Young children's conceptions of the biological world. *Current Directions in Psychological Science* 15:177–181.

Inhelder, B., and Piaget, J. 1969. *The early growth of logic in the child: Classification and seriation*. New York: W. W. Norton.

Jackendoff, R. 1992. What is a concept, that a person may grasp it? In *Languages of the mind: Essays on mental representation*, by R. Jackendoff, 21–52. Cambridge, MA: MIT Press.

James, W. [1890] 1950. *The principles of psychology.* New York: Dover Publications.
Johnson, C., and Keil, F. C. 2000. Explanatory understanding and conceptual combination. In *Explanation and cognition*, ed. F. C. Keil and R. A. Wilson, 327–359. Cambridge, MA: MIT Press.
Jones, G. V. 1983. Identifying basic categories. *Psychological Bulletin* 94:423–428.
Jones, S. S., and Smith, L. B. 1993. The place of perception in children's concepts. *Cognitive Development* 8:113–139.
Jönsson, M. L., and Hampton, J. A. 2007. On prototypes as defaults. *Cognition* 106:913–923.
Juslin, P., and Persson, M. 2002. PROBabilities from EXemplars: A "lazy" algorithm for probabilistic inference from generic knowledge. *Cognitive science* 26:133–156.
Kahneman, D., and Frederick, S. 2002. Representativeness revisited: Attribute substitution in intuitive judgment. In *Heuristics & biases: The psychology of intuitive judgment*, ed. T. Gilovich, D. Griffin, and D. Kahneman, 49–81. New York: Cambridge University Press.
Kamp, H., and Partee, B. 1995. Prototype theory and compositionality. *Cognition* 57:129–191.
Kan, I. P., Barsalou, L. W., Solomon, K. O., Minor, J. K., and Thompson-Schill, S. L. 2003. Role of mental imagery in a property verification task: fMRI evidence for perceptual representations of conceptual knowledge. *Cognitive Neuropsychology* 20:525–540.
Katz, J. J., and Fodor, J. A. 1963. The structure of a semantic theory. *Language* 39:170–210.
Keil, F. C. 1987. Category structure and patterns of conceptual change. In *Concepts and conceptual development: The ecological and intellectual factors in categorization*, ed. U. Neisser, 175–200. Cambridge: Cambridge University Press.
—— 1989. *Concepts, kinds, and cognitive development.* Cambridge, MA: MIT Press.
—— 1991. Theories, concepts, and word meaning. In *Perspectives on language and thought: Interrelations in development*, ed. S. A. Gelman and J. P. Byrnes, 197–224. Cambridge: Cambridge University Press.
—— 2003. Folkscience: Coarse interpretations of a complex reality. *Trends in Cognitive Sciences* 7:368–373.
Keil, F. C., and Wilson, R. A. eds. 2000. *Explanation and cognition.* Cambridge, MA: MIT Press.
Keil, F. C., Carter Smith, W., Simons, D. J., and Levin, D. T. 1998. Two dogmas of conceptual empiricism: Implications for hybrid models of the structure of knowledge. *Cognition* 65:103–135.
Keil, F. C., Levin, D., Gutheil, G., and Richman, B. 1999. Explanation, cause and mechanism: The case of contagion. In *Folkbiology*, ed. D. Medin and S. Atran, 285–320. Cambridge, MA: MIT Press.
Kemp, C. S., and Tenenbaum, J. B. 2003.Theory-based induction. In *Proceedings of the twenty-fifth annual conference of the Cognitive Science Society*, ed. R. Alterman and D. Kirsh, 658–663. Hillsdale, NJ: Erlbaum.
Kiefer, M., Sim, E.-J., Liebich, S., Hauk, O., and Tanaka, J. 2007. Experience-dependent plasticity of conceptual representations in human sensory—motor areas. *Journal of Cognitive Neuroscience* 19:525–542.
Kim, J. 1992. Multiple realization and the metaphysics of reduction. *Philosophy and Phenomenological Research* 52:1–26.

Knowlton, B. J. 1997. Declarative and nondeclarative knowledge: Insights from cognitive neuroscience. In *Knowledge, concepts, and categories*, ed. K. Lamberts and D. R. Shanks, 214–246. Cambridge, MA: MIT Press.
—— 1999. What can neuropsychology tell us about category learning. *Trends in Cognitive Sciences* 3:123–124.
Knowlton, B. J., and Squire, L. R. 1993. The learning of categories: Parallel brain systems for item memory and category knowledge. *Science* 262: 1747–1749.
Komatsu, L. K. 1992. Recent views of conceptual structure. *Psychological Bulletin* 112:500–526.
Kripke, S. A. [1972] 1980 *Naming and necessity.* Cambridge, MA: MIT Press.
Kruschke, J. K. 1992. ALCOVE: An exemplar-based connectionist model of category learning. *Psychological Review* 99:22–44.
Kunda, Z., Miller, D. T., and Claire, T. 1990. Combining social concepts: The role of causal reasoning. *Cognitive Science* 14:551–577.
Kuo, Z. Y. 1923. A behavioristic experiment on inductive inference. *Journal of Experimental Psychology* 6:247–293.
Labov, W. 1973. The boundaries of words and their meanings. In *New ways of analyzing variation in English*, ed. C. J. Baily and R. Shuy, 340–373. Washington, DC: Georgetown University Press.
Lakoff, G., and Johnson, M. 1999. *Philosophy in the flesh: The embodied mind and its challenge to western thought.* New York: Basic Books.
Lancaster, J. S., and Barsalou, L. W. 1997. Multiple organisations of events in memory. *Memory* 5:569–599.
Laporte, J. 1998. Living water. *Mind* 107:451–455.
Laurence, S., and Margolis, E. 1999. Concepts and cognitive science. In *Concepts: Core readings*, ed. E. Margolis and S. Laurence, 3–82. Cambridge, MA: MIT Press.
LeDoux, J. E. 1996. *The emotional brain.* New York: Simon and Schuster.
Leevers, H. J., and Harris, P. L. 2000. Counterfactual syllogistic reasoning in normal four-year-olds, children with learning disabilities, and children with autism. *Journal of Experimental Child Psychology* 76:64–87.
Locke, J. [1690] 1979. *An essay concerning human understanding.* Ed. P. H. Nidditch. Oxford: Oxford University Press.
Logan, G. D. 1988. Toward an instance theory of automaticity. *Psychological Review* 95:492–527.
López, A., Gelman, S. A., Gutheil, G., and Smith, E. E. 1992. The development of category based induction. *Child Development* 63:1070–1090.
López, A., Atran, S., Coley, J. D., Medin, D. L., and Smith E. E. 1997. The tree of life: Universal and cultural features of folkbiological taxonomies and inductions. *Cognitive Psychology* 32:251–295.
Luhmann, C. C., Ahn, W. K., and Palmeri, T. 2006. Theory-based categorization under speeded conditions. *Memory & Cognition* 34:1102–1111.
Lynch, E. B., Coley, J. D., and Medin, D. L. 2000. Tall is typical: Central tendency, ideal dimensions and graded category structure among tree experts and novices. *Memory & Cognition* 28:41–50.
Machamer, P., Darden, L., and Craver, C. 2000. Thinking about mechanisms. *Philosophy of Science* 67:1–25.
Machery, E. 2005. Concepts are not a natural kind. *Philosophy of Science* 72:444–467.

—— 2006a. How to split concepts: Reply to Piccinini and Scott. *Philosophy of Science* 73:410–418.

—— 2006b. Two dogmas of neo-empiricism. *Philosophy Compass* 1:398–412.

—— 2007a. Concept empiricism: A methodological critique. *Cognition* 104: 19–46.

—— 2007b. 100 Years of psychology of concepts: The theoretical notion of concept and its operationalization. *Studies in History and Philosophy of Biological and Biomedical Sciences* 38:63–84.

Machery, E., and Barrett, C. 2006. Debunking *Adapting Minds*. *Philosophy of Science* 73:232–246.

Machery, E., and Lederer, L. G. Forthcoming. Simple heuristics for concept composition. In *The Oxford handbook of compositionality*, ed. M. Werning, W. Hinzen, and E. Machery. Oxford: Oxford University Press.

Machery, E., and Seppälä, S. 2008. Against hybrid theories of concepts. Manuscript.

Machery, E., Mallon, R., Nichols, S., and Stich, S. P. 2004. Semantics, cross-cultural style. *Cognition* 92:B1–B12.

Maddox, W. T., Filoteo, J. V., Hejl, K. D., and Ing, A. D. 2004. Category number impacts rule-based, but not information-integration category learning: Further evidence for dissociable category learning systems. *Journal of Experimental Psychology: Learning, Memory, and Cognition* 30:227–235.

Mallon, R., Machery, E., Nichols, S., and Stich, S. P. Forthcoming. Against arguments from reference. *Philosophy and Phenomenological Research*.

Malt, B. C. 1989. An on-line investigation of prototype and exemplar strategies in classification. *Journal of Experimental Psychology: Learning, Memory, and Cognition* 15:539–555.

Malt, B. C. 1993. Concept structure and category boundaries. In *The psychology of learning and motivation*. Vol. 29, *Categorization by humans and machines*, ed. G. Nakamura, R. Taraban, and D. Medin, 363–390. Orlando, FL: Academic Press.

—— 1994. Water is not H_2O. *Cognitive Psychology* 27:41–70.

Malt, B. C., and Johnson, E. C. 1992. Do artifact concepts have cores? *Journal of Memory and Language* 31:195–217.

Malt, B. C., and Sloman, S. A. 2007. Category essence or essentially pragmatic? Creator's intention in naming and what's really what. *Cognition* 105:615–648.

Malt, B. C., Sloman, S. A., Gennari, S., Shi, M., and Wang, Y. 1999. Knowing versus naming: Similarity and the linguistic categorization of artifacts. *Journal of Memory and Language* 40:230–262.

Mandler, J. M. 1992. How to build a baby: II. Conceptual primitives. *Psychological Review* 99:587–604.

Marcus, G. F. 2000. *The algebraic mind: Integrating connectionism and cognitive science*. Cambridge, MA: MIT Press.

—— 2005. Opposites detract: Why rules and similarity should not be viewed as opposite ends of a continuum. *Behavioral and Brain Sciences* 28:28–29.

Margolis, E. 1994. A reassessment of the shift from the classical theory of concepts to prototype theory. *Cognition* 51:73–89.

—— 1995. The significance of the theory analogy in the psychological study of concepts. *Mind and Language* 10:45–71.

Margolis, E., and Laurence, S., eds. 1999. *Concepts: Core readings*. Cambridge, MA: MIT Press.

Margolis, E., and Laurence, S. 2004. Concepts. In *The Blackwell guide to the philosophy of mind*, ed. T. A. Warfield and S. P. Stich, 190–213. Oxford: Blackwell.

Markman, A. B. 1999. *Knowledge representation*. Mahwah, NJ: Lawrence Erlbaum Associates.

Marr, D. 1977. Artificial intelligence: A personal view. *Artificial Intelligence* 9:37–48.

—— 1982. *Vision: A computational investigation into the human representation and processing of visual information*. San Francisco, CA: W. H. Freeman.

Martin, A., and Chao, L. L. 2001. Semantic memory and the brain: Structure and processes. *Current Opinion in Neurobiology* 11:194–201.

McCloskey, M. 2003. Beyond task dissociation logic: A richer conception of cognitive neuropsychology. *Cortex* 39:196–202.

McCloskey, M., and Glucksberg, S. 1978. Natural categories: Well-defined or fuzzy sets? *Memory & Cognition* 6:462–472.

McDowell, J. 1994. *Mind and world*. Cambridge, MA: Harvard University Press.

McNamara, T. P., and Sternberg, R. J. 1983. Mental models of word meaning. *Journal of Verbal Learning and Verbal Behavior* 22:449–474.

Medin, D. L. 1989. Concepts and conceptual structure. *American Psychologist* 44:1469–1481.

Medin, D. L., and Atran, S., eds. 1999. *Folkbiology*. Cambridge, MA: MIT Press.

Medin, D. L., and Ortony, A. 1989. Psychological essentialism. In *Similarity and analogical reasoning*, ed. S. Vosniadou and A. Ortony, 179–195. Cambridge: Cambridge University Press.

Medin, D. L., and Schaffer, M. M. 1978. Context theory of classification learning. *Psychological Review* 85:207–238.

Medin, D. L., and Schwanenflugel, P. J. 1981. Linear separability in classification learning, *Journal of Experimental Psychology: Human Learning and Memory* 7:355–368.

Medin, D. L., and Shoben, E. J. 1988. Context and structure in conceptual combination. *Cognitive Psychology* 20:158–190.

Medin, D. L., and Smith, E. E. 1984. Concepts and concept formation. *Annual Review of Psychology* 35:113–118.

Medin, D. L., Lynch, E. B., and Solomon, K. O. 2000. Are there kinds of concepts? *Annual Review of Psychology* 51:121–147.

Medin, D. L., Coley, J. D., Storms, G., and Hayes, B. 2003. A relevance theory of induction. *Psychonomic Bulletin and Review* 3:517–532.

Mellor, J. S. 1977. Natural kinds. *British Journal for the Philosophy of Science* 28:299–312.

Mervis, C. B., and Rosch, E. 1981. Categorization of natural objects. *Annual Review of Psychology* 32:89–115.

Michalski, R. S. 1993. Beyond prototypes and frames: The two-tiered concept representation. In *Categories and concepts: Theoretical views and inductive data analysis*, ed. I. Van Mechelen, J. A. Hampton, R. S. Michalski, and P. Theuns, 141–172. New York: Academic Press.

Mill, J. S. 1843. *A system of logic*. London: J. W. Parker.

Miller, G. A., and Johnson-Laird, P. N. 1976. *Language and perception*. Cambridge, MA: Harvard University Press.

Millikan, R. G. 1998. A common structure for concepts of individuals, stuffs, and real kinds: More mama, more milk, and more mouse. *Behavioral and Brain Sciences* 21:55–100.

—— 2000. *On clear and confused ideas: An essay about substance concepts*. New York: Cambridge University Press.
Mineka, S., Davidson, M., Cook, M., and Keir, R. 1984. Observational conditioning of snake fear in rhesus monkey. *Journal of Abnormal Psychology* 93:355–372.
Moore, T. 1910. The process of abstraction: An experimental study. *University of California Publications in Psychology* 12:73–197.
Murphy, D., and Stich, S. P. 1999. Griffiths, elimination and psychopathology. *Metascience* 8:13–25.
Murphy, G. L. 1988. Comprehending complex concepts. *Cognitive Science* 12:529–562.
—— 1990. Noun phrase interpretation and conceptual combination. *Journal of Memory and Language* 29:259–288.
—— 2002. *The big book of concepts*. Cambridge, MA: MIT Press.
Murphy, G. L., and Allopenna, P. D. 1994. The locus of knowledge effects in concept learning. *Journal of Experimental Psychology: Learning, Memory, and Cognition* 20:904–919.
Murphy, G. L., and Brownell, H. H. 1985. Category differentiation in object recognition: Typicality constraints on the basic category advantage. *Journal of Experimental Psychology: Learning, Memory, and Cognition* 11:70–84.
Murphy, G. L., and Lassaline, M. E. 1997. Hierarchical structure in concepts and the basic level of categorization. In *Knowledge, concepts, and categories*, ed. K. Lamberts and D. Shanks, 93–132. Cambridge, MA: MIT Press.
Murphy, G. L., and Medin, D. L. 1985. The role of theories in conceptual coherence. *Psychological Review* 92:289–316.
Nazzi, T., and Gopnik, A. 2003. Sorting and acting with objects in early childhood: An exploration of the use of causal cues. *Cognitive Development* 18:219–237.
Newell, A., and Simon, H. A. 1976. Computer science as empirical inquiry: Symbols and search. *Communications of the ACM* 19:113–126.
Nichols, S., and Stich, S. P. 2003. *Mindreading*. New York: Oxford University Press.
Nichols, S., Stich, S. P., Leslie, A., and Klein, D. 1996. The varieties of off-line simulation. In *Theories of theories of mind*, ed. P. Carruthers and P. Smith, 39–74. Cambridge: Cambridge University Press.
Nisbett, R. E. 2003. *The geography of thought: How Asians and Westerners think differently... and why*. New York: Free Press.
Nisbett, R. E., Peng, K., Choi, I., and Norenzayan, A. 2001. Culture and systems of thought: Holistic vs. analytic cognition. *Psychological Review* 108:291–310.
Nosofsky, R. M. 1986. Attention, similarity, and the identification-categorization relationship. *Journal of Experimental Psychology: Learning, Memory, and Cognition* 115:39–57.
—— 1988. Exemplar-based accounts of relations between classification, recognition, and typicality. *Journal of Experimental Psychology: Learning, Memory & Cognition* 14:700–708.
—— 1992. Exemplar-based approach to relating categorization, identification, and recognition. In *Multidimensional models of perception and cognition*, ed. F. G. Ashby, 363–393. Hillsdale, NJ: Lawrence Erlbaum Associates.
—— 2000. Exemplar representation without generalization? Comment on Smith and Minda's 2000 "Thirty categorization results in search of a model."

Journal of Experimental Psychology: Learning, Memory, and Cognition 26:1735–1743.

Nosofsky, R. M., and Johansen, M. K. 2000. Exemplar-based accounts of multiple-system phenomena in perceptual categorization. *Psychonomic Bulletin & Review* 7:375–402.

Nosofsky, R. M., and Zaki, S. R. 1998. Dissociations between categorization and recognition in amnesic and normal individuals: An exemplar-based interpretation. *Psychological Science* 9:247–255.

Nosofsky, R. M., Palmeri, T. J., and McKinley, S. C. 1994. Rule-plus-exception model of classification learning. *Psychological Review* 101:53–79.

Osherson, D. N. 1978. Three conditions on conceptual naturalness. *Cognition* 4:263–89.

Osherson, D. N., and Smith, E. E. 1981. On the adequacy of prototype theory as a theory of concepts. *Cognition* 9:35–58.

—— 1997. On typicality and vagueness. *Cognition* 64:189–206.

Osherson, D. N., Smith, E. E., Wilkie, O., López, A., and Shafir, E. 1990. Category-based induction. *Psychological Review* 97:185–200.

Osherson, D. N., Stern, J., Wilkie, O., Stob, M., and Smith, E. E. 1991. Default probability. *Cognitive Science* 15: 251–269.

Paivio, A. 1986. *Mental representations: A dual coding approach.* New York: Oxford University Press.

Palmeri, T. J. 1997. Exemplar similarity and the development of automaticity. *Journal of Experimental Psychology: Learning, Memory, and Cognition* 23:324–354.

Palmeri, T. J., and Flanery, M. A. 1999. Learning about categories in the absence of training: Profound amnesia and the relationship between perceptual categorization and recognition memory. *Psychological Science* 10:526–530.

Palmeri, T. J., and Gauthier, I. 2004. Visual object understanding. *Nature Reviews Neuroscience* 5:291–304.

Peacocke, C. 1992. *A study of concepts.* Cambridge, MA: MIT Press.

—— 1996. Can possession conditions individuate concepts? *Philosophy and Phenomenological Research* 56:433–460.

—— 1998. Implicit conceptions, understanding and rationality. In *Philosophical issues.* Vol. 9, *Concepts*, ed. E. Villanueva, 43–88. Atascadero, CA: Ridgeview.

—— 2004. Interrelations: Concepts, knowledge, reference and structure. *Mind & Language* 19:85–98.

Peterson, D. M., and Bowler, D. M. 2000. Counterfactual reasoning and false belief understanding in children with autism. *Autism* 4:391–405.

Peterson, D. M., and Riggs, K. J. 1999. Adaptive modeling and mindreading. *Mind & Language* 14:80–112.

Piaget, J. 1954. *The construction of reality in the child.* New York: Basic Books.

Piccinini, G., and Scott, S. 2006. Splitting concepts. *Philosophy of Science* 73:390–409.

Pietroski, P. 2003. The character of natural language semantics. In *Epistemology of language*, ed. A. Barber, 217–256. Oxford: Oxford University Press.

Pinker, S. 1997. *How the mind works.* New York: W. W. Norton & Company.

Pinker, S., and Prince, A. 1999. The nature of human concepts: Evidence from an unusual source. In *Language, logic, and concepts*, ed. R. Jackendoff, P. Bloom, and K. Wynn, 221–261. Cambridge, MA: MIT Press.

Plaut, D. C. 1995. Double dissociation without modularity: Evidence from connectionist neuropsychology. *Journal of Clinical and Experimental Neuropsychology* 17:291–321.

Poirier, P., and Hardy-Vallée, B. 2005. The spatial-motor view. In *The compositionality of meaning and content: Applications to linguistics, psychology and neuroscience*, ed. E. Machery, M. Werning, and G. Schurz, 229–250. Frankfurt: Ontos.

Posner, M. I., and Keele, S. W. 1968. On the genesis of abstract ideas. *Journal of Experimental Psychology* 77:353–363.

—— 1970. Retention of abstract ideas. *Journal of Experimental Psychology* 83:304–308.

Pothos, E. M. 2005. The rules versus similarity distinction. *Behavioral and Brain Sciences* 28:1–14.

Potter, M. C., Kroll, J. F., Yachzel, B., Carpenter, E., and Sherman, J. 1986. Pictures in sentences: Understanding without words. *Journal of Experimental Psychology: General* 115:281–294.

Prinz, J. J. 2002. *Furnishing the mind: Concepts and their perceptual basis*. Cambridge, MA: MIT Press.

—— 2004. *Gut reactions*. New York: Oxford University Press.

Proffitt, J. B., Coley, J. D., and Medin, D. L. 2000. Expertise and category-based induction. *Journal of Experimental Psychology: Learning, Memory, and Cognition* 26:811–828.

Putnam, H. 1975. The meaning of "meaning." In *Mind, language, and reality*, by H. Putnam, 215–271. Cambridge: Cambridge University Press.

Pylyshyn, Z. W. 1984. *Computation and cognition: Toward a foundation for cognitive science*. Cambridge, MA: MIT Press.

—— 1999. Is vision continuous with cognition? The case for cognitive impenetrability of visual perception. *Behavioral and Brain Sciences* 22:341–365.

—— 2003. *Seeing and visualizing: It's not what you think*. Cambridge, MA: MIT Press.

Quine, W. V. O. 1951. Two dogmas of empiricism. *Philosophical Review* 60:20–43.

—— 1960. *Word and object*. Cambridge, MA: MIT Press.

—— 1969. Natural kinds. In *Ontological relativity and other essays*, by W. V. O. Quine, 114–138. New York: Columbia University Press.

Ramsey, W., Stich, S. P., and Garon, J. 1990. Connectionism, eliminativism and the future of folk psychology. *Philosophical perspectives*. Vol. 4, *Action theory and philosophy of mind*, 499–533.

Read, S. J. 1987. Constructing causal scenarios: A knowledge structure approach to causal reasoning. *Journal of Personality and Social Psychology* 52:288–302.

Read, S. J., Jones, D. K., and Miller, L. C. 1990. Traits as goal-based categories: The importance of goals in the coherence of dispositional categories. *Journal of Personality and Social Psychology* 58:1048–1061.

Reber, P. J., Stark, C. E. L., and Squire, L. R. 1998. Cortical areas supporting category learning identified using functional MRI. *Proceedings of the National Academy of Sciences of the United States of America* 95:747–750.

Reed, J. M., Squire, L. R., Patalano, A. L., Smith, E. E., and Jonides, J. 1999. Learning about categories that are defined by object-like stimuli despite impaired declarative memory. *Behavioral Neuroscience* 113:411–419.

Rehder, B. 2003a. Categorization as causal reasoning. *Cognitive Science*, 27: 709–748.

Rehder, B. 2003b. A causal-model theory of conceptual representation and categorization. *Journal of Experimental Psychology: Learning, Memory, and Cognition* 29:1141–1159.

——— 2006. When causality and similarity compete in category-based property induction. *Memory & Cognition* 34:3–16.

——— 2007. Property generalization as causal reasoning. In *Inductive reasoning: Experimental, developmental, and computational approaches*, ed. A. Feeney and E. Heit, 81–113. Cambridge: Cambridge University Press.

Rehder, B., and Hastie, R. 2004. Category coherence and category-based property induction. *Cognition* 91:113–153.

Rehder, B., and Kim, S. 2006. How causal knowledge affects classification: A generative theory of categorization. *Journal of Experimental Psychology: Learning, Memory, and Cognition* 32:659–683.

Rey, G. 1983. Concepts and stereotypes. *Cognition* 15:237–262.

——— 1985. Concepts and conceptions: A reply to Smith, Medin and Rips. *Cognition* 19:297–303.

Ribot, T. 1891. Enquête sur les idées générales. *Revue Philosophique* 32:376–388.

——— 1899. *The evolution of general ideas*. Trans. F. A. Welby. Chicago: Open Court Publishing Company. Translation of *L'évolution des idées générales*. Paris: Alcan, 1897.

Rieskamp, J., and Otto, P. E. 2006. SSL: A theory of how people learn to select strategies. *Journal of Experimental Psychology: General* 135:207–236.

Rips, L. J. 1975. Inductive judgments about natural categories. *Journal of Verbal Learning and Verbal Behavior* 14:665–681.

——— 1989. Similarity, typicality, and categorization. In *Similarity and analogical reasoning*, ed. S. Vosniadou and A. Ortony, 21–59. Cambridge: Cambridge University Press.

——— 1995. The current status of the research on concept combination. *Mind & Language* 10:72–104.

——— 2001. Necessity and natural categories. *Psychological Bulletin* 127:827–852.

Rips, L. J., Blok, S. V., and Newman, G. 2006. Tracing the identity of objects. *Psychological Review* 113:1–30.

Rips, L. J., Shoben, E. J., and Smith, E. E. 1973. Semantic distance and the verification of semantic relations. *Journal of Verbal Learning and Verbal Behavior* 12:1–20.

Roberts, W. A. 1998. *Principles of animal cognition*. Boston, MA: McGraw Hill.

Roese, N. J. 1997. Counterfactual thinking. *Psychological Bulletin* 121:133–148.

Rogers, T. T., and McClelland, J. L. 2004. *Semantic cognition: A parallel distributed processing approach*. Cambridge, MA: MIT Press.

Rosch, E. 1973. On the internal structure of perceptual and semantic categories. In *Cognitive development and acquisition of language*, ed. T. Moore, 111–144. New York: Academic Press.

——— 1975. Cognitive representations of semantic categories. *Journal of Experimental Psychology: General* 104:192–233.

——— 1978. Principles of categorization. In *Cognition and categorization*, ed. E. Rosch and B. B. Lloyd, 27–48. Hillsdale, NJ: Erlbaum.

Rosch, E., and Mervis, C. B. 1975. Family resemblance: Studies in the internal structure of categories. *Cognitive Psychology* 7:573–605.

Rosch, E., Mervis, C. B., Gray, W. D., Johnson, D., and Boyes-Braem, P. 1976. Basic objects in natural categories. *Cognitive Psychology* 7:573–605.

Ross, B. H., and Makin, V. S. 1999. Prototype versus exemplar models in cognition. In *The nature of cognition*, ed. R. J. Sternberg, 205–244. Cambridge, MA: MIT Press.
Ross, B. H., Perkins, S. J., and Tenpenny, P. L. 1990. Reminding-based category learning. *Cognitive Psychology* 22:460–492.
Russell, B. 1948. *Human knowledge: Its scope and its limits*. London: Routledge.
Ryle, G. 1951. *The concept of mind*. London: Hutchinson.
Salmon, W. 1971. Statistical explanation. In *Statistical explanation and statistical relevance*, ed. W. Salmon, 29–87. Pittsburgh: University of Pittsburgh Press.
——— 1989. Four decades of scientific explanation. In *Minnesota studies in the philosophy of science*, ed. P. Kitcher and W. Salmon, 13:3–219. Minneapolis, MN: University of Minnesota Press.
Schank, R. C., and Abelson, R. P. 1977. *Scripts, plans, goals and understanding*. Hillsdale, NJ: Erlbaum.
Schyns, P. G. 1999. The case for cognitive penetrability. *Behavioral and Brain Sciences* 22:394.
Scott, F. J., Baron-Cohen, S., and Leslie, A. 1999. 'If pigs could fly': A test of counterfactual reasoning and pretence in children with autism. *British Journal of Developmental Psychology* 17:349–362.
Searle, J. R. 1958. Proper names. *Mind* 67:166–173.
Seger, C. A., Poldrack, R. A., Prabhakaran, V., Zhao, M., Glover, G. H., Gabrieli, J. D. 2000. Hemispheric asymmetries and individual differences in visual concept learning as measured by functional MRI. *Neuropsychologia* 38:1316–1324.
Shallice, T. 1988. *From neuropsychology to mental structure*. Cambridge: Cambridge University Press.
Shanks, D. R. 1997. Distributed representations and implicit knowledge: A brief introduction. In *Knowledge, concepts, and categories*, ed. K. Lamberts and D. Shanks, 197–214. Cambridge, MA: MIT Press.
Shaver, P. R., Shelley, W., and Schwartz, J. C. 1992. Cross-cultural similarities and differences in emotion and its representation: A prototype approach. In *Review of personality and social psychology*. Vol. 13, *Emotion*, ed. M. S. Clark, 175–212. Newbury Park, CA: Sage.
Shepard, R. N. 1964. Attention and the metric structure of the stimulus space. *Journal of Mathematical Psychology* 1:54–87.
Shepard, R. N., and Metzler, J. 1971. Mental rotation of three dimensional objects. *Science* 171:701–703.
Simon, H. A. 1995. Machine as mind. In *Android epistemology*, ed. K. M. Ford, C. Glymour, and P. J. Hayes, 23–40. Cambridge, MA: MIT Press.
Sloman, S. A. 1993. Feature-based induction. *Cognitive Psychology* 25:231–280.
——— 1994. When explanations compete: The role of explanatory coherence on judgments of likelihood. *Cognition* 52:1–21.
——— 1996. The empirical case for two systems of reasoning. *Psychological Bulletin* 119:3–22.
——— 1998. Categorical inference is not a tree: The myth of inheritance hierarchies. *Cognitive Psychology* 35:1–33.
——— 2005. *Causal models: How people think about the world and its alternatives*. New York: Oxford University Press.
Sloman, S. A., and Lagnado, D. 2005. The problem of induction. In *The Cambridge handbook of thinking & reasoning*, ed. K. Holyoak and R. Morrison, 95–116. New York: Cambridge University Press.

Sloman, S. A., and Malt, B. C. 2003. Artifacts are not ascribed essences, nor are they treated as belonging to kinds. *Language and Cognitive Processes* 18:563–582.

Smith, E. E. 1989. Concepts and induction. In *Foundations of cognitive science*, ed. M. I. Posner, 501–526. Cambridge, MA: MIT Press.

Smith, E. E., and Medin, D. L. 1981. *Categories and concepts*. Cambridge, MA: Harvard University Press.

Smith, E. E., and Osherson, D. N. 1989. Similarity and decision making. In *Similarity and analogical reasoning*, ed. S. Vosniadou and A. Ortony, 60–75. Cambridge: Cambridge University Press.

Smith, E. E., and Sloman, S. A. 1994. Similarity- versus rule-based categorization. *Memory & Cognition* 22:377–386.

Smith, E. E., Patalano, A. L., and Jonides, J. 1998. Alternative strategies of categorization. *Cognition* 65:167–196.

Smith, E. E., Shoben, E. J., and Rips, L. J. 1974. Structure and process in semantic memory: A featural model for semantic decisions. *Psychological Review* 81:214–241.

Smith, E. E., Osherson, D. N., Rips, L. J., and Keane, M. 1988. Combining concepts: A selective modification model. *Cognitive Science* 12:485–527.

Smith, J. D. 2002. Exemplar theory's predicted typicality gradient can be tested and disconfirmed. *Psychological Science* 13:437–442.

Smith, J. D., and Minda, J. P. 1998. Prototypes in the mist: The early epochs of category learning. *Journal of Experimental Psychology: Learning, Memory, and Cognition* 24:1411–1436.

——— 2000. Thirty categorization results in search of a model. *Journal of Experimental Psychology: Learning, Memory, and Cognition* 26:3–27.

——— 2001. Journey to the center of the category: The dissociation in amnesia between categorization and recognition. *Journal of Experimental Psychology: Learning, Memory, and Cognition* 27:984–1002.

——— 2002. Distinguishing prototype-based and exemplar-based processes in category learning. *Journal of Experimental Psychology: Learning, Memory, and Cognition* 28:800–811.

Smith, J. D., Murray, M. J., and Minda, J. P. 1997. Straight talk about linear separability. *Journal of Experimental Psychology: Learning, Memory, and Cognition* 23:659–680.

Smith, L. B., and Samuelson, L. K. 1997. Perceiving and remembering: Category stability, variability and development. In *Knowledge, concepts, and categories*, ed. K. Lamberts and D. Shanks, 161–196. Cambridge, MA: MIT Press.

Smoke, K. L. 1932. An objective study of concept formation. *Psychological Monographs*, 42:1–46.

Smolensky, P. 1991. Connectionism, constituency, and the language of thought. In *Meaning in mind: Fodor and his critics*, ed. B. Loewer and G. Rey, 201–227. Oxford: Basil Blackwell.

Sobel, D., Tenenbaum, J., and Gopnik, A. 2004. Children's causal inferences from indirect evidence: Backwards blocking and Bayesian reasoning in preschoolers. *Cognitive Science* 28:303–333.

Solomon, K. O., and Barsalou, L. W. 2001. Representing properties locally. *Cognitive Psychology* 43:129–169.

——— 2004. Perceptual simulation in property verification. *Memory & Cognition* 32:244–259.

Solomon, K. O., Medin, D. L., and Lynch, E. L. 1999. Concepts do more than categorize. *Trends in Cognitive Sciences* 3:99–105.
Sousa, P., Atran, S., and Medin, D. L. 2002. Essentialism and folkbiology: Evidence from Brazil. *Journal of Cognition and Culture* 2:195–223.
Spalding, T. L., and Ross, B. H. 1994. Comparison-based learning: Effects of comparing instances during category learning. *Journal of Experimental Psychology: Learning, Memory, and Cognition* 20:1251–1263.
Spelke, E. S. 1994. Initial knowledge: Six suggestions. *Cognition* 50:431–445.
Spelke, E. S., Breinlinger, K., Macomber, J., and Jacobsen, K. 1992. Origins of knowledge. *Psychological Review*, 99:605–632.
Sperber, D., and Wilson, D., 1998. The mapping between the mental and the public lexicon. In *Language and thought: Interdisciplinary themes*, ed. P. Carruthers and J. Boucher, 184–200. Cambridge: Cambridge University Press.
Spirtes, P., Glymour, C., and Scheines, R. 2000. *Causation, prediction, and search*. 2d ed. Cambridge, MA: MIT Press.
Squire, L. R., and Knowlton, B. J. 1995. Learning about categories in the absence of memory. *Proceedings of the National Academy of Sciences of the United States of America* 92:12470–12474.
Stanovich, K. E. 1999. *Who is rational? Studies of individual differences in reasoning*. Mahweh, NJ: Erlbaum.
Stanovich, K. E., and West, R. F. 2000. Individual differences in reasoning: Implications for the rationality debate. *Behavioral and Brain Sciences* 23:645–726.
——— 2003. Evolutionary versus instrumental goals: How evolutionary psychology misconceives human rationality. In *Evolution and the psychology of thinking: The debate*, ed. D. E. Over, 171–230. Hove: Psychology Press.
Stein, L. A. 1995. Imagination and situated cognition. In *Android epistemology*, ed. K. M. Ford, C. Glymour, and P. Hayes, 167–182. Cambridge, MA: MIT Press.
Stich, S. P. 1978. Beliefs and sub-doxastic states. *Philosophy of Science* 45:499–518.
——— 1983. *From folk psychology to cognitive science: The case against belief*. Cambridge, MA: MIT Press.
——— 1996. *Deconstructing the mind*. Oxford: Oxford University Press.
Strevens, M. 2000. The essentialist aspect of naive theories. *Cognition* 74:149–175.
Taine, H. 1870. *De l'intelligence*. Paris: Hachette.
Tanaka, J. W. 2004. Object categorization, expertise, and neural plasticity. In *The cognitive neurosciences*, 3d ed., ed. M. S. Gazzaniga, 877–888. Cambridge, MA: MIT Press.
Tenenbaum, J. B., Griffiths, T. L., and Kemp, C. 2006. Theory-based Bayesian models of inductive learning and reasoning. *Trends in Cognitive Sciences* 10:309–318.
Tenenbaum, J. B., Griffiths, T. L., and Niyogi, S. 2007. Intuitive theories as grammars for causal inference. In *Causal learning: Psychology, philosophy, and computation*, ed. A. Gopnik and L. Schulz, 301–322. New York: Oxford University Press.
Teuber, H.-L. 1955. Physiological psychology. *Annual Review of Psychology* 6:267–296.
Thelen, E., and Smith, L. 1994. *A dynamic systems approach to the development of cognition and action*. Cambridge, MA: MIT Press.

Thompson-Schill, S. L. 2003. Neuroimaging studies of semantic memory: Inferring "how" from "where". *Neuropsychologia* 41:280–292.
Thorpe, S. J., Delorme, A., and VanRullen, R. 2001. Spike based strategies for rapid processing. *Neural Networks* 14:715–726.
Tinbergen, N. 1963. On aims and methods in ethology. *Zeitschrift für Tierpsychologie* 20:410–433.
Todd, P. M., and Dieckmann, A. 2005. Heuristics for ordering cue search in decision making. In *Advances in neural information processing systems*, Vol. 17, ed. L. K. Saul, Y. Weiss, and L. Bottou, 1393–1400. Cambridge, MA: MIT Press.
Todd, P. M., and Gigerenzer, G. 2000. Simple heuristics that make us smart. *Behavioral and Brain Sciences* 23:727–741.
Tversky, B., and Hemenway, K. 1984. Objects, parts, and categories. *Journal of Experimental Psychology: General* 113:169–193.
Ullman, S. 1996. *High-level vision*. Cambridge, MA: MIT Press.
Van Gelder, T. J. 1990. Compositionality: A connectionist variation on a classical theme. *Cognitive Science* 14:355–384.
—— 1995. What might cognition be, if not computation? *Journal of Philosophy* 91:345–381.
Van Orden, G. C., Pennington, B. F., and Stone, G. O. 2001. What do double dissociations prove? *Cognitive Science* 25:111–172.
Vygotsky, L. S. 1986. *Thought and language*. Revised edn. Cambridge, MA: MIT Press.
Wattenmaker, W. D., Dewey, G. I., Murphy, T. D., and Medin, D. L. 1986. Linear separability and concept learning: Context, relational properties, and concept naturalness. *Cognitive Psychology* 18:158–194.
Weiskopf, D. A. Forthcoming. The plurality of concepts. *Synthese*.
Weiskopf, D. A., and Bechtel, W. 2004. Remarks on Fodor on having concepts. *Mind & Language* 19:48–56.
Williamson, T. 2007. *The philosophy of philosophy*. Malden: Blackwell.
Wilson, T. D. 2002. *Strangers to ourselves: Discovering the adaptive unconscious*. Cambridge, MA: Harvard University Press.
Wisniewski, E. J. 1995. Prior knowledge and functionally relevant features in concept learning. *Journal of Experimental Psychology: Learning, Memory, and Cognition* 21:449–468.
Wisniewski, E. J., and Medin, D. L. 1994. On the interaction of theory and data in concept learning. *Cognitive Science* 18:221–281.
Wisniewski, E. J., and Wu, J. Forthcoming. Emergency!!!! Challenges to a compositional understanding of noun-noun combinations. In *The Oxford handbook of compositionality*, ed. M. Werning, W. Hinzen, and E. Machery. Oxford: Oxford University Press.
Wittgenstein, L. 1953. *Philosophical investigations*. Ed. G. E. M. Anscombe. Oxford: Blackwell.
Wood, J. N., and Grafman, J. 2003. Human prefrontal cortex function: Processing and representational perspectives. *Nature Reviews Neuroscience* 4:139–147.
Woodward, J. 2003a. *Making things happen: A theory of causal explanation*. New York: Oxford University Press.
—— 2003b. Scientific explanation. In *The Stanford encyclopedia of philosophy*, ed. E. N. Zalta, Winter 2003 Edition. Online. Available: http://plato.stanford.edu/entries/scientific-explanation/. Accessed 07/24/2007.

Wu, L. L. 1995. Perceptual representation in conceptual combination. Ph.D. diss., University of Chicago.

Young, M. P., Hilgetag, C.-C., and Scannell, J. W. 2000. On imputing function to structure from the behavioural effects of brain lesions. *Philosophical Transactions of the Royal Society of London* B355:147–161.

Zaki, S. R., and Nosofsky, R. M. 2001. A single-system interpretation of dissociations between recognition and categorization in a task involving object-like stimuli. *Cognitive, Affective & Behavioral Neuroscience* 1:344–359.

Zaki, S. R., Nosofsky, R. M., Jessup, N. M., and Unversagt, F. W. 2003. Categorization and recognition performance of a memory-impaired group: Evidence for single-system models. *Journal of the International Neuropsychological Society* 9:394–406.

Ziff, E. 1972. *Understanding understanding*. Ithaca, NY: Cornell University Press.

Zwaan, R. A., Stanfield, R. A., and Yaxley, R. H. 2002. Language comprehenders mentally represent the shapes of objects. *Psychological Science* 13:168–171.

Index of Names

Abbott, Barbara, 69–71
Ahn, Woo-kyoung, 161, 186, 188–190,
Anderson, John R., 20–21, 112, 137
Ashby, F. Gregory, 7, 26, 81–83, 99, 124, 141–146, 161, 250

Barsalou, Lawrence W., 10–15, 21–24, 84, 86–87, 91, 108–118, 165–166, 171, 223, 248
Berkeley, George, 94 n. 39, 109–11
Binet, Alfred, 77
Boghossian, Paul, 40–41
Boyd, Richard, 233
Brooks, Lee R., 92–93, 96, 195–196
Brooks, Rodney A., 220–222
Bruner, Jerome S., 79–80, 82
Burge, Tyler, 48–49

Carey, Susan E., 18, 35–36, 53, 62, 100–103, 158
Churchland, Paul M., 224, 241
Clark, Andy, 13, 225
Coltheart, Max, 137, 140

Dennett, Daniel C., 24–26
Descartes, René, 19, 77
Dunn, John C., 126, 134

Fisher, Sarah C., 77, 79, 157, 162
Fodor, Jerry A., 27, 32, 36–37, 80, 113–114, 155 n. 4, 232, 239

Gelman, Rochel, 64
Gelman, Susan A., 16, 54, 102–103, 199
Gigerenzer, Gerd, 122, 139–140, 148–150, 186, 250
Gleitman, Lila R., 64, 165, 169–171
Glymour, Clark N., 105
Gopnik, Alison, 16–17, 19, 62, 101–106, 161, 191–193
Greene, Joshua D., 128, 133, 140
Griffiths, Paul E., 232–241
Grush, Rick, 222

Hacking, Ian, 230
Hampton, James A., 12, 35–36, 62, 83–92, 153, 161, 163–168, 207–212

277

Hintzman, Douglas L., 171
Hull, Clark H., 78, 157–158, 162
Hume, David, 19, 77, 108 n. 54, 109–111

James, Williams, 222

Keil, Frank C., 54, 62, 85, 104, 106, 186–187
Knowlton, Barbara J., 141, 161, 214–218, 245
Komatsu, Lloyd K., 10–12, 21, 57–58, 76, 89
Kripke, Saul A., 37, 226–227

Labov, Williams, 166
Locke, John, 77–78, 108 n. 54

Machamer, Peter K., 101
Marr, David, 125–126
Malt, Barbara C., 12, 69–71, 154, 180–182, 193–194
Margolis, Eric, 26, 32, 36–37, 102
Markman, Arthur B., 14
McCloskey, Michael, 223–224
McDowell, John, 24
Medin, Douglas L., 10, 15–16, 18, 26, 55–56, 62, 84–85, 92–95, 97–98, 100–104, 106, 153, 161, 171–172, 177–179, 203–204, 208, 211, 240, 244–245
Mill, John Suart, 230
Millikan, Ruth G., 57 n. 8
Moore, Thomas, 77–78, 162
Murphy, Gregory L., 15, 28–29, 54, 62, 76, 81, 101–104, 106, 154, 161, 166, 178–179, 200

Nisbett, Richard E., 62, 226–227
Nosofsky, Robert M., 62, 66, 81, 92–94, 96–97, 98–100, 158, 173–174, 177, 215–217

Osherson, Daniel N., 65–67, 91, 95, 164, 199, 201–204, 207

Palmeri, Thomas J., 82, 96, 186, 216–217
Piaget, Jean, 17, 62
Peacocke, Christopher, 32, 33 n. 4, 34 n. 5, 38–47
Piccinini, Gualtiero, 58–60, 63
Posner, Michael I., 83, 98, 159–161, 166–167, 171, 214
Prinz, Jesse J., 24–26, 28–29, 36–37, 54–55, 101, 108–116
Pylyshyn, Zenon W., 8, 27
Putnam, Hilary, 37

Quine, W. V. O., 40, 230, 231 n. 9

Rehder, Bob, 101, 106–108, 161, 189–191, 198, 204–206, 249
Rey, George, 37, 73
Ribot, Théodule, 77
Rips, Lance J., 12–13, 83, 101, 166, 183–186, 199–201,
Rosch, Eleanor, 59, 83–88, 95–96, 98, 153–154, 161, 164–167

Searle, John R., 35
Sloman, Steve A., 91, 113, 140, 146, 184–186, 203–204, 249
Smith, David J., 62, 172–179, 182, 193–194
Smith, Edward E., 65–67, 83, 84–85, 88–89, 91–92, 94, 153, 164–166, 184–186, 195–196
Smith, Linda B., 28–29, 220, 222–224
Squire, Larry R., 141–142, 161, 214–217
Stanovich, Keith E., 113, 140, 146–148
Stich, Stephen P., 49–50, 224–230, 237–238

Van Gelder, Tim J., 27–28
Vygotsky, Lev, 62

Weiskopf, Daniel A., 240, 243–245

Zaki, Safa, R., 158, 215–217

Index of Subjects

amnesia, 214–217
amodal theories of concepts. *See* theories
analytic/synthetic distinction, 39–41
analyzable property. *See* dimension
Anderson's problem, 112–114
A-not-B search task. *See* task
anti-representationalism, 220–222
artifact, experimental, 44, 161, 176, 179, 189
artifacts, 12, 54, 103, 130, 166, 168, 186–187, 205,
   and natural kinds, 230 n. 8, 233–234, 236
associationism, 111

blank predicate, 199–200

categorization, 8–9, 22–24, 28–29, 96, 152–155, 158–196, 222–224
   and the classical theory of concepts, 78–79, 212–214
   and the exemplar paradigm of concepts, 96–100, 173–183, 214–218

   heterogeneity of, 53, 61, 63, 126–129, 133–134, 138–140, 193–196, 243
   and hybrid theories of concepts, 64–66
   implicit and explicit, 141–146
   inconsistent judgments of, 67–74
   phenomena as explananda, 55, 63
   and the prototype paradigm of concepts, 90–92, 163–173, 179–183, 214–218
   and reference, 35
   and the theory paradigm of concepts, 106–108, 183–193
category, 8, 14
   ad hoc, 22–23, 117, 165, 223
   artificial, 94–96, 145, 153–154, 158–162, 166–167, 250–251
   goal-derived, 117
   natural, 94–96, 166
   structure, 174–176, 179
category-specific deficits, 20
causal Bayes net, 105–106
causal centrality, 188–191, 203–204, 210

causal effects, 187–193, 202–203, 210
causal status hypothesis, 188–191
central tendency, 179, 194–195
classical architecture, 13
cognitive competence, 8–10, 16–17, 19–20, 58–59, 121–124, 138–139
  higher versus lower, 8–9
cognitive conflict, 67–74, 133–134, 147, 152, 196, 206
cognitive impenetrability, 8
cognitive process, 9, 124
  automatic, 24, 96, 113, 146–147, 185–186
  controlled, 146–147, 185–186
  exemplar-based, 96–100, 183
  prototype-based, 90–92, 183
  theory-based, 106–108, 191
concept
  abstract, 12, 58, 80, 168
  abstraction, 78, 156
  acquisition, 4, 19–20, 77–79, 82–83, 98, 142–146, 156, 158, 162–163, 245
  as a body of knowledge under organismic control, 24–26
  as a categorization device, 28–29
  as a constituent of thoughts, 26–28
  combination, 11, 16, 28, 65, 91, 207–212, 244–245
  complex, 65, 207–212
  as a component of a theory, 102–104
  of events, 11, 12, 18, 58, 75, 168
  format, 4, 19–21, 109–110
  fundamental kinds of, 52–53, 60–61, 116, 126, 244–245
  general properties of, 18–20, 55–56
  of individuals, 12–13
  individuation, 14, 33–34, 65
  innate, 82, 111
  knowledge stored in, 18–19, 78, 83–85, 92–94, 100–104
  learning, 20, 142–146, 155–158
  neural localization of, 4, 20, 212–218
  parts of, 64–66, 81
  in philosophy, 31–51
  in psychology, 7–21, 34–37
  of substances, 12, 56–57, 68–71
  as a temporary body of knowledge in working memory, 21–24
  use, 19, 90–92, 96–100, 106–108, 110–111, 117
concept learning design, 156–158, 160, 162–163
conceptual promiscuity, 16–17, 28–29
connectionism, 13–14
constituent of thoughts. See concept
Context Model, 93–95, 98, 174
context-sensitivity, 15, 21–24, 86–88, 222–224
counterfactual reasoning, 41–46
COVIS, 142–146
cue-valid property. See property

decision rule, 91–92, 98, 148–150
  deterministic, 92
  non-deterministic, 100, 107
default, 11–16, 63, 85, 93, 129–130 n. 2, 210–211
definition, 58, 62, 65–68, 74, 78–83, 169, 212–214, 249
diagnostic property. See property
dimension
  analyzable or separable, 99–100, 144
  non-analyzable or integral, 99–100
discovery scenario, 186–187
dissociation, 134–138, 214–217
  functional versus neuropsychological, 134–136
  simple versus double, 134–135
domain, 61, 102–103
dot-distortion category task. See task
dual-process theories. See theories
dynamical-systems approach, 220–222

ecological validity. See task
eliminativism, 53, 219–246
  applied to "concept," 241–245
  horizontal arguments for, 237–239
  old-fashioned, 224–230
  scientific, 230
  vertical arguments for, 237
embodied robotics, 220–222
essences, 78, 231–232
  belief in, 69, 72, 103
exemplar

and categorization, 173–183
and concept combination,
　211–212
effects, 173–178
featural and dimensional models of,
　93–94
paradigm of concepts, 17–18,
　52–53, 61–63, 92–100,
　118–119, 242–243, 248–249
experiment
　crucial, 137
　pizza, 183–186, 213
explanation, 101–104
　causal, 202–203, 205–206
　inference to the best, 106, 119, 183

fast and frugal heuristics. *See* heuristic
fastest-take-all rule. *See* rule
feature listing task. *See* task
feature production task. *See* task
feature verification task. *See* task
folk biology, 103–104

generalized context model, 98–100,
　177
generics, 199–200

Heterogeneity Hypothesis, 52–53,
　60–62, 81, 119, 121, 127, 139,
　153, 220
　evidence for, 193, 197, 201, 207,
　　217–218
heuristic
　fast and frugal, 148–140
　recognition, 148–149
　and system 1, 146
higher cognition. *See* cognitive
　competence
hybrid theories of concepts. *See*
　theories

ideals, 61, 116–118, 168, 249
imagery, mental, 110 n. 55, 112–116
induction, 8–9, 15–16, 29, 59, 84,
　103, 132–133, 140, 153,
　197–207, 223, 249
　categorical versus ampliative, 198
　category-based and categorical, 197
　feature-based model of, 202
　multi-process theory of, 204–206

and natural kinds, 230–234
similarity-based, 201–202
similarity-coverage model of,
　201–202
theory-based, 202–203
integration, 130–132, 139–140,
　143–144, 147, 193–196,
　205–206, 250

knowledge, 8
　background, 11–14, 22–23, 63,
　　118, 210, 248
　causal, 19, 64, 101–106, 119,
　　187–193, 195, 203–204, 210–211
　declarative versus non-declarative,
　　141–142
　implicit versus explicit, 8, 9, 141
　modal, 119, 185, 208, 209–211
　statistical, 83–85, 89, 119, 210

language of thought, 26–28
linear separability, 178–179

majority rule. *See* rule
matching, 90, 92,100, 106, 115, 167,
　185, 201, 218
memory, 13, 138, 161, 237
　declarative versus non-declarative,
　　141, 214–215
　discrimination in, 215–216
　encyclopedic, 11
　explicit versus implicit, 141
　long-term, 4, 9–11, 14, 21–24, 68,
　　82, 90–91, 93–94, 109, 113–114,
　　223–224
　semantic, 11, 14
　working, 15, 21–24, 216–217
method of cases, 226–229
most-confident-take-all rule. *See* rule
multi-process theories. *See* theories
natural kind, 230–236
　assumption, 241–242
　causal notion of, 232–234
　essentialist notion of, 231–232
　nomological notion of, 232
　splitting, 236–239

neo-empiricism, 108–116

old-items advantage, 173–174

parsimony, 126
perceptual representation, 19, 108–116
pluralism
   competence, 58–60
   concept, 239–240, 244–245
   scope, 57–58
problem from imagery, 114–116
production task. *See* task
property
   cue-valid (or diagnostic), 84–85, 163, 182
   emergence, 211–212
   inheritance, 209–211
   typical, 19, 35, 67, 84–85, 98, 119, 162–163, 182, 207–208
property listing task. *See* task
property verification task. *See* task
prototype
   and categorization, 163–173, 179–183
   and concept combination, 207–209
   featural and dimensional models of, 84
   versus ideal, 116–117
   and induction, 201–202
   paradigm of concepts, 17–19, 35–37, 52–53, 61–63, 83–93, 118–119, 242–243, 248–249
   proxytype, 108–111

Received View, 53–56,
reenactment, 110 (*see also* simulation)
reference
   and eliminativism, 225–226, 229–230
   intuitions about, 226–228
replication, importance of, 161–162
rule, 83, 142–146, 185, 195–196, 213–214
   of composition, 27
   and definition, 81–82
   explicit versus implicit, 142–146
   fastest-take-all, 132, 140
   majority, 131
   most-confident-take-all, 132
   and system 2, 146
   unidimensional, 142–146
   verbalizable, 142–146
RULEX, 66, 81

selection problem, 85, 94
separable property. *See* dimension
similarity, 90–91, 96–100, 106, 108, 119, 245
   and categorization, 144–146, 167–168, 171–174, 181, 183–187, 212–214, 215–217
   exponential measures of, 97, 100
   and induction, 201–202, 204–206
   linear measures of, 90–91, 98, 177
   multiplicative measures of, 97
   non-linear measures of, 97–100, 177
Simple Account, 38–47
simulation
   and counterfactual reasoning, 42–47
   perceptual, 110, 115–116
   and the Simple Account, 41

Take-the-Best, 149–150
task, 20–21, 58 n. 10, 122, 124–125
   A-not-B search, 17
   dot-distortion category, 159–160, 214–217
   ecologically valid and invalid, 83, 132–133, 163, 176–178, 250–251
   feature listing (or feature production or property listing), 23, 86–89, 112–114, 166
   feature verification (or property verification), 115–116, 166
   linguistic versus non-linguistic, 59–60
   recognition, 181
   Wason Selection, 147
theories
   amodal, 19, 109–116
   of concepts in psychology, 12, 17–20, 34–37, 54–55
   dual-process, 128–129, 133, 137, 143, 146–148, 185–186, 250
   hybrid, 63–75, 81
   multi-process, 121–150, 193–194, 204–206, 212, 243, 249–250
   type-1 versus type-2, 125–126
theory
   and categorization, 183–193
   and concept combination, 209–211
   framework, 103–104

and induction, 202–203
mini-, 101, 103, 105
paradigm of concepts, 52, 58,
    61–63, 76, 100–108, 242–243,
    248–249
transformation scenario, 186–187
typicality, 59–60, 92, 96, 117,
    163–166, 174, 176–178,
    202–206, 208–209, 214
    versus degree of membership, 164
    effects, 163–173, 201–202, 204
    measure of, 164–165, 166
    of properties. *See* property
    variation in, 22–23, 165,
    223–224

Unified View of Cognition, 125–127,
    138–139, 249–250

Wason Selection Task. *See* task

BF 443 .M33 2009
Machery, Edouard.
Doing without concepts

APR 28 2014